THE USES OF
CONTROVERSY
IN SOCIOLOGY

The Uses of
Controversy
in Sociology

edited by

Lewis A. Coser
and
Otto N. Larsen

A Publication of
The American
Sociological Association

THE FREE PRESS
A Division of Macmillan Publishing Co., Inc.
NEW YORK

Collier Macmillan Publishers
LONDON

The Free Press
A Division of Macmillan Publishing Co., Inc.
866 Third Avenue, New York, N.Y. 10022

Collier Macmillan Canada, Ltd.

Library of Congress Catalog Card Number: 76–7177

Printed in the United States of America

printing number

1 2 3 4 5 6 7 8 9 10

Library of Congress Cataloging in Publication Data

Main entry under title:

The Uses of controversy in sociology.

"All the contributions . . . were originally written for presentation at the 1975 annual meetings of the American Sociological Association at San Francisco, although some of them have been extensively rewritten since."
"A publication of the American Sociological Association."
Bibliography: p.
Includes index.
1. Sociology—Congresses. I. Coser, Lewis A. II. Larsen, Otto N. III. American Sociological Association.
HM13.U7   301   76-7177
ISBN 0-02-906830-4

Contents

**VIII. To Spur the Development of the Discipline by Pinpointing
Theoretical and Methodological Deficiencies**

About the Contributors

JAMES E. BLACKWELL received his B.A. and M.A. from Western Reserve University and his Ph.D. from Washington State University. He has taught at Grambling State University, San Jose State University, and the University of Massachusetts at Boston, where he is presently located and where, for five years, he chaired the department. He has served in various United States Foreign Service capacities in East and Central Africa and in Southeast Asia. He was the first President of the Caucus of Black Sociologists and has been a member of the Council of the American Sociological Association. Among his publications are *The Black Community: Diversity and Unity* and *Black Sociologists: Historical and Contemporary Perspectives* (coedited with M. Janowitz).

ALBERT K. COHEN was born in Boston. He received his B.A. from Harvard, his M.A. from Indiana University, and his Ph.D. from Harvard. He was Professor of Sociology at Indiana University and is now Professor of Sociology at the University of Connecticut. He is the author of *Delinquent Boys: The Culture of the Gang* and *Deviance and Control*.

JAMES S. COLEMAN was born in Bedford, Indiana, and earned a B.S. at Purdue. His Ph.D. is from Columbia. He has been Professor of Sociology at Johns Hopkins and currently is Professor of Sociology at the University of Chicago. He is a member of the National Academy of Science. Coleman is the author of *The Adolescent Society* and principal author of *Equality of Educational Opportunity,* the so-called Coleman Report.

PATRICK W. CONOVER was born in Washington, D. C., and earned his B.D. from the Chicago Theological Seminary and his Ph.D. from Florida State University. He is currently Assistant Professor of Sociology at the University of North Carolina at Greensboro.

LEWIS A. COSER was born in Berlin and studied at the Sorbonne. He has a Ph.D. from Columbia. He held the post of Professor of Sociology at Brandeis and currently is Professor of Sociology at the State University of New York at Stony Brook. Coser is a Past-President of the American Sociological Association. His publications include *The Functions of Social Conflict* and *Masters of Sociological Thought.*

RAYMOND D. DUVALL received an A.B. from the University of Pennsylvania and a Ph.D. from Northwestern University. He is currently an Assistant Professor of Political Science at Yale University and a member of the editorial board of the *Journal of Conflict Resolution.* He is coauthor of *Dependency and Imperialism* and *Conflict and Society.*

WILLIAM H. FORM was born in Rochester, New York, and received his B.A. from the University of Rochester and his Ph.D. from the University of Maryland. He is Professor of Sociology and Labor and Industrial Relations at the University of Illinois, Champaign–Urbana. He is currently the Secretary of the American Sociological Association. Among his recent publications are *Income and Ideology* and *Blue-Collar Stratification.*

ANTHONY GIDDENS was born in London and has a Ph.D. from Cambridge, where he is currently a Fellow of King's College and University Lecturer in Sociology. He is the author of *Capitalism and Modern Social Theory, The Class Structure of the Advanced Societies,* and, most recently, *New Rules of Sociological Method.*

WALTER R. GOVE was born in Holden, Massachusetts, and received a B.S. from the New York State University College of Forestry. He received his Ph.D. from the University of Washington. He is currently Professor of Sociology at Vanderbilt University. Among his publications is the edited volume, *Labeling Deviant Behavior: Evaluating a Perspective.*

TED ROBERT GURR has a B.A. from Reed College and a Ph.D. from New York University. He taught at Princeton University and is now Payson S. Wild Professor of Political Science at Northwestern University. Among his publications are *Violence in America: Historical and Comparative Perspectives, Why Men Rebel,* and *The Politics of Crime and Conflict: A Comparative History of Four Cities.*

RICHARD F. HAMILTON was educated at the University of Chicago and at Columbia University. He has taught at Princeton University and the University of Wisconsin. He is now Professor of Sociology at McGill University. He is the author of *Affluence and the French Worker, Class and Politics in the United States,* and *Restraining Myths.* He is currently working on a study of the electoral support for the National Socialists in Weimar Germany.

ALEX INKELES was born in Brooklyn, New York, and received his A.B. and A.M. from Cornell University and a Ph.D. from Columbia. He also studied at the Washington School of Psychiatry and the Boston Psycho-analytic Institute. Inkeles is now the Margaret Jacks Professor of Sociology and Education at Stanford University, to which he came after having been Professor of Sociology at Harvard. He is the author of *Public Opinion in Soviet Russia* and *What Is Sociology?* and the coauthor of *Social Change in Soviet Russia* and *Becoming Modern.*

OTTO N. LARSEN was born in Tyler, Minnesota. He received a B.A. and a Ph.D. from the University of Washington, where he is now Professor of Sociology. He was Fulbright Professor at the University of Copenhagen and served for three years as the Executive Officer of the American Sociological Association. Larsen was formerly editor of *Sociological Inquiry* and the *Pacific Sociological Review.* His publications include the edited book, *Violence and the Mass Media,* and the coauthored volumes on *The Flow of Information, Conceptual Sociology,* and *Sociology.*

EDWIN M. LEMERT was born in Cincinnati, Ohio. He received a B.A. at Miami University in Ohio and a Ph.D. from Ohio State University. He is now Professor of Sociology at the University of California, Davis, where he is involved in comparative studies of juvenile justice. He is a former President of the Society for the Study of Social Problems. Lemert is the author of *Human Deviance, Social Problems and Social Control,* and *Social Action and Legal Change.*

LAURA NADER is Professor of Anthropology at the University of California at Berkeley. She holds a Ph.D. from Harvard University and has done fieldwork in Mexico, Lebanon, and the United States. Nader is both editor and contributor to *The Ethnography of Law* and *Law in Culture and Society.* She is the author of *Talea and Juquila: A Comparison of Zapotec Social Organization,* has produced a film on Zapotec court procedure: *To Make the Balance,* and has coedited the volume *Cultural Illness and Health.* She is currently conducting a study of complaint management in the United States.

DAVID RIESMAN was born in Philadelphia, attended Harvard College, and has a J.D. from Harvard Law School. He taught in The College and the Department of Sociology at the University of Chicago and is Henry Ford II Professor of Social Sciences at Harvard. His writings include *Academic Values and Mass Education* (with J. Gusfield and Z. Gamson) and *Thorstein Veblen: A Critical Interpretation.* He founded and edited (from 1960 until 1965) *The Correspondent: Critical Dialogue and Research on Home and Foreign Affairs.*

PETER H. ROSSI was born in New York City and earned his B.S. at The College of the City of New York and his Ph.D. at Columbia. He has held faculty positions at Harvard, Chicago, and Johns Hopkins and is currently Professor of Sociology at the University of Massachusetts, Amherst, and Director of the Social and Demographic Institute. He also served as Director of the National Opinion Research Center at the University of Chicago and as Secretary of the American Sociological Association. His publications include *Why Families Move, Evaluating Social Programs,* and *The Roots of Urban Discontent.*

DAVID SERBER has a Ph.D. in anthropology from the University of California at Berkeley and is presently a post-doctoral fellow at the Health Policy Program, School of Medicine, University of California at San Francisco. His publications include articles on reform and regulation and on complaint management. Currently he is working on a study of the politics and development of national health insurance in the United States.

ARTHUR B. SHOSTAK was born in Brooklyn, New York, and earned a B.S. at the New York State School of Industrial and Labor Relations, Cornell University. He has a Ph.D. from Princeton University. He has served on the faculty at the University of Pennsylvania and is currently Professor of Psychology and Sociology at Drexel University in Philadelphia. Among his publications are *The "Eye" of Sociology, Modern Social Reforms, Putting Sociology to Work,* and *Privilege in America.*

THEDA SKOCPOL grew up in Wyandotte, Michigan, and earned a B.A. at Michigan State University. Her Ph.D. is from Harvard, where she is currently Assistant Professor of Sociology. She is the author of a dissertation on *Social Revolutions in France, Russia, and China: A Comparative-Historical and Structural Analysis* and related articles appearing in various journals.

ARTHUR L. STINCHCOMBE was born in Clare County, Michigan, studied at Central Michigan College of Education, and received his Ph.D. at the University of California at Berkeley. He has been Professor of Sociology at the University of California at Berkeley and is now a Senior Study Director at the National Opinion Research Center and Professor of Sociology at the University of Chicago. He has written *Constructing Social Theories, Rebellion in a High School,* and *Creating Efficient Industrial Administrations.*

IMMANUEL WALLERSTEIN has a Ph.D. from Columbia. He is currently Distinguished Professor of Sociology at the State University of New

York at Binghamton. He is the author of *The Modern World-System,* which was awarded the 1975 Sorokin Prize. He was President of the African Studies Association and is the author of several works on contemporary Africa.

DENNIS H. WRONG was born in Toronto and received his B.A. from the University of Toronto. His Ph.D. is from Columbia. He is Professor of Sociology at New York University. He was the first editor of *Contemporary Sociology: A Journal of Reviews.* He is the author of *Population and Society* and *Skeptical Sociology* and editor of *Max Weber.*

J. MILTON YINGER was born in Michigan and studied at DePauw (A.B.), Louisiana State (M.A.), and Wisconsin (Ph.D.). He is Professor of Sociology and Anthropology at Oberlin. A former Guggenheim Fellow and Senior Specialist at the East-West Center, he is currently a Fellow of the National Endowment for the Humanities and President-Elect of the American Sociological Association. Among his published works are *Toward a Field Theory of Behavior, The Scientific Study of Religion,* and *Racial and Cultural Minorities* (with G. E. Simpson).

Introduction

"It is what we think we know," Claude Bernard once remarked, "that prevents us from learning." This is why it seems imperative from time to time to reassess our stock of knowledge to determine whether the received wisdom on which we rely still stands up in the light of current experience and knowledge. Such a reassessment may take the form of systematic inventories of ideas and attempts at codification, but it may also proceed by way of critical dissection of past and present contributions. It is the second path that we have chosen in this volume.

"Conflict is the gadfly of thought," John Dewey has written; "it stirs us to observation and memory. It instigates to invention. It shocks us out of our sheep-like passivity, and sets us at noting and contriving. . . . Conflict is a *sine qua non* of reflection and ingenuity." It is in this spirit that we have entitled this volume *The Uses of Controversy in Sociology.* Not all controversies, alas, provide enlightenment; when the contenders argue from mutually exclusive positions and have no common ground to share, the result is usually, as the French say, a dialogue of the deaf. But when it is the case—as we think it is with all the contributors to this volume—that divergencies and debates proceed with a shared commitment to the growth of sociology as an intellectual discipline, controversy is likely to lead to needed clarification of issues and to a clearing of the ground for future advance. The controversies of today, we would contend, point to the cutting edge of future developments.

Many of the contributions we have collected in this volume take a dim view of established sociological pieties and of the fads and fashions currently on the ascendant. And this is as it should be since such countercyclical thinking, as David Riesman once called it, seems peculiarly apt to alert us to the perennial task of re-evaluating our fund of knowledge in the cool light of sociological reason. Controversy is surely not the only road to advancement of our discipline, but it is an important road. Hence, two cheers for the uses of controversy in sociology.

All the contributions gathered in this volume were originally written for presentation at the 1975 annual meetings of the American Sociological Association at San Francisco, although some of them have been extensively rewritten since. Many more papers were submitted to us than could possibly be accommodated within one volume, forcing us to make sometimes difficult choices about which ones to include. We may have made mistakes here and there, but we are convinced that on the whole we have chosen the cream of the crop. By no means all the controversies that are currently alive in sociology are being mirrored in these pages, but we think enough of them are included to provide a representative sample.

It would serve no purpose were we to follow in the footsteps of those editors who feel the need to spoonfeed their intended audience by providing capsule summaries of the papers they have selected. No intelligent reader can really gain an informed opinion from such truncated digests. We trust our readers to select for themselves which contributions speak more directly to their current concerns and which to approach with, as it were, more peripheral interest.

Some of the controversies being aired here concern the assessment of trends in American society, others address themselves to theoretical divergencies within contemporary sociology, and still others point to the gap between certified knowledge and commonsensical assumptions in the explanation of our current predicaments. On the face of it, there seems little in common between David Riesman's incisive and acerbic comments about contemporary American society and Peter Rossi's cool dissection of the failings of current research in stratification. Nor does there seem to be much relation between, say, the variant appraisals of the importance of ethnicity in Part V and the debate on the merits of the labeling approach in Part VI. Yet we are willing to argue that over and above such dissimilarities in focus and subject matter, this volume provides a unified perspective insofar as every contributor is committed to a probing examination—be it of the tools or the results—of the sociological enterprise.

This volume speaks through many voices, but all of them in their variant tones and modulations address themselves to the clarification of central issues in the explanation of the net of social relations and sociological determinants in which we are enmeshed. Whether used in the classroom or the scholar's study, it will, we hope, provide a measure of enlightened information about the trials and tribulations, as well as the joys, that await those who have dedicated their scholarly lives to the study of society.

I

To Provoke Concern for Societal Trends

Some Questions about Discontinuities in American Society

David Riesman

IN AN ESSAY written some years ago, Marcus Cunliffe chided students of American history for our preoccupation with the concept of "watersheds," radical breaks with the past, which from his British perspective did not look so dramatic. Indeed, in a kind of vanity, many of us who are students of American society have turned the Chinese curse—"May you live in interesting times!"—into "May you live in changing times." Many apparent breaks with the past may actually represent continuity with a part of the past that had been suppressed or buried. In other words what appears as discontinuous may be part of a cyclical or dialectical process in which, for example, conflicts between the competing values of liberty and equality are not resolved, but in which rather the overemphasis on one leads to the eventual revival of the other (Lipset, 1961; Parsons and White, 1961).

Precisely because academic social scientists and intellectuals are often purveyors of news of change, or invent and disseminate the terms by which change is delineated, we may be overimpressed by what turns out to be ephemeral—a tendency that can be enhanced by the probability that we live among a cenacle of the like-minded. Yet we are

☐ I am indebted to the Hazen Foundation and the Clark Foundation for assistance in making work on this chapter possible. I have also received helpful comments from Daniel Bell, Ernst Borinski, Harvey Brooks, Alphonse Buccino, Herbert Gans, Denis Hayes, Nathan Glazer, Edwin Harwood, Christopher Jencks, Joseph Kauffman, Samuel A. Klausner, Joseph Kraft, Eric Larrabee, Seymour Martin Lipset, Samuel Lubell, Michael Mandelbaum, Peter Mayer, Lee Rainwater, Richard Robbins, William Schneider, and Laurence H. Tribe.

not like those ethnographers who, on visiting a strange people and in the absence of archeology and oral history, see only its diurnal round of life, and mistake the momentary for the enduring. Historians of Western culture have become increasingly sophisticated in their use of the techniques developed in the social sciences. They have used gravestones, birth records, and demography as devices to infer opinion prior to the invention of formal public opinion surveys.

The Lonely Crowd took insufficient account of these new historical techniques. We not only extrapolated demographic trends which quickly changed, but we made the mistake in retrospect of being too provincial in our focus entirely on intra-American developments (Riesman and Glazer, 1961; Riesman, 1969). Similarly, I have repeatedly overestimated from survey data the strength of the right wing in America, most recently in the 1960s (e.g., Riesman, 1968a). However, in arguing with euphoric faculty and student radicals who for a short time believed they could remake America, I would sometimes contend that in some future year in which the United States received no increase in the amount of oil it had over that of the previous year, George Wallace would be elected president. That remains to be seen.

In my opinion it is the business of people like ourselves to be early warning stations for discontinuities whether we regard these as benign or otherwise. But the older I get, the less confidence I have in my own judgments, and experience has also taught me sobriety and skepticism when it comes to the judgments of others. In many respects, American society as a whole seems to me remarkably fluid: Ordinary citizens appear confused and bewildered, sometimes looking for leaders (but lacking good job descriptions for them), while others succeed in eliminating doubt although not anxiety by developing (as Gallup polls show, long before Watergate) conspiratorial views of the villains who run things and who are holding out on us, not only their secrets and trickster behaviors, but also the promised bounties of universal justice and affluence. The various elites, local, regional, and national, are not only divided among themselves, as often in the past, but frequently divided within themselves, less self-assured about their privileges and, like the rest of the population, frequently in doubt as to the directions toward which they should exercise their influence.

From the flux of events, principally in the post–World War II period, I want to discuss a few items concerning which the issue of discontinuity can be raised; there is no claim that these are the most significant themes. I shall deal first with what I regard as the radical discontinuity revealed by the explosion over Hiroshima; then with the consequences of the spread of affluence in the two decades following 1945; then with the shift in attitudes toward appropriate professions and careers; and finally, with the impact of the women's liberation movements, and the kind of social and moral traffic jams created by simultaneous movements toward liberation, democratization, and equality. As the last instance illustrates, my emphasis will be on continuities as well as discontinuities, and the question as to whether shifts of emphasis and degree constitute cyclical fluctuations or more or less irreversible developments.

Nuclearism [1]

The explosion of a nuclear bomb over Hiroshima marked, in my judgment, a truly irreversible discontinuity not only for the United States but for the planet. Prior to Hiroshima, mass bombings of German cities by both the British and Americans produced as much (or more) destruction and as many casualties as the bombs dropped on Hiroshima and even more inexcusably on Nagasaki; these earlier bombings would seem to discredit the notion common on the left here and abroad that Americans dropped atomic bombs on the Japanese and dropped so-called conventional bombs and napalm on the Vietnamese and Cambodians because we are racists; rather, this would seem to represent the Federal, as against the Confederate, style of warfare, which uses technical force rather than personal hardiness to assure victory; and the example of Sherman's march through Georgia, seems to illustrate an early example of Western industrial *Schrecklichkeit*.[2]

This latter reference suggests elements of continuity which lurk within radical discontinuities, for it can be said that in all our wars, however begun, Americans mobilize the population by using or calling on our civil religion, our Manichean idealism, and our sense of Manifest Destiny. Our temptation to overreach is something which Tocqueville saw as a danger, because of the way a mobilized and aroused democracy would conduct warfare. Nuclear weapons were, however, an overreaching of a different order of magnitude; I have shared the judgment of those scientists and others grouped around the *Bulletin of the Atomic Scientists* in opposing the efforts of Herman Kahn, Edward Teller, and (in an earlier period) Henry Kissinger to turn the issue into one of degree rather than of kind.[3]

[1] I borrow the term "nuclearism" from Lifton, 1968. (Riesman, 1968*b*.)

[2] Eric Larrabee acquainted me with the continuities of these two styles of warfare. (Riesman, 1963.)

[3] I cannot here enter into all the complex arguments as to whether, in the period from 1945 to the present, the existence of nuclear weapons may have stabilized relations among the great powers, no matter how ominous the future as nuclear technology spreads. As an admirer of the work of Gene Sharp on the possibilities of nonviolent but

For the average American, except in periods of crisis such as during the Cuban missile confrontation and the panic over fallout shelters, the existence of nuclear weapons brought few nightmares and no apparent discontinuities in daily life. Only in Japan has the issue been kept alive among the general population, with a slight wavering beginning to appear as to whether the line between conventional and nuclear weapons should continue to be held. But among American foreign policy elites, the issue has remained one of recurring importance. One element, I believe, in our initial involvement in Vietnam in 1961 was the effort by Secretary of Defense Robert McNamara and others to move away from the John Foster Dulles doctrine of massive retaliation, and to demonstrate (perhaps with the Congo or Latin America in mind) that the United States was prepared for both conventional and counterinsurgency warfare. But the nation's failure in Vietnam only makes the use of so-called tactical nuclear weapons look all the more likely in a situation of desperate resort. Now, with our military discredited and somewhat demoralized by the Vietnam war, as well as by the creation of a volunteer or mercenary army—also largely a result of that war—it is not surprising that the secretary of defense, James Schlesinger, and others are again openly discussing first use of nuclear weapons in South Korea and perhaps in Europe or in the Middle East, as in the Dulles era. Indeed, our allies may press for just such reassurance. They could well be anxious about the state of our combat troops (and perhaps also their own), and if they read the American polls, they must recognize that the unideological lack of interest in foreign adventures of less educated Americans has now been joined by an ideological and fervent antimilitarism of a large section of the educated elites.

Antimilitarism extends beyond the realm of defense, and the kind of defense (and periodic offense) represented by the CIA, to the whole realm of involvement in foreign affairs, including aid to the less developed countries, which can no longer be justified by the traditional cold war rhetoric and, except in cases of obvious disaster relief, is not easily justified in humanitarian terms when there is a domestication of American interests, a preoccupation with our grave internal problems, and a fear that the touch even of Peace Corps–type assistance is only another form of imperialism. I am constantly struck by the discrepancy between the marked concern among the educated about pollution of the atmosphere by the way we use energy in factories, fields, transport, and

active defense, instances of which he has studied from Norway to San Salvador, from Gandhi to Martin Luther King, Jr., I nonetheless find it hard to imagine the anarchic Americans learning the discipline necessary and possessing the morale for such a defense (Sharp, 1971, 1973). In 1945 it was possible for some to envisage a post-Hiroshima further discontinuity, which would move toward world federalism or even toward world government. Today I find it hard in a near-Hobbesian world of nation-states to envisage so radical a discontinuity.

buildings, and the widespread lack of concern with the current SALT negotiations and the wholly different magnitude of pollution that an exchange of nuclear weapons would produce. In this country, the Cuban missile crisis produced, after the initial shock, a state of calm which I regard as unjustified. John F. Kennedy took risks greater than any of his successors have taken, counting on Khrushchev to be sensible, even at the cost of the latter's political legitimacy in his own country. (I should add that the partial nuclear test ban is in my judgment President Kennedy's greatest accomplishment.)

As already suggested, in spite of our acceptance of nuclearism, the country has become less warlike, and this is not only a discontinuity produced by the bitter "loss" of Vietnam as viewed by some, the bitter shame and moral outrage of Vietnam as viewed by others. Korea, too, was not a popular war, although once engaged, the country went along with it. World War II was fought with less passion against the Nazis than World War I had been fought against the Germans. There is continuity rather than a sharp break with the past in this erosion of warlike sentiment among Americans, an erosion not contradicted by the fact that during the years of the cold war, patriotism remained strong, and anything labeled as communist was suspect.

The cold war drew part of its strength from the evangelism that is one strand in our Puritan past, while another strand, the fierce pessimism of the Calvinists, has remained muted; later, the peasant fatalism of many immigrant Catholics had minimal effect on foreign policy. General Grant insisted on unconditional surrender in the Civil War; the doctrine of unconditional surrender prolonged and made more fierce the Second World War, including the dropping of atomic bombs on Japan. In Korea, General MacArthur's crossing of the 38th parallel in the face of Chinese warnings was in the spirit of earlier modes of simplistic and self-righteous warfare, forgetting that we were not fighting a whole people and that we would need, after these wars, to become reconciled with former enemies.

Similarly, in our diplomacy during the early years of the United Nations, most Americans failed to appreciate that any possibility of international order would be destroyed by getting our own way too often, that is, by an uninterrupted string of victories;[4] while our patriotic,

---

[4] Some critics of my address have argued that the United States did not use its automatic UN majority to threaten the Soviet Union within its own sphere of vital interests, and cooperated with them in some peace-keeping measures (as at Suez). Even so, our heady rhetoric and seemingly ready use of our hegemony in the United Nations may have weakened that forum, as it weakens the American case when this country is now so often in a small minority in the UN. Furthermore, the Soviet Union (and the excluded Chinese) may have felt threatened, whatever covert assurances they had through diplomatic channels; the Korean case may have proved that it was not possible to be sure what the United States would regard as within the sphere of its vital interests.

cheering population could be nurtured on the conviction that any setback to national aims, as interpreted by foreign policy elites, went against the order of nature, and hence must result from a conspiracy in high places.

C. Vann Woodward (1968) contended in a reflective essay a few years ago that the South was different, and might provide a model for America as a whole because it had known defeat, tragedy, suffering. Southerners, he thought, could not interpret our history as a succession of victories, as did the rest of the country. There *is* a South for which Vann Woodward himself speaks. Its inhabitants are more regional, more attached to place, than most Americans; it has been poor and somewhat fatalistic. But the South has also been the habitat for some of our most hawkish officers and politicians. Many Southerners regard the War Between the States not as a defeat, but as a romantic memory of heroism. Southern military and civilian officials have been no more critical of nuclear weapons than other Americans have been. Moreover, today, worried about its textile and other threatened industries, and in contrast with its earlier, sometimes interventionist internationalism, the South has become isolationist and protectionist, like the rest of the country.

The term "isolationist" carries a connotation which can be misleading. For example, many who were termed isolationists in the First World War vis-à-vis aiding the Allied powers were quite happy about intervention in Mexico or elsewhere in Latin America; similarly, many who opposed fighting the Nazis and the Italian Fascists in alliance with imperial Britain and Communist Russia were not so much America Firsters as Asia Firsters. What Thorstein Veblen called the underlying population, though he saw it as jingoistic, has not been fond of war and sacrifice, even though, as already indicated, it could be mobilized by calls upon its patriotism; in general, terms like "isolationist" or "interventionist" are more applicable to educated elites. And it is these latter who are now often turning inward vis-à-vis the rest of the world, at a time when interdependence is increasingly urgent. Spanish seems to be the only foreign language which continues to be taught in many high schools, especially now that most colleges and many doctoral programs have dropped any foreign language requirements. Even during the last stages of the war in Vietnam, many in the antiwar movement had negligible interest in the intricate structures of Francophone Southeast Asia—it was enough to know that America was imperialist, racist, militaristic; and more notice was often paid to the resources, such as oil or tin, that South Vietnam might possess than to its tribal and religious divisions. China has captured the interest of a few, as Cuba did earlier, and Yugoslavia earlier still. But on the whole, limited arousal occurs only when an ethnic group takes an interest in what is happening in its ancestral homeland or country of identification. Larger concern occurs, as for instance with Soviet grain purchases, or the import of foreign cars, when some sectors of the American economy are threatened (though other sectors benefit). Here the possibility of American disengagement from the United Nations, just when it is most needed as a forum for mediation of potential armed conflict, and even occasionally to interpose troops, is dangerous. So, too, in our relations with the Soviet Union, elements in both countries are constantly tempted to overreach, renewing that tacit alliance in which the military nationalists in one country are the allies of their counterparts in the other, against the underlying populations of both. If America is seen as nonthreatening, the "worst case" fears of Soviet hawks might be neutralized, but they might also be strengthened by the argument that America becomes more dangerous as influential foreign policy elites feel diplomatically and politically isolated and powerless in the world.[5]

That sense of powerlessness can lead to intransigence in a nation or in groups within it—or even in an individual who may resort to terrorism or assassination or hijacking to say, in effect: "I am here. I count. You must take notice." The sense of powerlessness grows with the feeling that there is no one in charge of the country, or at any rate, no one who can be trusted—attitudes which preceded Watergate and even the heightening of tension over Vietnam. I had once thought that veto groups operated mainly in domestic affairs, leaving foreign policy, as suggested above, to elites. Later, with the rise of the cold war, some elites were discredited and others divided concerning proper relations with the Soviet Union and mainland China. But today, elites are not only divided but also discredited and often individually demoralized. The current coalition against détente may not be permanent, but it embraces not only large portions of attentive people among the highly educated who retain an interest in foreign affairs, including many Zionist and non-Zionist Jews understandably preoccupied with the security of Israel (but whose backing of intransigence may undercut that security), but also the strongly anti-Communist staffs of major labor leaders, as well as the working-class allies of the latter, for example, among longshoremen outside of the West Coast—and even usually peaceable housewives, worried about the price of bread and meat.

[5] Daniel Bell (1975: personal communication) has commented that the radical discontinuity here is not just nuclearism, but the eclipse of distance in that World War II was the last of the wars in which land mass could still serve as a basis for safety or, if need be, for retreat. He notes that even apart from nuclear weapons, modern logistics permits movement of thousands of troops readily to any part of the world. (See also Wohlstetter, 1975.) It seems likely that the space program and the moon landing also have served to increase the awareness of ecological hazards and also to decrease the feeling of security that the United States is buffered by distance and by the oceans from external invasion. The periodic flying saucer scares could be viewed in this perspective.

Some Effects of Affluence

The boycott of high meat prices by housewives several years ago may serve to introduce the second, though less dramatic discontinuity, namely, the consequences for American attitudes and expectations of the nearly uninterrupted prosperity for most, but not all Americans, which followed the Second World War. That ever-rising plateau of affluence led millions of Americans to believe that we could move simultaneously along three somewhat incompatible dimensions: toward more individual liberty, toward greater group equality, and toward more democratic participation. The housewives' boycott was spontaneous, although it later became organized by an elite of activist consumer groups among the highly educated. The initial housewives were no doubt protesting against what they regarded as profiteering, but they were also in effect saying: If my husband, working overtime, is making $15,000 a year as a truck driver or foreman, three times what my own father made, it's my right as an American to put steak on his table! The housewife was unlikely to realize that her husband's salary reflected a worldwide process in which, for example, the Japanese moved as fast as they could from a diet of rice and fish to one of beef, wheat, and pork. Nor would ecologically-minded people convince her that the worldwide feeding of soybeans to cattle was continuing even while people were lacking basic protein in Upper Volta or Northeastern Brazil. Indeed, her sense of grievance did not allow her to take account of the truly poverty-stricken within America, among whom meat is still a luxury. With the combination of recession and inflation, many working-class people whose greatest fear has been that they would lose their precarious hold on the standard consumer packages of affluence, have had to serve hamburger (or beans and rice) as ersatz steak, while grievances smolder.

George Foster (1972) has commented that envy and the fear of it, though pan-human, seem to have been less powerful among Americans than among many peasant and other cultures. But if scarcity promotes great envy among peasant cultures, widely advertised affluence maintains and may even increase feelings of relative deprivation and envy among Americans.[6] Lee Rainwater would agree with George Foster's implications in indicating that those who receive less than half the median income do not want total equality; but even if they live better than their parents did, they may regard their hopes as unfulfilled and do feel bitter and deprived (Rainwater, 1975, 1974; Sennett and Cobb,

[6] Since writing the foregoing, I have come across an essay by George P. Elliott (1974) discussing the relationship between American envy and egalitarianism.

1972). Nevertheless, the gross national product, huge as it appears, was not large enough even before the present recession to meet the expectations for private and for public goods.[7] Only a minority, chiefly among the educated, has turned against consumerism and wasteful production; but the plateau on which this style of life rests is still an elevated one (except perhaps for a few hardy subsistence craftsmen-farmers), and often depends on considerable use of public services (Goldsmith, 1973).

Samuel Lubell, an evocative interviewer, reports in *The Future While It Happened* interviews done at the time of the 1970 and 1972 elections (Lubell, 1973). Many he interviewed were resentful of what scholars have referred to as the liberty and equality revolutions. His respondents were aggrieved, indignant at rising prices and taxes, envious of those above, resentful of those below, especially those on welfare. Most of them distrusted politicians (thus making themselves vulnerable to those politicians who claimed not to be politicians); many distrusted the media, big business, the intelligentsia, who they felt were putting something over on them. Such distrust itself is no discontinuity; it was evident in fights over fluoridation in many localities, for example; it did not take Watergate and the revelations in its wake to create distrust—indeed, local and national demagogic prospectors could build on it in the past. Attitudes that came only sporadically to the national surface and were in general opposed by the educated minority have now become endemic, with that minority in self-mistrustful, sometimes guilty disarray.

Even the Great Depression of 1929, while it shook and then destroyed the legitimacy of Central European governments, did not shake the fundamental faith of most Americans in the legitimacy of the national institutions (bankers and big business only partially excepted) and the faith that the economy would rally, as in fact it only fully did when Allied war orders began pouring in and when the United States itself entered World War II. The upshot was to make military-spending Keynesians out of most Americans. And the fact that World War II was not followed, as had been predicted, by a depression, as the First World War had been, made it seem as if the boom-and-bust cycle could be controlled. After wrestling with the ghosts of both Malthus and Schumpeter, the authors of *The Lonely Crowd* decided that abundance was here to stay, a provincial judgment by what Daniel Bell (1960) has referred to as the prophets of play and abundance. Far from saving out of increasing incomes (as for example the Japanese so dramatically did), many Americans plunged readily into debt. Moderately well-to-do

---

[7] I recognize that this is a highly arguable proposition; one of my sources is the work of the Commission on National Goals of the National Planning Association, of which I was formerly a member (see Terleckyj, 1975).

Americans overspent and, again unlike the Japanese, did not save for their children's college education, but shifted the burden of subsidizing a large part of that education to the states. The free-standing suburban home with its getaway car became the American norm.

Given the situation thus created, it is not surprising that most Americans do not want to believe that there is a real crisis of energy.[8] Their cynicism has been fueled by populist politicians who attack the oil companies (whose profits have undercut their propaganda) and/or the Arab oil-producing states—though not in public the Israelis. (Ardent Zionists and the worldwide net of Israel's enemies have almost, but not completely, succeeded in linking suspicion of or antagonism to Israel with anti-Semitism, but happily there are still a few people like the present writer who make a distinction here.) Much of the population welcomes making villains of politicians, foreign countries, or "foreign" oil companies; for there is a continuity of American resistance to constraint, whether in the form of gun control, seatbelts, limits on engine horsepower, or indeed any limits on the consumption of scarce resources. While recognizing difficulties of enforcement and the long-run dislocations of (more or less) free market allocation, I have been sympathetic with the minority of economists who have urged rationing and wage and price control; but it seems clear that, even if the administration had pushed such policies, the country would not have accepted them.

During the Second World War, many Americans were persuaded to buy war savings bonds on the ground that this would help the war effort, whereas of course the war would have been financed anyway through borrowing and the printing press; the purchases of bonds inhibited spending and thus limited inflation. During the cold war, a number of idealistic Americans used cold war rhetoric to persuade their countrymen to be generous to some non-Americans even outside the range of the containment policy. Today, of course, such arguments are almost entirely discredited. Even so, Americans can be generous when there are immediate disasters dramatically requiring relief at home or abroad. But it would take a very drastic shift in leadership and in followership to persuade Middle Majority Americans, or any mobilized truly poor Americans, to share our fertilizer with Bangladesh or the Sahel, or to enter agreements to right balances of trade among the United States and other countries rich in food, vis-à-vis countries rich in zinc or chromium or the oil of the OPEC nations. The well-to-do would have to set an obvious and credible model of asceticism before the educated minority could persuade those only recently affluent to inhibit their own unsated desires for the standard American package of

---

[8] Nor is it clear how they would act even if they did believe in it. (See Schelling, 1971.)

consumer goods. And management would have to set a model of self-less effort, free of the supposed spur of stock options, before a campaign could be mounted to increase greatly the productivity of the industrial force. (The agricultural self-employed farmers have done this.) All this leads me to fear that there may be no peaceful solution to either our internal or external impending scarcities.

Without continued economic growth, the movement toward greater equality within as well as among nations is unlikely to mute still more resentments and envies than Lubell picked up on his surveys. What we have now within America is a covert class warfare. College-educated Americans, especially in the more selective colleges, have become concerned with the side effects in both pollution and world poverty of the wasteful use and abuse of goods and energy. Working through legislatures, government agencies, federal and local courts, as well as through mobilized veto groups, these legatees of early patrician conservationists see growth as cancerous, whether of population or of production. While the conservationist impulse may be tapering off because of the recession, its momentum continues through the use of litigation and the already established government agencies by mobilized veto groups such as the Sierra Club and local environmentalist lobbies.

Yet litigation—a point I shall return to—is not a substitute for careful trade-offs between those concerned for the long-run environmental future and those preoccupied with raising the standard of living and the feeling of economic security of the great bulk of Americans who have risen above absolute and even relative poverty, but only by what they fear is a narrow margin. These morally indignant, not quite poor Americans envy those above them and fear those below them. Other than a new religion, I see no alternative to the continuation of what I hope will be controlled growth, some of which can come about through more efficient use of now wasted resources and through the development of relatively inexpensive technologies for the control of pollution. That growth must operate at a level of workmanship and of reward which allows us to compete for scarce resources not only with the affluent majority in industrialized Western Europe and Japan, but with the small affluent minorities even in poor countries.

To increase growth will require investment in labor-intensive industries while at the same time breaking free of the bottlenecks imposed by inefficient managerial allocation of resources and occasional labor union strangleholds. No large liberal democracy seems to have been able to increase productivity, limit the growth in state expenditures, and slow down inflation to a tolerable minimum. While war and preparation for it have declined as a relative support for the economy, social services have more than taken the place of defense-spending Keynesian therapies, quite often (as in the case of a large proportion of state sub-

sidies to higher education) for the benefit of the middle class and not of
the really poor.

The Search for Humane Professions

The belief that America had entered a post-industrial era because
of the proportion of the labor force entering white-collar and especially
the human service areas has been misleading.[9] Just as industry earlier
had absorbed people fleeing from or ejected from farming by high-
technology agriculture, we were absorbing the ever-larger number of
women in the labor force, as well as many men and women from formerly blue-collar jobs, into the expanding government services, including education. Though white-collar positions sometimes do not pay as
well as unionized and/or skilled blue-collar tasks, they have often appeared to offer more security against layoffs. College-educated people
have generally managed even now to find white-collar jobs which pay
more than most blue-collar jobs, except in the most highly skilled and
strongly unionized trades. In addition, young people often attend college because they want, as they often put it, "to work with people";
from the outside, this appears humane—and not as arduous as the
skilled crafts and (again as seen from the outside) as routinized as industrial jobs.[10] We lack tool and die makers and other skilled crafts-
men. We need many more miners in spite of those aging ones who return from unemployment in Detroit to the hills of Appalachia.
Moreover, although able, mostly male students from principally less-
educated family backgrounds are flocking into engineering, the
country is still short of certain kinds of engineers, including those who
can deal with questions of environment and mass transport.

However, in the more selective undergraduate colleges such as my
own, both women and men students have been stampeding into medicine and law: Professions which appear to offer independence from
bureaucratic constraint, high economic security in the case of medicine
(and a good chance for it for the high-standing graduate of a major national law school), and in many cases the hope that one can be of use to
people, whether in saving health and lives or in securing justice. The

[9] As already indicated, I was one of those who shared this judgment. Since delivering this
address I have read Daniel Bell's sober assessment of current discontents, an essay
whose argument at many points is congruent with and extends my own discussion (Bell,
1975).

[10] For a fuller discussion of mismatching among labor force requirements, education,
and individual preferences, including references to recent studies and surveys, see
Weiss, Harwood, and Riesman, 1976.

surge of so many highly talented young people, including quite a number with Ph.D.'s, into medicine has something of the quality of a brain drain even if there were hope for a better distribution of physicians which would give us fewer surgeons in New Haven or Boston and more in upper Michigan or Appalachia, for much work that is now done by physicians could be done by people less expensively trained and hence less eager for "interesting" diseases rather than chronic complaints from patients with inchoate symptoms who seem obstinately to refuse the doctor's advice. We are beginning to realize that we need people trained in schools of public administration who can administer health care systems, that hospital administrators need not necessarily be M.D.'s, and that many tasks now performed by highly trained physicians can be handled at least as adequately by so-called paramedical persons—though it is also true that in an egalitarian society, what is culturally defined as the "best" health care is less and less able to be rationed on a market basis, just as has already happened in large measure with higher education and is beginning to happen with legal services.[11] The start-up costs and recruitment problems of beginning a new medical school are enormous, yet old ones have expanded and new ones have begun, and medical school places have increased by about 50 percent in recent years. In contrast, law schools are often moneymaking operations, and those not in the national league are like accordions, almost indefinitely expansible.[12]

There is no particular discontinuity here: so far as I know, America is unique in the world in the proportion of lawyers who create, mediate, resolve, and exacerbate disputes (Nader, 1975). The United States has ten times as many lawyers as the Japanese, who use go-betweens to settle disputes by mediated consensus—and who sometimes import lawyers from America who possess the requisite "un-Japanese" aggressiveness.[13] To be sure, law schools, like graduate schools of education, have often served as way-stations for the undecided—a kind of post-baccalaureate second undergraduate degree (at the master's level in education) which closes few options and may open some.

The hemorrhage of talent into the law, now perhaps just beginning to have the tourniquet of market forces applied to it, is as already sug-

[11] There are somewhat analogous problems of the distribution of effort among medical research scientists, who are tempted to concentrate on the "American" preoccupations with cancer and cardiovascular ailments, with less attention to other diseases which have been less investigated scientifically or dealt with clinically.

[12] Many of their graduates are likely to resemble the solo lawyers Jerome Carlin (1962) has described, who end up selling insurance and real estate and hoping for a lucrative malpractice suit or other such bonanza.

[13] I owe this Japanese-American comparison to Nathan Glazer (1975), and much of this discussion reflects conversations with him. Lipset (1967) provides a comparison of the proportion of lawyers in the population of the English-speaking democracies.

gested not a radical discontinuity. But I do want to emphasize that the desire to enter the high-status, people-serving professions which presently dominates the student bodies of the most selective colleges, and also the desire of many older people of both sexes, is responsive not only to market forces and the desire for security, but also to an allergy in the same circles to working in any sort of organizational harness, whether in private or public bureaucracies. What in my judgment the country—and the world—needs are managers and planners. In the most selective university colleges, able students until recently have turned away from graduate schools of business and management and from the few graduate schools of public policy. What sort of preparation women and men need for large managerial and planning tasks is arguable, but I would think of history, demography, economics, statistics, an introduction to the natural sciences and engineering, and some knowledge of a non-Western civilization as elements of such preparation. In spite of a few efforts in major national law schools to add electives in such fields, most students do not learn these things in law school, although some manage to pick up an education later. We stock our legislatures with lawyers; and to some extent, the supply creates its own demand. Particularly, we stock the United States Senate with lawyers (some of them primarily businessmen with law degrees); and we tend to draw for presidential candidates on individuals who have managed a staff of ten to twenty people, have come from a calling prone to solipsism, which was indeed one of its attractions, and have little experience of leading a large collective enterprise. To grasp the long-run consequences of what they do is hard for people in any sphere of life; it may be especially hard for those whose adult socialization consists of experience in adversary situations or even in many situations where the work of a lawyer consists of negotiation or of building defenses against future litigation.

Able law students taught by sharp professors are nurtured on a diet of judicial opinions written for the most part by judges of lower social and intellectual standing than the eminent bar (the federal courts are something of an exception, and one or two state courts); one can learn in six months to pick holes in the judges' reasoning, and often to graduate with an omnicompetent confidence that there is nothing, except perhaps a patent case, which a good lawyer cannot get up in a matter of a few weeks. A number of these highly trained lawyers will be prepared to take part in the not so covert class warfare that goes on between part of the educated minority and much of the rest of the population over the issue of distribution of resources already discussed, and also about environmental protection and safety. Some among the educated are willing to use the federal courts or the federal government to achieve greater equality in education and in other social benefits. Many want the amenities of clean air and undestroyed wilds; they are often willing to override local majorities of the poor and middle-income Americans who want jobs and the consumer goods that have been defined as the standard American package. While of course, litigation can sometimes protect the rights of an oppressed minority, this scarcely justifies so very many now entering law in the hope of careers as public defenders or as public-interest lawyers.[14] In other words, prolonged and costly litigation—costly in terms of the time of public and corporate officials as well as direct legal costs—frequently distorts the difficult questions of planning and public and private management by which trade-offs might be less badly and more expeditiously concluded. Only a few years ago it appeared as if consumers needed protection by governmental action against exploitation on the part of producers, but if one considers what has happened now with malpractice litigation against the "producers" of medical services, or environmental litigation against a variety of producers of power and energy, one may ask about the cost to the society of this tilting of the balance and the resources spent on litigation as against the resources that might be spent on the substantive issues involved.

In *Popular Culture and High Culture,* Herbert Gans (1974) describes conflicts of taste, and argues in favor of subcultural pluralism, in which each group can have its own preferred enjoyments and its share of public subsidy. Many of these issues can be resolved without the necessity of litigation, although with respect to network television, where resources are scarce, and in occasional censorship cases, divisiveness may be unavoidable. Eventually, cable television may ameliorate such conflicts, just as at present each subculture can have its FM stations and printed media. One can imagine a world in which a working-class vacationer who wants clean streams and well-stocked fishing areas quite as much as any Sierra Club member can secure such amenities while also keeping his industrial job, its safety precautions, and a minimal level of inflation. But our present economy in its international setting gives scant prospect of reaching such a nirvana in the immediately foreseeable future.

The push into law of the idealistic and talented students about whom I have been writing in part reflects the denigration until quite recently of careers in high-technology (often multinational) corporations or in banking as bureaucratic and hence constraining,[15] where not actually complicitous.

---

[14] Some, but by no means all *pro bono* lawyers are sensitive to the ethical and practical dilemmas of the class action suit which may not benefit a particular client in a particular battle, and which may result in a resounding and famous legal victory which can leave all parties poorer. (See Brill, 1973, 1975).

[15] As panic about the uncertain occupational future becomes contagious among students who are both affluent and able, there is a tendency to herdlike behavior. For example, many misapprehend the freedom of the so-called free professions: They have little sense of the enormous diversity among kinds of careers in medicine or law, or of the

Historically, litigation or the threat of it has often served as a substitute for violence and vigilantism—though in current controversies over busing it may lead to both. Judicial coercion is a poor substitute for politics. There has been much talk about the imperial presidency, but little about the imperial judiciary, which is an exception to the general movement today toward more democracy and more equality. A single judge (even in the presence of a lay jury) can decide momentous cases, subject of course to the appellate process. Likewise, litigation is a poor substitute for a national agenda, which of course a court cannot set, since it can only deal with cases brought by litigants (including governmental agencies) who, as already suggested, may be quite unrepresentative of any larger constituency or potential coalition. None of this is intended, of course, to suggest that the courts have not in many areas of national and local life brought about greater fairness and served, especially in the case of the federal courts, through their insulation from populist pressures, to correct abuses, public and private, and as in the case of civil rights and the Supreme Court decision on abortion, to give a voice to the previous voiceless or oppressed.[16] My point is that the delegitimation of other careers competing with that of the law (and medicine) has created a certain discontinuity in the allocation of scarce talents to the problems of an industrial society undergoing, in Daniel Bell's phrase, "the revolution of rising entitlements."

The concept of social character which assumed that societies got the slate of character types they "needed" to fit the requirements of past epochs, and then somehow through adult socialization or resocialization deployed people to do the necessary work, was explored by a good many students of culture and personality a quarter-century ago. The authors of The Lonely Crowd thought in these terms. But if one asks about the future, how Americans are suddenly to find the restraint

constraints imposed by clients and colleagues. To seek to enter a prestigious medical or law school makes the claim only that one can get in, and thus avoids the "elitist" claim that one has something special to contribute in art or science. Careers in the arts seem inevitably hazardous, at least outside of academic settings, but Ph.D. programs in selected fields may offer both academic and nonacademic opportunities superior to those offered to the growing surplus of law-trained individuals. Boom-and-bust thinking has led to overgeneralizations concerning the lack of jobs in colleges and universities, so that fields which once appeared hopelessly overcrowded, such as classics or art history, may soon be looking for recruits who are simply not around. Whatever may be our world record in industrial production, it remains outstanding in art, including architecture, and in the academic disciplines—a national asset that can easily be lost (Riesman, 1975). (I fear that we academicians sometimes unwittingly persuade our students that our own mode of life is unduly constraining. Misled by two decades of growth and prosperity, we complain about not only legislative but also internal administrative efforts to establish coherence in our teaching programs, and easily lose a sense of calling and enthusiasm about what we do.)

[16] Even here in the case of abortion, one could say that the use of the courts was an antidemocratic expedient. The poor or the frightened young who could not get reasonably safe abortions elsewhere had their civil rights delayed as the issue was fought out politically on a state-by-state basis. Although myself in favor of abortion on demand, I

which our position on Spaceship Earth requires of us, and the leadership and followership in large organizations that are necessary to keep all of us alive without succumbing to either Malthusian or Hobbesian ravages, I do not see any answer. It is, however, clear that those who preach restraint must themselves be prepared to exercise it; otherwise, they will be in the position of the rich person saying to the poor one: "Why do you want my ulcers?" or the rich country saying to the not yet rich one: "Why do you want our traffic jams?"

Changes in orientation toward careers can occur with great rapidity. There are economists and others prepared to think and to plan about the largest questions of the world economy and who are not afraid of being "contaminated" by applied work. Yet we lack the centralization in the United States which makes possible the French *Grandes Ecoles* which might train planners for positions which barely exist as yet.

There is the additional handicap, not uniquely American, that the terms "bureaucrat" and "politician" have for a long time been pejorative, no less so for those who seek colleagueship at work than those who prefer the individualistic competitiveness which characterizes academic life or the arts. The right and the left agree in attacking bureaucracy, sometimes with the preference for shedding red blood to cutting red tape. Bureaucracies imply boundaries: boundaries of status, of expertise, of jurisdiction. And the great movements toward more equality, and more liberty, by which is meant more expressiveness, of the last several decades have been movements opposed to boundaries and constraints.[17]

---

have recognized this issue also as having aspects of class warfare. Upper-class men and women are rightly concerned with the dangers, tragedies, and traumas involved in the choice between illegal and dangerous abortions and unwanted pregnancies. But very few realize that there are women who would rather trap a man than not to have one, and that even shotgun weddings, in many working-class and rural settings, have been a protection for women, whereas today, local men can tell such women that they can go get themselves an abortion and thus avoid an "arranged" marriage. There is also the sweeping judgment that the "right to life" advocates are nothing but bigots, mainly Catholic, wedded to a patriarchal view of the world.

More generally, overcoming what most of us in this audience would regard as popular prejudices through incremental efforts at persuasion is hard counsel to offer those who do not want to wait indefinitely for justice, and who have often believed that court decisions themselves would act as educative forces overcoming the superstitions of the unenlightened. Instead, it is often the latter now who feel powerless—not even fighting, as they once did, against fluoridation as a symbolic crusade against the hegemony of the educated.

[17] Christopher Jencks observes in a comment on the foregoing passage that a movement toward equality would have to be a movement toward more restraints and boundaries: restraints on the privileges and freedoms of the competent and powerful implemented by creation of stronger social norms and legal sanctions for redistribution of income and wealth (Christopher Jencks, 1975: personal communications; Jencks et al., 1972). Until recently and for many even today, the assumption has been widespread that there are no real scarcities and that therefore what Daniel Bell refers to as the revolution of rising entitlements makes it possible for everyone equally to do or express his own thing.

In this climate, those who do take on roles of leadership feel their work has become unrewarding and frustrating. Sometimes they are held to very rigid limits precisely so that those who work under and around them can behave in ways the latter feel are spontaneous and unpredictable; any administrator who behaved in the same way would be regarded as playing favorites or lacking in accountability. Others are free to abuse and insult them; the administrators in turn must remain calm and conciliatory, but at the same time, "human." Since the administrators also belong to a culture which values at least the appearance of authenticity, they are often seized by a bad conscience, whether they exercise restraint or lose their tempers. Shortly after the Watergate investigations began, I attended a meeting of a group of college and university presidents, where there was general agreement with the remark one president made: "Watergate has diminished us." In the United States currently, the cry for better leadership is endemic. Surely, leadership is required. But its efficacy depends also on willingness to follow politicians who do not claim that they are not politicians and do not make easy reputations by attacking bureaucracy and centralized authority. Such attacks add to the already endemic feeling of people that they are manipulated by conspiracies; even before the recent spate of revelations about abuse of authority, Gallup polls showed how widespread had been the belief that Oswald did not alone kill President Kennedy, despite the American record of loners who have killed or shot at presidents.

It is not only people at the bottom of society who harbor quasi-conspiratorial attitudes of constraint. Ralph Turner (1975) suggests on the basis of a sample of UCLA students that those who have been more active, more likely to challenge their professors (of whom they are not afraid) are also those who feel most in danger of reprisal from "the System," and in a sense most alienated—more so than students who have been less engaged and, generally, less successful. One might interpret Turner's finding to signify that the more active students are tempted to take risks and fear the consequences; perhaps they also attribute to others the hatred and aggression they themselves may possess.

Liberation and Stalemate

The United States has never been as homogeneous as those who talk about a "mainstream" of white Anglo-Saxon culture like to believe, for even within these once-dominant groups there were marked differences among, for example, Congregationalists, Presbyterians, and various branches of Methodism. There was even a minority tradition of fatalism among some New England writers and intellectuals. But on the whole, among what might be called the club of the white males, there was more liberty and more equality in the sense of lesser deference, than there had been in Europe, and there was hope that progress would bring both more liberty and more equality. But as immigration increased (especially of those from non-Protestant cultural traditions, including many who distrusted the legitimacy of the governments of their nation-states, or, as in the case of southern Italians, hardly knew they had a nation-state), differences of customs and beliefs led to the symbolic crusades Joseph Gusfield describes concerning what it means to be an American, who is entitled to offer the preferred definition, and hence who is to have more liberty and equality and who is to have less (Gusfield, 1964; Hofstadter, 1965).

In the affluent decades from 1948 through the 1960s, there was a series of symbolic crusades as well as pragmatic movements by previously excluded groups demanding their share of education, medical, occupational, and other resources. While in the American past, as Seymour M. Lipset (1967) contends, the seesaw between the demand for more liberty and the demand for more equality has been a persistent continuity, the glamorous invitations offered by affluence made it seem possible to achieve simultaneously more liberty, more equality, and more democracy. A series of previously unmobilized groups entered the political arena, sometimes making use of civil and occasionally uncivil disobedience: first white Southerners objecting to desegregation; then previously unorganized blacks, followed by other minorities of color and then by white ethnic groups; elite and then less elite college students; and currently, activist, liberationist women.[18]

In my (all too often fallible) judgment, the women's liberation movements are not a passing fad among highly educated white upper-middle-class women and some of their male contemporaries. Bachofen, Engels, and Veblen argued in the last century that matriarchy was an even older system of authority than patriarchy (Slater, 1968). However, while attacks on patriarchy have a long intellectual history, and feminist movements among bluestocking pioneers a long social and political history, I would contend that the present situation is neither recapitulation nor simple progression, but represents strong elements of discontinuity. The discontinuity reflects the momentum and scope of the women's movements and their impact on both sexes and many aspects of social, institutional, and personal life.

For generations there have been isolated women, protected by high status, who could defy the conventions of their sex because of the eccentricities allowed their social class. Even in an older America there

---

[18] Samuel P. Huntington (1975) discusses the traffic jam of powerlessness created by these simultaneous and overlapping mobilizations.

have been such women: sometimes high-status Bohemians like Amy Lowell or brave reformers such as the Grimké sisters or, in other ways, Jane Addams; and of course in the fight for suffrage women resorted to civil disobedience and other tactics then considered shocking. The social hierarchy helped give scope to Eleanor Roosevelt, Frances Perkins, and other less well known women as recently as the 1930s. But the New Deal, followed by the Second World War, helped undo the residual social hierarchies, and the baby boom, after the war, along with the affluence that made it possible, enhanced by the suburban spread which had begun much earlier, and egalitarianism, subjected women to same-sex inhibitions even if they were college graduates and as well educated as their menfolk, or better. They could have jobs before the first child came and after the last had grown and flown, but were discouraged by both sexes from entering traditionally male careers. As recently as 1963, when Alice Rossi proposed a more equitable division of gender roles in work and in family life, at a conference sponsored by the American Academy of Arts and Sciences, a number of liberal male and female participants regarded her propositions as *outré* (Rossi, 1965).

The more radical wings of the women's movements shock many today. They are often seen by the general population as an aspect of other crusades by affluent and provocative young people, as in the earlier drug cults, in the antiwar movement, or in countercultural activities generally. But in fact, these radical wings are in part a reaction *against* these other movements of protest: A number of college-educated women discovered that, in the civil rights and New Left crusades, they were being led and often exploited by domineering men under the guise of liberation and emancipation (Thorne, 1972). Women also adapted a tactic, namely the consciousness-raising group, which mixed the age-grades, and helped, or perhaps occasionally overpersuaded, women to reinterpret their situation as one of deprivation and subordination to male chauvinism (Freeman, 1975). Indeed, lacking any obvious territoriality such as some nationalist blacks, Spanish-speaking groups, and American Indians possess, these women found that they had forcibly to separate themselves from a network of relations to men as fathers, brothers, sons, lovers, and to create a metaphorical territoriality. The result has been to inaugurate profoundly unsettling changes in attitudes toward the family and the role of the sexes on a far larger scale than could be accomplished or often even imagined by the earlier isolated pioneers.[19]

[19] The movement in England for the suffrage prior to World War I, led by the Pankhursts, so affronted Victorian attitudes of both sexes as to move toward tactics more violent than the American movement for women's suffrage, which could proceed state by state as well as nationally, and which also involved episodes of passionate civil dis-

There are participants and observers, perhaps especially in this sociological audience, who believe not only that marriage as an institution is endangered, but that it should be. My own surmise is that marriage in some form is likely to survive in America, but it would seem unlikely that gender roles will lapse back into former taken-for-granted patterns. There is already a minority of husbands taking major responsibility for running households while their wives are the major breadwinners—an occasional pattern founded not on ideology but necessity at the economic bottom of society. Among the educated, the hope is widespread that men and women can choose their roles, and that women's liberation movements are leading to men's liberation from competitiveness, from the tyranny of the clock, from Max Weber's "iron cage," and other constraints. But I am inclined to think that the iron cage is worldwide (and that we are more likely to run out of iron than of cages); the vision I once held that a general relaxation of habits of work was possible for Americans may in the short term be quite unrealistic. It would increase the politically explosive effects of inflation to the extent that this is brought about by lowered productivity. As already suggested, I believe that in the years of scarcity ahead, we shall need more than ever to exert ourselves to produce, and may not be able to afford the slackening of the work ethic, and of the need for achievement which must be distinguished from competitiveness and the need to dominate and surpass others. Many women who would consider themselves in the forefront of the women's movements would agree with this, maintaining that women have historically been producers, while men, as Veblen contended, have been sportsmen and gamesmen, more concerned with display than with craftsmanship. But the more countercultural implications of other wings of the women's movements which would reorganize work and family in a more relaxed way, could in the world economy prove too costly.[20]

Jo Freeman (1972) has observed that the consciousness-raising groups, in rejecting what they regard as the "macho" model of division of labor and of expertise and hence supposed domination, occasionally have endangered their own political effectiveness, as well as subjecting members to covert manipulations from each other. Currently, the avant-garde wings of the movements have sought to widen their social class bases and to cooperate, for example, with leaders of NOW, the National Organization for Women.

Yet as more women attend college, and as more children of both

---

obedience. As when members of any oppressed group seek to break through long-established forms, they can set in motion escalating chains of repression, violence, counter-repression: Only the First World War brought a truce and then, in both the United Kingdom and the United States, equality of voting rights for women.

[20] Arlie Hochschild (1975) provides a persuasively argued alternative view.

sexes are raised in college-educated families, and as more working mothers adapt their views of what is proper to their actual behavior, the circles widen in which some aspects of liberationist ideology are accepted. Daniel Yankelovich's (1974) study comparing college and noncollege youth asserts that there is a "sharp cleavage in views and values now separating college and noncollege women," but his data indicate the degree to which noncollege women accept some tenets which in an earlier day would have been considered heretical; for example, only half of the noncollege women regard having children as an important personal value (nearly a third of college women do), and 38 percent of noncollege women do not regard having children outside of formal marriage as morally wrong.[21]

In a way, what is surprising is that in the symbolic clashes and crusades among cultural classes, so much of Middle America has responded to provocation, not by active violence, but by a slowly growing tolerance coupled with irritated bewilderment. In race relations, for example, except where urban villagers object to forced integration and busing, and also (like other city dwellers) to crime, poll data I have seen (as in the work of Andrew Greeley) show rising racial tolerance, notably so among Catholics. There is also a rise in acceptance of new styles of dress and behavior, including sexual freedom and communal modes of life. The Yankelovich survey reported that, except for the cleavage over women's liberation, many values of the counterculture of 1969 have now reached noncollege youth.[22] Undoubtedly, as with other publicized movements of participatory protest, the women's movements have been deeply offensive to many rural and working-class as well as some middle-class Americans. For these movements appear to delegitimate the role of housewife or part-time or periodic job-holder in comparison with women who pursue careers. Volunteer activity is denigrated, sometimes because capable women were given subordinate positions in organizations led by men, but also in groups such as the League of Women Voters and PTA which have served as social cement

[21] In a study which became available only after the meetings at which this paper was presented, Karen Oppenheim Mason, John Czajka, and Sara Arber (1975) use a series of public opinion polls to suggest that many liberationist ideas were in the early 1960s already influencing the attitudes of employed noncollege women and of college-educated women, with education as in other surveys the strongest single variable and with work experience both a cause and consequence of change in attitude. The results have to be teased out from not easily comparable surveys, and the authors regret their inability to report any comparable data con　ning male attitudes.

[22] In "Notes on a Natural History of Fads," Meyersohn and Katz (1957) describe the way in which fads and fashions—and, one might add, larger constellations of subcultural styles—are often picked up by educated impresarios from outgroups such as lower-class or rural blacks, "hillbillies," or Yiddish comedians; these then become, when suitably altered (in the case of the Beatles, trans-Atlantic passages), the innovations of the taste-makers, which then in turn filter down again to noncollege youth.

not only for participants but for the entire society. Similarly, to the extent that housework is seen as volunteer labor, "unliberated" breadwinner males are told that they are exploiting the unpaid labor of their wives.

Because the women's movements do not stand in isolation from other protest movements, the possibility of continuing class cleavage (despite the emphasis on sisterhood) and backlash exists; but one could argue that the women's movements are currently losing their revolutionary significance and becoming in some measure accepted in all cultural classes. The devotees of Herbert Marcuse would call this repressive tolerance or co-optation, whereas I would regard it as mutual infiltration among groups only partially insulated from each other.

There are pockets of insulation nevertheless, illustrated by the sometimes violent boycott of "modernist" textbooks in Kanawha County, West Virginia, and in the prosperous condition of some of the colleges controlled by evangelical Protestant sects which emphasize biblical literalism, though at times with little training in theological fundamentals. The fundamentalist churches flourish, while liberal Protestant and Catholic leaders come under attack for preaching up-to-date versions of the Social Gospel. It would be as unwise to take the post-Vietnam and post-Watergate victory of liberal Democrats in the 1974 congressional elections as representing a new liberal consensus in the United States as it was earlier to overestimate, as I did, the appeal of right-wing symbolic crusades to working-class voters whose current concerns are more with inflation and the sagging economy than with assaults on their traditional familistic values by the women's movements and other causes advanced by educated minorities. Although the several states of the federal system have lost much of their bulkhead or insular quality that so attracted Justice Louis D. Brandeis, the political apathy of large numbers of potential voters currently offers a certain buffer against the coalescence of the pockets of right-wing extremism whose inhabitants Governor Wallace and former Governor Reagan are trying to mobilize on a national basis.[23]

Authority in Question

In the judgment of people from more hierarchical societies, Americans have appeared as they did to Tocqueville, less deferential—although he thought America in principle governable thanks to freedom of association, talent in forming voluntary associations via the

[23] Riesman and Glazer (1950) provide fuller discussion of the uses of apathy.

free press, the social cement provided by religion, and the restraint of the semi-aristocracy of the legal profession. (He also presciently feared a possible oligarchy of manufacturers, although the America he visited was still largely pre-industrial, and he recognized that the evil of slavery might shatter the nation.) Moreover, the fact that young Americans often had more education than their parents (or were more "American" if the latter were immigrants) and the invitations offered by the frontier and the West and in the cities early gave rise to attitudes hostile to authority as well as to authoritarianism. However, one example may illustrate the discontinuity involved in the increasing loss of credibility by authorities drawing their legitimacy from the society rather than from personal charisma or glamor. The Civilian Conservation Corps was created under the New Deal to put unemployed youth to work building firebreaks and trails under the discipline of noncoms often drawn from the military services. The CCC has often been in my mind as I have observed Peace Corps volunteers, mostly but not entirely college-educated, disparage those involved in their training and their deployment overseas—the noncoms of this small agency for volunteers. I have also pondered the CCC in connection with proposals, most recently by the Panel on Youth (1974) headed by James Coleman, that young people be put to work in constructive volunteer employment rather than stored in schools or left to roam the streets. In small enclaves, there have been groups of young people who cleaned up a neighborhood, or Sierra Club members who helped work to clear firebreaks in the forests. In the 1930s, young men obeyed the authority of noncom types even if they disliked the work and hated the boss. Of course, not all of them obeyed; there were always Huckleberry Finns.

However, the affluence of recent decades has made Americans of all ages able to say openly what children like to say to adults: "You're not the boss of me!" But neither, as we have seen, are they bosses of themselves in terms of self-restraint. And as more and more people have sought their shares in America, their ability to cancel each other out both in symbolic terms and often in pragmatic results—that is, their inability to arrive at trade-offs regarded as for the time being equitable—has as we have suggested led people to feel less potent or efficacious, and hence to blame authority for such evident stalemates as the inability of all industrial, democratic societies to control simultaneously inflation and unemployment (though in terms of unemployment, America's record is among the worst). Robert Heilbroner (1974) addresses himself to these matters in *An Inquiry into the Human Prospect,* and since he is a reflective political economist, I find his work more persuasive than that of ecologists or demographers engaged in extrapolating the Malthusian variables. The anti-Vietnam-war elites were successful in destroying the authority of the "best and the brightest"—

now a term of sarcasm—who helped invent, support, and justify the war. But the antiwar elites are themselves fragmented, and indeed often opposed to elitism as such, and almost certainly unable to replace the authorities, many of them still in positions of responsibility, whose legitimacy has been undermined. Yet this fragmentation of power seems to me most dangerous in controlling the atom, only slightly less dangerous in controlling responses to a lower standard of living. Believing as I do in surprises and discontinuities, I think it conceivable that the mood of the country can change—but it may not change in time for us to find acceptable ways of managing a country of over 200 million energetic people pursuing both private and group destinies of material ambition as well as evangelical mandates.

In view of the perilous situation we have reached, we need not only intelligent and responsive local and national leadership but, as already argued, the willingness to follow it. Governors and mayors who have raised taxes to meet essential services have almost invariably been voted out of office, while those who have borrowed money to pay off voters (mostly middle and working class, organized in unions and pressure groups, rather than poor) have survived politically, like those Americans who so amazed Tocqueville by going through bankruptcy and emerging with reputations unscathed. Another long-run legacy is the endemic cynicism concerning the promises of politicians, which in turn leads to gullibility vis-à-vis those politicians who pretend to be against politics, against government itself.

However, thoughtful policy-makers who are not exploiters of voters' resentments, fears, and paranoias, are, along with many of the rest of us, puzzled as to what would be politically feasible courses of action that could set limits on the spiraling struggle of contending blocs to keep up with or outrun inflation by shifting its terrible penalties to others. After the euphoria which gripped many in the late 1960s, we are in a period when there are few imaginative human prospects, including visions of alternative societies which are realistic in the sense that they might be achieved, given who we are and what we have made of ourselves in the world. We can learn of course from the experience of other nations and we should, but I do not see models for us, or indeed for the planet, which are particularly helpful for the American case. The visions of the New Left, whether these looked outward to other countries or inward to native American radicalism, failed in this respect by oversimplification and then, feeling more powerless than was often in fact justified, resorting in a few instances to terror. But we also need at the same time something very different, namely, not visions, but faith in the ongoing human enterprise including a restored belief in the virtue of "thinking small," taking some difficult incremental steps along but a single dimension. The counterculture has some-

times done this in providing examples of life of greater simplicity and
concern for the environment, even though it has often surrounded
such practical steps with rather vague and perhaps endearing visions of
a communal society which might fit a country the size of Denmark.

But of course to "think small" is not enough. America has always
been in danger of reaching the limits of the antagonistic cooperation of
its competing and coexisting parishes of interest and passion. It has as-
tonished me that the Civil War, though seared and enshrined in the
memory of Southerners, has left such a small impact on most of the
country about the capacities for civil strife of a massive sort, and
the companion danger of seeking to cope with internal fragmentation
by a new surge of American nationalism. Nationalism, with its ethnic
variants, remains perhaps the strongest ideological power in the world,
although nation-states seem to be losing their monopoly of violence to
guerrillas willing to die for their cause—who may themselves some day
acquire nuclear as well as conventionally horrifying weapons. At the
same time, the history of the human race exhibits extraordinary re-
siliency and adaptability. Human beings became settled agriculturalists
and thus were capable, as Lewis Mumford reminds us, of organizing
"megamachines" to build such monumental things as the pyramids [24]
only a few thousand years ago. Agriculture and civilization did not disappear even though particular lands and cities were destroyed through
the centuries by waves of barbarians and raiding nomads. If we do not
destroy the carrying capacity of the planet in a nuclear catastrophe or
some biological equivalent, I can be encouraged about the extraordinary speed with which human beings have developed high cultures,
even as old empires have fallen. For us as Americans, we need also to
recognize that, however hostile much of the world may be toward some
aspects of American power and relative plenty (of which our own educated strata are increasingly critical), and while some of the world fears
our not having enough cohesion and power, most of the highly educated everywhere look to the United States for advances in science and
in scholarship, in architecture, in music and painting—and even, in
spite of what I have said about our scorn for the so-called organization
man, for the American managerial know-how which we often seem better able to export than to use at home. The United States remains a
world leader in high-technology agriculture, in certain kinds of computers and components, and, for worse as well as for better, in air-
planes. We need to strengthen these elements of productive energy
while, with due help for displaced workers, relinquishing the protec-
tionism (and/or domestic subsidies) by which we maintain industries

---

[24] It has been suggested that the pyramids were a WPA project in periods of unemployment.

such as textiles or shipbuilding in which we cannot effectively compete, facilitating a better economic division of labor in the world, aiding our own consumers, and retraining and relocating our displaced producers. We must also prepare ourselves for the possibility that we will not have organized enough technological substitutes for current fossil fuels and other shrinking resources, and hence to find ways of maintaining our civilization on a different level of consumership, without destroying the creativity of entrepreneurs while evoking the resourcefulness and if need be the stoicism manifested in wartime and in many families during the Great Depression of the 1930s.

I am thinking now in terms of decades, for I can conceive of another spurt of economic growth in the United States, although not of one which will end inflation and even more rapid depletion of resources than our husbandry and ingenuity can replace. Robert Bellah (forthcoming) sees hope, not so much in the civil religion of a largely Protestant and ancestral America, but in what he terms the new religious consciousness (sometimes oriented toward nature) emerging especially among young people shopping for sects he and others have studied in the Bay Area. But I doubt if necessity is an adequate mother for religious invention. And even such morally compelling leaders as the slain martyrs, Robert F. Kennedy and Martin Luther King, Jr., did not command the full assent of, I would suppose, more than at most a bare majority of Americans. Indeed, if a charismatic leader came along to respond to our hungers and dilemmas, we would probably fear him or her, especially when what our present situation calls for are "complexifiers" and not the "terrible simplifiers."

When I reflect on history, I cannot be sanguine about the future of any particular nation-state, legatee of crumbling empires—certainly not about the United States. But I also gain from history, as already suggested, a kind of religious faith in the human enterprise as a whole: its tenacity and powers of recovery—including recovery of past wisdoms and great works of art and science, and of the potential in men and women to stretch themselves to the limit of their abilities at once in moral and intellectual terms. These abilities are more than enough to cope with the current human prospect, created as it has been by the ingenuity as well as the greed of our contemporaries and of earlier generations. Mind is not at the end of its tether (Trilling, 1973).

2

Conventional Wisdom, Common Sense, and Empirical Knowledge: The Case of Stratification Research and Views of American Society

Peter H. Rossi

Introduction

To PROVIDE an overall perspective on American society and at the same time to remain on the level of concreteness, it is necessary to focus on a specific aspect of the society rather than employ a fish-eye lens on the whole. This is the strategy chosen to pursue in this paper: Through a discussion of the findings of research on social stratification in America and their implications, a perspective will be provided on our society as a whole.

In order to delimit this essay even further I have elected to de-emphasize the race and sex aspects of social stratification even though one must recognize that the castelike aspects of American social stratification is one of its distinguishing characteristics among industrialized societies. The topic of race and sex stratification is one that deserves special, separate treatment and will be treated only in passing here.[1]

There are several reasons for using the study of social stratification to provide a perspective on a total society. First of all, it is clear that stratification is a major subsystem of any society, since it can be regarded as an outcome, directly and indirectly, of a number of other important societal processes. The connections between social stratifi-

---

[1] Because men and women are linked together within the basic unit of social stratification, families and households, it is not at all clear that sex stratification ought to be considered within the same context as other distributional aspects of social inequality.

cation and the economic, political, ethnic, and kinship systems are strong and clear, if not always completely understood. Secondly, we have learned a great deal about social stratification in America from the empirical researches of the last decade, and hence perspectives derived from there on the society as a whole can be more firmly grounded in what we know. Hopefully one would be constrained by that knowledge to remain as concrete as possible.

Research on any topic does not proceed in a value and political vacuum. The last three decades have seen a considerable increase in our empirical knowledge of social stratification processes, a result in part of the political concerns of the post–World War II period. In the early years of this period emphasis on this topic stemmed from our concern with the supply of talent for the scientific manpower needs of the post-Sputnik era. Somewhat later, political concerns shifted to the processes of resource allocation and redistribution issues that have been at the heart of major political concerns of the 1960s and 1970s, as expressed in the rediscovery of poverty, the politicization of blacks, women, and other "minorities," as well as a questioning of the roles played by the educational system in the society.

A word of caution is necessary before plunging into specific topics within the field of social stratification. There is an imperfect match between societal concerns and our understanding of social stratification. Popular discussions of social mobility often have in mind quite spectacular changes in life circumstances represented in very unusual careers involving very dramatic differences between social origins and eventual status attainment, but when we study social mobility our instruments are more likely to pick up the more common shifts from farm laborer to retail salesman. We are also inclined to exaggerate the influence of social stratification position on a wide variety of correlates. Position in the social stratification system discriminates among people, *but not by very much*, at least within the usual range of SES covered by typical empirical studies.

I will take up a number of topics in the body of this chapter, the choices being conditioned by one consideration: The topic should be one on which there is some empirical evidence of more than minimum probity. Toward the end of the chapter I will also consider some issues of relevance that social stratification research has been somehow unable to address itself to, either for technical or for political reasons.

Perspectives on Social Mobility

The more glamorous topics that sociologists deal with have to be shared with a variety of other professions. Social mobility certainly fits this description, being both glamorous and a topic which we share with novelists, economists, historians and publicists, and even common garden moralists. A critical issue that agitates all groups is whether the positions in our society that carry with them resources, power, and prestige are being distributed equitably. Of course there are several models of equity, including one which defines equity as meritocratic (the best people get on top), another which defines equity as equal opportunity, and still another which defines equity as a mixture of merit and equal opportunity—equality of opportunity for persons of equal quality.

The empirical evidence that has accumulated on this score is somewhat contradictory. From studies of mass intergenerational mobility (e.g., Blau and Duncan, 1967; Sewell and Hauser, 1975) it is clear that our society is meritocratic, *if* emphasis is placed on the very important role played by formal education in status attainment; or one may view the society as having strong ascriptive tendencies *if* one weighs more heavily the roles played by parental status in the educational attainments of their offspring.

If we look to the evidence that has been gathered in the study of elites, it is clear that the men (and some women) who stand at the head of our major institutions are far from a random sample of our society. Nothing that has been collected since C. Wright Mills' (1956) study of the power elite contradicts his findings of the homogeneity of class origins of elites in a variety of settings.

Furthermore, there are a number of findings that tend to add complexity to any perspective on social mobility. First, it is clear that a major source of change in our society arises out of the shifts in occupational structure accompanying the increasingly complex nature of our industrial technology and the growth of secondary industrial activities. In the past more vacancies were being created in the upper reaches of the occupational system by technological changes than upper-middle-class parents could supply children for. Perhaps the most dramatic shift has been the decanting of the countryside into the cities as agricultural technology became increasingly efficient and productive and hence less labor-intensive.

Another set of findings that are critical to our understanding of American society arises out of cross-national social mobility studies and out of the activities of the new social historians who have been analyzing the nineteenth-century manuscript censuses. From the comparative studies we have learned that the United States is not very different from other industrialized societies (Lipset and Bendix, 1959). The much vaunted "land of opportunity" turns out to afford its members about as much social mobility as societies we thought were more status- and class-ridden. Similarly the social historians have destroyed the myth of a past of stability and a consequently more rigid class structure (Thermstrom, 1973). The new historians have shown that the nineteenth century was, if anything, a period of time in which social mobility was at least as great as our own twentieth century.

A third set of findings stems from the fact that the processes of status attainment we have been able to specify account for so little of the total variance in status attainment. Thus Blau and Duncan (1967) can account for about 25 percent of the variance in adult status attainment with their path model, and subsequent researches have been able to do only a little better (Duncan et al., 1972; Sewell and Hauser, 1975). In short, there is a lot of wiggle in the status attainment processes that we have been able to model. Of course, some part of the wiggle is measurement error, based, for example, on the difficulties respondents have in describing their fathers' occupations at the time they were sixteen, or their mothers' fathers' occupations in the same period, or other dimly remembered events. How much is measurement error is not known. But a large part of the unexplained variance is due to the fact that our model is only a very loose fit. A more complete specification would come closer to using up more of the variance. Indeed, it is this looseness of fit that Christopher Jencks has made so much of, claiming that it indicates that there are large elements of luck or stochastic capriciousness in our status allocation mechanisms.

If we stand back a bit from these findings and ask what they say about our society, it is tempting to conclude that we are neither as rigid as some thought nor as meritocratic as others thought. But such an assessment would not be particularly useful. I would prefer to regard these findings as indicating something more important: First of all, the elite studies certainly show that our society is run by an Establishment, composed of persons who are relatively homogeneous in background and prior accomplishments.[2] It is still not yet clear to me whether this homogeneity of background implies a homogeneity of interests, outlook, and action; but unless there is nothing at all to our study of social psychology, I cannot imagine that the intra-Establishment variances in such respects are greater than or equal to the variances to be found in the population as a whole.

A second implication I draw is that intergenerational shifts in status position, when viewed in the mass, show a decided tendency for ascriptive processes to dominate in the overall process of status attainment. Although it is true that educational attainment has more to do with eventual status attainment than parental status, yet the educational experiences of Americans are hardly independent of the status positions

[2] Of course, there is always an element of judgment in such a statement. One person's view of homogeneity may be in conflict with another's view to the extent that the same phenomenon is met with widely variant judgments.

of their parents. It should, of course, be borne in mind that the major ascriptive forces in the American stratification system are the barriers to status attainment represented by race, sex, and ethnicity: Blacks and other minority ethnic groups and women are simply unable to cash in their background and personal attainments for income and occupational status to the same extent as "standard" white males.

Finally, the process of status attainment is scarcely fully specified as yet. Our models concentrate largely on the level of individuals and ignore the actions of large-scale institutions. Thus we are able to determine that blacks and whites of comparable personal characteristics are far apart in earnings and occupational attainments, but we don't know how that comes about in any detailed way: Of course we are certain that discriminatory processes are at work, but the precise nature of these processes are as yet unrevealed. Much of the variance in status attainment and income goes unaccounted for in the best of our models quite likely because we have left out the action of employing organizations, the role played by interpersonal networks in recruitment and placement, and so on.[3] We know very well that going to the right school is important, but our researches ordinarily equate a year of high school in Mississippi with a year of high school in New Jersey.

In short, there is nothing in the empirical knowledge that we have gained over the past decade that would contradict a perspective on the American social stratification system that characterizes it as heavily ascriptive, dominated by an elite homogeneous in background, and as yet incompletely understood on the level of fine-grained movements and the institutional practices that sustain these patterns.

The Arcane Mysteries of Occupational Prestige

Nothing seemed clearer about America three decades ago than our quite different ordering of status and deference distinctions. In the twenties and thirties it was clear to the Lynds (1929) as they studied Middletown that our society gave precedence to the businessman over the intellectual and to the lawyer over other professionals. And, of course, nothing produced more surprises in this respect than our studies of occupational prestige (Reiss, 1961; Siegel, 1976). It turned out that despite our derogation of politicians, we regarded political positions very highly, and despite the fact of capitalism and business domi-

---

[3] For a first attempt to measure such organizational effects, see Rossi, Berk, and Eidson, 1974.

nation, we gave our intellectuals more prestige than we gave our industrial captains.

There are additional mysteries that were revealed in the study of occupational prestige. First of all, we discovered that the prestige ratings of occupations were extremely robust: Subgroups of the American population generated much the same set of ratings. We also discovered that we could ask the question of respondents in a variety of ways and still come out with very much the same results. Secondly, by searching through the literature we were able to find studies of occupational prestige that were undertaken as far back as 1925 (Hodge, Siegel, and Rossi, 1964). Comparing the earlier studies with later studies indicated that hardly anything changed in the period between 1925 and the mid-1960s. This stability obtained despite considerable shifts in the occupational structure including a large increase in technical and professional occupational groups and precipitous declines in farming and personal-service occupations. Thirdly, when we compared the hierarchy of occupational ratings derived in this country with those found in others, we were even more shocked at the similarities revealed: Correlations between the ordering in the United States and in such faraway places as Tanzania, not to mention West Germany and Great Britain, were extremely high, of the order of .8 or higher (Hodge, Treiman, and Rossi, 1966).

In many respects these findings were counterintuitive. It takes very little experience with another society to realize that Americans do regard and reward occupations differently. Thus, academics come away from visits to Europe and Asia with some envy of the greater prestige of professors in those countries as compared with the United States. Secondly, we have experienced changes personally in the public regard for scientists and scientific occupations in the post–World War II period. Thirdly, our own experiences in our day-to-day lives would give rise to a different hierarchy, especially among professional occupations, than is recognized by the mass-based scales.

The fact that a finding is counterintuitive may often mean that conventional wisdom is not necessarily wise, but it may also mean that we may need to re-examine our research to make sure that a counterintuitive finding is not a mis-specification error. There is a growing suspicion that we may be dealing with a problem in mis-specification in the case of occupational prestige.

To begin with, the finding of overall agreement on the prestige ratings of occupations drawn from the entire range of the occupational system is compatible with quite divergent orderings that might result when we look at ratings generated of occupations close to subgroups of respondents. In short, local comparisons can be different from those generated by comparisons en grosse. For example, European studies uniformly show that the position of college professor is more highly regarded than that of physician, a rank inversion difference that is obscured in the overall agreement between U.S. scores and European scores. Thus the overall agreement mainly properly registers the fact that both college professor and physician get very high ratings as compared to truck drivers and bellhops.

The difference between local and more distant comparisons is magnified when we look at ratings obtained when respondents are asked to rate occupations that usually rate close together in an overall rating task (Kriesberg, 1973). Thus among health professionals there may be a decided amount of disagreement about the relative ratings to be given to osteopaths and rural family doctors. Findings of this sort are particularly important because they help to reconcile our personal experiences with the findings of overall comparisons. Each of us lives within an environment in which mainly local comparisons matter. Thus it makes little difference to us that professors rank considerably higher than automobile assembly-line workers in Germany and the United States; what does make a difference is the local comparison between doctors and professors, comparisons that are more important to us personally because they take place within our immediate environments, within our neighborhoods, universities, circles of acquaintanceship, and so on.

A second problem centers around the interpretation of prestige ratings, an issue recently raised most cogently by Goldthorpe and Hope (Hope, 1972). They make the point that the prestige ratings are mislabeled, being more of the nature of "general goodness" ratings, and do not fairly represent the more traditional meanings of prestige, involving such things as deference behavior and authority. Goldthorpe and Hope view the occupational prestige hierarchies as expressing the extent to which the general population perceive occupations as being differentiated along a continuum of a goodness of style of life.

What does all this mean for a perspective on American society? First of all, it should be clear that the consensus on occupational ratings, whether they reflect prestige or not, implies that the relative ordering of occupations is among the most clearly perceived features of American society. This consensus bolsters our conception of occupations as being at the heart of our social stratification system.

A second implication for a perspective about American society is that this is a society that, relatively speaking, has a high regard for its activist occupations of political decision makers and high-level businessmen. The qualifier "relatively speaking" has as its referent other industrialized societies whose intellectuals and academics are more highly regarded.

Finally, the robustness of occupational prestige means that the inherent inequality implied by the differential evaluations involved is widely recognized in our society and is not subject to perceptual distortion. Members of our society know where each occupational group stands in the eyes of others and have few illusions about where their own positions lie in the overall hierarchy. If there is a false consciousness in our society, it is not one that denies inequality and claims that ours is a society of equals, at least as far as occupations are concerned.

The Controversy Over Work

If there is anything that marks off the intellectuals from the rest of society it is their obsession with work. For this group more than almost any other, work is so absorbing that the boundaries between it and other activities are unclear and work weeks of considerably more than the conventional thirty-eight hours are common. The higher-level managers, entrepreneurs, and officials share some of the intellectuals' work commitment, although work-nonwork boundaries may be more distinct for these latter groups.

It is no great wonder then that intellectuals and other elites continually raise that question of what work can possibly mean to others whose jobs are so different. In this question, the archetypical image of the manual worker in our society is an assembler in an automobile plant whose daily work existence is reputed to be a constant struggle to keep up with a line that is constantly accelerating, doing tasks that are unvarying repetitions of essential though intrinsically trivial contributions to the assembly of automobiles. Knowledge about the nature of work in other factories, offices, or in other large-scale organizations indicates that such work departs from the auto assembler's task in degree rather than kind. In short, the majority of jobs appear to be ones in which the division of labor has given little scope to worker control over the pace of work, which involve few decisions, and which place the worker under constant supervision. When we add to this image the fact that most jobs are regarded as low down on the totem pole of prestige (or general goodness), then the overall assessment by intellectuals of the major occupations in our society is one in which the work is intrinsically unsatisfying and the rewards are low. Workers must obviously be suffering alienation from their work. Hence whenever workers express dissatisfaction in their work in industrial disputes, intellectuals and other elites are prone to see signs that the consciousness of workers has finally been raised to the point that the alienation is beginning to be expressed. When the grievances in the dispute actually refer to the presumed sources of alienation, as in the Lordstown Vega strike of a few years ago, the portents of a new consciousness in workers seem clear: Workers were finally beginning to protest the systematic degradation of their humanity that goes along with holding down a rank-and-file job in our large-scale industrial structures. The discontent of the young workers at the Vega plant was seen as a leading indicator of a new phase in labor-industry relations in which workers would finally seek to humanize work, that is, make it more like the work of intellectuals and managers.

This view of widespread alienation among low and middle ranks of jobs in our country is perhaps best exemplified in the monograph produced by a Health, Education, and Welfare committee, *Work in America* (Special Task Force, 1973). Based on surveys of research on work, the volume ends with a call for the restructuring of work to provide more intrinsically satisfying work experiences involving enlarging the control of workers over their activities, more meaningful work, more opportunities for upward mobility, more participation in decision making, and so on.

The viewpoint expressed in *Work in America* recognizes widespread worker alienation and places the blame on the organization of work as still based on a Tayloristic model. There is another more conservative assessment, represented ironically by the same administration to which the report was addressed, which laments the loss of the work ethic. The background for this viewpoint stems from an image of the archetypical worker as a plumber whose union guarantees him an annual income of $20,000 for a work week of twenty hours but does not guarantee that the plumber can fix a leak in a sink drain. This Nixonian assessment regards the worker as someone who attempts to minimize his effort and maximize his return, at the same time refusing to become involved in doing as good a job as he is capable of doing. It is this same viewpoint that objects to a guaranteed income as providing too much of a temptation for workers to cease their work activity and rely on a dole for a minimum household income. The shirking worker who is quick to use his organized leverage to increase his income and who refuses to develop maximum involvement in work is at least a large minority in the working force, according to this conservative viewpoint.

Chords of sympathy can be struck in almost everyone by both viewpoints. We all have experienced highly paid incompetence—from automobile mechanics who can't fix our cars through programers who consistently lie about when they will finish that new program, to colleagues who are incapable of good teaching, good research, fine scholarship, or efficient administration and who also may be dangerous to the mental health of all around them. Hence the conservative viewpoint that some workers are operating below the level that could be afforded by maximum commitment has some basis in reality, although the finding of widespread indolence and incompetence need not be limited to those on the bottom reaches of the occupational structure. Of course, we may raise the question whether any society could stand to have more than a small percentage of go-getters with all-out commitment to their jobs, a question which is rarely put.

We can also sympathize with the assessment of widespread alienation among workers. Although many of us have served some time on a keypunch and lived to boast about it, the prospect of spending up to eight hours a day punching buttons that register numbers that have little meaning is not the least bit pleasant. In short, were we in the jobs that most workers hold down, we would be alienated and hence some at least undercurrent of alienation must be present and ready to be evoked.

What do the empirical studies have to say about this controversy? The best assessment that can be made from the many studies of worker attitudes toward their jobs is that both viewpoints are far from the mark. First of all, there is little evidence of widespread discontent with jobs and with various aspects of jobs. The latest (and apparently well-done) survey conducted by the Survey Research Center at Michigan (Quinn and Sheperd, 1973) finds that the vast majority of workers on all levels of the occupational structure are satisfied with their jobs. Secondly, although the lower one goes in the occupational structure the more discontent can be found, the differences among occupational groups are not very striking. Professional and managerial workers are more satisfied than semiskilled operatives, but the differences between the means of the two groups did not exceed one standard deviation of the measures used.

Thirdly, a major pocket of dissatisfaction lies among the younger persons in the labor force, most likely a reflection of the poor jobs that are available to workers entering the labor force than it is a harbinger of social trends. Similarly women are less satisfied than men, and blacks and other minorities less than standard whites, although the gap between the sexes and races are less than the gap between professionals and operatives.

Finally, there is no discernible trend over time. Putting together surveys over the past several decades, levels of job satisfaction appear to be about the same in the earliest surveys as compared with the latest. If Maslow's hierarchy of needs is a good model, it is obvious that workers have scarcely gotten very far up in the hierarchy.

Nor is there any evidence that there is little commitment to work or widespread indolence. Surveys among the poor show them to be as committed to the work ethic as the middle class. The New Jersey–Pennsylvania Income Maintenance Experiment (Rossi and Lyall, 1976) showed that there was little reduction in work effort when poor and near-poor families were offered an income maintenance plan that in effect reduced their marginal wage rates.

What does all this mean? Liberals and conservative intellectuals and leaders are discontented: That is for sure. But the vast majority of the labor force are able to take their jobs without either seething with discontent or rushing to the nearest retail outlet of the welfare state for handouts on the dole. Perhaps the issue is whether discontent leads change or change leads discontent. Most sociologists and social psychologists subscribe to a model of change in which objective conditions give rise to subjective definitions of the situation, assessments, and then to movements for change in the objective conditions. Perhaps a more appropriate model provides for a role for leadership in which leaders define noxious conditions and hence give rise to discontent. Something along these lines is apparently going on with respect to occupational safety: A comparison between the S.R.C. 1969 survey of quality of employment and the 1973 survey (Quinn and Sheperd, 1973) shows a decided rise in the level of dissatisfaction with this aspect of work. If we recall that the intervening period was one in which the Occupational Health and Safety Act was passed, perhaps what we are seeing was an example of how defining a problem by legislative activity can redefine a tolerable situation into one which gives rise to some discontent.

This suggests that the job reorganization recommendations of the *Work in America* volume need not be thrown away. There is reason to believe that the redesign of work to provide for more autonomy, more participation in decision making, more involvement in the total output of work, and more opportunity for advancement in the occupational hierarchy are a set of changes which would be welcomed by most workers. Indeed, jobs which have such characteristics are jobs held by people who think highly of their work. Hence a movement in that direction would be one that might initially produce more worker dissatisfaction but eventually settle on a higher level of job satisfaction. Of course, it is not entirely clear whether such a reorganization will lead to greater or lesser productivity; but a slight loss in productivity might be offset by a higher level of job satisfaction than presently exists.

Perhaps what we are presently experiencing in the criticisms of work from the liberal side are the beginnings of a social movement that may lead to a reorganization of work as profound as that brought about by Taylorism. I would be a bit more optimistic, however, if the movement were being led by management rather than by liberal intellectuals in or out of the federal bureaucracy.

The Controversy Over the Role of Education in Social Stratification

Our classical sociological theorists who tried to deal with the topic of social stratification gave scant attention to the status allocation roles of educational institutions and of educational experiences in status and income attainment. This relative neglect stems perhaps from the fact that education's role in this respect is a relatively new one, arising out of the bureaucratization of business enterprises and the building of a mass educational system. To be sure, Davis and Moore (1945), in their famous article on the functional theory of stratification, pay some attention to the role of skills in allocation, especially when those skills are valuable and in scarce supply. One can be charitable and assume that Davis and Moore had in mind educational attainment as at least an indicator of achieved skill levels.

In contrast, the empirical researchers dealing with social stratification have paid a great deal of attention to educational institutions and educational attainment. Hollingshead's (1949) classical study of Morris, Illinois, focused on how the Morris High School faculty acted as gatekeepers in allowing middle-class adolescents through to their diplomas (and possibly on to greater glory at the University of Illinois) and closing the door on working and lower-class adolescents. Those who have built indicators of social class position of level within the stratification position have used educational attainment routinely as an indicator usually in combination with occupational attainment (Reiss, 1961).

But the main attention given to educational attainment has been in the intergenerational mobility studies (e.g., Blau and Duncan, 1967; Sewell and Hauser, 1975), found to be the best predictor of eventual status and income attainment among the variables used in their models. The net relationships of educational attainment to status and income attainment were not very high but they were clearly higher than any other net relationships. It is important to dwell for a moment on what these findings are in detail: Typically a study will find that with each additional year of educational attainment there is an increment in the occupational prestige and in the income or wage rates attained by an adult some years later. The increments for each year are not always found to be identical—there appear to be knots or kinks in the relationship between education and an outcome located at the completion of conventional units of education, high school and college graduation being the prominent kink locations.

Economists have also been intrigued by these findings; indeed educational attainment has more of a place in economic theory (G. Becker, 1964; Juster, 1975) than in sociological theory through the development of the concept of human capital in which educational attainment is seen as a form of investment in human capital. Considerable effort on the part of economists has gone into investigating what are the returns on such investments both to the households or individuals who have made the investments and to the society that has invested in educational institutions.

Initially, these findings seemed to be quite understandable: After all, the more years of education an individual had, the more skills he can be thought to possess and the more valuable he would appear on the labor market and hence able to command a better place in the occupational structure and a higher wage. The findings become less understandable when one considers what sorts of skills are imparted in schools and their match or lack of match with the skills needed on jobs. It is obvious that medical schools prepare persons to become doctors, and it is almost as obvious that law schools prepare persons to become lawyers, but for a very large proportion of jobs, the skills learned in schools are not those that are used most on the job. To be sure, white-collar jobs rely heavily on workers' ability to use the written and spoken versions of the English language, but there are literally thousands of jobs in which the skills are very specific and have only a vague resemblance to those imparted in school. Yet the findings indicate that the more years of education, the better the blue-collar job.

Finally, when the performance of workers varying in educational attainment within the same occupation was examined (Berg, 1971), it was hard to find that educational attainment was significantly related to job performance. Of course, educational attainment might be a good surrogate for general intelligence, presumably a quality related to performance on the job, and hence employers who used educational attainment as a device for screening job applicants and for choosing employees to promote were simply using a criterion that was cheap to administer and predictive of job performance. Here again, the evidence was negative: Measures of general intelligence, while positively related to educational attainment (either as antecedent or consequent), were not found to be significantly related to job performance.

The evidence has been piling up (Levin, 1975) from study after study that for the vast majority of jobs educational attainment is more of a credential than a manifest of job performance skills. Indeed, it is only in the highly technical and professional occupations that educational attainment has some sort of direct implication for job performance. It is also clear why employers use educational attainment as a screening device. First, its use in this fashion is widely accepted and perceived as just. Second, it is easy to use and inexpensive, especially in comparison with the testing of specific skills. Finally, the use of any credential that was not negatively related to job performance certainly cannot do any damage to a work force: It would simply leave the composition of the work force unchanged. Incidentally, there is very little evidence to suggest that educational attainment is negatively related to job performance.

The educational system of our society can be viewed as having a number of roles to play in our total social system. Not only is it the guardian of a considerable cultural and scientific heritage and a significant producer of increases to that heritage; it also serves as an allocation device that meshes loosely with the occupational and hence the stratification system. It does so by processing young people through a set of learning experiences that may be intrinsically interesting and possibly useful, but it also provides a grading system at the end with its diplomas and certificates. The system is considerably differentiated, as we all know, so that there is a gradation of diplomas and degrees as well as a graduated scale of goodness of the schools that grant the degrees and hand out the diplomas. It is no accident that our elite schools train the elite and that a diploma from the best schools is worth more than one from an undistinguished place.

If we accept even partially this interpretation of the functions of the educational system, then we gain an increased understanding of the controversies that rock the educational field from time to time. Conservatives in educational matters often express concerns for educational quality and for the supposed dilution of higher education that comes about through loosened admissions criteria. Reinterpreted in this framework, the concern for quality may be viewed as a more acceptable way of stating a concern for the inflation of credentials that might occur as a consequence of turning out so many B.A.'s. It is feared that the B.A. degree would be used as a credential for entry into occupations somewhat down the line than at present, with higher-order credentials being needed for places where the B.A. used to be an admissions pass.

The credentialing role of education has not escaped attention, and it is possible that a direct attack may be made on the use of educational attainment as a screening device. The courts have already ruled that aptitude tests used by firms in screening employees must be shown to be related to job performance. It is only a logical next step to challenge education seeking a court ruling that educational attainment may be used as an admissions requirement only when it can be shown that educational attainment is relevant to on-the-job performance, although the chances of this occurring, given the enormous heterogeneity of jobs, seems relatively small. Perhaps the single-purpose proprietary vocational schools would come into their own under such circumstances.

Finally, it should be stated that our economists are finding it hard to justify, either for individuals or for society, investment in higher education in terms of returns to individuals or to society. The return on human capital investment is small, and academics will be disappointed to know that with the exception of medical training, the rate of return goes down as the level of educational experience advances beyond the B.A.

Gaps in the Social Stratification Knowledge

Up to this point, I have been confining my remarks to topics in social stratification about which there is some solid empirical knowledge. Now I would like to turn to areas about which less known in the way of hard "facts" but which are important areas nevertheless.

While the general outlines of the social stratification system are fairly well known, there are some points of critical concern about which we do not know very much at all. Particularly important is the study of elites. It is true that a number of studies have provided a fairly good description of the origins of a number of elites—the upper levels of government are fairly well known as well as the corporate elite and the higher professoriate. Origins, life styles, and so on are important to know, but more important—in fact, critical—is to know about the interconnections among elite members. We need to know how much they share with each other their views of the goals of our society, their perceptions of what is possible and impossible in political terms, and what are the interests of their organizations which they try to express in their actions. One may regard this topic as doing C. Wright Mills's *The Power Elite* (1956) over again with more and better evidence. I do not expect that we will find much that is at variance with Mills's analysis, for the events of the last two decades since the publication *The Power Elite* have tended to bear him out more than to contradict his overall characterizations of the ruling circles of our society. Of course, I do not share Mills's technical pessimism that the elite will never talk about their roles in ruling America, and this too is something that can be tested out in the field.

A second main topic that has been alluded to throughout this chapter is the lopsided emphasis in social stratification research on individuals as opposed to organizations. One almost gets the impression that an individual can do anything he wants provided that he has the proper credentials and is stoked up with enough achievement motivation. Yet it is obvious that large-scale organizations play an extremely important role in the allocation of prestige, power, and income.

Schools, businesses, and government agencies evaluate people, admit or reject them, endow them with training and skills as well as seniority, promote or fail them, keep them in a segregated labor market or pass them on to higher circles, and so on. These organizational mechanisms are not very well understood or studied, despite their undoubted importance.

Perhaps what is missing is the technical apparatus for conducting such studies. If so, here is an opportunity for someone to make a breakthrough and restore to sociology its proper role of studying social structure rather than individuals.

It is my contention that much of the unexplained variance in status and income attainment is to be sought in the workings of organizational processing of persons. Considerably more important than the attitudes of individuals summed in the mass are the institutionalized practices that make up admissions, promotion, hiring, firing, and credentialing practices of schools, firms, and government agencies.

A third area of less than adequate firm knowledge has also been alluded to earlier in our discussion of worker satisfaction. In a very real sense, given the value system of our society, almost everyone in the society falls short and is to some degree defined as a failure. An almost infinite hierarchy of positions faces the individual as he threads his way through the occupational system and is faced by the certain knowledge that he will never make it to the dimly seen top. The individual also undoubtedly quickly perceives that he will probably not go very far up at all and risks a good chance of slipping down among the disadvantaged. We know very little about how individuals come to accept these dismal facts of social stratification, namely that he is not worth very much in society's eyes and will never amount to much more. Obviously people do come to accept and perhaps even like their station in life. Is this because local comparisons insulate the individual from derogation with little interpersonal contact that bridges wide gaps in status and income? Or is it because the individual has available many substitute forms of satisfaction that permit him to place occupational status and income at a lower point in a hierarchy of a hierarchy of values to be maximized?

The answers to this question go straight to the heart of the issues involved in the struggle for a more egalitarian society. If the range of tolerance for hierarchy and skewed distribution of resources is relatively high, then perhaps it is not as important to push for radical income redistribution or widespread status upgrading as it is to achieve that level of redistribution that satisfies.

My own expectation is that there is tolerance for considerable inequality in the distributions of status, income, and power as long as the means of these distributions are high and as long as the bottom is truncated by a floor below which few persons and families are not allowed to sink. It also seems important that the system be justifiable in some universalistic sense: Discrimination in favor of high school graduates is easier to take than discrimination in favor of the sons and daughters of doctors. If ascriptive forces are purified by running them through universalistic-appearing institutions, then inequality is easier to bear. In short, equity and inequality are acceptable, and they can co-exist.

Finally, we know very little about the subjective experiences of status, income, and power inequalities.[4] In everyday life there are many occasions when one is reminded of his station in life—what do shipping clerks feel when they view Archie Bunker making an ass of himself? Or how does a person feel when he is stopped by a police officer for a traffic violation and asked for his occupation? Or when, upon entering an employment security office, he is asked to stand behind a white line that puts four feet between the applicant and the clerk behind the desk until the clerk asks him to step forward? Conversely, are there feelings of a positive sort that occur when a clerk's behavior changes when an applicant reveals his title of Doctor? Or his address?

We know that in circumstances in which persons from widely separated class levels are thrown together for protracted periods of time under conditions of formal equality, as in jury duty, status relationships tend to maintain themselves in differential participation and interpersonal influence. What does it feel like to swallow your opinions and scrape a bit? And does it give you any joy to know that your fellow jurors are deferring to your opinions?

On this score, I do believe that the stratification system gives out a lot of rewards and punishments, the former in terms of deference and the latter in terms of derogation. I am certain that these experiences help to reinforce patterns of differential association along status, income, and power lines. They are also the stuff out of which self-images as competents and incompetents are forged.

Although I have come to the end of the list of things I would like to see stratification researchers work on, I do not mean to imply that we would know all there is to know if these questions are answered. Rather, I am sure that the quest for the answers to these questions will in turn raise issues that demand additional answers.

A Perspective on America as Viewed from an Examination of Social Stratification

I hope that I have been able to show that an examination of recent research on American social stratification provides a useful perspective

---

[4] An interesting but very slight step in this direction is represented by Sennett's recent monograph (Sennett and Cobb, 1972).

on American society, which goes beyond identifying the United States as a stratified society. There are a number of salient features of American society that are highlighted from this viewpoint.

First of all, it is clear that there is a ruling elite in American society, marked by a homogeneity in origins and background, most likely well integrated in a set of interlocking circles of acquaintanceship and characterized by occupational substitutability. It is an elite that is certainly not completely unified in interests and ideology, although the range of differences may be smaller than might otherwise be the case. It is also an elite that may be more permeable than the elite groups in other societies, its permeability being aided by the relative openness of the allocation processes of military careers and university achievements.

Secondly, it is a society with strong ascriptive forces operating along racial and ethnic lines as well as through the educational institutions. Its ascriptive character is disguised behind the operation of institutions that appear to be universalistic in style. Discrimination against blacks and other derogated minority groups is more in evidence in the actions of a wide variety of institutions. But for whites, the ascriptive character of stratification institutions are less visible, although the system makes it possible for families to pass on their advantages to their children with some degree of certainty.

Finally, it is a society that manages to satisfy the vast majority of the population who are allocated minor and impoverished roles in the system. It is not a society that is on the brink of falling apart, even though the seamy side of its elite has been brought under public scrutiny. It satisfies by providing a relative affluence if not abundance to large proportions while still managing to retain considerable inequality in the distribution of status, income, and power.

II

To Detect Overlooked Cleavages in the Social Structure

3

Conflict Within the Working Class: The Skilled as a Special-Interest Group

William H. Form

Working-Class Stratification

HISTORICALLY, students of stratification have focused on the basic cleavage of American society, that between the working class and the middle class. Though the American labor movement did not become committed to socialism, many sociologists did not give up hope. Understandably, they worried that the top stratum of the working class might join the middle class and forever seal off the possibility of a socialist America. Therefore, they studied the question whether the elite of the working class (the skilled) was more like the bottom of the middle class (clerical workers) than like other manual workers. This overriding concern about the manual–white-collar division of society diverted attention from the persistent cleavages among manual workers.

Because they uncritically accepted three long-standing ideas, sociologists neglected to study the internal stratification of the working class. The first idea is that the mechanization of industry reduces the need for skilled and unskilled workers while it increases the need for semi-

☐ I am indebted to Robert C. Bibb for general research assistance, to Stephen J. Mc-Namee for preparing the political data, and to Joan Huber for important suggestions to improve the manuscript. Melvin Rothbaum, James Scoville, and especially Richard Hamilton will not be happy with my response to their vigorous criticisms, but they improved my writing if not my argument. I also wish to acknowledge the support of the Institute of Labor and Industrial Relations at the University of Illinois at Urbana-Champaign.

skilled workers, thereby homogenizing the working class. The second idea, borrowed from economics, is that the rising level of education that accompanies industrialization creates a flexible labor supply and thereby reduces wage differentials among the skill levels. Third, the rise of industrial unions has so weakened the power of craft workers and their unions that the interests of ordinary workers now dominate working-class politics. This chapter challenges these three ideas and suggests that class politics is better understood if conflict within the working class is accepted as a structural regularity of an "open" society.

The suggestion (Form, 1973) that the working class becomes more stratified with industrialization strikes many sociologists as absurd or as a conservative hope. The strike at Lordstown (Aronowitz, 1974:21–50), the Paris uprisings (Gorz, 1973), the rash of wildcat strikes (Weir, 1973), the appearance of radical cells in the labor movement (Case, 1973) convince many sociologists that the working class is uniting rather than splitting. The argument seems simple and irrefutable: As advancing technology wipes away skill differences, incomes become more uniform, with the consequence that status distinctions decline and political self-awareness increases.

Yet the evidence of deep cleavages within the American working class, defined here as manual workers, cannot be overlooked. Contemporary economic studies of dual or tripartite labor markets (Bluestone, 1970; Fusfeld, 1973) document what sociologists have long known; that blacks, Spanish-speaking groups, and poorly educated whites suffer many periods of unemployment and that, when employed, they are crowded into the low-paying insecure jobs of marginal industries and services.[1] They are permanently locked in poverty despite government efforts to enforce fair employment and affirmative action regulations. The billions of dollars spent to train the poor for better jobs and to abolish poverty has scarcely dented the castelike division within the working class. If anything, rising unemployment and inflation have deepened the cleavage.

Even upper-caste workers are stratified. The lower stratum is comprised of unskilled and semiskilled employees in moderately stable and typically nonunionized factories and service enterprises. Though occasionally unemployed, these workers manage over the years to accumulate a few amenities and stave off poverty. The upper stratum is composed of skilled and semiskilled workers employed in the large, profitable, and often unionized enterprises of the primary sector, government, and the services. There unions have been relatively successful

---

[1] The United States is not unique in having an ethnic undercaste: Britain has Caribbean and South Asians; France, Germany, Sweden, and Switzerland have "guest" workers; Japan has South Koreans and Eta; South Africa has its blacks (see Van den Berghe, 1967:30).

in providing medical benefits and supplementary unemployment and retirement insurance. Their members typically own their homes, accumulate some savings, and send their children to technical school or college.[2] They give little thought to problems of less fortunate workers and do not identify with them as a class. This chapter focuses on skilled workers or the upper stratum because they fight the hardest to maintain economic, status, and political inequalities within the working class.

The idea that economically privileged skilled workers constitute a separate and often a politically decisive stratum within the working class is shared by both radical and conservative observers.[3] Lenin (1943:92) condemned the conservative self-serving skilled workers who prevent working-class solidarity. Both Thompson's (1963) detailed and respected study of the British working class and Bauman's (1972) truncated Marxist analysis emphasized the early and persistent split between the skilled and other workers in the British labor movement, a split that haunts the movement to this day. The major historians of the American labor movement (Commons et al., 1918; Perlman and Taft, 1935) have shown that the skilled directed the labor movement from its inception and used it to serve their special interests. Michels (1959:289–96) believed that the skilled inevitably appear as a separate class in industrial society even within the socialist labor movement. Lipset's (1960:220–309) extensive review of working-class politics shows that craft workers are generally more conservative than the less skilled, but under special circumstances they are more radical (Zeitlin, 1967; Hamilton, 1967).

Despite this impressive array of scholarly opinion, many American sociologists feel that craft workers are genuinely a part of the working class. Hamilton (1964) concluded that though the skilled may constitute a separate stratum, they are not easily distinguishable from other manual workers in their values and politics.[4] Labor historians have reasoned (Hardman, 1959) that the rise of industrial unions ended the monopolistic control of the union movement by the craft unions and that the merger of the AFL and CIO demonstrated the common interests of all manual workers. Labor economists (Dunlop, 1944; Reder, 1955) have claimed that the economic basis of separate status for the

[2] The skilled report a higher rate of home ownership than the unskilled in large cities, suburbs, and small cities in all regions of the country, the differences ranging from 9 to 30 percent and averaging 27 for the nonfarm population (Katona et al., 1964:37, U.S. Department of Labor, 1956:48). Similar differences are reported in life insurance ownership (Katona et al., 1964:91).

[3] The skilled category includes foremen, independent artisans, the licensed crafts, and nonlicensed skilled in industry and services. I am primarily interested in employees in the urban-industrial sector.

[4] Similarly in England, Goldthorpe et al. (1969) argue that the increased affluence of the skilled failed to make them more conservative politically.

various skill levels declines as their wage differentials decline over the years. Generations of scholars (Carr-Saunders and Jones, 1937; Warner and Low, 1947; Friedmann, 1955; Marglin, 1974) have argued that mechanization and automation reduce the need for unskilled and skilled labor, thus creating a homogeneous working class of mostly semiskilled workers.

Soon after World War II, Bell (1949), Faris (1954), Galbraith (1958), and others thought they detected societal trends which trivialized the issue of working-class solidarity. As prosperity increased, as automation made factory and office work more alike, as the expanding service sector pulled workers out of factories, and as the incomes of manual workers and white-collar workers became more alike, working-class and middle-class distinctions became less important. Middle America emerged; the shape of the stratification system changed from a pyramid to a diamond. Manual workers were behaving like white-collar workers: buying similar things, moving to the suburbs, and sending their children to college (Wilensky, 1961; Westley and Westley, 1971). Three consecutive victories of the Conservative party in postwar Britain and two consecutive Republican party victories in the United States pointed to the political embourgeoisement of manual workers.

Richard Hamilton was quick to test the validity of these ideas. In a series of studies in the United States (1963, 1964, 1965b, 1966, 1972), Germany (1965a) and France (1967), he found that the traditional cleavage between the manual and white-collar workers survived; the skilled were closer to other manual workers than to white-collar workers in their political attitudes, voting behavior, and class identification. Goldthorpe and others (1969) pursued parallel studies in Britain; they too found that affluent industrial workers of all skill levels remained loyal to the Labour party even when they moved to white-collar neighborhoods.

The anti-embourgeoisement counterattack is now in full swing. Parker (1972) asserts that middle-class American society is a myth because manual and lower-middle-class workers still constitute the majority. Far from affluent, they are just a month away from poverty. Andrew Levinson (1974) suggests that manual workers still comprise the majority because most employees in the expanding service sector are manual. Aronowitz (1974) believes that today's young, well-educated industrial workers represent a new breed; they will not submit to dehumanizing factory bureaucracy or to repressive union bureaucracy. Though Aronowitz (1974:156, 417) recognizes the power of the skilled to prevent working-class solidarity, like others (Gorz, 1973; Marglin, 1974), he believes that skill distinctions are technologically superfluous and artificially maintained by a conspiracy between the skilled and management to prevent working-class solidarity.[5] The new class of workers will destroy skill distinctions as they change both the factory and society. In short, these writers conclude that the working class is still the majority, still poor, and still sufficiently united to fulfill its historic mission to bring progress to the nation.

These ideas regarding skilled workers and working-class solidarity will now be re-examined. My primary concern is to address the issue concerning the independence of the skilled, because it seems hardly necessary to prove that the American working class has never been sufficiently united to bring about important political change. Labor parties and socialism have never captured the imagination of more than a small minority of Americans. Compared to European movements, the achievements of American labor have been modest. Only 30 percent of the nonagricultural labor force has been unionized, the lowest of any major industrial democracy (Bok and Dunlop, 1970:44). Though labor has been wedded to the Democratic party, unions cannot control the party or deliver the vote. Labor leadership has become a bureaucratic and conservative gerontocracy with narrow political vision. Twenty years after unification, the AFL-CIO remains a loose cluster of unions with little internal discipline. Some of the largest and most effective unions, whose members comprise over one fifth of all of organized labor, do not belong to the AFL-CIO.[6] National officers of many unions are so preoccupied with collective bargaining and maintaining order that they have frustrated the traditional and almost unique genius of American unionism: the control of the job and working conditions in the shop. This neglect has been so extreme that officers have succeeded in doing what radical cells could never do—provoke a rash of wildcat strikes against union leadership and a high rate of rejection of negotiated contracts (Weir, 1973; Simkin, 1968; Burke, 1973).

The Decline of Skill Stratification?

THE RECEIVED VIEW

I shall first summarize the generally received view about skilled workers in the social science literature and then examine the evidence for it. The prevailing view is that most skilled workers are employed in

---

[5] None of these authors presents convincing evidence on either side of the issue.

[6] The United Auto ,Workers, United Mine Workers, the Teamsters, Brotherhood of Locomotive Engineers, United Electrical Workers, the Longshoremen's Union, The United Mine and Mill, and others.

manufacturing. With industrial and economic development, the percentage of the labor force in manufacturing declines and the percentage in services increases. At the same time, the mechanization of production reduces the need for skilled workers, and with this reduction they lose influence with management and the union. As the numbers and importance of craft workers decline, the working class becomes more homogeneous in skill and income. In the long run, this homogenization promotes class solidarity and class action. All these ideas bear re-examination.

LABOR FORCE TRENDS

Let us first examine the evidence concerning the alleged decline of craft workers in the labor force. It is true that skilled workers have been most heavily concentrated in manufacturing and construction. Yet since the turn of the century the percentage of the United States labor force in these two sectors has remained remarkably stable. The high point in manufacturing employment was 36 percent in 1950; yet in 1970 as in 1900, manufacturing employed one quarter of the labor force. Construction employment has been stable since 1900, fluctuating between 4 and 6 percent. The proportion of skilled workers in the labor force also has been constant since 1920, about 13 percent. Since 1940, the percentage of skilled workers in manufacturing has been constant, about 20 percent; and the percentage in construction has declined slightly, from 59 to 56 percent (see Table 1).

In three sectors, the skilled today are more highly represented than their 20 percent in manufacturing: 22 percent in transportation-communication-utilities; 25 percent in mining; and 50 percent in construction. More important, from 1940 to 1970 the representation of the

T A B L E 1. Percentage of craft workers and foremen by industry group, 1940–1970

Industry Group	1940	1950	1960	1970
Manufacturing	19	20	20	20
Construction	59	57	53	56
Mining	13	17	22	25
Transportation, etc.	17	21	21	22
Wholesale and retail trade	5	6	7	9
Government	4	8	8	7
Finance	2	2	2	2
Service	6	9	7	6
Agriculture	*	*	1	2

* Less than 1 percent.

skilled has increased in other sectors: 12 percent in mining, 5 percent in transportation, 4 percent in trade, 3 percent in government, and 2 percent in agriculture. In short, the skilled are holding their own in manufacturing, declining slowly in construction, but increasing at various rates in most other sectors of the economy (see Table 1).[7]

SKILL STRATIFICATION AND ECONOMIC DEVELOPMENT

Now let us examine the traditional argument of economists regarding the skilled. Ober (1948), Kerr et al. (1960:252–55), and others have argued that occupational wage differentials decrease with industrialization. In many parts of the less developed world, skilled work pays three or four times as much as unskilled labor, while in advanced industrial countries, the skilled typically receive only 20 to 30 percent more. Changing market conditions account for the declining ratio: The supply of skilled labor in advanced economies increases with rising levels of general education, the spread of technical education, the upgrading and training of employees on the job, the building of local labor pools, and labor union efforts to equalize wages especially during inflationary periods (International Labour Office, 1956:25–27). Within a given labor market, the skilled/unskilled wage differential varies with economic conditions. In periods of economic depression and high unemployment, the skilled replace the unskilled because the skilled can perform a wider range of jobs and, though wages decline, skill differentials tend to widen. During periods of inflation and full employment, all labor is scarce and wage differentials tend to decline (Reder, 1955).

Let us now examine some of the data bearing on each of these points. I know of no general study of skilled/unskilled wage differentials across industries in nations at different levels of economic development. Data in Table 2 are derived mostly from case studies of different industries in various countries. The lowest ratio reported (1.1) is for Austria's construction industry and the highest (4.0) for factories in Poland (Wesolowski, 1969) and India (Lambert, 1963). Although countries at lower levels of economic development report higher ratios than industrialized countries, wide variations are found at all levels in both socialist and nonsocialist countries. Table 3 presents data for two industries, printing and construction, in forty countries. Again, the ratios in the less developed countries tend to be higher than in the Western industrial countries, but they are more alike in the construction than in

---

[7] Dahrendorf (1959:49–51) argues that early manufacturing homogenized skill levels, early twentieth-century manufacturing expanded the semiskilled, and after 1950 more skilled workers were needed to operate the more complex machines.

T A B L E 2. Wage ratios (skilled/unskilled) of countries by level of economic development

Country	Source	Industry	Ratios	Date	Per Capita GNP *
India	Lambert (1963)	4 factories, Poona	2.0–4.0	1957	73
China	Giles (1975)	Factory workers	3.0	1974	73
Yugoslavia	Kolaja (1965)	1 factory	2.0–3.0	1959	265
Japan	Taira (1970)	Construction	1.5+	1945–66	306
Cuba	Zeitlin (1967)	Industrial nat. sample	2.5	1962	431
Poland	Wezolowski (1969)	Manual workers	1.15–4.00	1963	475
Argentina	BLS (1966)	All occupations, B.A.	1.23	1965	490
Italy	Rothbaum (1957)	Wage workers	1.25	1952–53	516
USSR	CIA (1963)	Wage workers	1.37	1928–61	600
USSR	Geiger (1969b)	Machine, Leningrad	1.22	1965	600
Austria	I.L.O. (1974)	Construction	1.1	1973	670
France	Rothbaum (1957)	Wage workers	1.23	1952–53	943
Britain	Hunter and Robertson (1969)	Engineering industrial	1.42	1967	1189
U.S.A.	Rothbaum (1957)	Wage workers	1.37	1952–53	2577

* Russett et al., 1964.

T A B L E 3. Skill pay differentials in printing and construction by country or city [1]

City and Country	Per Capita GNP [2]	Printing (1957) [3]	Construction [4]
Africa			
Elizabethville, Belgian Congo	92	2.27	1.09
Accra, Ghana	172	1.99	1.82
Sierra Leone (nation)	—	2.65	1.59
Kartoum, Sudan	60	2.14	2.29
Dar-es-Salaam, Tanganyika	61	3.16	2.04
Capetown, South Africa	395	2.02	3.39

City and Country	Per Capita GNP [2]	Printing (1957) [3]	Construction [4]
America			
Anchorage, Alaska	2577	2.40	1.12
New York, U.S.	2577	1.17	1.24
Buenos Aires, Argentina	490	1.84	1.33
Santiago, Chile	379	4.55	1.70
Jamaica	316	1.84	1.83
Guatemala City, Guatemala	189	1.27	—
Mexico D.F., Mexico	262	3.17	1.49
Puerto Rico	563	1.00	1.70
St. Vincent, West Indies	200	3.95	1.60
Asia			
Taiwan	161	1.48	1.89
Hong Kong	272	2.87	1.38
Bombay, India	73	3.17	—
Tel Aviv, Israel	726	1.45	1.17
Beirut, Lebanon	362	3.36	4.00
Singapore	400	2.60	2.00
Saigon, Vietnam	76	2.70	1.55
Malaya	356	1.74	2.02
Bangkok, Thailand	96	1.46	1.65
Europe			
Austria (nation)	670	1.57	1.31
Brussels, Belgium	1196	1.47	1.25
Helsinki, Finland	794	1.36	1.31
West Berlin, Germany	927	1.49	1.05
Athens, Greece	340	1.00	2.32
Hungary	490	1.46	1.43
Dublin, Ireland	550	1.32	1.18
Norway	1130	1.35	1.02
Lisbon, Portugal	224	2.22	1.74
Geneva, Switzerland	1428	1.51	1.23
London, England	1189	1.25	1.13
The Netherlands	836	1.30	1.22
Malta	377	1.40	1.21
Rome, Italy	516	1.54	1.14
Oceania			
Wellington, New Zealand	1310	1.24	1.09
Sydney, Australia	1316	1.29	1.20

[1] Source of data, International Labour Office, 1958.

[2] Russett et al., 1964.

[3] Ratio of wages of unskilled laborers to machine compositors.

[4] Ratio of wages of carpenters to construction laborers.

the printing, perhaps reflecting the simpler and more uniform technology of construction everywhere. Moreover, large variations in the ratios are reported in printing in countries at similar levels of economic development. Thus, no difference in wages by skill is reported for Puerto Rico and Greece (unbelievable), while wide differences are reported for Chile and Mexico. In short, economists are probably correct in the general observation that wage differentials lower with economic development, but many other factors obviously affect the ratio, such as the ideology of equality, the racial composition of the labor force, what employers can get away with, and government policy.

SKILL INCOME DIFFERENTIALS IN THE UNITED STATES

The case for low and diminishing wage ratios between the skilled and the unskilled in the United States is not conclusive. Economists claim the ratio should be between 1.2 and 1.3 for advanced industrial societies and declining. One obvious source of income data is the United States census since 1940. Economists do not like to use the census because the categories are too broad (Scoville, 1972:17–44); they prefer data on hourly wage rates for specific industries, particularly construction (Ober, 1948; Douty, 1953; Gustman and Segal, 1974). Yet, Schoeplein (1975:11) notes that employment in construction is subject to violent fluctuations and that wages rates vary widely between the unionized and nonunionized sectors. Census data have some obvious advantages; they are inclusive, they report actual earnings, they are longitudinal, and they are most accurate in the manual sector where skill differences are clearly specified (Scoville, 1972:108).

When the annual male earnings of craft workers are divided by those of unskilled laborers, the ratio was 1.47 in 1940 and increased to 1.82 in 1970.[8] These ratios are not only higher than those suggested by economists, but they seem to be increasing rather than decreasing. Moreover, the ratios clearly underestimate the actual situation because the lower earnings of apprentices are included with those of craft workers and the omission of women in the ratio deflates it because unskilled women workers earn lower wages than men. Also, census takers rely on the occupational titles provided by informants, many of whom report higher status titles than their jobs warrant. The annual

---

[8] For 1950 the ratio was 1.67 and for 1960, 1.80. These data are for craft workers, exclusive of foremen, and for laborers, except those in farms and mines. Parenthetically, the income ratio between foremen and craft workers has not changed since 1950, being 1.23. The skill ratios for women are consistently lower than for men, and they rose more slowly: from 1940, 1.28, to 1970, 1.52 (supervisors were included with craft workers). The skilled/unskilled ratio for hourly earning in manufacturing declined from 2.05 in 1907 to 1.37 in 1953 and rose to 1.42 in 1974 (Blackmore, 1968).

earnings of highly skilled workers may almost double those of unskilled labor.

The size of the income difference becomes politically important when it is large enough to be worth fighting to protect and large enough to inhibit class solidarity. The first difference is easy to specify; almost any wage advantage (above ten cents an hour) is worth fighting for. The income advantage of craft workers over the unskilled is large enough to be worth protecting; in 1970, for fully employed males, the skilled earned a median income which exceeded that of the unskilled by $3,788. The earnings of the oldest age cohort (55–64 years) of the skilled were about the same as the youngest age cohort (25–34 years), while for unskilled labor, the oldest cohort earned $470 less than the youngest (U.S. Bureau of the Census, 1973:Table 1). Finally, Herman Miller (1966:282, 293) reports that the lifetime earnings of all skilled male workers is 1.56 that of the unskilled. These large income advantages accompanied by an invidious status distinction (skilled versus unskilled) seem worthy of protection. Since 1940 the median annual income of all skilled workers (including foremen) has roughly equaled that of professionals and was surpassed only by managers, officials, and proprietors.

CHALLENGES TO THE COMPETITIVE MODEL OF SKILL STRATIFICATION

Some economists have challenged simple competitive market models to explain wage differentials among the skills. Ozanne (1962), who examined a century of wage rates in a manufacturing company, found no support for Kerr's hypothesis of narrowing wage differentials. Ozanne discovered that the early unions were dominated by craft workers and that they widened wage differentials. The Knights of Labor then narrowed them, but later unions widened them again even during prosperous periods. Ozanne concluded that wage differentials today are very carefully controlled by both the union and management. Richard Perlman (1958), in a careful study, analyzed forces narrowing and widening wage differentials in advanced industrial societies. He concluded that both ideological and economic conditions affect differentials. Thus unions in Italy and France are committed to wage equalization and tend to move toward that goal by centralizing bargaining, especially during inflationary periods. American unions are not committed to equalization and, contrary to marginal economic theory, they have increased wage differentials during periods of full employment, economic depression, and rapid technological change (automation).

Mahler (1961) concluded that economic and market conditions have had little effect on wage patterns of those large industries which are markets for each other, have similar technological and organizational structures, are geographically concentrated, and communicate with each other by virtue of bargaining with the same unions and being subject to similar government regulations. This pattern appears most clearly in oligopolistic industries such as steel, automobile, farm machinery, aircraft, rubber, petroleum, electrical equipment, aluminum, copper, ship building, and meat packing. Other economists (Phelps, 1957; Doeringer and Piore, 1971) have proposed market typologies based on differing economic, organizational, and labor requirements of industries. The demand for skilled workers is typically recognized in these typologies. Thus, Doeringer and Piore demonstrated that different wage patterns appeared in enterprise, craft, and competitive markets. They stress that large enterprises have internal markets which need not respond to community wage patterns because these companies have the requisite resources, training facilities, and traditions to shape wage patterns to their needs.

The final element in competitive models deals with the impact of inflation on wage patterns. Wage differentials are supposed to decline during inflation and periods of labor shortages and increase during economic depressions. The most careful study of this problem (Schoeplein, 1975) examined the skilled/unskilled wage differential in manufacturing and nonmanufacturing in sixteen metropolitan areas during the inflationary period 1952–1973, using annual Area Wage Surveys for representative SMSAs gathered by the Bureau of Labor Statistics for representative industries. Schoeplein incorporated two major improvements in his research design: the elimination of the construction industry because of its volatile wage patterns,[9] and the comparison of identical occupations in the manufacturing and nonmanufacturing sectors (e.g., electricians and janitors). Schoeplein's data confirmed my suspicion that the usual ratio reported by economists is too low. He found that a ratio of 1.50 held for manufacturing during the entire period and that the extent of unemployment did not affect it.

The nonmanufacturing sector hires almost the same number (3.5 million) of skilled workers as manufacturing. Wage differentials in nonmanufacturing not only widened especially after 1965 from 1.7 to 2.0, they widened even more during periods of inflation and labor scarcity. Thus in the more unionized manufacturing sector, wages of the unskilled moved up with inflation at the same rate as for the skilled, but in the service sector, the lower unionization of the unskilled had the effect of depressing their wages relative to the skilled. The higher

[9] To simplify the analysis he also omitted workers in government and mining.

wages for craft workers in nonmanufacturing resulted from the greater freedom of managers to change wages as they anticipate wage increases in manufacturing (Schoeplein, 1975:63–73).

In summary, I examined several aspects of the competitive model of wage differentials among the skill levels. I found little support for a monotonic correlation between a nation's level of economic development and the skilled/unskilled wage ratio. Census data for the United States for the last thirty years, an era of rapid technological change, showed that wage differentials have widened rather than narrowed. Case studies of wage patterns conducted by labor economists also challenged the received wisdom. Ozanne's (1962) study concluded that wage ratios are more strongly conditioned by union ideology and union-management decisions than by market conditions. Perlman's (1958) comprehensive review came to a similar conclusion, but he placed greater stress on changing market conditions. Mahler (1961) found administered wage patterns among large corporations with similar structures and interdependencies, and Doeringer and Piore (1971) argued that the enterprise may be sufficiently strong to stabilize wage patterns independent of the community wage structure. Finally, Schoeplein's (1975) study of an inflationary period demonstrated no tendency toward wage equalization in manufacturing and a tendency toward widening differentials in nonmanufacturing. The conclusion from these economic studies is clear: If the solidarity of the working class is dependent upon the economic homogenization predicted by competitive economic models, it must come from other avenues; economic stratification within the working class continues in the United States and it may be increasing in Europe (Archer and Giner, 1971:32).

Conflicts Over Income Differentials

An economic class or interest group does not engage in collective action without developing a self-justifying rationale. While it is difficult to prove that craft workers adhere to a distinct ideology, a preliminary survey of the literature convinces me that they subscribe to the tenets of functionalist stratification theory. They feel they deserve higher pay than the less skilled because they are more capable, because they perform more important work, and because they have invested more of their time, money, and energy to learn their skills and obtain the requisite experience. This rhetoric is most audible when wage differentials are declining.

The organization to implement this ideology is the union, where it exists, or the informal organization where it does not. Where the skilled are a near majority in the union, they easily control it and maintain wage differentials. Where they constitute a minority of less than 15 percent, they experience difficulty in dominating union affairs. However, craft workers are often in the minority and yet control the union because they typically are its most active members and officers (Tannenbaum and Kahn, 1958:109; Spinrad, 1960; Aronowitz, 1974:157, 181). Arnold Weber (1963) claims that the skilled are most active in unions when they comprise 15 to 30 percent of the membership; union control is possible only if they are very active and strongly united.

American workers may be divided into three strata: In the highest are those who have high social solidarity and union protection; in the second, those who have little social solidarity but strong union protection; in the third, those who have neither. The skilled are more likely than others to have both social solidarity and union protection.[10] Their solidarity derives from their greater freedom and autonomy on the job; they can move about, communicate, and organize for their own protection (Blauner, 1964; Form, 1973). Even though they need little help from the union to control their working conditions, compared to the less skilled, more of the skilled are organized, participate in union affairs, and hold local and national offices (Aronowitz, 1974:173). Thus, craft workers supplement the power of work group solidarity with union influence or control. The semiskilled, especially in mass-production industry, display little work group solidarity, but when unionized, they exercise considerable collective bargaining power. However, a few skilled workers in these unions can cause considerable turmoil over the issue of wage differentials. Later I shall describe such a struggle in the UAW. Finally, unskilled, nonunionized employees have the least amount of work group cohesion (Goode and Fowler, 1949) and union protection. Such is the situation in economically marginal enterprises which employ blacks, Spanish-speaking minorities, very young workers, and older and sick workers who cannot afford to retire (Miller and Rein, 1966:426–516).

Currently, in the United States, the skilled are more concerned with protecting their advantages than winning new ones. In the large industrial unions they fight to maintain wage differentials between themselves and the less skilled. In the craft unions, they struggle to prevent blacks and women from learning their jobs. Despite fair employment legislation and affirmative action guidelines, women and blacks have made only token incursions into the skilled trades. Even voluntary programs proposed by labor itself to integrate blacks and women (Chicago Plan, the Philadelphia Plan, and other hometown plans) have not

[10] Bok and Dunlop (1970:45) estimate that 60 percent of the skilled are unionized as opposed to 38 percent of laborers.

moved craft unions, especially in the building trades, to release their control over the apprentice system and other routes into the trades (Marshall, 1968, 1972).

What is not widely known is the success of the skilled in the ideologically liberal industrial unions to keep blacks and women out of their jobs. The experience of the United Auto Workers is illustrative. Widick (1972) describes in detail the matching of skill and racial stratification in the auto industry. In Detroit's General Motors plants, 65 percent of the employees are black, but 100 percent of the skilled are white. In forty years, the UAW has not become a class-conscious union; whatever social solidarity existed fifteen years ago is now gone because workers are obsessed with the race issue. Union elections are fought largely along racial lines. Without help from UAW officers, black autoworkers have organized to obtain representation if not control of the union. As some blacks win union elections and as management co-opts others, whites become more apprehensive about their security. In the fight to keep their advantages in the union and in the city, the skilled are in the vanguard.

Economic issues are not dead; the craft-industrial union struggle continues in different industries with different outcomes. Thus, while wage differentials in petroleum remained stable for years, they fell from 1.72 to 1.44 in the automobile industry in only three years, 1947–1950 (Weber, 1963). In 1966 the skilled won an amendment in the UAW constitution permitting separate rights to ratify contracts (Brown, 1967) and later they demanded veto rights over contracts which they considered unsatisfactory. They specifically protested company practices of upgrading production workers to perform single-skill jobs alongside journeymen, of failing to keep up with wage levels in craft unions, of failing to respect skill jurisdictions, and of failing to maintain wage differentials with respect to production workers.

The complex issue over whether skilled workers could veto proposed contracts was never satisfactorily resolved, and it was finally turned over for adjudication to the UAW Public Review Board in 1974. Though the board ruled against the skilled trades, the issue is not dead. The skilled hired an attorney to fight the decision in the courts; if unsuccessful there, they threaten to leave the UAW, form an independent union, or join another. From 1950 to 1959 alone, skilled workers submitted thirty-eight petitions to the National Labor Relations Board to have separate bargaining rights, and they formed the United National Caucus within the UAW to coordinate the fight at the national conventions (O'Donnell, 1974; Tillery, 1974). This class movement within a class bears closer sociological scrutiny.

Sex stratification within the working class is as severe as race stratification. The crowding of women into low-paying jobs of the service sector is similar to that of blacks (Fusfeld, 1973) and has been amply documented by Kreps (1971) and others. In a national study, Bibb and Form (1975) have shown that the unaccountably low wages of blue-collar women cannot be explained in terms of the human capital model proposed by economists or by the achievement model proposed by sociologists. Rather they are explained in terms of the stratification characteristics of the industries themselves (size, economic sector, capital investment per worker, location), the stratification of occupations (skill level, extent of unionization), and the sex composition of the labor force. Even where unions officially adopt the principle of equal pay for equal work, women are vastly underpaid compared to men doing the same jobs. In 1968 Cook replicated a study of women's positions in unions done twenty years earlier. She found little or no change in union policies or practices. On the whole, unions followed policies most advantageous to the majority of their members. Not uncommonly, unions had separate bargaining agreements for men and women, but craft unions relied on peer pressure to keep women out of men's jobs. Since most women were in unskilled and semiskilled jobs, women's issues rarely received a serious hearing from officers. Cook concluded that "tokenism" is the standard practice for the political life of women in unions.

This situation is not surprising. The AFL and later the AFL-CIO annually opposed the passage of the Equal Rights Amendment since 1923 when it was first proposed in Congress. The most vocal opponents have been the skilled trades. In 1973 the AFL-CIO reversed its public stand, but took few steps to demonstrate the authenticity of its conversion. In March 1974, the Coalition of Labor Union Women (CLUW) was organized to fight for women's rights within the trade union movement and to increase women's participation. CLUW has its work cut out. After World War II, as after World War I (Baker, 1925), unions and management successfully reduced women's representation in the skilled trades. Although women in 1974 constituted one fifth of union members, two surveys in 1972 and 1974 showed that women union officials were rare even in industries where women predominate. In 1972 as in 1952, of the 177 unions, only two had women presidents (union of stewards and stewardesses, and union of veterinarians). "Of the 187 elected national officers and appointed officials reported by twenty-four unions with at least 50,000 women members, six were women" (Berquist, 1974:5–7).

Under pressure from the federal government, the percentage of women in skilled trades increased from 1960 to 1970 by 3 to 5 percent, a figure they had attained during World War II. While the representation of women increased in some occupations (supervision, dental technician, inspector, printers), it is noteworthy that the goals and timetable requirements of the Office of Federal Contract Compliance do not extend to women in construction trades covered by Hometown Plans developed in seventy cities and counties, and that affirmative action steps toward indenturing minorities by the Bureau of Apprenticeship and Training do not extend to women (Hedges and Bemis, 1974). What CLUW can do about these problems is uncertain, but the organization receives no financial support from the ALF-CIO, nor is it formally recognized,[11] a strange situation in a labor organization which claims to support the Equal Rights Amendment. Finally, women, like blacks, have less seniority than white males. During periods of unemployment, they are the first to be released. As far as I am aware, the AFL-CIO has not devised or implemented a plan to overcome the problems which arise from the strict application of the seniority system. At a conference of CLUW, "sympathetic" male union officers put responsibility for remedying this situation on the victims of the seniority rules by asking the women what they intended to do about the seniority problem. Although sexism in the labor movement is not limited to the skilled workers, they are more successful than other workers in excluding women from their jobs; 4.3 percent of the skilled are women, in contrast to 38 percent of operatives.

Political Stratification of the Working Class

Sociological analysis of American politics is made difficult by two structural features of its party system: the existence of two middle-of-the-road parties and the extraordinarily wide political spectrum of the major (Democratic) party. Under these conditions, parties may lean toward working-class or middle-class interests, but too strong a commitment in either direction threatens the stability of its coalitions. Since organized labor traditionally participates in the unstable coalition which makes up the Democratic party, one should not expect one stratum of labor such as the skilled, when it is unhappy over a political issue, to shift allegiance to the Republican party, just as one should not expect one segment of business, such as the banks, when unhappy over a political issue, to shift their allegiance to the Democratic party. When disagreements occur within a coalition, dissidents threaten to withdraw their support and occasionally do so.

In the United States, the skilled are part of a union coalition which is in turn part of a coalition in the Democratic party. The skilled expect

---

[11] In contrast, the UAW funds a Director of the Women's Department and has a woman vice-president of the International (Raphael, 1974:32).

to make their major gains in factory and union struggles and not in party struggles; that is, their main rewards derive from success in internal and not external politics. In view of these considerations, to demonstrate the political stratification of the working class, the researcher needs only to show the presence of stratal variations in party attachment and political beliefs. Since detailed documentation is impossible in a short paper, I shall discuss two of the most important studies in this area.

The most comprehensive American studies of working-class politics are those of Richard Hamilton (1965), who examined the question whether the more affluent members of the working class tend to become politically conservative. Using skill level as an indicator of wealth, he examined the non-South Republican vote in three presidential elections: the 1948 contest between Truman and Dewey and the 1952 and 1956 contests between Eisenhower and Stevenson. To eliminate contaminating influences on skill-wealth, Hamilton excluded blacks, women, independent artisans, and foremen from the skilled category. He found only negligible differences in the vote of the various skill levels and concluded that economic differences within the working class do not affect the party vote, but sociological factors do, such as age, group membership, group pressures, and size of community of residence (see Table 4).

McNamee (1975) replicated Hamilton's analysis for three following presidential elections: the 1964 Johnson-Goldwater contest, the 1968 Nixon-Humphrey-Wallace contest, and the 1972 Nixon-McGovern election. McNamee made three important changes: He included manual workers in the sample from the service sector, he included women according to their occupations, and he analyzed the effect of income independently from skill. Using a path analytic model, McNamee found that workers with higher incomes were more disposed to vote Republican and that the relationship between income and skill has an indirect effect on party vote. He also concluded that sociological factors strongly affect party choice.

In addition to the economic effects, an analysis of the combined data from the Hamilton and McNamee studies points to several important findings (see Table 4). First, the skilled vote more regularly than the less skilled; in three elections, variation in participation was 4 percent for the skilled and 22 percent for the unskilled.[12] Second, in six elections, consensus among the skill levels varied considerably on presidential candidate preferred and on party identification. Some elections were highly consensual (Humphrey-Nixon, 1968), while others were highly nonconsensual (McGovern-Nixon, 1972). While party identifica-

[12] The 1964 data probably overestimate the voting participation of the unskilled.

TABLE 4. Skill and politics: percentage Republican,[a] party identification, and voter participation among non-South respondents [b]

ELECTION YEARS	SRC 417	UNSKILLED	SEMISKILLED	SKILLED
1948	Truman-Dewey	30	31	42
1952	Stevenson-Eisenhower	50	56	63
1956	Stevenson-Eisenhower	54	50	58
1964	Johnson-Goldwater	26	18	24
1968	Humphrey-Nixon	42	41	46
1972	McGovern-Nixon	48	58	72
Party Identification				
1955	NORC	33	28	35
1956		31	38	45
1968		29	13	24
1972		32	20	24
Voting Participation SRC				
1964 [c]		83	74	76
1968		73	67	72
1972		61	68	74

[a] Excludes independents, don't know, and nonvoters.

[b] All data for 1948, 1952, and 1956 taken from Hamilton (1965*b*), and all remaining data from McNamee (1975).

[c] Data from 1968 and 1970 surveys are in response to questions concerning voting behavior in the last (1964) presidential election.

tion was not as variable as voting behavior, it too varied considerably from one election to another. These fluctuations in voting and party identification held (although in different patterns) even when blacks, foremen, and independent artisans were removed from the analysis. Third, the loyalty of the skilled to the Democratic party was more volatile than that of the other manual workers; in the six elections, there was a 48 percentage point variation among the skilled in support for the Republican candidate compared to 28 for the unskilled. Fourth, in five of six elections, a larger percentage of the skilled than other workers voted Republican: In three of the elections, over half of the skilled voted Republican compared to one election for the unskilled.[13] In short, the skilled as a group are more regular voters than the less skilled, they are more inconstant in their party loyalty, and they lean more toward the Republican party.

The second study by Glenn and Alston (1968) examined 113 ques-

[13] Kornhauser (1965:225) found that both young and middle-aged skilled autoworkers consistently held more conservative socio-economic attitudes than workers who performed repetitive tasks.

tions from twenty-three national surveys to compare the culture of the major occupational groups, extending from the unskilled to professionals. Like Hamilton, they concluded that cultural differences between skilled and clerical workers are wider than between any other two occupational strata and that the working-class/middle-class distinction is more in accord with reality than the concept middle mass. From the perspective of this paper, two observations from the Glenn-Alston data are more important than their central findings. First, consensus was low on most of the cultural items both in the working and middle class, and the range of scores was greater among the manual than the nonmanual workers (Glenn and Alston, 1968:372). Thus, the conclusion that working-class culture is more distinctive than middle-class culture seemed overdrawn. The second and more important observation lies in the critical area of political values where the skilled resembled the clerical-sales workers and professionals more than other manual strata (Glenn and Alston, 1968:373). In two related items (reading and exposure to news on the radio and TV and attention given to current events), the skilled were closer to clerical and sales than other manual workers. In addition, the scores of manual workers in the area of political values and news exposure exhibited more variation than the scores of nonmanual workers. Finally, on "attitudes on child rearing and discipline, skilled workers [were] clearly grouped with the middle-class occupations, being as close to professionals as to other manual categories with the most similar scores" (Glenn and Alston, 1968:373). Glenn and Alston underplay these data by stressing that the skilled are more like other manual workers in authoritarianism, attitudes toward labor unions, optimism about the future state of the world, and drinking attitudes and behavior. Hamilton's conclusion that the skilled may constitute a separate stratum seems more in line with these data than the Glenn-Alston conclusions. In sum, while the data from these studies are not conclusive, they suggest that the skilled are more politically active, more conservative, and more independent politically than other manual workers. Given the structure of labor politics in the United States, the political deviancy of the skilled may indeed inhibit the political solidarity of the working class.

The Skilled in the Class Structure

Sociologists have polarized the class identification issue by asking whether the skilled belong to the working class or the middle class. That such a framework may not be very instructive is illustrated by the history of the embourgeoisement hypothesis. A number of social scientists (e.g., Lipset, 1960:403–417; Kerr et al., 1960) thought they detected certain trends emerging in all advanced industrial societies: Workers were becoming affluent, industrial disruptions were declining, incomes were drifting toward the mean, and class ideologies were declining. These ideas were labeled "the embourgeoisement hypothesis" by scholars in the Marxist tradition. Social scientists decided to test the hypothesis by comparing the top of the working class (skilled workers) to the bottom of the middle class (clerical workers) on such items as buying a house, moving to a suburb, voting Republican, and identifying with the middle class. They reasoned that if the skilled were more like clerical than the unskilled, they were becoming embourgeoisified; if not, they were still working class. Jehlin (1974) points out that such a research design violates historically important issues concerning control of property and government. Embourgeoisement means acquiring capital, political control, and business values and status. Obviously such a test is too rigorous. On the other hand, the indicators of conservatism used by many researchers were too crude. Buying a house, moving to a suburb, shifting vote from one to another nonideological party, and identifying with the middle class are weak indicators of ideology.

A more rewarding approach might be to examine the behavior of class members with reference to each other. Perhaps the working-class/middle-class cleavage is not the most important issue in class politics today. If the skilled fight harder to maintain their privileges, take a more conservative stand on working-class issues, and associate primarily with other skilled workers, they retard the social solidarity of the working class and thereby exert a political force in the society.

Though Hamilton (1964), Mayer and Buckley (1955:84), and Lenski (1961:84) have suggested that the skilled may constitute a separate stratum or a stratum of the working class, little research has been done on the subject. I have re-examined most of the research of Hamilton (1963–1967), Goldthorpe et al. (1969), DeFronzo (1973), Kornhauser (1965), Glenn and Alston (1968), and others and determined that their data report consistent differences among the skill levels as well as between manual and white-collar workers. But only Mackenzie (1973) organized his research to focus specifically on this problem. He studied skilled and white-collar workers in Providence, Rhode Island, and found evidence that the skilled were attaining separate status in the stratification system. They not only earned more than other manual and clerical workers, they were more concerned with job security and work satisfaction. They reared their children conservatively; to be, obedient, respectful, and honest and to have white-collar and university aspirations. The high levels of home ownership and rising consumption among the skilled did not signify a commitment to bourgeois values. Their allegiance to the Democratic party was relatively high, though two fifths claimed to be independent voters. However, party loyalty reflected their ethnic and religious identification more than their political commitment (see Greeley, 1972). Importantly, half of the craft workers believed they were not in the same class as the unskilled (Mackenzie, 1973:135). Like Weber, the skilled defined class on the basis of income and life chances. They also saw themselves as a status group in interactional terms; two thirds of their leisure-time companions were also skilled workers. But they were not class conscious in Marxist (power or conflict) terms. Finally, more of the skilled than any other occupational group considered the unskilled/skilled distinction to be important.

Conclusions

The widely debated issue whether manual workers identify with the working or middle class, I suggest, hides as much as it illuminates. A more important concern is the identification of factors that inhibit the political mobilization of manual workers as a class. I have tried to demonstrate that this mobilization is inhibited by the tendency of the skilled to define their interests as different from those of other manual workers. To some extent, their definition is based on objective differences in their class, status, and political situation. They earn significantly more money than other manual workers. They want others to honor their skills, and they realize that they must organize to preserve their historic advantages over other manual workers. In this struggle, both employers and the less skilled may represent the enemy, depending on the issues.

When the skilled resist the incursions of the unskilled, they appear to be conservative. But the label is misleading. They are not antagonistic to other manual workers in principle. Whenever the skilled feel they can improve their position with the help of other manual workers, they not only accept it, but assume leadership in the struggle against the opposition. Thus, in Norway, Cuba, Latin America, and the United States prior to 1940, where organized labor felt oppressed, the skilled not only led the working class movement, they embraced a revolutionary ideology of economic equality. Once labor achieves political legitimacy in pluralistic societies or once labor becomes part of the government, as in socialist or communist systems, the skilled may again press for special economic treatment. But this is a research problem rather than a settled issue.[14]

[14] See the symposium edited by Windmuller (1974, 1975) for the broad spectrum of structural arrangements found among the labor movements, parties, and governments in various countries.

The type of analysis I have pursued makes the skilled appear as the *bête noire* of working-class movements because they inhibit political solidarity. This impression is due in part to focusing on the American case and limiting the analysis to the problems of skilled workers. If the analysis focused on the semiskilled in the primary industrial sector, for example, they too would appear to be indifferent to the problems of the economically disadvantaged workers in marginal enterprises. In short, the American working class is deeply stratified, and more than one of its strata inhibits political mobilization. Of course, middle-class strata also repress working-class movements, but that is a separate issue.

The study of working-class mobilization must take into account the internal politics of organized labor at the national level. Unfortunately, little is known about this except its results: The labor elite propagates a union but not a class political program. Most of the elite of the American labor movement has been and continues to be recruited from the ranks of skilled labor. The growth of mass industrial unions has not changed class politics perhaps because they have not broken the power of the traditional working-class elite.

4

Politics, Conflict, and Young Blue-Collarites: Old Dissensus and New Consciousness

Arthur B. Shostak

WHERE THE POLITICS of conflict are concerned, young blue-collarites are variously represented as shifting left, or marching to the political right, or dropping out of politics altogether into a drug-hazed world of indifference and naiveté. While some can undoubtedly be found in all three camps, the issue is wide open concerning where the largest number are now, and are likely to be, found over the foreseeable future. Commentators impressed by the 1962 Gans classic, *The Urban Villagers,* persist in dismissing contemporary blue-collar youth as merely routinized Democratic party faithful.[1] Still other students of the subject disagree vigorously, and make much of the considerable Wallace support evident in the ranks of certain young manual workers, while a third bloc of writers is intrigued by the very different radicalizing impact possible here from the counterculture and the recent high levels of long-term unemployment. All that is really clear, then, about the politics of the subjects—the 16- to 24-year-old sons of Caucasian blue-collarites—is that argumentation far outweighs evidence or persuasive lines of reasoning in the entire matter.

□ The assistance, editorial skills, and personal knowledge of the subject of Miss Christina Murianka is owed considerable credit for whatever merit this essay may have. Mr. Ro-shan Attrey, my first typist, met a very difficult deadline with graciousness and editorial skills, for which he has my sincere appreciation. Mrs. Rita McMaster, Administrative Assistant, Drexel University, directed preparation of the final copy with characteristic craft and cool-headedness, both vital in completing this endeavor.

[1] Gans, 1962, is of great value in understanding the provincialism, fundamentalism, and contradictions of older blue-collarites. See also Fried, 1973.

As my limited contribution to this far-reaching dialogue, I propose to offer tentative answers to five critical subquestions: First, what are the decisive public events of the last twenty years that may have shaped the political styles of this cohort? Second, what do major polls suggest about the impact on this blue-collar bloc of the campus-based counterculture? Third, what is the political significance of each of the three leading life-style types found among young blue-collarites today—the subcultures I label Hard-hat Hipsters, Nostalgic Revisionists, and Vanguard Insurgents? Fourth, what sort of research remains to be done in this complex and dynamic matter? And finally, working cautiously and yet imaginatively with what is known or can be surmised, what role are young male blue-collarites likely to soon play in the conflictual or consensual politics of America?

Blue-Collar Youth

Nearly 5.4 million young Caucasian males, 16 to 24 years old, swell today's job-short labor force, themselves the product of the 1950–1960 decade of the greatest baby boom in U.S. history (U.S. Bureau of the Census, 1974).[2] Impressive on many counts, this cohort presently equals 25 percent of all male Caucasian blue-collarites of any age (U.S. Bureau of the Census, 1974). Their ranks, even when restricted as in this essay to young members of one race of the male sex, are still so discordantly diverse as to include both an overrepresentation of the sons of white ethnics of polyglot variety, and of new young urban migrants.[3] This time the migrants are not off of Ellis Island, but are down from the Appalachian hills and are in from the back country (they are labeled now not "dagos" or "hunkies," but hillbillies, crackers, stump-jumpers, and ridge-runners). Overall, nevertheless, and of great relevance to their politics, this entire cohort boasts the highest average educational attainment of any to ever enter the blue-collar plurality of the American labor force.

Looking back over their 16- to 24-year life span, their style of poli-

[2] My figure of 5.4 million is an estimate from data that frustrate arriving at a more exact count. Note that I am excluding service workers from this count, and have made a guess-estimate deduction for the blacks originally included in the Bureau of the Census data.

[3] I restrict the essay as I do because the data on young blue-collar females and nonwhites is very rare and quite uneven. As well, their situation has its own unique components, and warrants a separate, lengthy, and complex treatment. Similarly I exclude from consideration an unknown number of blue-collar sons matriculating at two-year or four-year colleges, and intent on leaving the blue-collar life as fast and as far behind as possible. While I discuss these mobile types in *Blue Collar Life* (Shostak, 1969), I need more space than possible here to go into the matter.

tics (attitudes, values, and actions) appears deeply affected by their experience of two unpopular wars (Korea and Vietnam), four substantial recessions (1958, 1961, 1967, 1974–1975), and persistent, even double-digit inflation. As well, there have been three major domestic political assassinations, the confrontation 1960s, the persistent agitation by aggrieved minorities (along with women's liberation protest), détente and the trade-with-China collapse of anticommunist shibboleths, along with the Watergate augmentation of public cynicism regarding politics and politicians.

Most recently these young men have been abruptly challenged to make sense of and accommodate unemployment levels of over 15 percent in their ranks, the end of the draft and voluntary military service as an "easy out," the return to the factories of often aggrieved and troubled young veterans of the Indochina wars, the lure of the community college, and the persistent media-aided rumors of the fast-approaching disappearance of millions of (pre-automation) blue-collar jobs. (Some may know, for example, that Detroit manufactures the same number of cars now—six million—as it did a decade ago, but does so with 20 percent fewer workers).[4]

Pulling all this together, the conceding its suggestive nature, this cohort of 16- to 24-year-olds has known a remarkably turbulent and question-provoking history. Theirs appears to be a life-span record of political "happenings" of the most disorganizing sort—a representation that should be kept in mind as a case is made later for the willingness, even eagerness, of some of these young workers to experiment with new life styles and political modes.

The Old Consciousness

Throughout the 1960s the central explanatory fact concerning the class-linked politics of young workers was allegedly the light-years of attitudinal and value differences that apparently separated them from their college-going peers (that is, the "cutting-edge" counterculture proponents among matriculants). Indeed, this gap was represented as critical in containing the radicalism of the left on the campus, and in isolating campus activists from a large and invaluable pool of potential, converging allies among noncampus blue-collarites.[5]

Typical of reports emphasizing the gulf between blue-collar and

[4] The Detroit data are from Prof. Lewis Ferman, University of Michigan. Invaluable on the subject of job prospects is Rosenthal and Dillon (1974).

[5] The earliest relevant writing to contradict this well-entrenched notion of sharp interclass divisiveness between blue- and white-collar youth is that of Paul Goodman (1960).

other youth is a volume based on numerous annual Purdue Opinion Polls of high-schoolers.[6] According to sociologist Frank E. Armbruster these nationwide polls supported four major contentions:

1. Young people generally repeated the politics of their parents: The continuity of inherited ways was dominant where value choices and systems were concerned.
2. High-schoolers evidenced little or no change in fundamentals since 1951 (religion, views on democracy, support for free enterprise systems, etc.).
3. Blue-collar youngsters in particular resisted political attitude pressures of a nonfamily or minority youth sponsorship, both left and right.
4. Blue-collar youngsters wanted nothing so much as the opportunity to make it "big" within the system.

Overall, Armbruster made much of his conclusion that there might be a greater gap in the early 1970s between the attitudes of ultraliberal college-goers and those of noncollege-goers than between most youth and adults (the so-called generation gap).

Another study published that year by Kasschau and associates focused on 287 young Americans, 18 to 22 years of age, and came up with very similar findings:

Noncollege blue-collar youth showed the lowest commitment to New Left youth ideology of all research categories (including blue-collar college, white-collar noncollege and college). On issues of avoiding the draft or creating a revolutionary party, blue-collar noncollege-goers were especially nonsupportive.

Noncollege blue-collar youth had a uniquely high action potential for right-wing political activities. They were not only least likely to support a New Left ideology, but they were most likely instead to participate in a demonstration to reaffirm loyalty to the traditional system.

Overall, the authors concluded there simply was no empirical evidence in 1972 of a "relentlessly mounting and uniform general movement based on conflict, as has been so sensationally discussed in the mass media" (Kasschau, Ransford, and Bengtson, 1974).

The New Consciousness

Other students of the same phenomena at the same time saw it quite differently, however, and Milton Mankoff and Richard Flacks

---

[6] Armbruster, 1972: 174, 181, 327, 328, *passim.* I am appreciative to Robert Johanson for calling this volume to my attention.

(1971), for example, wrote approvingly in 1972 of the alleged spread of the youth revolt and counterculture conflict off of the campus and into the life experience of young blue-collarites.

In an especially illuminating way, Frank Riessman (1972) added his thoughts to this steadily growing academic fray with a major essay. Riessman was persuaded that young workers were exploring and adapting (rather than merely adopting) a wide range of youth culture components, such as the language, hairstyles, costumes, music, drug use, and sexual permissiveness of the new bohemians. Provocatively, this extended to include new doubts of theirs about the Calvinist work ethic, along with deep-set opposition to authoritarianism in all things, and especially to dehumanization in work.

Riessman, however, did *not* think this attitude change included a tolerance for challenges to conventional Western religions or conventional capitalist political policies. In his view young blue-collarites were open then only to youth culture components that were convenient, faddish, and casual: When things got sticky, as in a deep-reaching struggle between esoteric Far Eastern faiths and the old-time religion, their pro-tradition socialization would take over. Similarly, Riessman felt the challenge to job creation that young workers perceived in the advocacy by others of a no-growth or low-growth economy sharply divided hip blue-collarites from hip counterculture peers among the college-going, ashram-building, or Haight-Ashbury set.

Two years later, in 1974, the results of a major 1973 national survey were published. As the book analyzed 1969–1973 longitudinal data, it shed unique and invaluable light on the entire subject of the so-called New Consciousness among blue-collarites. Commissioned by the Rockefeller Fund and conducted by a commercial social research company, Daniel Yankelovich, Inc., the project entailed interviews with a representative sample of 3,522 young Americans, including about 2,200 Caucasians, 16 to 24 years of age. Excluding service workers, some 30 percent of these 2,200 young adults were blue-collarites, women making up an unknown proportion of the group (Yankelovich, 1974*b*:82).

To the apparent surprise of the survey researchers, their attitudinal data comparing young workers with college-goers revealed a remarkable unidirectional and widespread convergence:

> Perhaps the single most striking finding of the study is the extent to which the gap between college and noncollege youth has closed over these past six years. . . . To an almost uncanny degree, . . . noncollege youth today is just about where the college population was in 1969. Virtually every aspect of the New Values have deeply penetrated noncollege youth. Moral norms have changed dramatically. Social values with regard to money, work, and family are slowly being transformed. And the same intangible conflict between self-fulfillment and economic

security is spreading throughout every group in the youth population.
[Yankelovich, 1974*b*:23]

Specifically, young blue-collarites were markedly more liberal than they
had ever been in any earlier survey concerning abortion on request,
drug use, premarital relations, a de-emphasis on money, and other
controversial subjects. They broke with tradition and tended to down-
grade the importance of religion in their lives, the importance of patriotism as a personal value, and the belief that "hard work always pays
off." Like their college-going peers they placed the same high value (75
percent) on self-expression and self-fulfillment.

Nevertheless, consistent with the Riessman analysis of two years earlier, the Yankelovich data proved ambivalent and ripe for conflicting
interpretation where political attitudes were concerned. On the one
hand, there was evidence of a new-found disillusionment with patriotic
shibboleths, a gap growing possibly so wide as to permit inroads by
anti-Establishment political philosophies:

1. We suffered a moral loss in Vietnam—we had no right to be there
   (32%)
2. We are a sick society (35%)
3. Things are going very/fairly badly (50%)
4. Society is democratic in name only—special interests run things
   (58%)
5. Political parties need fundamental reform or elimination (64%)
6. Business is too concerned with profits and not with public responsibility (92%)

Trend data also lent additional support to those who sensed a proconflict, proreform edge to the New Consciousness:

In 1969, only 24 percent of noncollege youth found big business non-
viable as an institution. By 1973 the figure had reached 45 percent.

Similarly, political parties were thought to require fundamental reform
by 44 percent of noncollege youth in 1969, and by 64 percent four
years later.

On the other hand, vestiges of older blue-collar political attitudes were
also present:

There is too much concern with equality, and not enough with law and
order (71%)

There is too much concern with the welfare "bum" (77%)

Taking all into account, the researchers concluded that noncollege
youth tended to be "more conservative" in their views about political
issues and candidates than did their college peers:

Noncollege youth are, in fact, considerably less political than campus youth. Their politics are, if anything, pragmatic rather than idealistic, stemming in part from their own feelings that society is overly concerned with the needs of others (college students, minorities, etc.) and not enough with the needs of average young people who have to work for a living. [Yankelovich, 1974b:115]

Less likely to vote and more conservative in their outlook than their college peers, 78 percent of noncollege youth interviewed in 1973 claimed that they were "sick and tired of hearing people attack patriotism, morality, and traditional American values" (Yankelovich, 1974b:118). With this declaration they veered sharply back in the direction of the Old Consciousness—at least in this peevish particular.

Variations on the Theme

The New Consciousness that Armbruster and Kasschau deny, that Yankelovich defines and qualifies, and that Riessman divides, faces formidable obstacles in the way of four class-linked legacies. First, the socialization of young blue-collarities largely rears them to adjust and make do, not to question and ask why. Second, then neighborhoods are generally tight and defensive enclaves that orient residents to privatism and accommodation, not to privilege-questioning and action-taking. Third, their schooling essentially prepares them for ordinary lives of anonymous self-effacement and patriotic appreciation, not for proud self-assertion and goal reassessment. And finally, their experiences at work, as unionists, and even as mates and parents, fundamentally school them in a "make no waves," "deaf, dumb, and blind" kind of obsequiousness, not a "reach for the sky" kind of odyssey.[7]

Not surprisingly, then, the resulting politics of young blue-collarites has closely resembled that of their fathers: In many telling ways it has mixed self-effacing retreatism (apathetic or cynical nonvoting), self-inflating ritualism (straight party-line voting every time), or self-gratifying recklessness (minimally productive support of isolated right-wingers, reactionaries, Birchers, or Wallacites).

At present, however, the beachhold of the New Consciousness helps support three important variations on older blue-collar political styles. The first, belonging to Hard-hat Hipsters, is a fun-oriented, pleasure-promoting mode that has considerable latent political possibilities. The second, belonging to Nostalgic Revisionists, is an "uptight," backward-looking style that raises irreverent questions about social policies that "good people" are not supposed to question. And the third, the style of

[7] A thoroughgoing review of this material can be found in Shostak, 1969. See also Fried, 1973.

Vanguard Insurgents, is a change-seeking, ideology-revamping mode that could just help partisans evolve an authentic American radicalism.

Each of these three political styles has generic ties to either yesteryear's bohemianism, conservatism, or radicalism:

TIME FRAME			
1975	Hard-hat Hipsters	Nostalgic Revisionist	Vanguard Insurgents
Circa 1970s	Convergence with youth culture around a New Consciousness		
1960s and earlier	Bohemianism	Conservatism	Radicalism

T A B L E 1. Political styles of young blue-collarites: variations predicated in a new consciousness

	HARD-HAT HIPSTERS	NOSTALGIC REVISIONISTS	VANGUARD INSURGENTS
Political activism	[Latent]	Erratic; predicated on local flare-ups	Erratic; wildcat strikes and local issues
Political goals	Libertarian and laissez-faire Ethos	Restoration of predictability, equity, and integrity	Thoroughgoing overhaul of the entire system
Political weaknesses (viewed from outside)	Dis-inclination to contront through direct political action; distractions of play centrism	Impotence in face of stronger modernity trends; aura of irrelevance	Stigma of unpatriotic foreign sponsorship; internecine fractionalism
Political prospects	Hinges on efforts outsiders make to win adherents for permissiveness and entitlement politics (legal pot, guaranteed income, decriminalization, etc.)	Hinges on efforts to coalesce around more forward-looking matters, e.g., ethnic contributions to larger society	Hinges on efforts to nurture native radical leadership among coworkers; can gain from possession of a theory of history and a reform blueprint (the dialectic and socialist tenets; the conservative papers and tenets of modified welfare capitalism)

Each of the styles, however, differs from its progenitor more than it resembles it, as the transforming influence of the New Consciousness is pervasive. In combination with the zesty, convention-upsetting, two-and-a-half-decade history of this cohort, the influence of the New Consciousness promotes new political styles of a fresh and invigorating experience (see Table 1). Indeed, it is just this fresh slant—and the uneasy coexistence of these distinctive styles—that appears to raise a host of new possibilities where the class politics of this cohort is concerned.

HARD-HAT HIPSTERS

It is important to look beyond the outward posturing in colorful language, unisex costume, and "smooth" behavior of this New Consciousness variation, this blue-collar updating and modernization of yesteryear's bohemianism. To help accomplish this we will consider some telling aspects of the lives of young blue-collar drug users, and those of young steel mill workers, along with that of a young electrician I have interviewed in the course of my own recent research into blue-collar realities.

An essay by Gary Schwartz and others (1973), based on their 1971–1972 field research with 18- and 19-year-old working-class drug users, is especially helpful in explaining important aspects of the hipster style where deviance is central. As Schwartz and associates saw it, young "hippie greasers" improbably combined two youthful styles with opposing ideological connotations. As "greasers" they were tough-minded realists, preoccupied with gaining power, affirming their manhood, endorsing "rugged individualism," and controlling the things and people important in their immediate environment. As "hippies," however, they valued self-fulfillment, and continually monitored their own mood and their perceptions of significant others. Indifferent to other major aspects of hippie ideology (neoreligious communion with nature; the search for universal forms of human solidarity; belief in an organic community), blue-collar hipsters combined "the greaser's street wisdom and personal toughness with the hippie's dedication to drugs and rock music without any regard for the ostensibly contradictory meanings of these two orientations toward life" (Schwartz et al., 1973:290. See also Simon et al., 1971).

Ambivalent about, or antagonistic toward, societal structures that interfered with their personal freedom, the hippie greasers felt that only a lesser human being would yield to pro-subservience pressures. Accordingly, anxious to minimize hassles, they went so far as to redefine traditional machismo elements in their lives. The exaggerated, sardonic manner in which they joked about sexual conquests, for example, actually belied a low-keyed and relatively open way they had of dealing with women. Most seemed unwilling to allow traditional conceptions of the "war between the sexes" to grip and upset them: Most declined to make an issue of personal dominance in male-female relations. In same-sex relations, as well, nobody told anyone else what to do or how to do it. Zealous in protecting the completely relaxed atmosphere of their club, they rarely pursued tricks of persuasion and never indulged in direct confrontation. (Their membership, however, included some of the toughest "bikers" around, as well as several formidable street fighters.)

Moral codes were situationally defined: One group member, for example, stole from chain stores, and viewed it as merely taking back some of the money they "ripped off" from ordinary people. This stealing, however, had no political or revolutionary overtones, and was done simply as a matter of *quid pro quo*. Overall, greasers were bothered not by bourgeois materialism, but by bourgeois morality. They relied on their native skepticism where the motives of those who spoke on behalf of public morality were concerned. Some viewed public morality itself as little more than a handy set of self-serving platitudes useful to those who needed to rationalize meaningless lives or irrational behavior.

Work, while taken as grimly inevitable, was viewed with casual disinterest, the greasers being totally disengaged from career interest or pursuit: If something came along that seemed interesting, they took it. Otherwise they tried to get by as best they could. Insisting that the material rewards of work did not justify a life whose predictable routines would be broken only on weekends, they inverted the attitudes of their parents toward the basic requirements for a decent life: Many made it a point of honor *not* to take work seriously at all. Instead, they dealt with the reality of having to work at dull jobs by denying it, and never tried to justify it in terms of money made.

Prizing inner hardness, greaser politics took a comparably hard edge: Many retained the social conservatism of their parents, and viewed the world as a tough place where one learned to bear misfortune without exaggerated self-pity. They argued that you got what you deserved in this world, but only by dint of your own efforts (although it was vital to have "clout," influence, and "connections"). In a related way they directed more scorn than sympathy at the have-nots. Greasers shared the hostility of their parents toward blacks, and contended that people on welfare were inherently incapable of doing anything to change their situation. Efforts by aggressive blacks or the organized poor to do so, however, were sharply put down as the pushiness of people who didn't know where they rightly belonged. (Greasers scoffed at the romantic utopianism of the adherents of communes and radical politics, contending that these naive peers were ignoring the hard facts of life.)

Greasers, however, were not entirely without their own form of political radicalism, albeit one confined to an attitudinal stance. Many, for example, dwelt on the absurdities and trivialities of American culture, and enjoyed comics (such as *Mad*) preoccupied with the ridiculous underside of social reality. Most urged one another not to take anything at face value, especially the inanities of American life and politics. With all of this debunking fervor, however, their politics remained fundamentally a defensive and staying operation, as they were handicapped by a lack of a vision, dream, blueprint, or plan of how it might be otherwise:

> Rather than dreaming about a better world or a more perfect mode of existence, their political and social attitudes remain definitely antiutopian. Their response to their amorphous position in the "real" world is to "vegetate." [Schwartz et al., 1973:310] [8]

Illustrative was the situation one night when the club's record player broke down: Someone immediately suggested that they ought to smoke more dope so that they would not care whether it worked or not.

Turning from this 1971–1972 pen portrait, we can usefully compare more current observations of young steel mill hipsters, as recounted to me during the 1975 Sociological Association Meeting by John Maiolo (observations based indirectly on his 1973–1975 research while at Purdue University in Gary, Indiana).

Dead set against making work a central life interest, young mill workers strongly rejected identification with the work-defeated fate of their older mill-working brothers or fathers. Instead, they appeared persuaded that play was the best antidote to work: Costumed in high heels and wide-cuff treads, they were focused on owning a boat, a cabin, or a vampish van. Utterly rejecting of the self-depreciation pathos of older blue-collarites (as captured in the masterful Sennett-Cobb volume, *The Hidden Injuries of Class,* 1972), these young buccaneers based their own high self-esteem on their success at living the singles' life (a flat away from home; access to liberated, promiscuous "chicks" from all social classes; access to legalized abortion; and access to newly acceptable living-together arrangements). Many shunned the so-called ethnic revival as a backward-looking shuck, and most declined to believe that any—even those on campus—had it any better than they did.

Finally, there is the very different variation here of a remarkable young life-style adventurer I encountered in my spring 1975 research:

[8] See also Fred Davis, 1971.

"Aaron," 24 years old, graduated from high school and proceeded to score highest among 700 candidates for ten openings in the Electric Union's apprenticeship program. Now a foreman over electricians at construction sites, he shares a $25,000 gross income with his school-teacher wife. Intent on working only half a year, he devotes the other six months to such avocations as learning to fly, organic gardening, home repairs, carpentry. A dedicated reader, he goes through twenty or more books a year, and subscribes to the *Wall Street Journal, Flying, Playboy, Barron's, Organic Gardening,* and others.

When we discussed politics "Aaron" traced his liberal views to his compassion for the "poor slobs" he heard on the radio talk shows he listened to daily, and to his concern over the effects of frequent and even long-term involuntary unemployment on his coworkers. Persuaded that a smart fellow could still make it big in America, he also felt that the "big boys" had it all wrapped up and "pulled the strings" for the rest of us.

Overall, then, what can be made of the class-linked politics of three kinds of Hard-hat Hipsterism? It would seem clear that certain critical pro-conflict elements are conspicuously absent from the scene. First, there is no intention to wrestle improvements in economic fundamentals from a perceived class of exploitative others. Second, there is no spur of envy over the alleged undeserved and stolen wealth, happiness, and general well-being of these damnable others. Third, there is a lack of the inspiration and controlling mechanism of a guiding vision of how it all might be if it were to be made better for all.

I am reminded of the tavern-based observations of E. E. LeMasters in his *Blue-Collar Aristocrats* (1975). Drinking with the "boys down at Kelsey's" over a five-year period, LeMasters was struck by the fact that the elbow-bending members of this generation of young blue-collar sports were uniquely without spokesmen, leaders, or worse still, heroes. While possibly more liberal in their social attitudes and values than any earlier blue-collar cohort, they were preoccupied with local softball nitty-gritty, were sullenly quiet about their Vietnam maladventure, and were decidedly naive or apathetic in political matters.

NOSTALGIC REVISIONISTS

The second major political style here, the oldest and most respectable of the three variations on the New Consciousness, dismisses pop-culture hedonism of Hard-hat Hipsters as exaggerated, short-lived, and inconsequential. Instead, emphasis is placed on the new political headiness and independence of an assertive working class.

Central here is the contention that all blue-collar politics are at heart an extension of the worker's "gut feelings" about life in his own immediate neighborhood: When that is strained, his politics lash out at bungling planners, meddling do-gooders, and inadequate protectors of law and order. When things are balmy and secure in his "urban village" the worker registers his approval and appreciation by withdrawing back into the shell of personal life and immediate concerns, relieved to turn politics back once again to others "who are paid to worry about those sorts of things." [9]

Survey data offered in 1976 by Donald I. Warren suggest that many young blue-collarites are more prone than ever to leave the ranks of the "silent majority," and to lash out with ballots and/or brickbats in favor of the reinstitution of structures and rules that promote "law and order." While not opposed to government action-taking or to the large-scale collective programs of the New Deal, these blue-collarites impress Warren as being bitterly opposed to all that smacks now of promoting differential access to scarce rewards (such as benign job quotas, the ERA, and other aids to "protestors").

At the same time, however, they are also utterly rejecting of left or right calls to restructure social and political institutions. Instead, they prefer to replace the people heading offending institutions. (Similarly, blacks are thought prone to poverty and crime because of their underlying poor character, and not because of any fundamental processes of American social structure.) Young workers of this political persuasion are especially opposed to the forced busing of their school-age children, and to the collapse of adequate municipal services to their old working-class neighborhoods.

Overall, then, what are we to make of the class-linked politics of Nostalgic Revisionists? Skeptical of radical political ideologies of all persuasions, and suspicious of conventional political parties and their leaders, young blue-collar revisionists see themselves at the first stage of their own political maturation, as just beginning to actively "get themselves together." Appealed to by the right-wing likes of ROAR (Restore Our Alienated Rights), and Boston's anti-integrationists, they are also the focus of totally opposite organizing efforts by Baltimore's ethnic radical Barbara Milkowski, and the Fred Harris populist primary campaign. Even at this incubus stage, however, it seems clear that their politics of nostalgia will long focus on the restoration of new certainties and old securities in an America that otherwise strikes them as spinning out of control. In short, these young blue-collarites share not only in the hip pop culture, but also in a widespread nostalgia for simpler (mythical) days past, when hierarchy and oligarchy went seemingly

---

[9] Valuable here is Rainwater, 1971.

unchallenged, and life was plain, predictable, and modestly pleasurable—at least to hear certain quixotic retirees tell about it now.

VANGUARD INSURGENTS

The third and seemingly least popular of the major perspectives differs dramatically from the preceding two: Embracing elements of both, it parts from them to endorse the classic radical expectation of profound political insurgency coming soon from the ranks of vanguard blue-collar youth.

Seemingly typical of the young men involved is an eighteen-year-old white Southerner, Bobby Joe Wright, profiled by Gitlin and Hollander. The son of a sawmill worker, Bobby boasts a wild youth that many a Hard-hat Hipster would envy: sex at age ten, pistol holdups at twelve, male hustler at fifteen, porno film star at sixteen, truant and runaway from ten on, professional pool-hustler from twelve on, and "a different girl every night . . . like from fifteen till now I never made it with a girl under twenty-one" (Gitlin and Hollander, 1970:399. See also Kahn, 1972).

Turned in to the police by his father at age fourteen, Bobby spent time in three different reformatories (including solitary) before being released at sixteen years of age. Out two months, he was sent back for nine more after he and his brother battled with the local police. On his release he finished school and began a haphazard string of unskilled office and factory jobs.

Drawn in short order to a radical South Chicago activist group, JOIN, Bobby found their analysis of things helpful in "getting it together":

> . . . through the years I've heard people mention how the government really fucks over the people—it says that the people are supposed to have the right to decide for themselves, which they don't have that right at all, there's always somebody to decide for them and that's how I got to run into JOIN and everything. I found out I was a radical about four weeks ago, as soon as I found out what the word meant. . . . [Gitlin and Hollander, 1970:413] [10]

At the same time, however, his New Consciousness came at a price deemed too high by willful apathetic types and backward-glancing Nostalgic Revisionists:

> Now that I heard about all this war in Vietnam and how the government's runnin''over people and the people with money are runnin' over

---

[10] See also Howell, 1973.

the people, I'm twisted around. I'm not happy. The only time I'm happy now is when I'm on that pot. That's the only time I'm happy. Cause I got this carefree attitude like I did before I found out about all these things. [p. 416]

Nevertheless, Bobby worked with JOIN to organize white Southern workers, on his "own free will," all the time expecting a "little war" to soon break out locally, pitting his young buddies against the local police ("cause a lot of people are getting sick of 'em pushing 'em around and everything" [p. 419]).

Soon retained as a teacher for JOIN, Bobby wrote poems and articles for its newsletter, started a play, and read his first books. After eighteen months as a radical organizer, his New Consciousness had come a long way:

> I feel more dedicated than when I started cause things are startin' to happen and I was partly responsible for buildin' things that happened. . . . You get a great feelin' when you see a group of people standin' around demanding stuff that is rightfully theirs. . . . Now we gotta start findin' out how to get like people elected on the urban renewal board, get community police. . . . [p. 425]

His jerry-built political platform also called for requiring aldermen to live in the slum section of their election districts, relocating the draft board from downtown into the neighborhood, and lobbying for both a guaranteed annual wage and a reduction of the earnings of politicians to the "standard wage."

Sensitive to his own changes, Bobby insisted that they were irrevocable:

> . . . now knowin' all the stuff that I do know, I don't think I could drop back into the society which I came from. I can't go into a factory and work eight hours a day for twenty years, not unless I know that I'm buildin' for somethin' in that factory, somethin' that's not just gonna better me. I'm lookin' for better me, I'm lookin' for better everybody. . . . It's not easy at all but I can't see me stoppin' the work I'm doin'. [p. 428]

Drawing their book of portraits of Bobby and similar others to a close, Gitlin and Hollander note in passing that while JOIN soon disappeared, it did "train a band of leaders who will not be easily stopped, who work on the other side of hope and despair, because they've been, as they say, 'turned around,' because they have no choice . . . " (p. 434).

How significant is Bobby? A clue is available in a brief note contained in the 1971–1972 research on young "hippie greaser" drug users:

> Nick, an original member of the group, now departed for the West
> Coast and, living in a commune, was a self-styled radical who worked in a
> factory. While the group ridiculed his political rhetoric, they liked Nick
> personally and now joke about his search for the "Cosmic High." They
> do not believe there is an ideological solution to their situation.
> [G. Schwartz et al., 1973:302]

This cordial but deep-set rejection by accommodating peers would
seem the fate, the Achilles heel, of the entire vanguard effort at
present.

At least one major student of the subject, however, disagrees. Stanley Aronowitz remains optimistic that an original combination of JOIN-
like organizing efforts (vastly improved), along with the "inside" efforts
of Bobby and Nick, can make a substantial difference soon in favor of
radicalizing a style-setting cadre of young blue-collar youth. In his book
False Promises (1974) Aronowitz tries to calm the misgivings of activists
put off by the hedonism of the New Consciousness, explaining that it
should be welcomed for its ability to help free young men of Calvinist
and Horatio Alger misperceptions. Looking at the same 16-to-24-year-
old sons of manual workers that have preoccupied us throughout,
Aronowitz stressed their alleged novelty:

> They have not been cowered by having to survive through the Great
> Depression.
>
> They have transcended the bonds of divisive ethnicity.
>
> Vietnam and Watergate have helped disavow them of parochial patrio-
> tism.
>
> They have been disenchanted with traditional trade unionism and con-
> ventional anticommunism.
>
> They are animated with the ideals of self-fulfillment sown by American
> education.
>
> They are fast discovering the limits of high levels of consumership.

In sum, the present generation of workers is thought "qualitatively different from any in the history of American capitalism. (Aronowitz,
1974:407).

Aronowitz contends that since 1960, and hidden from surface view,
there has been a radical transformation of the American working class.
The true archetypical figure in working-class life has passed from being
an "Archie Bunker" or William Bendix–"Riley" sort of clod, living his
life in fear of layoffs and repossessions, to being a "Michael" or "Gloria
Stivak" type of adventurer, a young adult whose life experience has
been radically different from that of *all* previous blue-collar generations. Unlike their parents, and many of their peers, these new workers

TABLE 2. Interclass relations

RESEARCH UNKNOWNS: IMPACT OF—	PRO-HARMONY FINDING	PRO-CONFLICT FINDING
1. *Heterogeneity of the cohort* (race, income, skill, ethnicity, style of life, etc.)	Impedes growth of class consciousness, class unity, and class militancy	Diverse source of grievances and ideas; capable of quick coalescence at the right time
2. *Widespread resort to career education in public schools* (all leave with specific marketable skill)	Recreates the working-class ethic; puts emphasis on "correct" attitudes; scales back pro-middle-class bias	Erodes support for slavish job attachment; heightens expectations of off-work rewards; whets appetite for job enrichment
3. *Community college enrollment*	Creams off leadership talent; reinforces draw of individual rather than class upward mobility	Infuriates with poor quality and post-graduation failure to pay off; exposes some to New Left teachers
4. *Devaluation of college evaluation*	Defuses class rivalries; up grades self-esteem of non-college-goers	Angers aspirants to mobility through higher education; provokes suspicion; it is a self-serving middle-class ruse
5. *High rates of youth unemployment*	Demoralizing; heightens value of job retention; discourages workplace or union militancy	Infuriating; devalues dream of job-career advancement; encourages countermilitancy
6. *Job competition with women and minorities*	Distracts from other problems; fractionates the class; weakens union militancy	Focuses anger on failure of capitalism to generate adequate job opportunities
7. *Return of Vietnam veterans*	Preoccupied with making up lost time and	Angry over sense of loss; distrust in gov-

are *not* avid consumers or patriots, and they have *not* joined the American celebration or the embourgeoisification drift of certain others.

Accordingly, in words pregnant with political promise, Aronowitz (1974:407) solemnly contends that "the objective possibility for the emergence of a new revolutionary subject is in the process of formation." (See also Lynd, 1975; Packard, 1975; Nill, 1975.) Conceding that it will take more than a generation to root out the sexism and racism of the cohort, Aronowitz (and Marcuse before him) nevertheless represents young blue-collarites as helping *now* to build an autonomous popular culture on values subversive to the prevailing social system.

RESEARCH UNKNOWNS: IMPACT OF—	PRO-HARMONY FINDING	PRO-CONFLICT FINDING
	earnings; cowered and cynical	ernment; bitter over "lousy" benefits; volatile
8. *Young blue-collar women*	Eager to enjoy material comforts and faddish goods; acquisitive and status-hungry	Liberated from goods fetishism; eager to achieve personal growth; available for housewives' boycotts and Coalition of Labor Union Women
9. *Life-stage pre-occupations*	Marriage and child-rearing starts will sober and tame young bucks; "reinforcing events"	Escalating costs of family-man status will exacerbate class hostilities and rivalries
10. *Absence of political heroes* (FDR, JFK, etc.)	Steers political interests into conventional channels	Leaves openings for new leaders, such as Harris, Brown, Milkowski, Grasso, Abzug
11. *Pro-capitalist orientation of labor unions*	Depresses class militancy; isolates Vanguard Insurgents	Disillusions embittered workers; puts the spotlight on alternative offered by insurgents
12. *Role of organized crime in labor* (Hoffa disappearance, etc.)	Intimidates would-be insurgents; distracts from labor campaigns for job enrichment, etc.	Insults and infuriates proud men; spurs search for ways to · clean up the entire mess
13. *Revival of ethnic power campaigns*	Further divides the ranks; distracts from class-cohesive militancy	Reinvigorates the ranks; swells self-esteem and appetite for reforms; offers experience in action-taking

Open Questions

For all of the progress we may be making in strengthening our understanding of the style of life and political realities here, we remain hard pressed to assess the significance of several little-explored matters of possibly decisive importance. They are set out in Table 2 in terms of their alleged and contradictory impact on the class-linked politics of young workers.

As if these unanswered questions were not enough, there is considerable additional work ahead in strengthening the basis of what it is we like to think we already know: Our foundation appears flimsy, for example, when it remains based as at present on a cell of only thirty-nine respondents (Kasschau et al.), half of that number (Schwartz et al.), or the combination in a single category of all noncollege-goers, regardless of sex, race, or occupation (Yankelovich). The case could not be stronger for *more* research on larger, better-defined samples, using a wide array of sophisticated research methods (attitudinal surveys only one among many).

Scenarios

Keeping in mind the gaps in what we only tentatively grasp, and remaining sensitive to the considerable amount of sociological research and analysis still to be done, we can proceed to outline two major scenarios concerned with the class-linked politics of young male blue-collarites.

The first posits little or no change in the status quo over the foreseeable future. Pop culture, in whatever faddish format, will continue to mesmerize a large plurality of "good-time Charlies" among working-class youth, and their politics will reduce only to a low registration tally and to poor voter turnouts. The sights of many will be set on maximizing personal enjoyment in the here and now, this based on an unquestioning faith in the Keynesian macro-economic promise of continued national well-being. Relieved not to have to hassle now with the "heavy" controversial matters of recent years (such as how should the nation end the Vietnam war, decide the abortion question, respond to school segregation patterns), many young male blue-collarites will resist being drawn into a new agenda of comparably wrenching political questions. And their resistance, in turn, will increasingly demoralize and isolate the politicized Revisionists and Insurgents in their own ranks, thereby rolling things back toward the ritualism and retreatism that dominated blue-collar politics before the short-lived impact of the New Consciousness in the 1960s.

A very different scenario in this matter posits a steady growth of political concern, sophistication, and action-taking. Two potential prods are especially valued. First, the economic security that undergirds the Hipster style will be eroded by ceaseless inflation, erratic and high rates of post-1976 unemployment, and a steady loss of blue-collar posts to automation. Second, outside elements will increasingly help invigorate the ranks of youthful Revisionists and Insurgents (the former receive unrelenting recruitment attention from ethnic power organizations, such as EMPAC, the Ethnic Millions Political Action Committee, "a national civil rights committee, dedicated to a politics of family and neighborhood, to equality and fairness, to a new America"; similarly, leftist writers contend that "many of the most dedicated people in the New Left . . . have turned their organizing energies toward the working class" [J. Green, 1975]).

This combination of two developments—economic adversity compelling attention to activist politics, and outside political forces securing political alliances inside the cohort—could not be more problematic. Not only does it have to contend with traditional blue-collar wariness of outside proselytizing, but it also struggles against an influential piece of current events well known to young workers: When youth culture was in full flower on the campus, its adherents remained essentially powerless and vulnerable. Today, traces of this *Weltanschauung* are hard to identify (save for new moral libertarianism), on or off the campus. Noting this caustically, many young workers are likely to feel under little or no obligation to do very much more with their New Consciousness—as a lever for political change—than did the youth culture pioneers, or do the job-anxious careerists of the contemporary campus.

Implications

Viewed from outside the cohort, what seems to be at stake is a fledgling effort by a small but possibly a style-setting cadre of young blue-collarites to mature beyond their own political inheritance. Yesteryear's bohemianism appears challenged by the political *potential* of Hard-hat Hipsters, young men who may yet be drawn out of drug-induced fogs or funky dream worlds into political campaigns for decriminalization measures, libertarian gains, and other leisure-centered goals. Similarly, the "silent majority" conservatism of the fathers of Revisionists is presently challenged by an action-taking, question-raising, and irreverent style of hard-nosed politics. And the pre-Freudian radicalism of the past is being reworked today by Bobby, Nick, and others intent on incorporating into it a young worker's vision of realism, hedonism, and native American populism.

Should these New Consciousness variations prosper in the second half of the 1970s, the class-politics of the nation will stand to earn a valuable infusion of modernity, volatility, and pro-change momentum. The other way lies an ominous return by young workers to the political retreatism, ritualism, and recklessness of their elders, a bleak prospect that will set us all back in our pursuit of national political maturity.

Summary

Young male blue-collarites appear at a profound junction concerning their class-linked politics: They can slip back to the situation that long prevailed before a native version of the youth culture began to take hold in the late 1960s, or their New Consciousness can gain momentum and alter the scene here for decades to come. Three variations—Hipsterism, Revisionism, and (new) Radicalism—vie with older, well-entrenched, and more comfortable political modes. All that seems clear is that conflict and dissensus in American political life will be substantially altered by the outcome of the cohort's uncertainty—and their resolution of this matter will go far to shape the American Third Century for us all.

5

Old Issues and New Directions for Research

Richard F. Hamilton

ALL KINDS of claims exist about the important divisions within modern societies. Some of these have an "ancient" history, going back well over a century. Some are of more recent vintage. New claims, in fact, appear at the drop of a hat as the speculative theorists "do their thing."

For decades now commentators have focused on the manual-nonmanual distinction, arguing that it provides the crucial dividing line in the society. One recent secondary analysis, however, reviewing an immense quantity of Gallup data, was not able to confirm the claim as to the importance of this cleavage. While that division was the largest of any revealed, the size of the differences in a wide range of attitude and opinion questions were so small as to seriously challenge that initial assumption (Glenn and Alston, 1968).[1]

The basic problem may be indicated in another way: many commentators refer to something called "middle-class values." One might undertake a brief investigation beginning with a request for a list of, let us say, the ten most important "middle-class values." Assuming one is able to successfully accomplish this step, one could then raise the question: How do I know these are specifically middle-class values? Or, putting the question somewhat differently: Where will I find the evidence to support those claims? And, if successful in this second step, one may then undertake an examination of that evidence: Are we

[1] Glenn and Alston's conclusion reads: ". . . Our findings reveal no great 'cultural chasm' between manual and nonmanual workers and suggest that the distinction does not warrant the great importance often attributed to it in the sociological literature" (381). For another *investigation* of the question, one reaching a somewhat different conclusion, see Hamilton, 1972, chap. 5.

dealing with values that are "widely accepted" by Class A and, with similar frequency, rejected by Class B? Or is it rather a question of a 70 percent frequency in Class A and a 60 percent frequency in Class B? If the latter, then why are we speaking of the values of a specific class? If one found frequencies of 45 and 25 per cent one could raise the same question—why the class specific label? The basic question, in short, is this: How many cases will one find in which the assumption of contrasting predicates is justified?

The same kinds of questions may be raised about some of the other much discussed cleavages. Around the turn of the century, beginning in Germany, a conceptual distinction crept into the literature, one which distinguished between the "old" and "new" middle classes, that is, between those in independent and salaried white-collar employment. There was, and is, a general agreement that the independent business "class" is made up of the most thoroughgoing and unreconciled reactionaries imaginable. To the best of my knowledge for the period from 1900–1950 no German *study* exists which has established that claim. The most frequently cited American study on the subject is based on a sample in Bennington, Vermont, in 1954, over twenty years ago (Trow, 1958). A less well known study, based on a large eleven-state sample (Lipset, 1963:340–41), did not support the conclusion of the Bennington study. And yet it is the latter study that is cited and known. As far as I know, the only study of the subject in Canada is based on a small sample in Wetaskiwin, Alberta, a community of 6,000 located some forty miles south of Edmonton (Nolan and Schneck, 1969). The hypothesis was confirmed at the .10 level, an accomplishment which depended, if I remember correctly, on the answers of five respondents.[2]

What does this all amount to? It means either that one of the "big" claims about contemporary society has not been researched at all, or alternatively that it depends on rather flimsy wisps of evidence.

Another one of the "big" claims involves the distinction of "lower middle" and "upper middle" classes. Here too one has an ancient conceptual distinction—and a striking paucity of research. But, one will object, we *know* about that from the German experience, from the studies of the support for National Socialism. A question must be raised: Which studies?

Some illustrations may be useful. William Kornhauser (1959:203–4) indicates the basic position on the subject. "Another section of the middle class," he declares "that disproportionately supported the Nazis consisted of the lower white-collar employees. This is evidenced by the growth of the antidemocratic and pro-Nazi organizations of white-

---

[2] For an extensive *empirical* review of this question, see Hamilton, 1975, chap. 2, "The Politics of Independent Business." This review finds essentially no support for the claim.

collar people, and the concomitant decline in white-collar organizations that favored democracy." Again one may ask the question: How do we know that? Kornhauser cites the work of Peter Gay in support of the claim. Gay (1952:209–11) in turn provides us with some figures and statements that would generally support the Kornhauser assertions. A federation linked with the Social Democrats was undergoing a decline. A conservative-nationalist federation was growing. And a third union, the Gewerkschaftsbund der Angestellten, which he says "contained many National Socialists," also increased its membership.

And if one were to ask: How do we know that? What is the source for these statements? Gay refers us to Rudolf Küstermeier's, *Die Mittelschichten und ihr politischer Weg*. Speaking of this same union, the Gewerkschaftsbund der Angestellten, we find a *lack* of support for Gay's claim. Küstermeier (1933:45) says: "The leadership of the Federation is, as before, oriented toward the Democratic-State Party, while the members, in increasing measure, lean toward a socialist outlook. The National Socialist influence has remained relatively small." The trend, in other words, at least in this union, was not at all in the direction Gay has claimed. And this was a growing union. Küstermeier's statement, it should be noted, is also pure assertion. He provides no supporting evidence.

Tracing the genealogy of this idea, then, we have Kornhauser, who uncritically accepts his source, then Gay, who misrepresents his source, and Küstermeier, who presents no source.

One might, in the search for more solid evidence, turn to the statistical study of voting in Germany's cities, to the much cited, justifiably so, M.A. thesis of Samuel A. Pratt dating from 1948. Pratt calculated correlations between the proportions in the "lower middle" and "upper middle" classes in German cities and the vote for the National Socialists. Dividing the cities into three size classes, he found essentially *no* difference in the correlations in any of the three comparisons. Lipset (1960:147–48) claims that Pratt erred in his labeling and that the two ought to be reversed. Even if he were correct in that judgment, it still would make no difference in the point being made here—that no substantial differences were indicated in the support given by those classes for Hitler's party. Lipset's objection does point up a closely related difficulty. The best available research on the subject is of such a character that one cannot even be sure of the original designations.

In recent years, in what has been presented as a significant new breakthrough, some writers have focused on something called the "new working class." For those familiar with the literature, this "new" class will have a familiar appearance. In fact, it looks very much like what other commentators for some decades have been calling the "new *middle* class." That being the case, the new effort amounts to little more than a change of label. The same problems are found associated with the "new working class" as with the preceding "new middle class"—many claims, many declarations, accompanied by a dearth of research.

In most of the accounts, this "new" class is portrayed as leaning to the "left" in some way or else as having the potential for a "left" mobilization. There *is* some evidence available on this "class." Two of the largest occupations in the category are schoolteachers and engineers. Teachers do appear, in general, to have vague liberal-leftist tendencies. Engineers, however, prove to be one of the most conservative occupations in the entire society. One wonders what is accomplished by lumping them together and by providing *one* line of analysis for their *two* very diverse manifest tendencies.[3]

The conclusion: there is a need for fundamental descriptive work in the area of social class. Such work would aim to *discover* the location of cleavages present in the society. It would attempt to *discover* the values of the various "classes" found in this research. The emphasis is on the word *discover*—as opposed to *declare*. Declarations are a dime a dozen. Grounded conclusions are considerably more costly. But then, of course, they have considerably greater value.

A Postscript

Some curious things happened in the course of the discussion that followed the presentation of this paper. One panelist said, yes, we are all in favor of having data, but then too, he declared, on many questions, poverty for instance, the "jury is already in" and besides, having data has not proved too useful in many spheres of endeavor.

One might agree that where the "jury is in" there is no need for further work. One might—or one might not. Even jury decisions are subject to appeal. New evidence leading to a different verdict has appeared from time to time. The analogy moreover is inappropriate. In the sciences decisions are not made by a select jury. And *all* decisions are subject to continuous review. At least that is how it is supposed to be.

As should be clear from my initial remarks, that continuous research-review process, regrettably, has not been the case in the instances cited. It is difficult to see how an invitation to know-nothingism will serve to improve the situation.

Pursuing the same theme, a member of the audience pointed to the difficulty of doing some kinds of research. How would one get a "sam-

[3] For discussion and some evidence, see Hamilton, 1975:120–22.

ple of Watergates"? he asked. In response to my question whether anyone in the room had asked for such a sample, he said that he felt I had been saying something like that; he had heard it somehow in my remarks. It was necessary to assure him that he had not heard correctly.

Those comments provide some clues as to the sources of the problems pointed to in my brief observations. Here were social science practitioners actively opposing the suggestion that one undertake needed research.

It should also be noted perhaps that their marvelously irrelevant remarks gained rounds of applause from a small but clearly devoted coterie.

III

To Challenge the Meaning of Modernity for Person and Society

6

Understanding and Misunderstanding Individual Modernity

Alex Inkeles

ONE CAN GET rather good agreement as to what should be noted on a simple checklist of the important changes in human existence over the last several hundred years: Most everyone's list will include the emergence and florescence of the nation-state; the vast expansion of industry; the mechanization of agriculture; the prominence of science; the spread of bureaucracy; the diffusion of education; the growth of cities; and so on. Although we can get agreement as to the discrete items on the list, every attempt to offer a *general* characterization of all these changes is greeted by a barrage of challenges. Even more dissension is generated by every proposed *explanation* of these phenomena. Marx was surely telling us something terribly important when he urged us to concentrate on the mode of production and the resultant class relations. Nevertheless, Weber has convinced many that the ethic of social action embedded in religious and other transcendent world views impinges significantly on economic behavior. And Sorokin is not readily faulted in his assertion that we have witnessed the displacement of an ideational supercultural system by one of the sensate type. While the debate over these conceptions continued, the phenomena these grand theories confronted have persisted, and many of the trends they identified have deepened and accelerated.

In approaching this process of global change, my generation of sociologists had a number of obvious options. One was to take up one of the grand schemes which were part of their heritage, and to apply it to newly emerging phenomena. Another alternative was to emulate

103

one's precursors by devising and promulgating new overarching systems, as Talcott Parsons did with his "pattern variables." We found neither course suitable. The grand schemes of the past seemed too much
like actual or potential orthodoxies, and in an era committed to the end
of ideologies, one eschewed orthodoxies. Moreover, critical analysis
and more systematic research made us aware of how limited were the
perspectives, implicit or explicit, adopted by both the classic models
and the newer general systems.

A new spirit was abroad in the sixties which was more eclectic, less
ideological, more interdisciplinary. The lead was taken by economists
in the study of what they called development or growth. Relying heavily on factor analysis, they sought to identify the common socio-
economic characteristics of the "advanced" countries, and to discover
the common paths, if any, that had led to economic growth.[1] Political
scientists concentrated their attention on the development of the nation
state.[2] Anthropologists looked at the process as one of acculturation
and community development.[3] Population experts studied the demographic transition.[4] Psychologists delineated personality characteristics
they assumed to be critical in fostering entrepreneurial behavior,[5] or
measured the psychic adjustment of the individual exposed to rapid
change.[6]

Each discipline was, of course, studying but one aspect of a larger
process of social change which was widely diffused and deeply pene-
trating. For a decade or so during the fifties, economists played the
primary role in research in this field, and their concept, "economic development," served as the rubric under which other aspects of the
problem were subsumed. But as other disciplines turned their attention
to the issues, and other dimensions of social life came under scrutiny,
there was an obvious need for a more general term which would better
reflect the wide range of institutions under study and the diverse disciplinary perspectives being brought to bear. Throughout the sixties the

[1] For a sophisticated example of such analysis see Adelman and Morris, 1971. For one of
the most fundamental statements on the subject of economic growth see Kuznets, 1966.

[2] For a general treatise on modernization and government see Huntington, 1968. For
systematic analysis of data on the historic development of the state see Eisenstadt and
Rokkan, 1973.

[3] For a general review of the literature and statement of the anthropological view see
Goodenough, 1963. For a succinct analysis of peasant communities see Halpern, 1967.

[4] A comprehensive review of the interaction of population and modernization will be
found in Goldscheider, 1971.

[5] The most seminal work has been McClelland's (1961), focused predominantly on the
role in economic development of the need for achievement. For a more impressionistic
case-study approach sharing many of the same assumptions see Hagen, 1962.

[6] For a general review see Murphy, 1961. For a detailed application in the context of development and modernization see Inkeles and Smith, 1970.

term "modernization" gained increasing currency, and came to be widely accepted as the general designation for the process of common interest for numerous social scientists.[7] Society and institutions were then regularly characterized as more or less modern, and a polarity delineated between "modern" and "traditional" systems and their components.[8]

The total body of research on modernization is organized around a series of discrete foci of analysis. Most of the work is concerned with the institutional level. The investigators ask what are the institutional forms characteristic of more developed nations, or they interrelate the degree of change in one realm, say industry, with that in another, such as education.[9] A minority, however, have concerned themselves with the place of the *individual* in the process of modernization. They study the characteristics of individuals in relation to the properties of institutions and societies. Among those focusing on such system-person relations, several different lines of work may be discerned. One set of studies concerns itself with the process of psychosocial change and adaptation in individuals as they come increasingly into contact with modern institutions and participate in the socio-economic and political roles characteristic of more modern societies. It is specifically to such studies that my remarks in this communication are largely limited.

A number of sociologists and social psychologists have addressed themselves to this process, and they have generated a substantial body of empirical research.[10] Although some of this work is richly informative, many basic issues continue unresolved. Indeed, the study of individual modernity in its relation to social change has generated more than its share of misunderstandings as to what researchers are trying to do, what they have found out, and what their findings mean. In the hope of reducing such misunderstanding, I have here set down my an-

[7] A wide-ranging review of the study of modernization by leading scholars from different disciplines is Weiner, 1966. The most systematic integrative effort, also incorporating a historical perspective, is Black, 1966. Among the more useful bibliographies, Geiger (1969a) focuses on national development while Brode (1969) gives special emphasis to sociocultural themes.

[8] One of the major forces in casting the discussion in this mold was the appearance, in 1958, of Daniel Lerner's *The Passing of Traditional Society: Modernizing the Middle East*. For one of many criticisms of this polarity see Gusfield, 1967.

[9] The classic statement arguing the case for education as a stimulus to growth is found in Harbison and Myers (1964). For a much more cautious and sobering conclusion see Meyer et al., 1973. For an example relating growth to income inequality see Adelman and Morris, 1973.

[10] The best review extant as of this moment, by Brislin et al. (1973), is more oriented to issues of method rather than substance, but it reflects a rather comprehensive perspective and provides an excellent bibliography. For later and more substantive surveys: From a sociological perspective see Suzman (forthcoming in 1977), and for a psychological and anthropological perspective see Berry (forthcoming in 1977).

swers to some ten questions which are frequently asked about research on individual modernity.[11]

1. *Why study the individual? Doesn't the nature of the social system determine the characteristics of the individuals in it?*

Whether one studies individuals or institutions and social systems is partly a matter of sheer taste. For some, social change means more or less exclusively institutional and system change. Either they have no interest in the individual, or they feel that some other discipline should concern itself with the personal aspect of the change process. To take this stand is to adopt a narrow definition of the proper scope of sociology, and one at variance with some of the major tendencies of the sociological tradition. But as a matter of taste the position simply cannot be argued. All one can say is that others feel that the study of individuals is obviously important in its own right, and should be dealt with by sociologists.

One has, however, gone beyond matters of taste when one asserts that it is, after all, the social system which determines the nature of the individual. That is a testable proposition. Moreover, we may concede the general proposition, which obviously must in some degree be true, without at all concluding the discussion. Much more interesting than the general statement is its specification. We want to know what aspects of the social system change which individuals, in which respects, at which speed, and under what conditions?

If, in fact, the social system simply and totally determined the characteristics of the individuals in it, we should be able to state those characteristics with precision solely on the basis of knowing the nature of the social system and the position of the person in it. But, as many a social scientist has discovered to his chagrin, he can perform this feat very imperfectly if he can perform it at all.[12] The basic starting point of research on individual modernity is that the relation of social structure and personal attributes is *problematic.* Whatever their other differences

---

[11] In selecting these ten questions I tried to minimize overlap with the "issues" and "challenges" dealt with in the concluding chapter of *Becoming Modern* (Inkeles and Smith, 1974). That source should be consulted as a supplement to the arguments presented in this chapter.

[12] The work of Blau and Duncan (1967) on status attainment has been widely hailed as a milestone in modern sociology, yet the obvious variables measuring the individual's social antecedents used by them explained only 26 percent of the variance in the educational attainment, and 33 percent of the variance in the first jobs, of their American sample. When Sewell and Hauser (1975) restricted their model "to a simple accounting of the inheritance of status positions" in a sample of Wisconsin youths, they found that they could explain no more than 16 percent of the variance in the educational attainment and 12 percent of the variance in occupational status. As an example of the limits on our power to predict the obvious in the context of developing countries, see the evidence in Nelson (1969) that objective social characteristics such as low income and marginal status predict less about political orientation than is commonly assumed.

in emphasis, the common concern of the scholars who have done research on individual modernity has been to test empirically the widespread assumptions about the relations of social systems to the personal attributes of the individuals whose properties those systems presumably "determine." The special responsibility of the scholars involved has been to specify the concrete indicators of social structure and the exact personal attributes which should be measured; to measure those features in research designs which are relevant to theoretical concerns; and to interpret the findings with the objective of confirming, or disconfirming, revising, and extending the original theory.

Neither the general desire to test the theory that social structure determines personality, nor the urge to specify more precisely the scope of the theory's application, should be interpreted as a challenge to it, and even less as a rejection. On the contrary, in my experience virtually all those working within the framework sketched above believe that what we find in individuals does, in good part, reflect the nature of the social system they live in and their particular statuses within that system.[13] Moreover, commitment to studying the individual in the modernization process implies no automatic judgment as to either the primacy or the relative importance of the individual as against the system. In fact, the majority of those studying individual change actually see it as more caused by than causing institutional modernity, and in explaining the variance in levels of societal modernity they usually assign much greater weight to historical, economic, or political factors than to the impact of modern personalities.[14]

2. *Should changes in "objective" status characteristics or in "subjective" personality attributes be the focus of attention?*

If by a modern person is meant someone with a particular set of socio-economic characteristics, such as "employment in industry rather than agriculture" or "urban rather than rural residence," then it follows that to assess how far individual modernity is determined by changes in the socio-economic system, one should indeed trace changes in the distribution of this type of SES attribute *in individuals* as correlated with prior *social system* changes. In some instances, such measurement may highlight issues of considerable importance.[15] In most cases, however, individual characteristics of the objective SES type only express in another form what we already know from the aggregate system level statistics.

[13] For the origin and first elaboration of this argument see Inkeles, 1960. The position is more fully explicated on pages 139–43, 154–64, and 302–8 of Inkeles and Smith, 1974.

[14] Notable exceptions, however, will be found in the works of McClelland (1961) and Hagen (1962, 1975).

[15] As, for example, when census data on education indicate school graduates multiplying at a much higher rate than the number of available jobs.

An attractive alternative, therefore, is to define individual modernity exclusively in terms of psychosocial attributes—as values, orientations, opinions, and action propensities. This has the obvious advantage of eliminating the redundance and circularity built into many measures taken at the individual level. Thus, it is true by definition that if a nation has become "predominantly urban," then at least 50 percent of its citizens will be found to be "urban residents." But it is by no means true by definition that in a predominantly urban country, the majority of its citizens must be more efficacious or feel more alienated.

Building such presumed outcomes of the process of modernization into the definition of individual modernity precludes testing the most important proposition. Thus, in the otherwise illuminating research of Daniel Lerner, the definition and classification of individuals as "modern," "transitional," or "traditional" simultaneously took into account the individuals' social characteristics *and* their scores on a test of empathy. This made it impossible to tell with any precision whether and how far empathy, seen as a subjective outcome, had resulted from changed objective conditions such as exposure to education, urban residence, and mass media exposure, since these other variables were also built into the general index of individual modernity.[16] To facilitate testing the relation between the facts of social structure and the properties of individuals, a series of investigators have all defined the modern individual exclusively in psychosocial terms. This approach has been common to the work of Armer·and Youtz (1971), Doob (1960), Dawson (1967), Galtung (1971), Guthrie (1970), Inkeles and Smith (1974) and most users of the OM scale, Kahl (1968) and those who use his modernization scale, Klineberg (1973), and Stephenson (1968).

Here, again, it needs to be emphasized that merely by focusing on attitudes, values, needs, modes of acting we do not prejudge the question as to whether such qualities lead to or are merely determined by socio-economic status. In fact, most of the research in this field starts with the assumption that it is status which determines personality rather than the reverse.[17]

3. Which psychosocial characteristics should define an individual as modern?

[16] See the construction of the basic typology of modern, transitional, and traditional types in Lerner, 1958: chap. 2 and especially pp. 69–71. Lerner is not alone in electing to measure individual modernity by a scale which combines objective social characteristics with attitude and value measure. For other examples, see Schnaiberg's (1970) modernity scale and Rogers's (1969) "orientation to change" factor. Insofar as one seeks the most complete *description* of the psychological *and social* attributes of the modern individual, this procedure is quite sensible. But, as we have indicated, it limits our ability to test how far objective and subjective factors interact as cause and effect.

[17] For an extension of this perspective to American occupational settings see Kohn and Schooler, 1973.

So long as we are still operating at the level of definition, the decision is, of course, a matter of preference. In deciding which psychosocial qualities of individuals should be the focus of one's attention, one may be guided by a theory, by one's special purpose in a particular research, by one's reading of the empirical evidence so far collected, or by observation, casual or systematic, of real people in natural settings. Durkheimian analysis might lead you to expect anomie; Marxian thinking might point to alienation; a Freudian perspective could suggest high levels of anxiety; and a Parsonian view would focus on qualities such as affective neutrality. Being interested in the role of mass communication in the modernization process, Lerner (1958) selected as the key personal quality the holding of opinions, while Rogers (1969), concerned about the productivity of peasants, emphasized the importance of innovativeness and the adoption of new technology in agriculture.

In the Harvard six-nation study we were guided by a particular theoretical perspective. In most general terms, the main purpose of the research was to test whether, where, and how far individuals come to incorporate as personal attributes qualities which are analogous to or derive from the organizational properties of the institutions and the roles in which these individuals are regularly and deeply involved. To give this model greater specificity we selected the factory as the embodiment of one major type of modern institution, so that our general question could be rephrased more concretely as follows: "What are some of the personal qualities which extended service in a factory might inculcate in individuals who moved into such service after growing up in the typical agricultural village of one of the less developed countries?" [18]

From an analysis of factory characteristics such as the use of inanimate power, the extensive division of labor, the system for allocating working time, the technical hierarchy, and so on, we derived a set of qualities which we assumed would likely be "learned" and incorporated as personal attributes by men engaged in factory work. Among the qualities we expected under these conditions were a sense of personal efficacy; openness to new experience; respect for science and technology; acceptance of the necessity for strict scheduling of time; and a positive orientation toward planning ahead. Each of these characteristics we then designated as components in our definition of the modern man conceived in psychosocial terms.

[18] Although I use the term "individuals," the reader should be aware that the Harvard six-nation study, as reported in Inkeles and Smith (1974), was limited to men. However, a variety of later researches using comparable modernity scales give reason to argue that the concept applies equally to women, and that the modernity syndrome among women has fundamentally the same content as it does in men. For citation of the relevant research see footnote 25 below.

To this first set we added a second, derived on a different basis, following a "social demand" model. The roles which the citizen of a modern large-scale, industrial, urban social system is expected to play presumably require, or at least favor, his having certain personal attributes. In the political realm, for example, the modern polity, whether in a capitalist democracy or a socialist dictatorship of the proletariat, expects individuals to be participant citizens, that is, to take an interest in the news, to identify with the national system as against more local, parochial, or primordial ties, to be active in voting, campaigning, rallying, and so on. We applied the same mode of analysis to other institutions and the roles associated with them. For example, in the family realm we defined as more modern the insistence on selecting one's own spouse rather than accepting a wife chosen by one's parents or other "elders"; the preference for small rather than large families; and the willingness to practice birth control and the actual limitation of family size, as against the passive acceptance of "whatever number of children God might send."

The result of this series of analyses was a list of some twenty-four main themes, each defining a dimension which we considered part of the larger set of qualities defining individual modernity. Long as it was, the list was certainly not exhaustive. It reflected a definite theoretical position, which we believe it should have, since that permitted testing whether certain explicit expectations underlying the definition were sound.

A challenge often put to such a definition is that it excludes the possibility of testing other assumptions which, if granted, would place the matter under investigation in a different light. For example, it may be argued that our definition highlighted the "positive" qualities of the modern man, but failed to acknowledge how far he was also alienated, under psychic stress, and unfaithful to his obligations to kith and kin.

There are two responses possible to such a challenge. One can say, and quite properly, that it is not the obligation of a researcher to test someone else's theory. If others believe that men who are otherwise modern are likely also to be alienated, distressed, and unreliable, it is incumbent on them to test the assumption. There is, however, an alternative response, which we on the Harvard project adopted: One can accept the challenge, and oneself test the externally given assumptions. Following this principle, we introduced into our interview measures of anomie, alienation, psychic adjustment, and readiness to fulfill conventional obligations to kith and kin. We did not, however, include those qualities in our definition of the modern man. Thus, our field work created the basis for testing not only our own assumptions, but also others not made by us.

In actual fact, the personal qualities defined as modern in many different researches show a remarkable degree of overlap. Variants on the themes of fatalism, empathy, efficacy, innovativeness, flexibility, achievement orientation, information, and active citizenship abound. Almost as frequently the students of individual modernity have felt it appropriate to measure stress, alienation, and anomie. This recurrence of certain themes may result merely from diffusion and imitation, perhaps suggesting some lack of imagination in those who entered the field later. The phenomenon could also have resulted from differential recruitment, that is, from the fact that only individuals following a particular theoretical perspective have entered on this field. But I prefer to interpret the observed convergence as indicating that there is a compelling theoretical case to be made for the relevance of the core elements built into most psychosocial definitions of individual modernity.

4. *Is not the idea of individual modernity essentially a Western conception? And if it is, isn't its exportation to the less developed countries just another form of cultural imperialism?*

To settle this question we must agree on some rule for saying what *is* "Western." The attributes by which we have defined individual modernity, such as a sense of efficacy and openness to new experience, are rather general human qualities which obviously can appear, and surely have done so, in some degree in many places and times. It follows that the syndrome certainly cannot be considered Western in the same sense as are Christianity or the Germanic languages. Nevertheless, it will be said that the cultural traditions of the West are, in general, comparatively more congenial to, or more likely to foster, the qualities we identify as modern. To this contention one might respond by noting that the Dark Ages were hardly eras in which the traits delineating individual modernity were favored or widely distributed in Europe. Indeed, from the ninth to the twelfth century the qualities of individual modernity were probably much more common in those parts of the world dominated by Islam.

Nevertheless, in the twentieth century the qualities we have identified were most favored and most widely diffused in the populations of Europe or of European origin. And, in the last fifty or seventy-five years, many individuals in other parts of the world have come to be more like those we call psychologically modern. Some may, therefore, insist that such individuals have become "Westernized," or, at least, more *like* Westerners. I prefer to think of them as having become more modern, because I personally find it more appropriate to think of the qualities which make up the modernity syndrome as not being the distinctive property of any single cultural tradition. Rather, those characteristics seem to me to represent a general model expressing one form of the human potential, a form which comes more to prominence in certain historical times under certain types of social conditions. Nevertheless, if some prefer to call ours a Western model, I see little to be gained by spilling a great deal of ink over the issue. It seems much less important to settle whether individual modernity is Western or not, than it is to decide what consequences follow from its spread.

If the new institutions being widely adopted by developing countries, such as the factory, the school, the modern hospital, and the mass media, are thought of as Western, and if the habits, attitudes, values, and behaviors which are built into the social roles associated with these institutions are also defined as Western, then some sort of psychological Westernization may be a practical necessity for any country which seeks to modernize its institutions. New institutions remain at best empty shells, and at worst become graveyards of national resources, if they cannot be staffed by people who have the requisite personal qualities to fill effectively the role demands necessary to the operation of those institutions. Each nation and each people should be free to make the choice either to import the set of institutions which are generally considered to be modern, to live as they have always lived, to borrow some other pattern, or to invent wholly new institutional arrangements of their own. Each path will make its own distinctive demands on the psychology of the population. But if a people choose modern schools, mass production, mass communication, science-based technology, and scientific management, then the personal qualities we have called modern will be sorely needed, whether considered a Western import or not. Moreover, they will be needed whether the new society is socialist or capitalist, and if communist, whether the system follows either the Stalinist or the Maoist model. Imperialism can export Coca-Cola, blue jeans, Hollywood movies, and capital intensive production. But it cannot export individual modernity. Individual modernity may develop as a response to prior colonial action, but, being built into the psyches of the people, it must of necessity be a native product, home-grown, no matter how foreign was the origin of the seed.

4. *Does definition make it real? What is the empirical status of the concept of individual modernity?*

There is a long-standing tradition in sociology and social psychology of inventing types of men—the most famous of the recent models being David Riesman's typology of inner-, other-, and self-directed men.[19] Although such types of men were only theoretical constructs, the custom in sociology, at least in the past, has been to accept them as if they were real. Little or no systematic effort went into testing whether these types could in fact be found in nature, and if they existed, to ascertain the frequency of their distribution in different

[19] The almost invariant linking of sociological typologies to men is another heritage from the era in which we were all less sensitive to the prevalence of sexism in our professional terminologies.

societies and social strata. By contrast, the hypothetical construct of the modern man has been extensively tested empirically. Indeed, it has probably been as widely and systematically tested in field studies as any other comparable conception of a "type" of man.[20]

There are two main methods for testing the realism of a conception about human types. Each approach is identified with a school of scale construction, one known as the external criterion method, the other the coherence method.

The coherence method addresses itself directly to the issue of whether or not the personal qualities delineated in the conceptual model of a given researcher really constitute a "type," rather than being a mere assemblage of discrete and unrelated characteristics. In measuring coherence one takes no necessary position as to the frequency with which the type appears, nor, necessarily, with regard to where in the social structure that type may be found. Initially, therefore, the validity of a type delineated by the coherence method is necessarily limited to theoretical or face validity. The coherence test may be applied to what is conceived of as a single, discrete quality, say the sense of personal efficacy, or to a set of such qualities, as in testing a multidimensional model of "the modern man."

The criterion method for testing the soundness of a conception rests, as its name suggests, on one or more criteria external to the qualities being studied. In the case of individual modernity, the criteria which suggest themselves as obviously relevant are the objective social status characteristics associated with modern institutions and modern societies.[21] Thus, to show whether it is sound to define individual modernity in terms of greater efficacy or more openness to new experience, one should demonstrate that these qualities are found more often among those with more formal schooling, or among industrial workers as against farmers, or among urban as against rural residents, selecting the particular criteria used in accord with either some theory or common expectation. The criterion method, clearly, is valuable for establishing the validity of the elements of a definition. But it tells us nothing, directly, about the existence of a "type of man," that is, of a *set* of qualities which cohere and form an identifiable syndrome.

The criterion and coherence approaches, although quite discrete

[20] If the authoritarian personality syndrome is acknowledged to represent a "type" in the sense we have used the term, then it almost certainly can claim to be the most extensively assessed type. For a review of relevant studies see Kirscht and Dillehay, 1967. Research measuring individual modernity is reviewed in Suzman, 1977.

[21] Observed *behavior* may be used as an alternative criterion. Thus, the individual more modern in attitude might be expected to join organizations more often or to adopt new innovations in agricultural practice more quickly. Examples of the validation of scales of modern values through utilizing such behavioral indicators will be found in Inkeles and Smith, 1974: chap. 18, and in Rogers, 1969.

methods, are not mutually exclusive. Once a syndrome has been shown to exist, one may still seek to validate it against known criteria. And once a set of qualities has been identified by the criterion method, one can still test to see how well the qualities cohere and delineate a discrete "type."

Whether any given research finds a meaningful syndrome depends, of course, on a number of factors. If one's theory misleads one into attempting to put together things not joined in nature, no coherence will be found. What coheres in one population may not go together in another.[22] And what qualifies as coherent by one standard, will be judged by another to be only a conglomeration of discrete elements.[23] Considering all the opportunities to go wrong, it is notable that a substantial number of studies, conducted relatively independently and applying to diverse populations, have found a syndrome of individual modernity meeting fairly rigorous standards of coherence based both on factor analysis and on tests of scale reliability.[24] This is true for the

[22] This fact makes it extremely dangerous to offer sweeping generalizations on the basis of studying a single sample. An example of how misleading this propensity may be is found in Armer and Schnaiberg, 1972. They sought to cast doubt on the discriminant validity of several different modernity scales, including the OM scale, on the grounds that they found higher correlations between the measures of modernity and a scale to assess anomie. Actually, there are no sound theoretical grounds for refusing to consider nonanomic attitudes to be one element in a modernity scale conceived to be a multidimensional measure. But the available evidence argues against that because, from sample to sample, anomie bears no consistent relation to the other modernity dimensions. Thus Almond and Verba's (1963) five-nation study gave reason to believe that measures of political modernity related differently to anomie in Italy and Mexico than in the U.S. The absence of a consistent relation across countries of a political modernity scale and anomie was later conclusively demonstrated for the Harvard six-nation study in Inkeles, 1969. Armer and Schnaiberg had data from only one quite unrepresentative sample from one American city. Yet even if the relationship they observed were to hold up in other American samples, it would be ethnocentric to settle the relation of anomie to modernity on the basis of the results from one country. In stating their sweeping conclusions, Armer and Schnaiberg simply ignored the massive contrary evidence from these earlier country-wide studies. Some of that evidence is briefly discussed below as part of the response to question 8.

[23] Some will insist on scale reliabilities of .8 or above, others will be content with .6 or even less. Factor loadings of .3 are considered adequate by some, but will be dismissed by others as trivial. For an extensive discussion of the different standards for testing the coherence of scales of modernity see Inkeles and Smith, 1974: chap. 7, especially the technical footnotes. Particular attention is there drawn to the different impression of coherence one may get by using a measure of scale reliability such as the Kuder-Richardson as against a measure of the variance explained by a principal components factor analysis. Portes (1973) also devotes considerable attention to the factorial structure of modernity, and Armer and Schnaiberg (1972) stress discriminant validity, although they apply that standard in a rigid and mechanical way.

[24] For example, the main (OM) modernity scale used by Inkeles and Smith (1974) had a median reliability of .82 across six countries; the Schnaiberg (1970) "average modernism" scale, based on 46 items, yielded a reliability of .81 for a sample of Turkish women; Portes (1973), working with lower-class respondents in Guatemala, found his first principal components factor, weighing attitudes, values, and knowledge, to explain 19 percent of the total variance. This pattern is matched in many other studies,

largest and most complex studies, as well as for many smaller-scale operations, and applies to both sexes and across a wide range of nations, occupations, educational levels, ethnic groups, and ages.[25]

A comparable range of studies may be noted which have tested the internal coherence not of a multidimensional syndrome but rather of one of the subthemes which the more global measures treat as components of the more complex whole. Empathy, the sense of efficacy, the need for achievement, and fatalism are among the concepts which have been put to the test.[26] There are clear-cut theoretical and empirical justifications for insisting on such more limited measures as one's unit of analysis. It is, nevertheless, noteworthy in the perspective of our discussion of coherence that the level of reliability attained by these more restricted measures proves generally to be no higher than that of the multidimensional measures, indicating there has been little loss of coherence paid as the price for emphasizing the multidimensional syndrome.[27]

The criterion method also has its vicissitudes. There is, for example, no general agreement as to whether the criterion should be some

---

but some researchers do report less satisfying results. Thus, Klineberg (1973) found his first factor could explain only 11 percent of the total variance in parents' modernity scores, and concluded that "by these criteria, the evidence for a single dimension underlying the 30 items is mixed, if not negative." But Klineberg did not present a Spearman-Brown or Kuder-Richardson reliability estimate for comparison.

[25] Several of the most elaborate studies of modernity were limited to men only, as in Kahl's (1968) Mexican and Brazilian samples, and the six nations of Inkeles and Smith (1974). Therefore, special interest attaches to the question of whether the same approach, and the same measures, are appropriate for studying women. Scales to measure modernity developed explicitly for application to women, or based on the responses of both males and females, were reported by Cunningham (1972), Holsinger (1973), Kahl (1968), Klineberg (1973), Portes (1973), Schnaiberg (1970), and Stephenson (1968), among others. A separate analysis of the same scale for parallel male and female samples is rare, but an important exception will be found in Suzman, 1973a. In general, the same elements enter into the definition of modernity in females as in males, and the internal structure of the scale is similar, although there are important differences in emphasis. Insofar as men may score higher on these scales than women, that fact is almost entirely accounted for by differences in the average education and the occupational experience of the sexes. Thus, Cunningham (1972) reported there were no statistically significant differences in the modernity (OM) scores of those young men and women who were at the same grade level in her Puerto Rican high school.

[26] For description and analysis of various subscales measuring dimensions conceived to be part of the general modernity syndrome, in some cases including separate reliability estimates and factor analyses, see Armer and Youtz, 1971; Galtung, 1971; Inkeles and Miller, 1974; Kahl, 1968; Klineberg, 1973; Rogers, 1969; Sack, 1973; Suzman, 1973a; and Williamson, 1970.

[27] For example, the 14-question subjective efficacy scale used by Williamson (1970) had a median Spearman-Brown reliability of .69 across the six nations of the Harvard study, whereas the overall modernity scale, also with 14 items, but touching on many different themes at once, had a median reliability of .73, as reported in Smith and Inkeles, 1966. For other comparable results see the sources cited in footnote 26 above.

group having "known" status characteristics, such as higher education or wealth, or whether another familiar scale, presumed to measure the same qualities as one's new scale, can serve as a criterion. Moreover, those who insist that validity can only be established by showing that one's scale (or a single question) discriminates among "known groups," must face inherent difficulties in deciding which groups are appropriate candidates to serve as criteria, and how fully a scale must discriminate between groups before it is considered a truly valid instrument.

Despite all these pitfalls, it is again gratifying to note that both the large-scale and the more limited researches yield numerous instances of the criterion validity of both the subcomponents and of the summary scales of individual modernity. For example, across five villages in Colombia, both modern and traditional, Rogers (1969) found empathy scores to correlate with innovativeness in agricultural practice at .25. Moving up to the level of the more general syndrome of individual modernity, Armer and Youtz (1971) found among youth in Kano, Nigeria, that only 37 percent of those with no education scored "high" on their modernity measure, but among those with some secondary schooling the percentage modern jumped to 84. In six developing countries we found that among those with least exposure to modern institutions, as few as 2 percent scored as modern, whereas among those in the upper decile of exposure to modern experiences, as many as 90 percent showed modern attitudes and values.[28] Again, comparable results are available from numerous other studies, large and small, by different investigators proceeding relatively independently.

There is, then, massive evidence for the existence of a syndrome of individual modernity, tested both by the method of coherence and by the criterion method. In *Becoming Modern* we described this syndrome as follows:

> The modern man's character, as it emerges from our study, may be summed up under four major headings.[29] He is an informed participant citizen; he has a marked sense of personal efficacy; he is highly independent and autonomous in his relations to traditional sources of influence especially when he is making basic decisions about how to conduct his personal affairs; and he is ready for new experiences and ideas, that is, he is relatively open-minded and cognitively flexible.
>
> Although these are the principal components, they by no means exhaust the list of qualities which cohere as part of the modernity syndrome. The modern man is also different in his approach to time, to

---

[28] See Inkeles and Smith, 1974:121–24. For a discussion of the six-nation data addressed explicitly to the issue of validity judged by reference to known groups see Smith and Inkeles, 1975.

[29] Use of the term "modern *man*" in this context is meant literally, since the six-nation study was limited to samples of men between the ages of 18 and 32.

personal and social planning, to the rights of persons dependent on or subordinate to him, and to the use of formal rules as a basis for running things. In other words, psychological modernity emerges as a quite complex, multifaceted and multidimensional syndrome. [Inkeles and Smith, 1974:290–91]

Working independently from a related but distinctive perspective, Everett Rogers (1969) summed up the opposite pole of the modernity dimension, with specific reference to the "subculture of peasants," as including: "(1) mutual distrust in interpersonal relations; (2) perceived limited good; (3) dependence on the hostility toward government authority; (4) familism; (5) lack of innovativeness; (6) fatalism; (7) limited aspiration; (8) lack of deferred gratification; (9) limited view of the world; (10) low empathy."

We assume that there are some populations in which the modernity syndrome would not be found, that some elements of the syndrome would combine differently in some populations than in others, and that some measures of modernity would not discriminate among at least certain criterion groups. But to acknowledge all this is rather like affirming that in human affairs nothing is certain beyond death and taxes, and not even taxes are certain. What is so notable about the qualities of individual modernity, as tested by both the coherence and the criterion method, is how pervasive are the confirmations that the original definitions are, in fact, matched by what one may observe in real people. Third-grade children in Brasilia, high school students in Puerto Rico, peasant farmers in Nigeria, street hawkers in Bangladesh, and industrial workers in Chile all manifest the syndrome (see Holsinger, 1973; Cunningham, 1972; Inkeles and Smith, 1974). One may use it to discriminate between those with more or less education in Mexico, and between those who do and do not listen to news broadcasts in Colombia (see Kahl, 1968, and Rogers, 1969). It distinguishes within sets of the young and the old, within white and black communities in the United States, among males and females, and within all religious and ethnic groups in Chile, Argentina, India, Bangladesh, Nigeria and Israel (see Klineberg, 1973; Suzman, 1973*a;* and Inkeles, 1976*b*).

While it is clear that the concept of individual modernity has very general utility, we yet cannot assert it to be universal in its applicability. It may be that in China or Cuba the same qualities would not cohere, nor be associated with the same criteria in the same way. It seems quite possible that in those countries qualities not elsewhere observed to be part of the syndrome, such as self-effacement, collectivism, or subordination of individual choice to group goals, would figure centrally in the syndrome, whereas that has not been the case in populations so far tested. But it does seem highly likely that in China and Cuba, qualities such as the sense of efficacy, openness to new experiences, and commitment to planning will go together, and will be associated with distinctive external criteria, just as in most of the populations so far studied.[30]

6. *What makes people modern?*

At least five major theoretical perspectives may be distinguished among the answers which are regularly given to this question. Some of these positions are supported by evidence in great depth. Others have been the object of very little systematic research. The available evidence also varies in character, ranging from the most systematic field studies, through historical illustration, to the purely anecdotal.

MODERNITY AS AN INNATE TENDENCY

No one seems vigorously to argue this position explicitly, but it comes up repeatedly in efforts to explain why it is that people coming from the same background, and even having the same subsequent exposures to modern institutions, nevertheless vary so greatly in how modern they have become.

Given the specifically social content of individual modernity, it is obvious that in a strict sense no one is born modern. People can be modern only by *becoming* modern, through either maturation, or socialization, or both. Nevertheless, if qualities such as intelligence, dominance and assertiveness, activeness, curiosity, or flexibility are in part innate dispositions, then they could influence individual modernity as it is measured.[31] Some of that influence could be direct, since some modernity tests, in part, measure the very qualities mentioned above. But the main effects would, presumably, be indirect, leading those innately more curious or dominant either to search out modernizing experiences, or to be better "learners" in situations having the intrinsic ability to "teach" lessons in modernity.

I know of no research which has gone forward from systematic measures of early personality to later measures of "individual modernity," although existing panel studies of individual development could be used for this purpose. Working back from the current modernity of individuals to their early traits is an attractive alternative, although the procedure is subject to imposing methodological obstacles.[32] In any event, there is very little evidence, if any, bearing on the issue.

[30] For evidence concerning the assertion that modernity values are stressed in the schools of Communist China see Inkeles, 1976*a*.

[31] For an extremely valuable summary and evaluation of the evidence on the role of early manifestations of temperament in shaping later qualities of personality see Buss and Plomin, 1975.

[32] For a vigorous exposition of the view that the early experiences of the individual are the predominant factor explaining later individual modernity see Hagen, 1975. Hagen's statement is presented in the form of a challenge to the evidence in *Becoming*

MODERNITY AS A PRODUCT OF EARLY FAMILY MILIEU

Those who stress this explanation accept learning as the cause of modernity, but assume that the learning occurs mainly early in life, as a result of distinctive family constellations, and that the resultant qualities remain more or less fixed in the person for life.

To assume that differences in the home environment are what account for differences in individual modernity is, in effect, to state a special case of a much more general model. There is no obvious reason to expect greater success in predicting modernity from knowledge of the home environment than there has been in predicting other personality outcomes on that basis. My own reading of the evidence suggests that families are more successful in endowing offspring with socio-economic status characteristics than they are in transmitting to them a set of predetermined personality characteristics. Nevertheless, there is substantial evidence of the transmission of personality from generation to generation at levels of statistical association far from trivial. And we must acknowledge the important studies which rest on the assumption that the decisive factor in determining the modernity of individuals, now adults, was the special character of the early experience provided by parents and families.

Everett Hagen (1962) argues vigorously for the influence of the home environment in shaping the innovative personality, although his data are essentially anecdotal and his conclusions not based on the direct study of living individuals. The work of McClelland (1961) and his associates provides more systematic evidence on the familial antecedents of high need achievement. A pattern of significant correlation between the modernity scores of parents and those of their children has been found by Cunningham (1972) in Puerto Rico, Holsinger (1973) in Brazil, Klineberg (1973) in Tunisia, and Pandey (1971) in India. Pandey (1971), moreover, shows the outcome to result from the different approaches parents took to socialization in regard to achievement, authority, and human concerns. All this suggests some significant direct transmission of modernity from home to child.[33] But the

---

Modern, which showed that about half of the variance in OM modernity scores is accounted for by socialization experiences coming after adolescence. The defense of that evidence is presented in Inkeles's (1975) rejoinder to Hagen.

[33] One must, of course, consider the alternative explanation, namely that the modernity of the child shapes the modernity of the parents. This model is most plausible where the children secure much more schooling than their parents did, and then carry into the home the modernizing influence embedded in this advanced education. Although this alternative explanation is plausible, it cannot be the whole story since Holsinger (1973) found the mother's modernity score already made a difference in the third grade, and Klineberg (1973) found the strongest correlation, specifically .42, between parental and adolescent modernity in his sample of male school-leavers.

evidence is, unfortunately, not consistent.[34] Moreover, in the Harvard
six-nation study a measure of home-school background, based on perceptions of the behavior of parents and teachers in such matters as
keeping promises, and respecting one's feelings, proved only a weak
and inconsistent predictor of individual modernity, especially once
other factors were controlled.[35] In sum, it seems that the home environment, while significant, may be a less important factor than many
had assumed it to be.

MODERNITY AS AN EXPRESSION OF SHARED GROUP CULTURE

Each of us is the carrier of at least one culture, and those who come
from complex societies may embody elements of one or more distinct
cultural traditions. Cultures are differentiated by the values they inculcate, the behaviors they encourage, and the skills they transmit. It follows that some cultures might much more emphasize the qualities
which are considered modern. Individuals from those cultures would
then be more modern, at least insofar as they had been successfully
socialized into their culture.

Weber's analysis of the Protestant ethic is the prototype for this
mode of analysis. Hagen's (1962) characterization of the Antioqueños
of Colombia, and other groups, is a variant on the theme. McClelland's
research provides more systematic evidence across a large number of
societies, his characterization of the cultures being based on children's readers. But McClelland's (1961) study lacked the validation of
testing for differences in individuals from the cultures whose readers
he rated. LeVine's (1966) comparison of the Yoruba and the Ibo over-
came this difficulty, although without very compelling results. In the
Harvard six-nation study we found the men from some countries, notably Argentina and Israel, much more modern than those from other
countries, especially East Pakistan (now Bangladesh). Since the samples
differed greatly in education and income, the differences might have
been attributed mainly to "wealth" rather than to culture. But the dif-

[34] As examples of inconsistency, we may note that for high school students in the top
quartile academically in Puerto Rico, the mother-daughter correlation of modernity
scores of .35 was strong and highly significant, but for students in the bottom quartile
academically the comparable correlation was negative and not significant, as reported
in Cunningham (1972). In Tunisia, the modernity of male school-leavers correlated .42
with parental modernity, but was at only .06 for boys who continued in school. Bringing other variables under control by means of a regression analysis did not eliminate
the inconsistency. See Klineberg, 1973. In his path analysis, Pandey (1971) found no
important "direct" casual effects of the subjective aspects of parental modernity on either child socialization or child development variables.

[35] The evidence is presented in chapter 17 of Inkeles and Smith (1974). Also see the criticism of this effort by Hagen (1975) and its defense by Inkeles (1975).

ferences persisted, even if somewhat muted, when we compared groups from different countries selected to be alike on such characteristics as education and occupation. In one typical matching, for example, only 8 percent of those from East Pakistan scored as modern, whereas 30 percent of the otherwise comparable Argentinians did so.[36]

Now that we have strictly comparable measures of modernity which can be used cross-nationally, this mode of analysis can be extended to other countries. Pending a more systematic survey, we may tentatively conclude that some national populations do indeed seem much more modern than others. Moreover, since such differences persist after matching for education and occupation, we must grant the assumption that such differences may stem from distinctive cultural systems shared by particular populations.

DIFFUSION-IMITATION-DEPENDENCY THEORIES

If the set of institutions defined as modern, and the sentiments and behaviors associated with them, are seen as a distinctive cultural product of "the West," then modernization may readily be interpreted as only a special case of the general process of cultural diffusion. Certainly, the system of industrial production, of scientific management, and of mass communication originated in and diffused from the West, and a good case can be made that many other institutions making up the set we usually call modern had a similar origin.[37]

It is relatively easy to imagine how one can transplant a complete factory, or even a university. But what of the attitudes, values, skills, and patterns of interpersonal relations which are typically associated with these institutions at their Western point of origin? Behaviors can, of course, be imitated, and attitudes simulated. But most skills must be more nearly authentic, else the consequences become rather painfully apparent. And the basic, deeper-lying personal dispositions and psychic tendencies, such as cognitive flexibility or field independence, seem by their very nature not subject to imitation, but rather come about only through slow development after long learning.

The extent to which the modern attitudes, values, and behaviors found outside the West got there mainly because of diffusion, is intrinsically difficult to test with any precision. Where certain social classes in developing countries come directly in contact with the international bearers of this new culture, the case for imitation can easily be made.

---

[36] See Inkeles, 1974, for details. Also relevant is Inkeles, 1976*b*.

[37] Whether it still is realistic to speak of these institutions as "Western" when, for example, they have been introduced by Japanese into the societies of Southeast Asia, is clearly moot. The issue is, however, beyond our responsibility here.

For other classes lacking this direct contact, one can claim that the mass media, especially the movies and television, have likely had considerable impact in diffusing superficial forms of adherence to some Western model. This is essentially the logic followed in dependency theory, which stresses the extent to which the power of the advanced (colonial) system drives out the indigenous culture patterns and replaces them wholesale with foreign models. But to explain the deeper changes in personal dispositions which we observe in factory workers who are located in provincial areas and do not have foreigners present as models, would seem to require adopting a rather different theoretical perspective, based on the concept of social learning.

SOCIAL LEARNING THEORY

Following the leads Marx provided when he declared that one's relationship to the mode of production shapes one's consciousness, we may expect individuals to learn to be modern by incorporating within themselves principles which are embedded in the organizational practice of the institutions in which they live and work.

This general perspective, which I first presented in the paper "Industrial Man" (Inkeles, 1960), influenced the research design adopted by Joseph Kahl (1968) for *The Measurement of Modernism,* and was given a more explicit test in the Harvard six-nation study (Inkeles and Smith, 1974). As the theory predicted, work in factories, in modern bureaucratic organizations, and in agricultural cooperatives all produced significant and substantial increases in the sense of personal efficacy, in openness to new experience, and in the approval of science and technology. Similar changes, even more marked for any given year of exposure, were brought about by attending school. Yet neither the school nor the bureaucracy rely heavily on the use of the sort of machinery typically found in factories. We were stimulated, therefore, to conclude that school and factory produce the same result because they both expose individuals to certain common principles of organization, procedures for assigning power and prestige, modes for allocating rewards and punishment, and approaches to the management of time. Individual modernity then becomes a quality learned by the incorporation into the self-system of certain qualities characteristic in certain institutional environments.

I believe that the five approaches described above would together account for most of the variance in individual modernity, if we could but find some way to represent them all in a single study. Moreover, I am convinced that of the five, the social learning theory would account for by the far greater proportion of the variance explained. Indeed, in my opinion, the point is already established by the evidence presented in *Becoming Modern*. Nevertheless, it remains true that a definitive test of this assumption has not been made. And it is also true we have far to go in understanding precisely which features of schools and factories make them effective teachers of modernity, and how such features achieve their results.

7. *What consequences does modernization have for the individual's psychic adjustment? Can modernization only be gained at the cost of psychic stress?*

To answer this question we must get agreement on what we mean by adjustment, and how we shall measure it. Moreover, interpretation of any results obtained should take into account not only how the individuals we study feel now, but should also consider their adjustment prior to their exposure to modern institutions.

A great many anthropological field reports, along with other types of observation, provide extensive evidence of the extremely deleterious personal consequences regularly accompanying the impingement of powerful European nations on the peoples of relatively small, insular cultures not having the benefit of advanced technologies. Although there are clearly important exceptions, such as the Manus described by Margaret Mead, this type of contact seems to produce a high frequency of deculturation, personal disorganization, alcoholism or other forms of addiction, lassitude, depression, anxiety, hyperaggressivity, and evidence of stress.[38]

By contrast, individuals from nonmodern societies with their own high culture, especially if they are part of a more or less autonomous nation state, seem to fare quite differently as a result of their contact with the institutions introduced by the modernization process. In our six-nation study we found that, in general, there were no consistent differences in the psychic adjustment of those who were more exposed to factory work, urban living, or the mass media. (See Inkeles and Smith, 1970.) We did not interpret these findings as meaning such exposure was intrinsically tonic. Rather, we suggested that the pursuit of agriculture in the typical traditional village was much less gratifying an experience than many Western intellectuals imagined it to be. Consequently, in relative terms, the urbanized, industrially employed ex-migrant tends to be no worse off psychically than his cousin who stayed on the farm.

We believe that our findings accord well with the results of other systematic researches of the impact of modernization on individual adjustment, but the picture is complex, and no definite conclusion can hope to win general adherence at this time.[39]

[38] For a summary of evidence concerning the American Indian see Stewart, 1952.
[39] For a discussion of relevant evidence see Murphy, 1961; Inkeles and Smith, 1970.

8. *What does becoming modern do to the individual's politics? Is alienation an inevitable accompaniment of modernization? And is individual modernity antithetical to political radicalism?*

One senses that the New Left sees the concept of modernization as a rival doctrine to the Marxist laws of capitalist development, or as some kind of new opiate of the masses which will detract them from the struggle to build socialism.[40] In such an atmosphere it is extremely difficult to develop a dispassionate discussion of the implications which becoming modern has for an individual's political role. Nevertheless, the issue is fundamental, and one must take an initial position, however tentative.

One fact seems unmistakable, indeed it seems to come as close to being a law as anything to be observed in social science. As individuals move up the scale of individual modernity, whether judged by objective status characteristics or by psychological attributes, they regularly become more informed, active, participant citizens. With exceptional regularity, increasing individual modernity is associated with voting, joining public organizations and participating in public actions, interacting with politicians and public figures, taking an interest in political news and keeping up with political events.[41]

So far as concerns moving to the left or the right on the political spectrum, it seems reasonable to assume that the concomitant of becoming modern, at least for most people in most developing countries, should be a move to the left. This would seem to follow from the fact that, as many studies have shown, more modern individuals are more desirous of change, more open to new experience, less fatalistic, and less in awe of authority and received tradition.

Of the six nations in the Harvard modernity study, it was only in Argentina and Chile that our local advisors agreed to our intention to ask questions which tested radicalism and conservatism. In both countries, the more modern men were more "radical," in that they much more favored an immediate and profound transformation of the basic institutions of their respective societies (see Inkeles, 1969). The point is not well documented elsewhere, but I read the existing evidence as in general agreement with our results (see Nelson, 1969, and Cornelius, 1975).

Since political and economic change is generally slow, and political systems often unresponsive, it might seem to follow that change-

---

[40] See Chapter 7 of this book.

[41] Although they were not oriented to testing a theory of individual modernity, Almond and Verba (1963) provided fundamental comparative evidence relating these dimensions of political participation to increasing education. That the same patterns of response were to be found in developing countries, and that they constituted a syndrome of participant citizenship, was established in Inkeles, 1969.

oriented modern individuals would be more alienated. But the firmness of this association should, presumably, depend on the larger political and social context. Thus, in societies in which the government was especially responsive, or was bringing about rapid social change, the more modern men might well be *less* alienated.

There is less evidence on this issue than one might like. Two studies in the United States, one in inner city Chicago (Armer and Schnaiberg, 1972), the other in the suburbs of Boston (Suzman, 1973*a*), found modernity to be strongly associated with lack of alienation and non-anomic feelings. In our six-nation study we found the same thing to be true only of East Pakistan and Chile, and then less sharply so. In Nigeria, by contrast, the more modern were more anomic and more alienated. The other countries showed other patterns still, and we were forced to conclude:

> The participant citizen is not also consistently nonanomic, nonhostile, and satisfied with the performance of his government. Rather, we must say, "it depends" on the country—and no doubt on the segment of the population being studied. [Inkeles, 1969]

Clearly, we need to do much more research before any firm conclusions can be drawn. But it seems likely that quality of participant citizenship will be consistent in being almost everywhere strongly associated with individual modernity, whereas alienation and anomie will behave inconsistently, sometimes being associated with modernity and sometimes not, depending on the national and community context.[42]

9. *What are the consequences for kith and kin of a person's becoming modern? Does individual modernity automatically lead to defaulting on traditional interpersonal obligations?*

There is a widespread impression that modernity, whatever the advantages it may bring to individuals, is always bought at high cost to the local native community because it leads people to default on their traditional obligations, most notably those owed to kith and kin. This assumption is strengthened by the common tendency of both theoretical discussion and empirical research to establish a polarity between the modern and the traditional, thus encouraging the presumption that supporting most modern modes necessarily implies rejecting all traditional ones.[43]

---

[42] For relevant evidence and explication, see footnote 22 above. For further discussion of the role played by variation in local and national community contexts, see Cornelius, 1975; Verba et al., 1971.

[43] An exception to the tendency to measure modernity and traditionalism as contrasting poles will be found in the work of Dawson (1967; Dawson et al., 1971), who gives each individual a score expressing his simultaneous acceptance of both traditional and modern positions bearing on the same issue. Pandey (1971) also develops some complex typologies by factor rotation and the use of canonical correlation.

Such direct conflict is probably inevitable in some realms. For example, one cannot, without contradiction, favor relaxed and informal scheduling, while simultaneously insisting that individuals be at the school or the factory by a fixed hour. And if, in a given culture, "respect for elders" means explicitly accepting their choice of one's occupation or spouse, then modern individuals will quite consistently be found failing in this virtue. Such direct confrontation of principle, and such inherent incompatibility of different acts are, however, much less common than is often assumed. While effective participation in modern institutions fosters some selected psychic dispositions, it does not determine, or even have implications for action in, *all* particulars of *all* realms of life. Indeed, so long as the minimum imperatives of the industrial-bureaucratic system of production and administration are met, the individual's behavior in other realms may vary widely without serious conflict with the norms of modernity as we have defined and tested them. In fact, individual modernity is found, and apparently lives compatibly, alongside of many orientations and behaviors which some analysts consider to be part of traditionalism.[44]

The realm of religious commitment and observance provides an important illustration. Numerous conceptions of modernization assume, by definition, that the modern spirit is antithetical to religion, and that becoming modern means giving up one's religious tradition. However, even a moment's reflection on this proposition brings to mind evidence so glaringly in contradiction to this expectation as to immediately call into question the soundness of the underlying theory. Consider, for example, the United States, which by almost any measure is one of the most modern nations in the world, yet which also has one of the highest rates of church membership and one of the highest levels of regular church attendance.

So far as concerns obligations to kith and kin, we found in our six-nation study that becoming modern was not at all consistently associated with the rejection of, or defaulting on, traditional obligations. Indeed, very often those who had left the village to take up industrial work in town were more willing than their country cousins to give financial aid to a relative in dire need. They also were equally ready to

[44] This point has been an important element in the general theory of modernization as presented by Eisenstadt (1973) and Gusfield (1967), and suffuses the Rudolphs' analysis of modernization in India. Unfortunately, the force of the argument depends on creating a straw man. In common practice, most measures of modernity give individuals a summary score based on numerous questions. Since most people get a middling score, and almost no one gets a "perfect" score, it follows that even those classified as "modern" by this means must be holding many attitudes which are theoretically defined as "traditional." When, therefore, critics point so vigorously to nominally "modern" individuals whom they know to also engage in certain "traditional" practices, they are only restating in words what every scale of modernity has already repeatedly expressed in numbers.

give respect to the aged, on the simple ground that age deserved respect. And they were, in general, not less exacting in carrying out the basic practices required by their traditional religion.[45]

Further research will be required to assess whether this seemingly peaceful coexistence of the modern and traditional is characteristic only of the early stages of modernization. I am of the opinion that it may be found at later stages as well. But to specify which forms of coexistence are possible, and in what contexts, will require much additional research over a wider range of situations and in a diversity of settings.

10. *What are the consequences of individual modernity for one's society? Does individual change of this sort do anything to bring about social change, or to improve the lot of the rest of the people?*

We have come full circle, returning to our first issue, but now viewing it in a different perspective. Because we committed ourselves to studying how individuals change as a result of living in modernizing societies or of coming into contact with modern institutions, we are often charged with presuming that individual change must precede societal change, or that personal change is more important than system change. No misunderstanding of the work on individual modernity is more pervasive, nor more serious in its ability to misrepresent the actual views of those engaged in research on this topic.

Just as the impact of institutions on individuals must be taken as problematic, so should the impact of individual properties on the social system be recognized as a matter for study. Merely to put a question is in no way to prejudge the answer. Moreover, confusion is inevitable if discussions are couched in extremely general terms rather than by specifying precisely what types and degree of social change are in question.

No doubt a systematic search can turn up some quotation from some work which will demonstrate that at least some people have made extreme and implausible claims for the ability of psychological properties to shape social forces. But if one focuses more on the main thrust of the argument made by the corps of scholars who have been studying individual modernity, one finds common a more modest, indeed a highly qualified, set of claims. Specifying more precisely the different levels of system change, the prevalent positions may be characterized as follows:

A. Basic structural transformations of a radical or revolutionary kind, involving the social system as a whole, are rather uniformly acknowledged to be very little determined, if at all, by the psychological

---

[45] Only a small part of the relevant evidence is so far published in chapter 7 of Inkeles and Smith, 1974. Specifically with regard to attitudes toward the aged, see Bengston et al., 1975.

properties of a national character or by the modal personality of significant subordinate strata. In the case of the political revolutions such as
those of Russia, China, or Cuba, it is obvious that the transformation of
society rested not on the diffusion of new personality patterns but on a
sudden rupture of power. But even in the case of the more gradual
transformations, as in the successive industrialization of England,
France, and Germany, it seems clear that institutional change did not
need to wait on prior personal transformations.

B. Nevertheless, we are not in a position to deny that under conditions of equal opportunity, peoples with a distinctive "national character" may manifest a differential propensity to adopt new institutions,
and may enjoy very different rates of success in getting those institutions "to work" effectively. The Japanese are the obvious case in point.
Stalin's effort to create "the new Soviet man" may serve to highlight the
sense of frustration national leaders can feel when they are mounting
massive efforts of social change but find, to their chagrin, that the
human material they have to work with seems not suited to their purpose.[46]

Only now that we have the technical means to measure the average
level of individual modernity in national populations are we in a position to achieve a more objective assessment of the relative contribution
of the psychological characteristics of a people to the overall modernization of their society. Measures of such qualities could be weighed,
along with other factors in the standard matrix of measures, to predict
how the properties of nations in an earlier period predict their standing at later points in time. This is basically what McClelland tried to do
in *The Achieving Society,* but his method of measuring the personal qualities of the populations concerned was so indirect as to leave a residue
of profound doubt as to the reliability and validity of his conclusions.[47]

C. Certain religious, ethnic, or other cultural subgroups seem to
play a distinctive role in the modernization process by generating in
their members qualities which attract them to, and make them especially effective in, certain roles, notably that of entrepreneur.

Weber's stunning analysis of the Protestant ethic, McClelland's
study of family patterns generating high need achievement, Hagen's
case studies of innovative personalities, all start with this assumption.
They also present extensive documentation which they see as proving
their thesis. But it seems more accurate to say that theirs are essentially
case studies which merely *illustrate* the thesis without establishing its
general validity. Later, more extensive studies with large samples of en-

---

[46] On the problems of fitting individuals to the new role demands of a society undergoing
a revolutionary transformation, see Bauer (1952), Inkeles, Hanfmann, and Beier,
1958; Inkeles, 1976*a*.

[47] For an elaboration of this point see Inkeles, 1971.

trepreneurs seem not to turn up much evidence that the incumbents of this role came from distinctive family milieus.

D. The case for the social consequences of individual modernity rests mainly on evidence showing that becoming more modern leads individuals to undertake new transformative social roles within their societies and in their more immediate social networks.

Individuals who attain psychological modernity, especially in less developed societies where that character is not yet the predominant norm, adopt different social roles than do their less modern countrymen. They are more active in voluntary organizations and participate more in politics; they practice birth control more regularly and have fewer children as a result; they are quicker to adopt innovative practices in agriculture and are more productive as workers in industry; they keep their children longer in school and encourage them to take up more technical occupations; and, in general, they press more actively for social change. This catalog of behavioral differences could be considerably extended. And although such differences cannot be guaranteed to appear in all groups and in all settings, they are well documented in a strikingly large number of groups and places.[48]

Such behavior may be viewed as merely a more effective means of coping that is of advantage to the modern individual and his dependents, but is no particular boon to society at large. But when it is cumulated across large numbers of individuals, such modern behavior may also become a collective input essential to the overall success of any program of national development. And this may be true even in those cases in which a revolutionary transformation of the ownership of the means of production has already been accomplished.

In Communist China the national leaders are constantly urging the local community not to become dependent on grandiose national plans, nor to seek constantly for help from the central authorities, but instead to cultivate and practice self-reliance in all things The soundness of this advice is evidently well grasped in numerous other countries by people who have not had the benefit of Mao's teaching, but who have come to the same conclusion in the process of becoming modern. In our six-nation study we asked the question: "Which is more important for the future of your country?"

There followed four alternatives:

The hard work of the people.
Good planning on the part of the government.
God's help.
Good luck.

[48] See Inkeles and Smith, 1974: chap. 18; Rogers, 1969.

It will be no surprise that the more traditional selected the last two alternatives, the more modern the first two. But of the first two, the most frequent first choice of the more modern men was not the government plan but rather "the hard work of the people." Was this choice merely a manifestation of individual self-interest, or did it express some fundamental collective wisdom?

7

Modernization: Requiescat in Pace

Immanuel Wallerstein

WHEN A CONCEPT HAS DIED, some try to revive it by invoking it as ritual incantation, some regret its passing wistfully, some pretend it never existed, and some are impatient with any reference to it. But only the American Sociological Association holds a funeral service.

De mortuis nil nisi bonum? A good slogan perhaps for personal matters, but not very helpful in intellectual or political ones. I should like therefore very briefly to review how world social science ever got into this cul-de-sac known as modernization theory and, now that some of us are out of it, what lies on the horizon ahead.

I hesitate to review the history of this idea since it seems to me that this has been done already on a number of occasions. But memorials involve familiar memories. Until 1945 it still seemed reasonable to assume that Europe was the center of the world. Even anti-imperialist movements outside of Europe and against Europe often tended to assume it. But the world moved inexorably on. And everyone's geographical horizons expanded. To cope with this changing world, Western scholars invented development, invented the Third World, invented modernization.

Let us start by citing the merits of these inventions. The new terms replaced older, distasteful ones. Backward nations were only underdeveloped. The Yellow Horde became instead the Third World. And progress no longer involved Westernization. Now one could antiseptically modernize.

Above all, the new concepts offered hope. No doubt Africa had never invented the wheel, no doubt Asian religions were fatalist, no doubt Islam preached submission, no doubt Latins combined racial

131

miscegenation with a lack of entrepreneurial thrift; but it could now be asserted confidently that these failings were not biological, merely cultural. And if, like the Japanese, the underdeveloped were clever enough to invent an indigenous version of Calvinism, or if they could be induced to change the content of their childrens' readers (the children first being taught to read, of course), or if transistors were placed in remote villages, or if farsighted elites mobilized benighted masses with the aid of altruistic outsiders, or if . . . , then the underdeveloped too would cross the river Jordan and come into a land flowing with milk and honey. This was the hope offered up by the modernization theorists.

It was unquestionably a worthy parable for the times. It would be easy to show how this parable was manipulated by the masters of the world. Let us recognize nonetheless that it served to spur devoted and well-intentioned scholarship and liberal social action. But the time has come to put away childish things, and look reality in its face.

We do not live in a modernizing world but in a capitalist world. What makes this world tick is not the need for achievement but the need for profit. The problem for oppressed strata is not how to communicate within this world but how to overthrow it. Neither Great Britain nor the United States nor the Soviet Union is a model for anyone's future. They are state-structures of the present, partial (not total) institutions operating within a singular world-system, which however is and always has been an evolving one.

The last thing we need to do is to make comparative measurements of noncomparable and nonautonomous entities when the social system in which we all operate is for the first time in human history a single unit in which the entire game is resumed in the internal relationships to be found within the capitalist world-economy: of core to periphery, of bourgeois to proletarian, of hegemonic culture to cultures of resistance, of dominant strata with their demand for universalistic individual measurement to institutionally oppressed racial and ethnic strata, of the party of order to the party of movement. These relationships can be measured too, but we have not been measuring them.

The first step we must make if we wish to understand our world is radically to reject any and all distinction between history and social science, and to recognize that we are part of a single discipline of study: the study of human societies as they have historically evolved. There are no generalizations that are not historically time-bound, because there are no systems and no structures that are unchanging. And there is no set or sequence of social events that is comprehensible without reference to a theoretical construct whose function is to create meaning out of reality.

What was primarily wrong with all the concepts linked to the paradigm of modernization was that they were so ahistorical. After all, the modern world did not come out of nowhere. It involved the *transformation* of a particular variant of the redistributive mode of production, that found in feudal Europe, into a European world-economy based on a capitalist mode of production. It involved the strengthening of state-structures in the core areas of this world-economy and the correlative weakening of them in the periphery.

And once capitalism was consolidated as a system and there was no turnback, the internal logic of its functioning, the search for maximum profit, forced it continuously to expand—extensively to cover the globe, and intensively via the constant (if not steady) accumulation of capital, the pressure to mechanize work in order to make possible still further expansion of production, the tendency to facilitate and optimize rapid response to the permutations of the world market by the proletarianization of labor and the commercialization of land. This is what modernization is about, if one wants to use such a contentless word.

But whatever word we use, let us remember that the suffix "-ization" in the English language contains an antinomy. It refers both to the state of something and to the process of becoming that something. The capitalist world-economy has not yet, after four to five hundred years of existence, realized a free market, free labor, unentailed land, unbounded flows of capital. Nor do I believe it ever will do so. For I believe that the essence of the capitalist mode of production is the *partial* freedom of the factors of production. It will in fact only be with a socialist world-system that we will realize true freedom (including the free flow of the factors of production). This is indeed what lies behind Marx's phrase about moving from the "realm of necessity into the realm of freedom."

I do not intend here to preach a faith. Those who wish will believe. And those who do not will struggle against it. I wish rather to suggest an agenda of intellectual work for those who are seeking to understand the world-systemic transition from capitalism to socialism in which we are living, and thereby to contribute to it.

I think top priority must go to the original concern of the nineteenth-century fathers of social science, the understanding of the capitalist world-economy in which we live as a gestalt. But how do we do that? I see five major arenas of research, each large in scope.

1. The first arena is the internal functioning of the capitalist world-economy as a system: the institutional ways in which areas get located at the core, the periphery, and the semiperiphery of that system, and how units can and do change their location; the mechanisms of transfers of surplus toward the core; the ways in which classes emerge, consolidate, and disintegrate; the multiple expressions of class struggle; the creation, sustenance, and destruction of all varieties of "status-groups"

(ethnonational groups, racial castes, age and sex groups), and the ways these "status" groupings interweave with class structure; the cultural expressions of conflicting interests; the pattern of interplay between cyclical processes of expansion and contraction and the secular evolutionary processes that undermine the basic stability of the system; the modalities of and resistances to the proletarianization of labor and the commercialization of land; the role of the state in affecting the world market and aiding specific groups within it; the rise of antisystemic revolutionary movements.

This is a long list, but it is only one arena. We must also and simultaneously work in other arenas:

2. We must reopen the question of how and when the capitalist world-economy was created in the first place: why the transition took place in feudal Europe and not elsewhere; why it took place when it did and not earlier or later; why earlier attempts of transition failed. This is not merely an exercise in archeological reconstruction; it is rather essential to the full comprehension of the nature of our present system.

3. Allied with this issue is another on which almost no work has been done. For at least three centuries (the sixteenth to the eighteenth), the capitalist world-economy functioned side by side with noncapitalist social systems outside it. How did it relate to them? And in particular, what were the processes that made it possible for the capitalist world-economy to incorporate them?

4. In the light of these interests, it will be clear why we must also turn to a comparative study of the various historical forms of social system, the alternative modes of production. I myself believe there have only been three such modes up to now: the reciprocal (lineage) mode found in minisystems; the redistributive (tributary) mode found in world-empires (either full blown or largely disintegrated); the capitalist (market) mode found in world-economies. But this is a contentious formulation. In any case enormous work has to be done simply to identify properly which historical constructs reflected which modes and to make appropriate comparisons primarily within the systems or modes and secondarily among them.

5. This then brings me to the fourth system based on a socialist mode of production, our future world-government. We are living in the transition to it, which has begun and will continue for some time to come. But how are we relating to it? As rational militants contributing to it, or as clever obstructors of it (whether of the malicious or cynical variety)? In any case, here too we must look afresh at the various "socialist" experiences, seen as regimes that are seeking both to transform the world-system and partially to prefigure the future one, with greater or lesser success. And we must look to the relationship of revolution-

ary movements in the various political subdivisions of the world-system to each other.

You may ask whether this agenda is not far wider than the narrow field "modernization" was to cover. Yes, indeed it is. But that is the point. Modernization theory has served to deflect us from the agenda that would be able to speak to the problems with which it was supposedly concerned. This agenda requires redoing our historical narratives, accumulating new world-systemic quantitative data (almost from scratch), and above all reviewing and refining our conceptual baggage.

There are those who will say that such an agenda is a throwback from the scientific advances of modern social science to the imprecise and ideological musings of the nineteenth century. To such a contention, one can only give the answer of Thomas Kuhn when he discussed the problem of the historical use of measurement in physical science:

> [M]uch qualitative research, both empirical and theoretical, is normally prerequisite to fruitful quantification of a given research field. In the absence of such prior work, the methodological directive, "Go ye forth and measure," may well prove only an invitation to waste time. . . .
>
> The full and intimate quantification of any science is a consummation devoutly to be wished. Nevertheless, it is not a consummation that can effectively be sought by measuring. As in individual development, so in the scientific group, maturity comes most surely to those who know how to wait. [1961:55, 60]

We have been impatient for the past thirty years. And the wine has turned sour. Let us go back to where we once were: understanding the reality of our world, which is that of a capitalist world-economy in the early stages of its transition to a socialist world-government. The road is hard, intellectually and politically. But it is the road both of scholarly integrity and of scientific promise.

IV

To Reorient Theories of Conflict and Revolution

8

Introduction to a Formal Theory of Political Conflict

Ted Robert Gurr and Raymond D. Duvall

THIS CHAPTER IS an introduction to a fully specified and formalized theory of the social origins of manifest political conflict to be published under the title *Conflict and Society: A Formal Theory and Some Contemporary Evidence.* Since it is a theme-setting chapter it leaves unanswered many of the questions it raises, but it should suffice to give the reader a clear idea of our basic argument and of how the theory is to be formulated and tested.

We believe that virtually all extant works on social and political conflict entail "theory" only in the loose sense of that term which pervades most of the social sciences: They are built up of discrete hypotheses which offer general functional relationships among sets of variables, but they provide neither a precisely specified set of basic principles from which the discrete hypotheses can be derived, nor a clear statement of the logical relationships among the hypotheses through which the deduction of additional hypotheses would be made possible. By contrast, we offer an argument that is more nearly theory in the rigorous scientific sense. That is, we develop our argument from a set of basic principles, given as definitions and axioms, which, in combination, enable the deduction of "theorems," or testable hypotheses. And as is generally true of scientific theories, our argument results in the deduction of hypotheses, some of which are counterintuitive, and most of

☐ This work is being carried out with the support of a grant from the National Science Foundation. We should like to thank Mark Levine of Northwestern University and William Foltz of Yale for their comments on this version of the theoretical argument.

139

which are a good deal more complex than the linear additive relations that, by default, are characteristic of arguments constructed from discrete hypotheses.

Three types of assumptions underlie our theory and must be made clear if it is to be fully understood. First are assumptions about the nature of the phenomenon which is the object of theory, manifest political conflict and one of its properties, "magnitude." Second are assumptions about the major determinants of this phenomenon, that is, about the basic nature and form of the theory. To anticipate the subsequent presentation, it can be said here that we assume the central importance of three macrosocial variables in interaction: the social aggregate of individuals' potentials for remedial action; collective dispositions to conflict behavior; and the organizational strength of collectivities. Third are assumptions about the contexts (kinds of circumstances) in which a theory of this nature can be expected to be valid. In this paper we present only our assumptions about these three issues. The full formal theory derived from these and additional assumptions is not given here.

The Concept of Manifest Political Conflict

The central concept around which this theory is constructed and for which it is intended as an explanation is manifest political conflict, and, in particular, the magnitude, as variable property, of such conflict. It is convenient to begin with a precise definition, the elements and implications of which require extended discussion.

DEFINITION M1. *The magnitude of manifest political conflict (MPC) is the extent and intensity of physical confrontation between collective actors contending over the structures, incumbents, or policies of the most inclusive authority patterns in the social system.*

The most basic element in this definition is conflict, which we view simply as contention among members of a social system over the production or allocation of some limited goods (or bads). Conflict as contention is not necessarily expressed in overt behavior. However, we *do* assume that it is ubiquitous, both across systems and over time for any system. In our view, a continuous process of contention over scarce goods is characteristic of all social systems. Awareness of conflict processes in national systems usually comes to our attention through the occurrence of particular events, which range in form from political demonstrations and riots to terrorism, coups, and revolutionary warfare. Moreover it proves useful, for operational purposes, to index magnitudes of conflict by reference to the summed properties (not numbers) of diverse conflict events. But this is a measurement issue. What the theory accounts for is the magnitudes of conflict in social systems, not the occurrence of particular numbers or kinds of conflict events.[1] Said differently, ours is not a theory of conflict probability because it does not specify the probability that a riot, a revolution, or a civil war will occur. It is instead a probabilistic theory of the conditions which determine the processual ebbs and flows in the manifest severity and intensity of conflict, conceived of as a continuous, or constant, phenomenon.[2]

A second element of the definition that needs comment is the issue of what is "political." We regard the political issues in any social system as those which concern the structure and exercise of authority at the most inclusive levels. In the nation-state the most inclusive levels are the political regime and its subordinate elements; in universities they are usually the governing administrative and faculty bodies; in tribal societies they are the chief and his supporting institutions; and so forth.[3] Any demands or disagreements about the structure or procedures of these bodies, or about the identity of those who staff them, or the policies that they carry out, constitute *political* conflict. Or, in other terms, political conflict is distinguished from other types of conflict by the particular goods over which there is contention—for political conflict contention takes place over the nature, occupancy, and outputs of socially inclusive authority patterns.

The term "manifest" conflict signifies our special concern with phys-

---

[1] The distinction between conflict properties and events is often overlooked by students of conflict, the results being frequent confusion over the status of the concept, and inappropriate empirical procedures. A prominent example is the "Correlates of War Project," which has been criticized on these grounds by Raymond Duvall (1976). This project at least gives substantial attention to conflict properties, which is more than can be said of most collections of data on conflict within nations.. See the critique in Gurr, 1974.

[2] The theory is tested by reference to conditions in a cross section of societies in the 1960s, but those tests cannot be criticized as inappropriate to a theory which is concerned with the conflict process. The reason is that what follows is not a process theory (i.e., one closed with respect to causal variables, and hence one in which time is an integral concept), but rather a theory about a property *of* a process. That property, magnitude, is said to be the result of a set of conditions; variation in the antecedent conditions is associated with or "causes" variation in magnitude. There is nothing inherent in the logic of the theory which implies that the variation must be assessed in reference to time rather than space. The argument is of the classic "if . . . , then . . ." form, where the ifs and thens specify "statist" concepts—that is, concepts which refer to the state of a system or a process during some limited period of time. Thus, time need enter into tests of our theory only to demarcate periods of reference and to provide the observational basis for concepts which are defined in reference to time, such as lags and changes. It is useful to test theories about political processes with longitudinal data, of course, but there are no epistemological grounds for rejecting the use of cross-sectional tests where they are theoretically appropriate, as they are here.

[3] This conception of the "political" is proposed by Eckstein, 1973.

ical confrontation between collective actors. It is virtually a truism that the process of conflict is a social universal; indeed, we have committed ourselves to that position immediately above—at least in the context of systems composed of collective actors. Moreover, conflict has innumerable manifestations. Election campaigns, cabinet instability, high absenteeism of workers, and high rates of murder and alcoholism all *may* be aspects of conflict, and some of them may even be political conflict. But we explicitly restrict our interest, and the theory, to group or collective action which overspills the bounds of "institutionalized" social interaction [4] and is expressed in actual physical clashes (e.g., armed attacks, riots) or in symbolic ones (e.g., general strikes, political demonstrations). For the purpose of this theory, political conflict is "manifest" if and only if it involves actual or symbolic physical confrontation between groups expressing or resisting demands for political change. The theory is not intended to apply to other forms of political conflict.

The notion of "collective actors" is elaborated presently, but because earlier versions of this theory have been criticized for their "one-sided" emphasis on the characteristics of "rebels," [5] it is worth pointing out here as an aside that this version of the theory explicitly includes political authorities and their various elements and agencies as "collective actors." They usually are one party to episodes of manifest political conflict because what they possess and do are, by definition, its principal issue and object. And, as will become evident below, the theory is intended to account for the manifest conflict behavior of authorities just as much as it accounts for the actions of those who contend with them over questions of policy and power.

Manifest political conflict has numerous properties. The object of our theory is a single variable property, "magnitude," which signifies the "extent" and "intensity" of collective physical confrontations. Because neither of these terms is entirely unambiguous, and because definitional precision for the central object of theory is desirable and necessary for the development of measurement rules that permit precise comparisons across time and social systems, the elements of magnitude are defined explicitly below.

DEFINITION M2. *The extent of manifest political conflict is the relative amount of human effort expended in physical confrontations between collective actors.*

DEFINITION M3. *The intensity of manifest political conflict is the relative de-*

---

[4] By "uninstitutionalized" social interaction we mean interactions which occur outside the formal structures of the political system, not interactions which are normatively unacceptable or exceptional—some kinds of manifest conflict may be unacceptable and rare, others are not.

[5] The principal earlier statement of this theory is Gurr, 1970. Two critics of its alleged omission of characteristics of the state are Nardin, 1971, and Jenkins, 1971.

gree of human and material destruction incurred in physical confrontations between collective actors.

Social systems vary greatly in numbers of members and there is little point in "explaining" differences among them in extent and intensity of conflict that are due merely to their size differences. The theory which follows is intended to account not for absolute differences in magnitudes of conflict among systems, but for differences relative to their populations. Therefore we index "extent" of MPC by reference to man-days of participation per 100,000 population and "intensity" by reference to conflict deaths per 10 million population. These measurement rules by no means exhaust the possibilities but have the advantages of being straightforward and usually ascertainable for the national systems we study.

Manifest political conflict takes many different forms; a further question is what theoretical distinctions might be made among them. Virtually all the extensive literature on "types" of conflict is concerned with distinguishing among classes of conflict *events*,[6] whereas this theory deals with magnitudes of conflict. However there is reason to think that the nature of conflict processes differs systematically with the *issues* of conflict. Definition M1 distinguishes among policies, incumbents, and structures of authority as objects of contention in conflict. It has been commonly observed that conflict which is limited to the first of these issues, namely the policies followed by governments, typically involves substantial but short-lived participation by members of conventional association groups. Ordinarily both parties to limited conflict of this sort are restrained in their use of force, hence their confrontations are usually low in intensity. The typical forms in which such conflict is manifest are demonstrations, strikes, riots, and clashes. Conflict over who (usually, which groups) shall rule and through what structures, by contrast, is often protracted and frequently involves combat between military or quasi-military organizations. Both parties are often unrestrained in their use of force, so intensity may be high. The forms of conflict over these basic political issues also are distinctive: They include terrorism, coups d'état, civil and guerrilla war, and revolutionary warfare.[7] But the difference appears to be one of kind (the dominant

---

[6] Conceptual discussion of types of conflict include David Bell, 1974: chap. 4, and Johnson, 1964: 26–31. There is also a substantial empirical literature which purports to distinguish among types of conflict events on the basis of factor analyses which show that some events tend to co-occur with regularity. The pioneering study is Rummel, 1963. A critical review of the findings of this and other such studies is Morrison and Stevenson, 1971.

[7] There are exceptions to these generalizations but there is little doubt about their overall accuracy. Relevant quantitative evidence about the properties of conflict events is reported in Gurr, 1969.

issues of conflict) more than of degree, and provides the basis for a distinction between what we call "protest" and "rebellion."

DEFINITION M4. *Protest is manifest political conflict in which the principal issues are the policies of political authority.*

DEFINITION M5. *Rebellion is manifest political conflict in which the principal issues include the incumbents or structures of political authority.*

Rebellion ordinarily entails opposition to policies as well as to incumbents and structures, so it is the presence of the latter issues, not the absence of the former, that distinguishes rebellion from protest. There is thus some empirical blurring between the two forms of conflict, which is increased by the fact that many conflict events we would characterize as rebellion began as protests over more limited issues. Nonetheless it is possible, and empirically useful, to distinguish between the two forms of MPC in a social system, and to assess separately their relative extent and intensity. It should be clear that we do not assume and necessary correspondence between the form and the magnitude of conflict—magnitude is not "explained" in our theory through conceptual reference to distinct forms of conflict. It is rather that the magnitudes of the separate forms of conflict are themselves subject to explanation.

The Major Determinants of Manifest Political Conflict

Conflict within societies is shaped by the motives of individuals, and the behavioral dispositions and organized strength of contending groups. This statement is deceptively simple and potentially controversial. In more elaborate form it is the basic premise of our theory: To explain to what extent and with what intensity groups of men confront one another, it is necessary to know what it is they want, or fear, and how badly; to understand their beliefs about manifest conflict as a mode of action; and to assess their collective means for acting on their convictions. The argument is essentially the same as the one made in *Why Men Rebel*, except that little was said there about the motives and beliefs which shape the actions of the powerful and advantaged groups who are a party to most political conflict processes. We assume, first, that personal desires to maintain or increase one's well-being are a necessary precondition for manifest conflict behavior: Satiated men do not engage in physical confrontations, dissatisfied and fearful men may. But dissatisfied men do not necessarily challenge other groups in open conflict, because they may not believe manifest conflict to be appropriate and/or because they lack the collective strength to confront others successfully. Thus, the magnitude of manifest conflict depends on three kinds of conditions. The first is the general intensity of individuals' motivations to take remedial action, that is, the size and the "depth" of the pool of individuals potentially mobilized by collectivities in conflict. The second is the orientation to manifest conflict characteristic of each of the various collectivities which compose the society. This, in turn, is a function of their cultural and ideological dispositions, calculations about the relative costs and gains of conflict, and the immediacy of threat posed by opponents. The final factor in the calculus of conflict is the relative capacity of groups for taking concerted conflictual action.

But what, precisely, is the form of the relationship by which these three variables determine the magnitude of manifest political conflict? At least part of the answer is implied in the preceding discussion, which states that motivation for remedial action is a *necessary* precondition, and that *either* believed inappropriateness *or* a lack of effective strength is sufficient to preclude a resort to manifest conflict behavior, even by those strongly motivated to remedial action. The clear implication of this is that if *any* of these three conditions is absent, the magnitude of conflict can be expected to be zero. Thus, the three variables are fully interactive with one another—each contributes to conflict magnitude to the degree that the others are present. Moreover, and finally, because manifest conflict entails confrontation between or among groups, it is likely to be particularly prolonged and intense if contenders are evenly matched. Social systems in which one cohesive group controls virtually all power and resources have inherently low potentials for manifest conflict. They can be assumed to be unique in that regard.

The ramifications of the basic argument just sketched are not simple at all; a great deal of careful thought is needed to translate them into explicit, testable theory. The task can begin here with a formal presentation of the central assumption about the form and nature of theory. That assumption is:

AXIOM M1: In any social system, s,

$$MPC_s = \left[\sum_i PA_i\right]^{\theta_1} \frac{\left\{\left[\sum_c (DC_c)(OS_c)\right] - \left[(DC_1)(OS_1)\right]\right\}^{\theta_2}}{i} + \omega_{s,MPC}$$

where

MPC$_s$ is the magnitude of manifest political conflict in s;

PA$_i$ is the potential for goal-directed or remedial action by individual i;

DC$_c$ is the disposition to manifest conflict behavior of collectivity c;

OS_c is the organizational strength of collectivity c;

DC_1 is the disposition to manifest conflict behavior of the strongest collectivity in the system;

OS_1 is the organizational strength of the strongest collectivity in the system;

i is the number of individuals in the system;

c is the number of distinct politically relevant collectivities in the system;

θ_1, θ_2 are elasticities, or sensitivity coefficients, for the determinants of MPC; and

$\omega_{s,MPC}$ is error in the specification of the MPC model for system s.[8]

Because Axiom M1 is the backbone of our entire theory, a substantial elaboration of it is required. First, it is not of itself a theory of manifest political conflict because the three explanatory concepts, PA, DC, and OS, are constructs: they represent dispositions and potentials that in principle are not directly observable. If Axiom M1 is to become empirical theory it is necessary to specify some measureable determinants of each of its three variables. That is our strategy: to develop formal subtheories, each of which specifies observable determinants of the three variables. Thus our theory of conflict is fully integrated with, and indistinguishable from theory about, individual potentials for action, collective dispositions to action, and organizational strength. We turn to those subtheories in *Conflict and Society,* where we develop what are essentially measurement models for the components of this central theoretical assumption that is presented formally here.

Second, we offer no rejoinder to critics who maintain that general theories of conflict cannot or should not be attempted.[9] They have spared themselves both the trouble of trying and the obligation of reading what is written by those who think otherwise. The controversy which we do address is the question of whether "causes" at different

[8] The symbol ω (omega) represents all other causes of MPC not specified in our model, and may even include some of the concepts which are included in our model (e.g., $\sum_i PA_i$), if we have misspecified, or only partially specified, the functional form of the relationship between them and MPC. In effect, ω is our acknowledgment that the model is not wholly deterministic, or complete, even under conditions of perfect measurement. We do not intend it to connote the set of assumptions that are made about "error" in most statistical work, such as that it is normally distributed with mean zero, and so forth. We are not constructing a regression model here; rather, we are specifying formally the postulated functional forms of relationship and have no immediate need or desire to be constrained by the assumptions of statistical theory. Thus, in this theory, ω represents some unspecified functional form, with unknown properties, that might be represented in more conventional mathematical terms as $g_M(\mathbf{Z})_s$. We use $\omega_{s,MPC}$ to simplify an already complex notation.

[9] Two essays that are highly critical of the systematic (comparative, theoretical) analysis of "revolution" (and, by implication, violent conflict generally) are MacIntyre, 1973, and Wolin, 1973. Their charges are epistemological (it cannot be done) and ethical (the purposes and consequence of attempting to do so are evil).

levels of analysis need to be included in a general explanation of group conflict. There is a distinct tendency when theorizing about conflict to give primary emphasis to one (kind of) factor. Some writers argue that psychological conditions are primary, as one of us has in the past. Others prefer explanations phrased in terms of cultural dispositions and normative systems, social structure and social movements. The clash of groups contending for power and privilege is a favorite theme of historians and some political scientists. Rulers and revolutionaries are disposed to emphasize those aspects of collective organization, force, strategy, and tactics that are subject to their manipulation.[10] Virtually all contemporary writers acknowledge that "other conditions" than their chosen explanation may have some bearing on the outcome, but they usually add, "only a little." None that we know of has been willing to base theory on the premise that conditions at all levels of social analysis—psychological, structural, cultural, and political—are of interdependent importance for comprehensive explanation of the phenomenon of group conflict. We make that assumption and add one more: Any general explanation which neglects any of these levels of analysis is seriously incomplete as a theory of the magnitude of manifest conflict.

Nothing said thus far should be taken to imply that social systems are entirely self-contained, or that this theory applies only to conflict in such systems. Quite the contrary. In *Conflict and Society* we show how external constraints, dependencies, and acts of intervention affect each of the three primary causes of manifest political conflict. In general we think that the explanation of conflict within a social system lies at the junction of three paths, one from characteristics of its individual members, the second from its aggregate systemic properties, and the third from its external environment.

Third, and in spite of our use of explanatory variables at multiple levels, it should be emphasized that the theory is not intended to account for the processes of conflict at the microlevel: It does not deal directly with such issues as why particular individuals choose to join revo-

[10] Much of the relevant literature through 1968 is surveyed in Gurr, 1970, a study which proposes a multilevel explanation while giving primacy to psychological preconditions. Other kinds of psychological approaches to group conflict are the works of James C. Davies and Ivo K. and Rosalind L. Feierabend (see their contributions in Feierabend, Feierabend, and Gurr, 1972); Daniels et al., 1970; David Schwartz, 1973; and Wolfenstein, 1967. A synthesis of ideas and evidence from the social psychological point of view is Scherer et al., 1975. Some recent books offering sociological perspectives on group conflict are Kriesberg, 1973, and Oberschall, 1973. An elementary survey of sociological approaches to collective behavior is Berk, 1974. Major non-Marxist contributions to the class conflict mode of theory include Dahrendorf, 1959; Moore, 1966; and the writings of Charles Tilly, especially Tilly, 1975. The theories of revolutionaries are at least as numerous as scholarly theories of conflict and probably more widely read. A useful survey of current revolutionary theory is Martíc, 1975.

lutionary movements, or how leaders of conflict groups mobilize support, or why politicos choose particular policies of concession or repression. Thus, criticisms commonly raised against previous versions of this theory—that revolutionaries are not the most dissatisfied members of society—are inappropriate here. We do not assume this to be the case, nor is it necessary to do so. All that we claim in this regard is that manifest conflict is apt to be of greater magnitude to the extent that individuals in the social system are deeply and extensively dissatisfied. What the theory does deal with are conflict processes at the macro- or system level. It specifies the changing properties of social systems, and their environments, that set conflict processes in train, and it shows how the properties of conflict (and other social conditions) act to dampen or escalate subsequent conflict. In short, we are concerned with explaining conflict as a macrosocial process, which requires a theory that accounts for both its varying properties over time within systems and its variance among systems, but not its microscopic features.

Fourth, the interactive, or multiplicative, formulation of the causes of manifest political conflict clarifies some common misunderstandings of the theoretical arguments in *Why Men Rebel*. In particular, the individual-level variable, "potential for action," does not necessarily, or even commonly, lead directly to manifest conflict behavior. It may show up instead in increased productivity, conventional political action, emigration, crime, or innumerable other kinds of individual and collective behavior. Our assumption is that manifest conflict behavior will be evidenced only to the extent that individuals are organized into collectivities which have the two properties given above.[11] The first of these, a "collective disposition to conflict behavior," is the orientation the members of a group share about the relative desirability and utility of conflict behavior. We think of these dispositions as an emergent property of the collectivity. They have individual bases—different people feel differently about conflict behavior—but they are not a simple aggregation or average of individual dispositions. The dispositions of members of a group are substantially modified—intensified or constrained—by the dispositions of other members, especially but not only leaders,[12] so that the group takes on a characteristic disposition which is

[11] This is a clarification rather than a revision of a basic assumption in *Why Men Rebel*. Two potentially inconsistent statements on this issue are made there, one that "deprivation-induced discontent is a general spur to action" (p. 13), the other that "men who are frustrated have an innate disposition to do violence to its source. . ." (p. 37). We assume here that the first statement is the more accurate; the task is to identify the circumstances in which PA, or discontent, is likely to lead to attacks on others. It is possible to accept the likelihood of its doing so without necessarily assuming that there is an innate, unobservable disposition to that end.

[12] This is the crux of the reason we treat "collective dispositions to conflict behavior" as an unobservable. It would not be sufficient to ascertain those dispositions through sur-

not necessarily an exact equivalent to that of any single member of the group.

The multiplicative formulation reflects our position that groups collectively disposed to conflict behavior still do not necessarily effect a great deal of manifest conflict. They must have the organizational means to take *concerted* action, and in particular they must be strong enough to challenge opposing groups in order to affect appreciably the magnitude of conflict. The mathematical expressions (DC) (OS) summarizes the interdependency of these two conditions: A collectivity's potential for contributing to open conflict depends on its having some significant level of both proconflict dispositions and organizational strength. If either is very low, the collectivity is unlikely to participate appreciably in conflict.

The following complex expression represents the argument that the magnitude of conflict in a system varies according to the relative strengths of its constituent collectivities.

$$\left[\sum_{c}(DC_c)\,(OS_c)\right] - \left[(DC_1)\,(OS_1)\right]$$

If a system consists of a large number of collectivities of appreciable strength, some of which have high dispositions to conflict, then MPC will tend to be high. Such a situation is analogous to one of "perfect competition" among many producers. But to the extent that there are "monopolistic" tendencies in the system, the magnitude of manifest conflict will decline: Collectivities which are relatively weak will be discouraged, on rationalistic grounds, from attacking powerful and aggressive opponents. When the weak *do* attack the strong, or vice versa, or when weak collectivities confront one another, the consequent magnitudes of conflict are likely to be a good deal less than when conflict occurs between stronger, more equal opponents. A similar argument was made in *Why Men Rebel,* to the effect that the magnitude of political violence varies (*ceteris paribus*) with the balance of support and coercion between dissidents and regimes.[13] The basic axiom of this theory takes account of the fact that most systems consist of many potentially contentious collectivities—it would not be sensible to talk of a monopoly over dispositions to conflict by one collectivity because (according to subsequent parts of our theory) dispositions are partly dependent on the dispositions and actions of others. A monopoly over conflict dispositions will not long remain a monopoly, and hence we cannot expect the complex term to approximate zero through any other avenue than a highly concentrated distribution of organizational strength. The es-

vey techniques, even by weighing leaders' responses more heavily, because group context and pressures are crucial in determining the *operant* collective dispositions.
[13] *Why Men Rebel,* chaps. 8–10.

sential principle is that the more potent the strongest collectivity by comparison with all other conflict-disposed collectivities combined, the lower MPC is likely to be. The extreme case is that in which a social system consists of one strong cohesive collectivity—in which case the axiom implies that MPC is expected to be zero. We might add, parenthetically, that such a system might well initiate warfare against other systems—as did postrevolutionary France in the 1790s, for example. This idea is not further explored, but the resulting intersystem conflict could be explained by this theory if the analyst moved to the level of the larger, international system, provided that larger system satisfied the assumptions of theory context given below.

The nature of the basic causal relationship in Axiom M1 now should be clear. Its first term, $\sum_i PA_i$, signifies the total potential for action among members of a social system. That potential varies markedly among systems, within systems over time, and also among groups within systems. But manifest political conflict is not a function of the simple aggregation of individual potentials for action, independent of other conditions. Social conflict is collective conflict, therefore the magnitude of political conflict is dependent upon the orientations and organizational properties of collectivities in the system. The nature of those effects is to amplify (or minimize) the conflictful consequences of high potentials for action. It follows that if $\sum_i PA_i$ is high but the aggregate potential for collective conflict, $\left[\sum_c (DC_c)\,(OS_c)\right] - \left[(DC_1)\,(OS_1)\right]$, is low, then manifest political conflict in the system will be low. The converse is also true: The existence of strong organizations and pervasive proconflict dispositions do not of themselves generate collective conflict, not if $\sum_i PA_i$ is low.[14]

In everyday language, organized physical confrontations are apt to be severe if and only if three things are simultaneously true. First, many people are intensely dissatisfied with what they have. Second, dissatisfied collectivities feel that fighting is a satisfying or useful thing to do under the circumstances. And third, some of those groups have the capacity to turn their desires into action. If any one of those things is not true, then other kinds of individual and social consequences follow—but not intense or extensive conflict behavior. Axiom M1 implies more than that, of course, and we should be able to further elabo-

---

[14] In *Why Men Rebel,* chap. 10, the basic theoretical argument is misleadingly depicted as an additive one, whereby the magnitude of political violence is said to be a function of relative deprivation *plus* justifications *plus* balance (see pp. 320, 341–42, and 349). The text, however, implies that this basic relationship is multiplicative (see especially pp. 159 and 319–47 *passim*), as it is treated in this revision of the theory. Peter Abell has diagnosed the problem and suggested more appropriate formulations in "Why *do* men rebel? A Discussion of Ted Robert Gurr's *Why Men Rebel,*" *Race,* 13 (July 1971), 85–89.

rate the general argument for it by saying why we chose this particular formulation and not one of two alternatives. These are the two alternatives in equation form:

1) $\text{MPC} = \left(\sum_i \text{PA}_i\right)\left(\sum_i \text{DC}_i\right)\left(\sum_c \text{OS}_c - \text{OS}_1\right)$

2) $\text{MPC} = \left[\sum_c (\text{PA}_c)\,(\text{DC}_c)\,(\text{OS}_c)\right] - \left[(\text{PA}_1)\,(\text{DC}_1)\,(\text{OS}_1)\right]$

Verbally, the first equation implies that the three variables shall be evaluated, and aggregated, separately across all actors in a social system. We reject this formulation because it misrepresents the role of collectivities in conflict. Not all organizations contribute to manifest conflict, only those in which there are significant proconflict dispositions. Moreover, proconflict dispositions are not merely or mainly properties of individuals: They usually are reinforced and transmitted within particular collectivities; hence it is the general disposition of the group which is consequential for manifest conflict.

The second alternative formulation is more plausible than the first, and in fact is precisely accurate for any given point in time: The extent of manifest conflict today in a social system should depend upon the potentials for action only of those people who are now mobilized by conflict-prone collectivities. However, we do not think it possible in principle, nor instructive in practice, to deal with magnitudes of manifest conflict at narrow points in time. Since this is a probabilistic theory, whose causal mechanisms take varying lengths of time to work themselves out, the theory applies more accurately to magnitudes of conflict measured during periods of time rather than at instants in time. And during such longer periods there are microprocesses which affect the participants in conflict. In particular, in most social systems people move in and out of organized collectivities depending on how well these suit their interests—and sometimes create new groups when old ones prove inadequate. In a theory which takes account of conflict processes and examines the manifestations of those processes during a *period* of time, the action potentials of all individuals in a system need separate assessment because those potentials will affect the growth and decline of conflict-prone groups.

In summary, the objection to the first alternative to Axiom M1 is that it gives too little attention to the special properties of collectivities in mobilizing people for conflict, while the second alternative errs in the opposite direction. If dissatisfied people have any choice among the collectivities to which they commit their hopes and efforts, then Axiom M1 should be the appropriate formulation of the central theoretical assumption of this theory of conflict.

Assumptions about Context

Our final task here is to determine and specify the conditions under which the theory ought to apply. Physical scientists may hope to develop universal theories, ones which are valid within small margins of error in all times and in all places. In the social sciences, though, the goal of deterministic theories (i.e., theories virtually closed with respect to context) seems too grand an expectation. Rather, social scientists should ordinarily expect to set boundaries for any given theory, by making explicit assumptions about the context in which the theory can be expected to be valid.

Our basic contextual assumption is that this theory of manifest political conflict should hold for *all social systems in which inclusive positions of authority are distinguishable, and which are composed of collective purposeful actors.* The terms "social system" and "collective purposeful actors" require definition and explanation. A "social system" is a collectivity of actors—individuals or groups—who are bound together by a high degree of interaction which persists over time. The systemic bonds among members may be ones of common fate, or ones of regular causation and constraint among elements, but in either case the defining property of a social system is that the attributes and behaviors of each element are substantially and recurrently (not necessarily totally) affected by the attributes and behaviors of the other elements. In short, a social system has entitivity and is to be distinguished from nominal systems, like the United Nations and most religious congregations in Western societies, which are characterized by little regular interaction. This contextual limitation is basic to the definition of "potential for action" which is developed below, and to subsequent axioms about actors' dispositions to conflict behavior. In a nominal system actors rarely act as though their fate depends upon their position in that system.

The set of systems to which this theory is applicable thus is much larger than the nation-states to which earlier theoretical statements referred. On the other hand not all states necessarily belong in the set, for one of two reasons: Some, like the historical Holy Roman Empire and the minimal states that still prevail in parts of the Third World, are little more than nominal systems; others, like the Congo (now Zaïre) in the early 1960s and South Vietnam t' roughout the decade, were temporarily sets of contending systems rather than single social entities. So there is some question about the appropriateness of a few of the eighty-six states used in empirical analyses to be reported in *Conflict and Society*.[15] Insofar as these states include entities which are nominal, our abil-

---

[15] For an initial empirical assessment of the revised theory, using data on eighty-six countries, see Gurr and Duvall, 1973.

ity to test the theory is impaired. In any event we have eliminated from the set of test cases those "entities" whose entitivity was most in doubt in the 1960s, such as Laos, Papua-New Guinea, and Mozambique.

The theory also assumes that the systems to which it refers are comprised of "collective purposeful actors." Supra-individual entities such as firms within cartels, departments within universities, clans within tribes, communal groups and provinces within nations, and nations within alliances are all potentially "purposeful actors." To qualify as a purposeful actor, however, a supra-individual group must be a "real" system in precisely the same sense as the larger system of which it is part. The individuals who comprise it must be sufficiently interrelated that individual-level phenomena give rise to emergent group properties such as group goals, group behavior, and group response.[16] Note that by "purposeful" we do not imply an assumption that actors are always rational. The point of this delimitation is that the theory is inappropriate for systems comprised of collective actors who never act so as to realize goals. The point also may be trivial, because it is unlikely that any such systems have more than a fleeting existence.

We have cast much of our theory at the level of collectivities within systems, which may raise questions about the use of "psychological" concepts such as motivation and rationality. We deal with the problem by restricting the context of theory such that referent actors are "real" systems. That is, composition rules or organizational principles are assumed to exist which join individuals together into corporate entities which are capable of concerted action. The composition rules may be as diffuse as shared symbols and group identity, acquired through common socialization, or as explicit as highly directive, hierarchical patterns of authority. The composition rules are not specified here, nor do we think it necessary to do so. The real-world existence of supra-individual actors is manifestly obvious, and so long as they exist and operate, the theory is appropriate, regardless of the level of aggregation of actors and regardless of the principles by which those aggregations acquire entitivity. However, because the observations we use to test this theory do not contain information about the rules of composition which link individuals to groups, and because the test we offer does involve collective conflict behavior, it is quite possible that the theory is being tested in *some* inappropriate contexts. It is not that we are testing a "psychological" theory at the wrong level of analysis, a criticism that is inapplicable to this formulation of the theory. The potential source of difficulty here is that our observations are generated under the assumption that collectivities such as suppressed communal and political groups, and

---

[16] To avoid conceptual nitpicking we must be explicit on one other point. Not all individuals and actors who are nominally members of a system are equally or completely plugged into it; some may be almost wholly isolated from it. The larger the proportion of such isolated or insulated actors in a system, the less accurately our theory applies.

the people of separatist regions, are purposeful actors. If, in some na-tion-states, the groups we identify are not purposeful entities, then it is inappropriate to test the theory *in those nation-states.*

Finally, because ours is a theory of *political* conflict, the system must be marked by different roles of subordination and superordination; that is, there must be recognizable authority patterns. The "ordered anarchy" of pure market systems is not a context in which this theory could be expected to be valid.

In sum, we believe the theory outlined here, and elaborated in *Conflict and Society,* to be of wide but not limitless scope. It is appropri-ate to the explanation and prediction of manifest conflict behavior in any real political system composed of any types of collective social actors that engage in goal-seeking behavior.

9

Explaining Revolutions: In Quest of a Social-Structural Approach

Theda Skocpol

THE EXPLANATION of revolutions poses a unique challenge for social science. Success depends upon finding some way to hypothesize about complex, large-scale events in which patterned group conflicts and sudden societal transformations intrinsically coincide. Undoubtedly the most difficult cases are social revolutions, in which societal political conflicts occurring in conjuncture with class upheavals from below lead to "rapid, fundamental, and violent domestic change in the dominant values and myths of a society, in its political institutions, social structure, leadership, and government activities and policies" (Huntington, 1968:264). To be sure, the historical occurrences that unequivocally measure up to this definition are few: France, 1789; Russia, 1917; Mexico, 1911–1936; and China, 1911–1949 are the obvious clear-cut instances. Many would argue that a phenomenon of which there are so few instances does not deserve theoretical attention. Yet the enormous impact and continuing historical significance of social revolutions are surely sufficient to override the fact of their generic scarcity and render them a fit object of explanatory effort for social scientists.

What explains revolutions? Why do they (or might they) occur in certain societies at given times, while not in other societies, or at other times in the same societies? Apparently, recent American social science should have much to say in answer to this question, for, like a hundred flowers blooming, theories of revolution have sprung up thick and fast during the past fifteen years. Most recent attempts to explain either revolutions per se, or some broader class of phenomena explicitly conceived as subsuming revolutions, can be identified primarily with one or another of three major approaches: (1) *aggregate-psychological* theories, which attempt to explain revolutions in terms of people's motivations for engaging in political violence or joining oppositional movements; (2) *systems/value-consensus* theories, which attempt to explain revolutions as violent responses of ideological movements to severe disequilibrium in social systems; and (3) *political conflict* theories, which argue that conflict between governments and organized groups contending for political power must be placed at the center of attention.

Yet it will be the burden of argument in this essay that recent social scientific theories of revolution in fact fail to elucidate or explain revolutions. The basic differences are both methodological (in the broad meaning of the term) and substantive. Substantively, the chief difficulty is that existing theories attempt to explain the occurrence of revolutions through hypotheses about the situation and states of mind of rebellious masses or the emergence of consciously revolutionary vanguards, rather than through hypotheses about patterns of institutional development in specific types of complex societies in given sorts of historical circumstances. Methodologically the difficulty lies with attempts to explain revolutions directly in terms of abstract, deductive hypotheses about human behavior or societal processes in general, and to put such hypotheses to statistical tests based on large numbers of units, rather than engaging in comparative-historical analyses to generate and test hypotheses inductively through systematic contrast of the few positive cases of revolution with negative cases of failure or nonoccurrence. Thus I shall be arguing that a major theoretical reorientation—away from social psychological and universalist-deductive modes of explanation, and toward a structural and comparative-historical approach—is required if progress toward the adequate explanation of revolutions is to be made in the social sciences.

Aggregate-Psychological Theories of Revolution

Aggregate-psychological theorists assume that "revolutions, like all political phenomena, originate in the minds of men. . . ." (Schwartz, 1972: 58), and so they turn for explanatory power to various theories of motivational dynamics. Some of these theorists (e.g., Geschwender, 1968; Eckstein, 1965; Schwartz, 1971, 1972) rely upon various cognitive psychological theories. But the most prevalent and fully developed type of aggregate-psychological explanation of revolution begins "with the seemingly self-evident premise that discontent is the root cause of violent conflict" (Gurr, 1973:364), and then seeks to explicate this premise with the aid of psychological theories that link frustration to violent, aggressive behavior against the perceived agents of frustration. James Davies (1962, 1969), Ivo and Rosalind Feierabend (1972), the Feierabends and Nesvold (1969, 1973), and Ted Robert Gurr (1968*a*, 1968*b*, 1970) have been the leading proponents of this approach. Gurr's book, *Why Men Rebel,* represents the most sophisticated and thoroughly elaborated presentation of a complex model based on frustration-aggression theory. Thus in our discussion of the aggregate-psychological approach to explaining revolutions, we shall focus primarily upon the frustration-aggression variant, and especially upon Ted Gurr's presentations of it.

Frustration-aggression theorists tend to "see" revolutions as just one possible form of violent and illicit political behavior that is fundamentally instigated by a certain frame of mind. Thus Gurr seeks to explain "political violence," by which he means

> all collective attacks within a political community against the political regime, its actors—including competing political groups as well as incumbents—or its policies. The concept represents a set of events, a common property of which is the actual or threatened use of violence. . . . The concept subsumes revolution, ordinarily defined as fundamental sociopolitical change accomplished through violence. It also includes guerilla wars, coups d'état, rebellions, and riots [1970:3–4]

The concerns which dictate this theoretical focus are openly stated:

> [A]ll such acts pose a threat to the political system in two senses; they challenge the monopoly of force imputed to the state in political theory; and in functional terms, they are likely to interfere with and, if severe, to destroy normal political processes. [1970:4]

Clearly Gurr is interested in explaining only the "destructiveness" of revolutions, an aspect shared with other types of events, and not the amounts or kinds of societal change that revolutions, specifically, bring about. He focuses upon a style of behavior, "resort to illicit violence," as the defining property that distinguishes these collective events from others. This focus, in turn, "has the crucial theoretical consequence: to direct attention to psychological theories about the sources of human aggression" (Gurr, 1968*b*:247).

Gurr's theory is not mainly psychological in manifest content, however, for he concentrates upon specifying many interrelated societal conditions, which according to his ultimately psychological logic, might operate to initiate and then to focus and channel potentials for collective political violence. Relative deprivation—"a perceived discrepancy between men's value expectations [the goods and conditions of life to which people believe they are rightfully entitled] and their value capabilities [the goods and conditions they think they are capable of attaining or maintaining]" (Gurr, 1970:13)—is specified as the frustrating condition that produces the potential for political violence. Relative deprivation is supposedly to some degree generated in people whenever societies undergo changes. (However, frustration-aggression theorists ultimately specify so many different kinds of social circumstances that might generate feelings of relative deprivation [see especially Gurr, 1970: chaps. 3–5], that the skeptical observer is left wondering whether discontent attributable to relative deprivation could not be attributed by these theorists to any group in any society at any time or place.) Once discontent due to relative deprivation is generated, the magnitudes and forms of collective political violence to which it gives rise depend both upon the intensity and widespreadness among people in society of the feelings of relative deprivation, and upon the effects of various mediating variables that channel and regulate the particular expression of generalized potentials for political violence. Among the important mediating variables that Gurr specifies are cultural conditions such as the degree of legitimation of existing authorities and normative approval for engaging in political violence to express grievances, and institutional conditions such as the degree of organizational strength of dissidents versus regime incumbents (Gurr, 1970:chaps. 6–9).

Still, relative deprivation remains the strategic explanatory variable. For it induces frustration that cannot be entirely suppressed by mediating conditions. Moreover, the possible effects of the mediating variables are all assessed in terms of their imputed psychological impact upon actors already experiencing feelings of relative deprivation—and this gives a distinctive slant to all of Gurr's conclusions about the effects of social conditions. Thus, for example, Gurr concludes that coercive repression is likely to exacerbate political violence, not because he considers government coercion as "political violence" (he does not—he excludes government actions by definition), but because he reasons that government coercion, unless it is extremely intense and totally consistent and efficient, will only increase dissidents' frustration levels and make them even more prone to violence (Gurr, 1970: chap. 8).

Within Gurr's overall model, revolutions in particular are explained merely as responses to widespread and intense relative deprivation that touches *both* "masses" and marginal "elites" in society, thus creating at once both widespread participation in and deliberate organization of violence. Relative deprivation confined merely to the masses would, according to Gurr, produce only "turmoil," since the "ability to rationalize, plan, and put to instrumental use their own and others' discontent is likely to be most common among the more skilled, highly educated members of a society—its elite aspirants" (Gurr, 1968*b:*276).

What does empirical evidence tell us about the validity of frustra-tion-aggression theories? Relative deprivation theorists have collected cross-national aggregate data to test their theories of political violence. Especially noteworthy are the attempts by Gurr (1968a) and the Feiera-bends (1972). On the face of it, "relative deprivation" emerges in these studies as a strong predictor of political violence in a large number of societies around the world. However, Gurr and the Feierabends have not *directly* operationalized their central explanatory variables. While the exact testing of relative deprivation theories, as Davies has aptly argued, requires "the assessment of the state of mind—or more pre-cisely, the mood—of a people" ideally over "an extended period of time in a particular society" (Davies, 1962:17–18), Gurr and the Feierabends have not taken this approach. As they themselves admit, their studies "resort to an indirect method of measuring psychological variables, employing structural and ecological indicators" (Feierabends and Gurr, 1972:121) for numerous nations for years since World War II. There-fore, the reader must take their theoretical interpretations of the evi-dence on faith.

A number of researchers have devised more direct tests of relative-deprivation/frustration-aggression theory than those offered by its leading proponents, and these outside investigators have found little empirical support for this approach to explaining political violence. Using survey data on the attitudes as well as the characteristics and situ-ations of Chilean slum dwellers, Alejandro Portes (1971:29) found ab-solutely no relationship between objective or subjective measures of de-privation and frustration, and declarations of willingness to accept "revolution and revolutionary violence as legitimate means to over-throw an economic and political order." Similarly, in a survey of politi-cal attitudes employing Cantril's Self-Anchoring Striving Scale, a sub-jective "deprivation measure recommended by Gurr," Edward Muller found

> little support for an explanation of potential for political violence which ascribes strong—or any—direct effect to relative deprivation, or which casts relative deprivation as an important precondition that might be related to potential for political violence indirectly through effect on a factor such as belief in the legitimacy-illegitimacy of the regime. Rela-tive deprivation . . . was found to be the *least* consequential predictor of potential for political violence. [1972:954]

Finally, David Snyder and Charles Tilly did a study that used objec-tive indicators of relative deprivation, yet improved upon Gurr and the Feierabends by investigating patterns over time. Working with time-series data from France, 1830–1960, Snyder and Tilly (1972) attempted to predict changes in numbers of incidents of collective violence events and participants therein from fluctuations in indices of food prices,

prices of manufactured goods, and levels of manufacturing production. They tested a wide variety of models based upon the hypotheses and operationalizations of Gurr, Davies, and the Feierabends, but found no significant relationships.

A few writers, for example Lupsha (1971) and Muller (1972), have responded to the increasingly evident inadequacy of frustration-aggression theories by suggesting that the willingness of individuals to resort to political violence could be better explained by their commitment to moral standards at variance with prevailing ideals or practices in society. Gurr himself (1968a) has accepted "legitimation" as an important "state of mind" variable independent of relative deprivation. Yet, while attention to the moral dimensions of consciousness may produce more powerful theories of the political orientations of individuals, it seems unlikely that any sort of theorizing grounded on the psychological level will produce an adequate explanation of either collective patterns of political violence or revolutions.

For the fundamental difficulty with all aggregate-psychological theories is that they attempt to explain social processes more or less directly on the basis of hypotheses about subjective orientations attributed to aggregates of individuals. Such a theoretical strategy can have even surface plausibility only to the extent that the events to be explained are conceived as the direct manifestations of individual behavior—hence the preferred focus on "political violence." But revolutions, coups, rebellions, even riots, all are events in which not amorphous aggregates but rather collectively mobilized and organized groups engage in violence in the process of striving for objects which bring them into conflict with other mobilized groups. Moreover, the various types of political violence are normally labeled and differentiated not only on the basis of whether primarily skillful and farsighted ("elite") or emotional and shortsighted ("nonelite") people participate in them, but rather on the basis of the social-structural locations of actors and the sociopolitical consequences brought about (or not) by the processes of political conflict. Revolutions above all are not mere extreme manifestations of some homogeneous type of individual behavior. Rather they are complex conjunctures of unfolding conflicts involving differently situated and motivated (and at least minimally organized) groups, and resulting not just in violent destruction of a polity, but also in the emergence of new sociopolitical arrangements. Thus it seems entirely in order to conclude that, even if frustration-aggression theorists could explain either individual predispositions to political violence or sheer aggregate amounts of all types added together (and the studies cited above show that they cannot even do this), they still could not enlighten us as to the causes of revolutions—or any other distinctive form of political conflict.

"To extrapolate from sums or proportions of individual attitudes to the occurrence of structural transformations," says Alejandro Portes (1971:28) in a critique of frustration-aggression theory, "is to accept a naive additive image of society and its structure." In contrast, the two alternative prominent approaches to explaining revolution both employ social-structural logics to correct shortcomings of the aggregate psychological approaches. Thus systems/value-consensus theorists derive their hypotheses about why revolutions happen and what they accomplish by working directly from a theoretical model of an equilibrated social system. And political conflict theorists derive hypotheses about political violence and revolutions from a model of the group political processes that they consider central to all politically organized populations. But even though both of these approaches begin with social-structural perspectives, nevertheless both end up offering fundamental social psychological explanations of the roots of revolutions. Let us investigate why this has happened.

Systems/Value-Consensus Theories

While *mass discontent* is the crucial factor for explaining revolutions for frustration-aggression theorists, *systemic crises* and, especially, *revolutionary ideology* are the key factors for systems/value-consensus theorists. In broad outline the systems/value-consensus perspective on revolution is shared by a number of theorists, including, most prominently, the sociological theorist Talcott Parsons (1951: chap. 9), along with his onetime students Edward Tiryakian (1967) and Neil Smelser (1963). However, the perspective has been most thoroughly and judiciously applied specifically to the explanation of political revolutions by the political scientist Chalmers Johnson, in his 1966 book, *Revolutionary Change*. Let us review the argument that Johnson presents.

For Johnson (1966:1) revolution "is a special kind of social change, one that involves the intrusion of violence into civil social relations" which normally function to restrict violence. Like Gurr, then, Johnson makes violence central to his definition of revolution. However, Johnson (1966:57) considers violence not as an emotional urge toward destruction, but rather as a rational strategy intended to accomplish change involving societal reconstruction along with destruction. Therefore, he concludes that the analysis and explanation of revolution must be done with reference to some theory of social structure. Fatefully, though, the sociological theory with which Johnson decides to work is Parsonian systems theory, and this theory's perspective on societal integration and change inexorably pushes Johnson back toward social-psychological explanations for revolutionary change.

Following the Parsonians, Johnson (1966:chaps, 2–4) posits that a normal, or crisis-free, society should be conceived as an internally consistent set of institutions that express and specify in norms and roles core societal value-orientations—value-orientations which have also been internalized through processes of socialization to become the personal moral and reality-defining standards of the vast normal majority of the adult members of society. It follows from this conception of the bases of societal integration that close parallels should exist between the dominant world-views of a society and individuals' feelings of personal orientation, and that any objective social-structural crises should automatically be reflected both in the breakdown of the dominant world-views and in the emergence and popular acceptance of an ideology embodying alternative societal value-orientations. Johnson readily accepts these logical consequences of the Parsonian theory of societal integration.

Thus, according to Johnson, crises in society develop whenever a society's values and environment become significantly "dissychronized." The instigators of crises can be either endogenous innovations (especially of values or technologies) or exogenous influences or intrusions (Johnson, 1966:chap. 4). Yet impetuses to crisis, whatever their source, are always realized via the societal members' experience of disorientation. "The single most generalized characteristic of the disequilibrated system is that values no longer provide an acceptable symbolic definition and explanation of existence" (Johnson, 1966:72–73). As a result "personal disequilibrium" is widely experienced, and there is an increase of individual and group behavior heretofore considered "deviant" in terms of the previous value consensus.

At this point, a revolutionary situation develops only if, and because, ideological movements focused around alternative, innovative value-orientations coalesce and begin to attract large numbers of adherents.

> The dynamic element which . . . leads to the development of lines of cleavage is ideology. Without ideology, deviant subcultural groups—such as delinquent gangs, religious sects, and deviant patriotic associations—will not form alliances, and the tensions of the system which led particular groups to form these associations will be dissipated without directly influencing the social structure. [Johnson, 1966:81]

But even given a full-blown revolutionary situation, whether a revolution will actually succeed depends, according to Johnson (1966:91), primarily upon whether or not the legitimate authorities are willing and able to develop policies "which will maintain the confidence of nondeviant actors in the system and its capacity to move toward re-synchronization" of values and environment. For Johnson (1966:xiv, 94) insists that authorities can—theoretically speaking—always modify existing values and institutions so as to avert the crisis and the need for revolution.

While the authorities seek to implement policies of "resynchroniza-tion," they may of necessity have to rely on coercion to prevent success-ful revolution. However, Johnson sees this as an entirely chancy situa-tion, and one which cannot last for long. He maintains that a wide variety of "accelerators," which he regards as "not sets of conditions but single events," could at any time "rupture a system's pseudo-integration based on deterrence" (Johnson, 1966:99). He asserts that

> superior force may delay the eruption of violence; nevertheless, a divi-sion of labor maintained by Cossacks is no longer a community of value-sharers, and in such a situation (e.g., South Africa, today [1966]), revolution is endemic and, *ceteris paribus,* an insurrection is inevita-ble. [1966:32]

Because he views the "authorities" as necessarily legitimated by consen-sual societal norms and values, Johnson is most reluctant to admit that a strong, efficient government could repress revolutionary tendencies over a prolonged period—a situation that has, for example, prevailed in South Africa for fifteen years (see Adam, 1971). If Johnson, or any other theorist of the systems/value-consensus persuasion, were ever to admit such a possibility, that would, of course, call into question the basic "value-consensus" model of societal integration and dynamics which underpins this approach to explaining revolutions.

In sum Johnson, like the aggregate psychologists, believes that gov-ernments must satisfy their citizens if they are to escape revolution. Only for Johnson it is the citizens' internalized value standards, not merely their customary or acquired appetites, that must be appeased. Further, just as revolutionary movements succeed for the frustration-aggression theorists because they express the anger of the discon-tented, similarly for the systems/value-consensus theorists they succeed because they allow the disoriented to express commitments to new societal values. In both cases, essentially social-psychological modes of explaining revolutions are grounded on consensual images of societal order and change, the one implicit and utilitarian, the other explicit and moralistic.

Nor has this brand of essentially social-psychological explanation been demonstrated to have any greater empirical validity than frustra-tion-aggression theories. As steps toward more rigorous empirical tests of their theories, Tiryakian (1967:92–95) and Johnson (1966:132, chap. 6) have suggested specific components of indices of "revolutionary potential" or system "disequilibrium." Thus far, however, no systems/value-consensus theorist has used these or other indicators systematically to test the theory cross-nationally after the manner of the relative-deprivation theorists.

Perhaps more important, no systems/value-consensus advocate has seriously confronted historical materials with two straightforward questions: Are revolutions really *made by* ideological movements, consisting of elites and masses committed to alternative societal values? And are there cases where ideological movements have been strong—as strong as or stronger than they have been in successful revolutions—but where no revolution has resulted, even after a considerable time lag?

Had these simple questions been seriously posed, the answers would by now have eliminated systems/value-consensus theories as plausible explanations of revolutions. In the Third World, "disequilibrated social systems" and ideological movements questioning the legitimacy of established authorities and arrangements abound, and yet actual revolutions are rare. It is even more telling to point out that in no successful revolution to date has it been true that a mass-based movement sharing a revolutionary ideology has in any sense "made" the revolution. True enough, revolutionary ideologies and charismatic leaders have in some instances helped to cement the solidarity of radical vanguards before and/or during revolutionary crises, and have greatly facilitated the institution of new national patterns afterward. But in no sense did such vanguards, let alone vanguards with large, ideologically imbued mass followings, ever create the essentially politico-military revolutionary crises they exploited. In the French Revolution the emergence of the revolutionary crisis in 1788–1789 stimulated the articulation and widespread acceptance of the initial revolutionary ideology, rather than vice versa as a systems/value-consensus theory of revolution would suggest (Taylor, 1972). In the Russian Revolution, the Bolshevik ideologues were but a tiny, faction-ridden sect of the intelligentsia before mid-1917, when the war-induced collapse of the tsarist government gave them suddenly enhanced opportunities for political leverage and mass manipulation. And in the Chinese and Mexican revolutions, the ideological movements that ultimately triumphed in the struggles among competing elites during the revolutionary interregnums did not even yet exist when the old regimes were toppled in 1911.

Moreover peasants—the most important lower-stratum in revolutionary dramas heretofore—typically have not thought or acted in "revolutionary" ways at all. Even as they have fueled the greatest social revolutions, peasants—and often the urban poor as well—have fought for traditional and either specific or parochial values and goals. As Trotsky perceptively put it, "the masses go into a revolution not with a prepared plan of social reconstruction but with a sharp feeling that they cannot endure the old regime" (Trotsky, 1932:x). And it is usually the concrete aspects of the old regime that they avowedly reject, not its overall structure and values. Thus peasants have helped to launch revolutions by seizing the property of landlords in the name of the king and traditional anti-aristocratic myths (Lefebvre, 1932), or else through appeals to traditional ideals of community justice (L. Tilly, 1971; Chamberlin, 1935:chap. 11; Womack, 1968), while urban workers have tipped the balance in struggles for state power between moderate and radical revolutionary elites in the process of themselves fighting to achieve more immediate goals such as lower food prices (Rudé, 1959) or workers' control of factories (Avrich, 1963).

The Political Conflict Perspective

To explain collective violence and revolutions, aggregate-psychological and systems/value-consensus theorists alike end up focusing on discontent or disorientation and relegating institutional and organizational factors to the role of intervening variables. But writers converging on what I shall call a political conflict perspective (e.g., Oberschall, 1969, 1973; Overholt, 1972; Russell, 1974; Tilly, 1969, 1975) argue that instead there should be an emphasis on the role of organized group conflicts for political goals. The most articulate and prolific spokesman for the new departure is Charles Tilly; moreover, his preliminary statements about revolution (1973, 1974, 1975) demonstrate the internal contradictions that yet remain within this perspective.

The political conflict perspective has developed mainly in critical response to discontent and societal disintegration explanations of political violence. According to Tilly (1975:484–96), theorists such as Gurr and Davies and Johnson and Smelser have failed to see that political violence is essentially a by-product of omnipresent processes of political conflict among mobilized—that is, organized and resource-controlling—groups and governments. Castigating these theorists for concentrating "their theorizing and their research on individual attitudes or on the condition of the social system as a whole" (1975:488), Tilly contends

> that revolutions and collective violence tend to flow directly out of a population's central political process, instead of expressing diffuse strains and discontents within the population; . . . that the specific claims and counterclaims being made on the existing government by various mobilized groups are more important than the general satisfac-

tion or discontent of these groups, and that claims for established places within the structure of power are crucial. [1973:436]

Tilly therefore places "political conflict" at the center of attention. And he proposes to analyze it with the aid of a general model whose major elements are governments ("organizations which control the principal means of coercion") and contenders for power, including both polity members and challengers (Tilly, 1975:501–3). Working with this model and some inductive generalizations about the social structural conditions and European historical trends that have affected the capacities and occasions for groups to mobilize and for governments to repress mobilized contenders, Charles, Louise, and Richard Tilly have recently demonstrated in *The Rebellious Century* (1975) that, for a one-hundred-year period (1830–1930) in France, Italy, and Germany, their approach can make better sense of the overall patterns of incidence of changing forms of collective political violence than can the alternative discontent or social dislocation theories.

Ironically, though, when Tilly turns from criticizing and countering competing explanations of political violence to his own attempt to characterize and explain revolutions in particular, he ends up falling back upon the shopworn hypotheses of relative deprivation and ideological conversion. This happens because of several seemingly innocent pretheoretical choices made by Tilly before he begins to speculate about the possible causes of revolutions. Although Tilly (1975:485–86) correctly stresses that revolutions are complex events whose occurrence probably depends upon a convergence of several relatively independent processes, nevertheless he chooses to ignore aspects of class conflict and social change and to separate out only the single aspect of struggle for political sovereignty for analytic and explanatory attention. Along with civil wars, international conquests, and national separatist movements, Tilly conceives of revolutions simply as situations of multiple sovereignty:

> A revolution begins when a government previously under the control of a single sovereign polity becomes the object of effective, competing, mutually exclusive claims on the part of two or more distinct polities; it ends when a single sovereign polity regains control over the government. [1975:519]

It is easy enough to see that this approach appeals to Tilly because it allows him to generalize from his group conflict model already developed for analyzing political violence: Revolutions can be conceived as a special case of group conflict in which the contenders are both (or all) fighting for ultimate political sovereignty over a population. Yet if what makes revolutionary situations special is precisely *the extraordinary nature of the goal* for which contending groups are struggling, then it naturally seems to follow that what needs to be explained about revolutions is the emergence and appeal of contenders who *intend* to achieve these special goals. And, indeed, when Tilly comes to the point of suggesting causes of revolution, he relies upon social-psychological hypotheses to explain the emergence of revolutionary contenders and the increase of their followings. Echoing Chalmers Johnson, Tilly declares (1975:525) that potential contenders are "always with us in the form of millennial cults, radical cells, or rejects from the positions of power. The real question is when such contenders proliferate and/or mobilize." Charismatic individuals and the rise or decline of social groups are possible explanatory factors, Tilly suggests. Yet he notes that one factor is especially important:

> The elaboration of new ideologies, new theories of how the world works, new creeds, is part and parcel of both paths to a revolutionary position: the emergence of brand-new challengers and the turning [to revolutionary goals] of existing contenders. [1975:526]

As for "the commitment to the [revolutionary contenders'] claims by a significant segment of the subject population," Tilly suggests (1975:526) that it "is in accounting for the expansion and contracting of this sort of commitment that attitudinal analyses of the type conducted by Ted Gurr, James Davies, and Neil Smelser should have their greatest power." Discontent re-emerges as a central explanatory factor—only with the dependent variable no longer violent behavior but, instead, acquiescence in the support of a revolutionary elite, coalition, or organization.

There is still another tension within the political conflict perspective. On the one hand, because emphasis is placed upon organized political activity, the state becomes central. Indeed Tilly argues that structural transformations of states have provided the opportunities and provocations for a large proportion of violent political conflicts; that agents of the state are the most active perpetrators of violence; and that "war bears a crucial relationship to revolution" both through its impact upon coercive capacities and through its effect on governmental demands upon subject populations (Tilly, 1975:532–37). But, on the other hand, Tilly's stress upon multiple sovereignty as the defining characteristic of revolution trivializes—inadvertently, no doubt—the role of the state. The state is not seen as determining by its own strength or weakness whether or not a revolutionary situation can emerge at all. Instead it is portrayed as an organization competing for popular support on more or less equal terms with one or more fully formed revolutionary organizations or blocs. Societal members are envisaged as able to choose freely and deliberately whether to support the government or a revolutionary organization, with their choices determining whether or not a revolutionary situation develops. Thus, according to Tilly:

> The revolutionary moment arrives when previously acquiescent members of . . . [a] population find themselves confronted with strictly incompatible demands from the government and from an alternative body claiming control over the government—and obey the alternative body. They pay taxes to it, provide men for its armies, feed its functionaries, honor its symbols, give time to its service, or yield other resources, despite the prohibition of a still-existing government they formerly obeyed. Multiple sovereignty has begun. [1975:520–21]

In sum, while the political conflict theorists explicitly reject the notions of discontented or disoriented or morally outraged people directly turning to revolutionary behavior that destroys or overturns the regime or the social system, nevertheless they maintain a largely social-psychological perspective on the causes of revolution. For they retain the image of organized, conscious revolutionaries arising to challenge governmental organizations through appeals for social support from discontented or ideologically converted people.

Toward a Structural and Comparative-Historical Approach

Indeed, if one steps back from the clashes among the leading perspectives on revolution just reviewed, what seems most striking is the sameness of the image of the overall revolutionary process that underlies and informs all three approaches. According to that shared image: First, changes in or affecting societies, social systems, or populations give rise to grievances, social disorientation, or new groups and potentials for collective mobilization. Then there develops a purposive, broadly based movement—coalescing with the aid of ideology and organization—which consciously undertakes to overthrow the existing government, and perhaps the entire social order. Finally, the revolutionary movement fights it out with the "authorities" or the "government" and, if it wins, undertakes to establish its own control, authority, or program of societal transformation. What no one ever seems to doubt is that the basic condition for the occurrence of a revolution is the emergence from society or a people of a deliberate effort, tying together leaders and followers, aimed at overthrowing the existing political or social order. Adherence to this image naturally coaxes even theories intended to be social-structural into social-psychological explanations, for it inexorably pushes analysts' attention toward people's feelings and consciousness—of dissatisfactions and of fundamentally oppositional goals and values—as the central problematic issue in the explanation of revolutions.

But in fact the assumptions about societal order and change that underpin the revolutionary movement image are internally contradictory. If the stability of the core institutions of societies truly rested upon the voluntary support of people who could readily withdraw it and force readjustments if and when those institutions ceased to meet their needs or accord with their values, then revolutions should either happen continually (perhaps every generation, as Thomas Jefferson once proposed) or else, if reform movements were the typical mechanism of adjustment, never at all. On the other hand, if societal order (in general, or in specific types of societies) does *not* rest upon value consensus and/or member satisfactions, if, conversely, institutionalized domination of the many by the few prevails, then revolutions—although according to the existing theoretical perspectives they might be especially "needed" and likely under such circumstances—could hardly develop according to the pattern of the liberal reform movement, in which people coalesce around an explicit program of change and strive to achieve its adoption. For the *normal* functioning of institutionalized domination would surely prevent the emergence of any full-blown, well-organized, and extensively supported movement ideologically and actively committed to revolution. Such a movement would be likely to emerge only *after* a crisis in the normal patterns of state, and perhaps also class, domination, thus rendering the development of such a crisis one of the crucial things to be explained in order to account for revolutions.

Moreover, in any revolutionary crisis, differentially situated and motivated groups become participants in a complex unfolding of multiple conflicts that ultimately give rise to outcomes not originally foreseen or intended by any of the particular groups involved. As the historian Gordon Wood argues:

> It is not that men's motives are unimportant; they indeed make events, including revolutions. But the purposes of men, especially in a revolution, are so numerous, so varied, and so contradictory that their complex interaction produces results that no one intended or could even foresee. It is this interaction and these results that recent historians are referring to when they speak so disparagingly of these "underlying determinants" and "impersonal and inexorable forces" bringing on the Revolution. Historical explanation which does not account for these "forces," which, in other words, relies simply on understanding the conscious intentions of the actors, will thus be limited. [1973:129]

Any valid theory of revolution rests on the possibility and the necessity of the analyst "rising above" the participants' viewpoints to find, across given historical instances, similar institutional and historical-circumstantial patterns in the situations where revolutions have occurred and in the processes by which they have developed.

An explanation of revolutions must find problematic, first, the emergence of a revolutionary situation, wholistically conceived, and second, the complex and unintended intermeshing of the various motivated actions of the differentially situated groups which take part in the revolution—an intermeshing that produces overall changes which never correspond to the original intentions of any one group, no matter how "central" it may seem. One can begin to make sense of such complexity only by focusing simultaneously on the interrelated situations of groups within specified societal institutional nexuses, and the interrelations of societies within dynamic international fields. To take such an impersonal and nonsubjective viewpoint—and one which emphasizes patterns of institutionalized relationships among persons, positions, and groups—is to work from what may in some generic sense be called a structural perspective on sociohistorical reality.

How, then, does one proceed from a generalized commitment to such a social-structural frame of reference to the actual development of explanatory hypotheses about revolutions? Shall we plunge directly from our very general notions about how societies are integrated and what revolutionary processes are like, into an attempt to deduce general propositions about some generic revolutionary process conceived to be possible and similar in all times, places, and types of sociopolitical orders? This sort of generalizing, deductive strategy is currently fashionable in social science, and has been the approach followed by all recent theorists of revolution. Thus, for example, Gurr, Johnson, and Tilly alike have attempted to describe and explain revolutions *directly* in terms of general processes occurring within universal entities, individual or collective: that is, relative deprivation leading to frustration and political violence in aggregates of individuals; strains giving rise to value redefinition in social systems; and the occurrence and resolution of multiple sovereignty in polities.

But when it comes to explaining phenomena such as revolutions, the difficulties with such generalizing, deductive strategies for theory-building are threefold. First, highly general theoretical propositions seem to work best in the social sciences, given their existing levels of theoretical development, only to explain phenomena which can be characterized very simply, if not literally, one-dimensionally. But, as virtually all will agree, revolutions are by nature complex and multidimensional.

Second, if one is to take a social-structural approach toward explaining revolutions, one really must theorize in terms of various specific types of societies, for there is little or nothing of any significance that can be said about the political or socio-economic institutions of all kinds of known human societies lumped together. Moreover all successful revolutions to date have occurred in one or another sort of agrarian state, and nothing is to be gained by ignoring this fact in order to develop a theory putatively capable of explaining revolutions in any sort of society from a band or tribe to an advanced industrial nation. If one wishes to generalize from findings about past revolutions in agrarian states to speculation about future possibilities for revolutions in, say, industrial societies, then the more fruitful way to proceed is to attempt to identify the conceivable functional equivalents of, or alternatives for, the causal patterns that can be directly established for revolutionary transformations of agrarian sociopolitical structures.

Third, a primarily deductive and universalizing mode of theory-building makes no real sense for explaining revolutions, because there have been, by any well-focused definition, only a small number of cases, and all of them, as the etiology of the concept "revolution" implies, have occurred during the era of "modernization," in the last several hundred years of world history (Hatto, 1949; Griewank, 1971; Arendt, 1965:chap. 1; Huntington, 1968:chap. 5). Indeed, modernizing trends operative at international as well as intranational levels—for example, commercialization and industrialization, and the rise of national states and of the European states system—have been intrinsically related both to the causes and consequences of revolutions. Of course, to aid in disentangling the multiple, complex processes of revolutions, the investigator can and must make use of whatever available insights there are about human behavior and social processes in general. But the revolutionary processes themselves should be assumed to be, in part, specific to particular, nonuniversal types of sociopolitical structures, and, for the rest, specific to particular sorts of world-historical circumstances.

A critic might well argue at this point that, precisely because they are so few in number and tied to particular world-historical developments, revolutions as such should be studied only by "narrative historians," leaving social scientists free to theorize about more general phenomena. But no such drastic response is necessary. Revolutions *can* be treated as "a theoretical subject." To generalize inductively about them and verify hypotheses about their causes and consequences one can employ the comparative historical method, with selected national historical trajectories as the units of comparison. According to this method—which has a long and distinguished pedigree in social science—one looks for concomitant variations, contrasting cases where the phenomenon one seeks to explain is present with cases where it is absent, controlling in the process for as many sources of extraneous variation as possible by contrasting positive and negative instances which are otherwise as similar as possible (Nagel, 1950; Sewell, 1967; Smelser, 1971; Smelser, unpublished, 1966; Lijphart, 1971).

As the mode of multivariate analysis to which one necessarily resorts when there are too many variables and not enough cases (Smelser, unpublished, 1966; Lijphart, 1971), comparative analysis is likely to remain the only scientific tool available to the macrosociologist who is interested in national political conflicts and developments, and who is also sensitive to the enormous impacts of world-contextual variables upon national developments (see Hopkins and Wallerstein, 1967). Given the combined variability of "internal" patterns and external situations, analyses of phenomena such as revolutions will make sense only for carefully delineated categories containing a few cases apiece. In contrast to the past practice of the "natural historians" (Edwards, 1927; Brinton, 1938), there should be included in any study both positive and negative cases, so that hypotheses about the causes of the phenomena under investigation can be checked against cases where that phenomenon did not occur (e.g., Skocpol, 1976). Ultimately, cases can be grouped and regrouped in different ways according to what questions are being investigated or according to what hypotheses are being tested, so that the end result of proliferating historically sensitive comparisons will be far richer than the products of studies which try to pretend that historical developments and world contexts are irrelevant.

What About Marxism?

On the face of it, there is an already well-established theoretical tradition—Marxism—that seems to meet the need for a historically grounded, social-structural approach to explaining revolutions. In many respects, Marxist explanations of revolutions are exemplary. First, the general image of revolutionary processes to which Marxists adhere emphasizes the importance of social-structural contradictions in generating revolutionary crises:

> At a certain stage of their development the material forces of production in society come into conflict with the existing relations of production, or—what is but a legal expression of the same thing—with the property relations within which they had been at work before. From forms of development of the forces of production these relations turn into their fetters. Then comes the period of social revolution. [Marx, in Feuer, 1959:43–44]

Second, Marxists do not assume that all revolutions are, for theoretical purposes, the same. Instead Marxists distinguish between "bourgeois" and "socialist" revolutions according to which mode of production, "feudal" or "bourgeois," is being transformed, and among particular variants of each type of revolution through concrete historical analyses of the forces and relations of production and class structures of the various particular societies in which revolutions have occurred. Finally, Marxists do not fail to treat revolutions as intrinsically related to broader processes of large-scale social change, for they argue that both the causes and consequences of revolutions are directly related to socio-economic developments.

Moreover, some very rich social-historical studies of revolutions have been published in recent years by American social scientists operating within Marxist-derived theoretical frames of reference. Both Barrington Moore, Jr., in his *Social Origins of Dictatorship and Democracy* (1966), and Eric R. Wolf, in his *Peasant Wars of the Twentieth Century* (1969), extended Marxist concepts and hypotheses to analyze revolutions in predominately agrarian countries. Specifically, Moore and Wolf developed path-breaking hypotheses about the historical and social-structural conditions that determine when and how agrarian classes, especially landlords on the one hand, and peasant communities on the other, will engage in collective actions that affect the outcomes of societal political upheavals which occur as agrarian countries are subjected to the effects of capitalist developments. Since peasant revolts have played key roles in every historical instance of social revolution, the advances achieved by Moore and Wolf can and must be incorporated into any historically oriented, social-structural theory of revolutions.

Nevertheless, Marxist-derived theories of revolutionary processes cannot be uncritically accepted as rigorous, empirically validated explanations. The reason why can be straightforwardly stated: The basic Marxist explanation sketch—which argues that revolutions are caused by socio-economic developments that lead to the outbreak of class struggles which, in turn, transform and mark the divide between distinct modes of production—simply does not succeed in laying bare the overall logic of actual historical revolutions. Thus the roles of peasants and urban lower strata, not to mention the dominant strata, in the French, Russian, Mexican, and Chinese revolutions cannot be understood without detailed analysis of the class positions of the various groups, yet political struggles central to these revolutions cannot be comprehended in strictly class terms. Likewise, the causes and consequences of revolutions cannot be comprehended without knowledge of modes of production and their dynamics, yet revolutionary situations involve political-military as well as economic "contradictions." Nor does the juxtaposition of modes of production—feudal/bourgeois for the French and Mexican revolutions, and bourgeois/socialist for the Russian and Chinese—at all adequately characterize the transformations wrought by these revolutions.

Marxist-inspired investigators have rested content with applying or modifying the existing conceptual categories to illuminate the class and group conflicts that occur during revolutions, and have not actually put to empirical test explicit Marxist propositions about the causes of revolutions—using the comparative historical method of checking common patterns identified for positive cases against evidence from similar negative cases. As a result it has been possible for them to downplay for theoretical purposes the very central role of the state in revolutions. In accounting for the causes of revolutions the theoretical emphasis is always placed upon economic developments and class contradictions, while the capacities of political rulers, given the state organizations at hand, to cope with international pressures and, internally, with upper-class political dissidence and lower-class rebellions, are matters often treated descriptively, but never examined theoretically with an eye to identifying the social-structural conditions that might systematically affect such political capacities. Marxist scholars have failed to notice that causal variables referring to the strength and structure of states and the relations of state organizations to class structures may discriminate between cases of successful revolution and cases of failure or nonoccurrence far better than do variables referring to class structures and patterns of economic development alone. Moreover, in their characterizations of the outcomes of revolutions, Marxist-oriented scholars emphasize changes in class structures and even very long-run economic developments, while virtually ignoring the often much more striking and immediate transformations that occur in the structure and functions of state organizations such as armies and administrations, and in the relations between the state and social classes. And, again, this has meant that they have missed identifying the distinctive political-institutional changes that set revolutions apart from nonrevolutionary patterns of national development.

To pull together, then, the strands of the argument made in the course of this review essay: I am suggesting that substantial progress can be made toward explaining revolutions only through a new theoretical strategy—one which synthesizes *an historically grounded, social-structural style of explanation,* akin to the Marxist approach to explaining revolution but differing in substantive emphases, *with a comparative historical method of hypothesis testing,* akin to the statistical techniques idealized by contemporary social scientists, but specifically tailored to handle many variables when there are but a small number of cases. By thus combining, on the one hand, that fusion of theoretical understanding and historical relevance characteristic of a great and enduring macro-theoretical tradition with, on the other hand, the concern of contemporary social science for rigorous hypothesis testing, students of revolution can avoid the twin dangers of abstract, irrelevant theorizing and empirical inadequacy that have long plagued explanatory efforts in this area of inquiry.

V

To Appraise the Resurgence of Ethnicity

10

The Power Basis of Ethnic Conflict in American Society

James E. Blackwell

DURING THE PAST DECADE, the American society has witnessed what may be called a "resurgence of ethnicity" among ethnic groups of European ancestry. This new ethnicity was preceded by an articulation of a sense of ethnicity by blacks and Third World or non-European minorities in the United States. Some sociologists, such as Milton Gordon (1964:24–25), argued quite forcefully that "the sense of ethnicity . . . has proved to be hardy. . . . It has survived in various forms and with various names, but it has not perished." Whether we argue that ethnicity has survived but in an almost dormant state or that what we see today among European ethnic groups represents a resurgence of ethnic identification, may be less important than a higher fact: that this resurgence of ethnic identification, unity, and solidarity among Americans of European descent has occurred precisely at the time that blacks and Third World minorities have asserted their claim for an increased share of power and those values we cherish in American society. It is a reaction to presumed gains accrued from black ethnicity. The convergence of competing claims for available resources has brought into sharp focus the power basis of ethnic conflicts in our society.

It can be argued that a strong relationship exists between power—specifically, the inequality of power distribution—and the escalation of various forms of social conflict between ethnic groups in American society. It is, then, my thesis that *the most fundamental variables which undergird conflicts in the American society are those of differential power and race.* It is the unequal distribution of power, especially between racial

179

groups, and to a lesser degree between ethnic groups, that is the critical dimension of interethnic competition and of hierarchical arrangements between the races. It is useful to at least recognize the importance of (1) intranational and cross-national comparisons of ethnicity; (2) the fact that all ethnic groups have neither identical histories nor historical legacies in the United States; (3) the existence of certain continuities between the social, economic, and political experiences of Third World groups and ethnic groups of European descent in the United States (Glazer, 1971); (4) the fact that all ethnic groups in the United States initially suffered at the hands of the powerful dominant Anglo-Saxon ruling class; and (5) the observation that there are similarities today between blacks and Third World groups as well as between these minorities and the powerless whites, and that the powerlessness of each of these groups is admittedly relative. Notwithstanding these observations, because of space considerations, I have chosen to specify the prototypicality of blacks in the United States for other Third World groups. Thus, uniqueness of blacks as an ethnic group is stressed in relation to white ethnics of European origin.

Hence, in my view, black experience in America is distinctive and unique. The differences between black experience and that of white ethnic groups in American life outweigh what Nathan Glazer (1971) has discussed as "continuities" between these groups. The uniqueness of black experience lies in a number of factors and conditions including its nature and quality; the racial component of black identity; the persistence of social control mechanisms over all aspects of social living among blacks by the dominant group; the manipulation of power by the dominant group over blacks for its advantage; perpetuation of categorization of the black population and the treatment of blacks as an internally colonized population.

Several sociologists have addressed the power basis of intergroup relations or have developed power theory to explain other dimensions of human interaction and behavior. Among these are Robert Bierstedt (1951), H. M. Blalock (1960, 1967), Richard Schermerhorn (1970), William J. Wilson (1973a), Tamotsu Shibutani and Kian M. Kwan (1972), and, more recently, Milton Gordon (1975) as well as this writer in his volume on the black community (Blackwell, 1975b). Perhaps the most visible recent proponent for the application of the internal colonialism model to interpret black experience in the United States has been Robert Blauner (1969).[1] The seminal work of Michael Hechter (1974) on internal colonialism is also acknowledged. Thus, I am indebted to these writers for their original ideas employed in my theoret-

---

[1] Blauner acknowledges his indebtedness to Kenneth Clark and Harold Cruse for their ideas on this theory.

ical interpretations which follow. Here it should be stressed that I see a theoretical convergence in power analysis and internal colonialism when applied to the situation of black Americans that is not of equal utility when interpreting the experiences of white ethnic groups in America. This point is amplified later in this discussion.

Power Theory: One of the more apparent differences between dominant and subordinate groups is that the dominant groups possess superior power in contrast to the relative powerlessness of subordinate groups. That power is manifested in the dominant group's control over the decision-making processes of the society as a whole, and to some degree it is reflected in the extension of control over the decision-making processes observed within subgroups, particularly as they relate to structural conditions within the larger society. It is manifested in the ability of the dominant group to establish the legitimacy of its normative structure as the model governing acceptable behavior, to change laws to suit their needs, and to apply appropriate sanctions against those who overtly violate those norms. It is apparent in the ability of the dominant group to reward individuals whose behavior approximates the norms and values it espouses and to deny access to scarce values to those persons and groups regarded as outsiders, pariahs, or unworthy. Dominant group members share in what Melvin Tumin once called "an ideology of entitlements"—those values commonly shared among them by virtue of their pre-eminent position vis-à-vis the subordinate groups. But, significantly, dominant groups tend to maximize their power, institutionalize and legitimate it to such a degree that they, in the words of Vander Zanden (1972:92), "actualize their claim," to a larger share of the scarce values and highly prized resources of the society. Thus, dominance is in itself equated with power, and the absence of power subordinates individuals and groups in position, status, privilege, and in their unequal access to shared values and scarce resources of the society. Dominant group culture becomes imperial while subordinate group culture is perceived as weak, inferior, primitive, deprived, or nonexistent. Moreover, the actualization of the imperial quality of dominant group culture can be assured by virtue of the capacity of the dominant group to use force and violence if necessary. Hence, this potential or threat of force and violence, not necessarily their implementation, fosters acceptable degrees of confomity even as normative standards undergo change within the social system.

Similarly, this potential use of force and violence, as well as legitimated authority, enables the power group to promulgate legal systems for governance and the regulation of normative behavior. Sometimes, as in the United States, laws have been employed to establish boundary-maintenance devises between the powerful and those who possessed lesser power within a hierarchy of group ranks. For example, some restrictive covenants, various housing ordinances and Van Sweiergenan agreements, and violence have made some ethnic groups less equal than others. And they have denied blacks equal access to housing. The Jim Crow legislation of the first half of the twentieth century placed blacks firmly at the bottom of the social ladder in relation to all white groups in the United States. Such legal constraints were buttressed by the use or the threat of use of both force and violence against overt dissenters. However, it should be noted that the use of force or even its potential use requires group consensus. It cannot be sustained for long without group approbation, whether explicit or implied by silence. Few problems are encountered in that attainment when disfavored subordinate groups fail to adhere to normative expectations, "step out of place"—or threaten the position of privilege groups in power. Thus, the observations made by Shibutani and Kwan (1972) that power or dominant groups have "control over economic resources, means of violence, and communication channels" is of special salience here.

Of equal importance is the position taken by Bierstedt (1951) that power involves considerably more: It is derived from numbers, in some instances, a high degree of social organization, as well as resources. But the possession of resources is not a sufficient precondition for power. This is so whether we are speaking of such resources as money, prestige, education, superior technology, expertise labor, the ability to employ violence to fulfill one's desires, or the use of deceit or fraud. Power is also, as Blalock (1960) has demonstrated, a function of the effective mobilization of the resources that a group possesses. And it is only when those resources are effectively mobilized that a dominant group can compel adherence to its normative structure by subordinate and powerless groups.

Among the consequences of mobilized resources are the maximization of power among those who already possess it and a struggle for power among the powerless or among those whose power is limited by the dominant group. It is, then, this inequality of power or its unequal distribution among groups and subgroups within a society that is fundamental and basic to intergroup conflict. It fosters disruptive relationships and, if it leads to what Richard Schermerhorn (1970) calls a "pure form of conflict," it is likely to prevent full integration or assimilation of minority groups into the larger society. The struggle for power between dominant and subordinate groups, as well as between the various subordinate groups who want to move along the pole toward dominant group power, escalates as all contenders engage in a contentious battle for what Blalock (1960) and Wilson (1973:16–17) agree are constraint, pressure and competitive resources. We are referring to what are essentially behavioral inducements—abilities to persuade and influence without the actualization of threats—the essence of political and economic power—the use of boycotts, strikes, demonstrations, social and political disruption—as well as the use of an expertise and skills or knowledge that others want.

Some groups are, for one reason or another, more successful than others in the use of the various types of resources for effecting changes in power relations. Consequently, this success carries into movement in the direction of the entitlements possessed by the dominant group. Others are not as successful, for special reasons, and hence remain near the polar opposite of the dominant group, notwithstanding that some of their members do move more rapidly along the power continuum. White ethnic groups in America have been more successful in this endeavor as well as in societal integration and assimilation. But, if Andrew Greeley (1975) is correct, many of them have paid a heavy price for their assimilation and their success in the attainment of relative power.

European Ethnics in American Society

A brief review of the experience of white ethnics in American society may be instructive at this point. Although the conditions of economic deprivation, political and religious oppression, and the psychological disabilities which compelled Europeans to emigrate to the United States during the nineteenth and early twentieth centuries are recognized, two essential facts are inescapable in their importance for the success of European immigrants in moving toward the dominant group pole: the fact of their *race,* since they were white, and *the voluntary character of their immigration.* While it is true that they came in large numbers and some possessed a high degree of social organization, the degree of social organization, for example, was not uniformly high among all ethnic groups of European descent. Nevertheless, European white ethnics had the advantage of being white and, in many instances, of having come from nations of some degree of power and respect among the community of nations then recognized as "civilized." These remarks are cautioned by the observation that both the sovereign nations of Great Britain and Germany did have a habit of sending to America their derelicts, paupers, and convicts—and it is reasonable to assume that many of these people in time would become members of the dominant groups with maximum power over Indians who were here first and of blacks who preceded white ethnics. In the case of white ethnic groups, it was possible that the external condition, engendered by the respect for the nations of their origins, helped to facilitate comparatively better treatment in the United States than that accorded Native Indians, blacks, and other Third World groups.

The voluntary character of their immigration suggests that, despite the push factors which led to their departure from Europe, white ethnic groups had a choice—though admittedly the options open to them were not always palatable, as for example the limited options open to the Irish during and following the potato famine. But there were options as to which country to select as their new homes since, as the evidence shows, the Irish did not all enter the United States upon leaving Ireland. Some did immigrate to Canada (cf. Greeley and McCready, 1975; Glazer and Moynihan, 1963). In both the nineteenth and twentieth centuries, some white ethnics went to other European nations where opportunities were open to them, and some still do, in varying degrees. As white, voluntary immigrants, they were and have always been a free people, entering as both equal and unequal members of the dominant white group.

The Formation of Ethnic Communities

Initially, white ethnic groups were encouraged to enter the cities, particularly in the North and East to provide labor in an industrializing and modernizing society. They were encouraged to move westward to help open up new areas and establish new settlements and to provide a larger population base for political purposes. In this process, these groups were attracted to each other because of the ethnolinguistic homogenization and the commonality of their culture—their language, religion, national origins, life styles, and social institutions. Within these communities, established within the cities and in farming areas initially by a process of natural selection,[2] members of each group could find comfort in practicing a familiar culture. Hence we are familiar with the rise of ethnic language newspapers and of ethnically oriented churches, schools, banks, clubs, recreational facilities, and meeting halls in which the idea of ethnic politics was formulated, nurtured, and given substance. The persistence of these structures exemplifies the functional basis of ethnic solidarity.

Within this context, the traditions, values, and social norms of the social system of origin would be protected and perpetuated as these new and sometimes reluctant Americans came to terms with an unfamiliar and often hostile American social system. Individual members found themselves torn between those centripetal forces which pulled them toward institutional closure and parallelism, ethnic cohesion, and

[2] See Shibutani and Kwan, 1972:234, for an elaboration of this process.

those centrifugal forces which attracted them away from their own in-group toward the dominant group culture and institutions as the norm. Moreover, the highly visible distinctiveness of their culture—their language, customs, dress, and social institutions—set them apart from the dominant group. This also fostered an ideology of ethnic solidarity in the face of attack from the outside. Hence the persistence of ethnic communities is also a reaction to external forces.

Further, the natural selection which initially led to the formation of ethnic areas and neighborhoods now gave way either to the involuntary formation and perpetuation of ethnic communities because they could not move into other residential areas, or to the voluntary continuation of such communities because of the satisfaction derived from living together with people of a common ancestry and culture. In many instances, these communities became a sacred and particularized territory with specific boundaries—open exclusively to members of one specific ethnic group or persons who married exogamously—from which people emigrated voluntarily as they became assimilated into mainstream American society, or within which they lived the remainder of their lives. The rigidity of such communities is in evidence today in a city like Boston with its Irish South Boston and its Italian North End. Other cities, such as Cleveland, have their Little Italys, Little Bohemias, Slavic communities, Jewish enclaves, and similar areas inhabited almost exclusively by a single ethnic group.

As blacks emigrated from the rural South to the urban North, not only did they succeed some European ethnic groups in residential areas, but for a time blacks and these groups coexisted in the same neighborhoods. The relationship between blacks and these groups ranged from toleration to overt hostility. However, the hostile reactions to these new black urban emigrants were dominant in the labor force in which blacks were now perceived as a threat to the economic security and upward mobility of ethnic minorities such as the Irish.

The pre–Civil War Irish were initially relegated near the bottom of the economic, political, and social scale. They were never the lumpenproletariats of the economic structure, since that position was reserved for the black population, Native Americans, and, later, other Third World minorities. Nevertheless, as economic competition between blacks and the Irish and other nineteenth-century European immigrants intensified, racial and ethnic riots also escalated as whites sought to protect their gains against the intrusion of blacks and European white ethnics. There is one factor of prime importance in any comparison between blacks and European white ethnics, and that is the factor of remuneration for labor. Although blacks were not always remunerated for their labor, as in the case of slaves, whenever they were paid, their wages were more often than not far below the level of the European white ethnics. This inequity existed even when the two groups engaged in the same type of work.

As the Irish climbed the power ladder, other immigrant groups replaced them near the bottom of the occupational structure. As Greeley (1973) indicated, the Irish had an advantage of language and an understanding of the political processes in America. This enabled them to more effectively use the strategy of ethnic politics to their advantage and to seize political control of many American cities. The Irish, like other European ethnic groups who followed them, were in a position to maximize political advantage, and to make even the civil service work for them. Other groups such as the Greeks have also used the political institutions to effectively promote their collective interests. Literally, all ethnic groups and collectives have acted in their own best interests in making decisions regarding employment, occupational choices, wage distribution, the allocation of resources, and group protection when they had the opportunity to do so. And they still do! Thus, the initial practice of hiring relatives and friends still exists in the construction industry, in specialized trades such as plumbing and electrical repair, and in higher education. At the same time, it might be noted, as blacks gain a measure of political control or when they are in a position to follow the same path that European ethnic groups followed, and to give better credence to Glazer's view of "continuities," there is an outcry for the application of universalistic criteria in each of these processes. It should be noted that I have absolutely no objection to the application of universalistic criteria as long as they are not particularized! There appears to be, however, a convenient application of such criteria for discriminatory and exclusionary purposes and not for the necessary maintenance of high standards and not for affirmative action purposes. Therefore, the enforcement of corrective affirmative action policies may indeed be the best prevention against particularism and exclusion.

Of course, other ethnic groups followed the Irish and were met with similar, if not worse, forms of prejudice and discrimination. Many Jews, Italians, and Slavs from eastern and southern Europe were a darker people marked by language and cultural differences. Almost at the same time, the old immigrants in the West had become threatened by the competition posed by the Chinese. And it is here that, for the first time, these colored minorities are categorically treated as an inferior and subordinated race of people, against whom the force of law should be directed to curtail their immigration to the United States and to speed up their departure from this country. Racial considerations promoted the Chinese Exclusion Act of 1882 and racial considerations, as then interpreted, were the compulsion to Congress to enact a series of anti-immigrant legislation between 1917 and 1924. Similarly, racial considerations were the prime movers behind Jim Crow legislation to protect white supremacy in the United States.

However, like their predecessors from northern and western Europe, the new immigrants also had options opened to them, since the inevitability of their assimilation was taken for granted. Nevertheless, it is obvious that not all immigrant group members sought either eventual or immediate assimilation. The diversity within these groups can be exemplified by the differences between Israel Zangwill's famous celebration of the "melting pot" and Horace Kallen and Issac Berkson's prolific discourses on cultural pluralism among American Jews. In either case, a conscious decision was made to use the demands of the dominant group normative structure to the advantage of the ethnic group as a special-interest group in search of higher status, acceptance, and eventual power.

Subsequently, the old and new voluntary immigrant groups argue in the language of Irving Kristol (1966) that they made it, and maybe the blacks too will make it in time, since "the Negro of today is the immigrant of yesterday." That is, of course, a highly optimistic view that is not fully supported by the evidence. Further, the times and conditions are different and the European white ethnics do not carry the mark of racial subjugation, nor was their low status more than a transitory phenomenon.

However, many formerly low-status white ethnic groups now reflect the negative attitudes and stereotypes toward blacks that were once more specifically directed against them as a group. Stereotypes die hard! Similarly, "ethnophaulisms" also tend to persist. Unfortunately, as Greeley noted in a recent *New York Times* article (1975) and from my own research findings (Blackwell, 1975*b*), these groups may not recognize that old stereotypes against them still prevail in the mass media. Merely reflect on the "blacksploitation" films and ethnic TV programs and the likes of Superfly, Shaft, Kojack, The Mack, Columbo, Baretta, Petrocelli, Sanford and Son, and All in the Family. Aside from their perpetuation of stereotypes, increasing utilization of blacks on stage, screen, and television called attention to the immense ethnic diversity in this country and, in a sense, precipitated the arrival of the ethnic dimension in entertainment.

What, then, are those attitudes of white ethnic immigrant groups toward blacks? It should be stressed that the attitudes lack uniformity. They also reflect the frustrations, fears, and insecurities of groups who are still uncertain about their position in the American social structure.

Perhaps nowhere was this situation more apparent than in the events leading to the local and, especially, the national elections of 1972. The historic alliance between blacks and Jews, already badly eroded by a series of events and situations to be identified below, was all but severed by the end of the election. Much attention had been given to the position of American Jews regarding support for Israel and their support for candidates depending upon their identification as "hard" or "soft" on Israel. But Irving Louis Horowitz (1972) warned that the real issue for Jews in the 1972 election was not Israel but "their survival as an ethnic group in their own right." In his view, this identity would permit Jews to join coalitions of blacks, poor Catholics, Poles, Slovaks, urban poor, and college youths. The choice for Jews, as Horowitz saw it, was

> whether the historic sense of equity, built up by the strong and powerful identification from the New Deal period to the New Frontier period, would yield to a sense of fear and a sentiment of loathing for the newer minority groups, particularly the blacks and Spanish-speaking groups, who have gotten beyond philanthropy in their dealings with Jews. There can be no question of this as the main issue. [1972:32]

Horowitz further stated his view that to assert that Jews would vote solely on the basis of a candidate's position as "hard" or "soft" on Israel and not on the basis of the domestic interest of American Jews, such as their interest in New York's Forest Hills housing project, would be a cruel disguise. A similar conclusion was reached by Jack Nusan Porter (1972) in his discussion of the trend toward conservatism among American Jews. He allowed that one reason for the Jewish swing to Nixon in the 1972 presidential election was the feeling among Jews that "McGovern will take from the middle class (read: Jews) and give to the blacks, the Puerto Ricans, and the young. The old zero-sum game: What they get, we lose." [3]

The antiblack position among white ethnic groups is noted by Martin Kilson in the Glazer-Moynihan volume, *Ethnicity: Theory and Experience*. Kilson points to a study by William Schneider of the political attitudes of 600 Jewish voters in New York's 1972 Democratic mayoralty primary. He examined the characteristics of supporters of Mario Biaggi, who was regarded as the foremost proponent of "white neo-ethnicity in city politics." He found that "the hard-core Jewish supporters of Mario Biaggi . . . were typically older, poorer, and less educated than the typical Jewish voter. . . . Some 62 percent of Biaggi's Jewish supporters believed the city government is doing too much for blacks and minorities; 84 percent supported the militant demonstrations against low-income public housing in the middle-class Forest Hills district, and 90 percent supported the boycotts by Catholics and Jewish parents and pupils of schools slated for integration in the

---

[3] For further information on the historic relationship between blacks and Jews and explanations of the current conflicts between these two groups, see Ben Halpern, 1971, and Howe, 1971.

Canarise school district" (Kilson, 1975:264). Kilson also notes that "the strength of the ideological element in the appeal of white neo-ethnicity is underlined by the fact that although 65 percent of the Jews in Schneider's survey were characterized as 'liberal,' more than half (52 percent) of the 'liberals' supported the demonstration against public housing in Forest Hills and 51 percent of these backed the Canarsie school boycotts" (p. 263). In contrast to the liberalism and support of blacks indicated among the Jewish population during the early sixties, the Schneider evidence appears to support Jack Porter's conclusions which noted a significant shift in attitudes toward a more conservative position. A similar type of conflict could be observed in the clashes between blacks and Italians over the attempts of black nationalists to construct Kawaida Towers in what was regarded as an Italian district in Newark.

How can this shift in attitudes, especially among Jews, be explained? Murray Freidman contends that the shift in Jewish sentiments is based in an interlocking network of complex factors including those mentioned above, the school conflicts in Ocean Hill–Brownsville, as well as others. He points to problems of changing special interests, conflicting values, an emerging black bourgeoisie who saw Jews as an impediment to their progress (since Jews were prominent among ghetto merchants, landlords, social workers, civil rights officials, and government bureaucrats) and to Jews threatened by the new black militancy, while blacks in turn perceived Jews as a threat to their own upward mobility (Friedman, 1973:150).

This situation was exacerbated by the anti-Semitism revealed among some blacks in the school and housing conflicts in New York; by attacks against Jewish merchants in various cities; by the fostering of an ideology of anti-Semitism among militant black extremists; by the anti-Israel resolution adopted at the Gary, Indiana, Black Power Conference; by the support of many blacks for the Arab position in disputes with Israel; and by what Earl Rabb (1969:30) calls the "Jewish nightmare": the "possible alliance between white upper classes and the black underclass at the expense of the Jews." Friedman (1973:157) also notes that "Jewish attitudes toward blacks are sharply divided along class lines." It is his contention that the upper classes among Jews remain more sympathetic and liberal in their orientation toward blacks but that the greatest degree of resistance is found among the lower middle class who "send their children to public and not to private or suburban schools, or to municipal colleges instead of the elite universities" and people most likely to encounter blacks in their daily lives on the job, in the neighborhood, in small businesses, or in taxis. In recent years, however, it should be noted that special efforts have been made among black leaders, especially Bayard Rustin, to demonstrate that the anti-

Semitic sentiments attributed to various black Americans is not uniformly distributed among black people. Joint conferences have been recently sponsored between various traditionally black and integrated civil rights organizations and Jewish leaders and organizations in such cities as New York and Chicago to foster cooperation between blacks and Jews and to re-establish the alliances that worked effectively in the fifties and sixties to promote mutual interests.

The Uniqueness of the Black Experience in America

Earlier on, I stated that the black experience in America was unique and is in a large measure predicated on the magnitude of the race factor in fostering powerlessness among the black American population. This position should be amplified at this point.

As has been noted, a major difference between blacks and white ethnic groups is the fact that the immigration of blacks to America was involuntary. The choices open to white ethnics were not available to those 15 to 20 million blacks who were captured, sold, tricked, and deceived into slavery. Except for a few black indentured servants and some free men of color, the overwhelming majority of blacks were not financially remunerated for their labor. Furthermore, there is voluminous evidence to show that the institution of slavery supported the ideology of white supremacy and its accompanying white group dominance. It also assured acquisition of power resources by whites as well as their utilization in social, political, and economic exploitation of the black population. White supremacy justified categorical treatment of blacks because of their presumed biological and cultural inferiority. It established boundary-maintenance systems which separated blacks from whites and endorsed the privilege of white men to initiate sexual unions with black women whenever desired.

Structural conditions imposed by slavery induced the first system of stratification among blacks as found in the bifurcation between house slaves and field hands. I have argued elsewhere that the type of environment in which house slaves (largely a mulatto-octoroon group) lived was conducive to their internalization of dominant-group norms and values, and hence made them more acceptable to the dominant group and its rewards than was the case among field hands. On the other hand,

> the field hands were likely to retain their African heritage. . . . [T]he plantation structure crystallized the division between master and slave

and bifurcated the slave social system. In each system institutions arose to meet certain socially defined needs. The differences among the institutions within these basic stratification subsystems were a function of the intensity of cultural homogenization or isolation between slaves and masters. The differences were greater among field slaves. . . . As ethnolinguistic units remained relatively intact, institutional differences between the superordinates and the subordinates were maximum. In both cases there occurred unique adaptations to the American experience that formed the framework for the development of parallel institutions and a form of pluralism. [Blackwell, 1975*b*:8–9]

Hence the formation of the black community was reactive in the sense that it was formed in response to the forces of white racism against black people and the success in the utilization of the power of the dominant group to effect social, political, and economic boundaries between black and white people. This was accomplished through the promulgation of slave codes, black codes during post-Reconstruction, Jim Crow legislation, intimidation, terror, force, and violence. All of these means enabled the dominant group to subject blacks to categorical treatment, prejudice, and discrimination, while at the same time mounting their economic and political gains at the expense of blacks (cf. Glenn, 1963; Cutright, 1965).

By virtue of discriminatory regulatory norms and manipulation of the legal institutions by whites, in order to maximize the power advantage and privilege of the white population, blacks in America became increasingly restricted to geographical and residential areas within which a segregated institutional pattern was fostered and a black culture was nurtured.

Significantly, this separation also permitted blacks to be treated as an internal colony, manipulated and controlled by white administrators and caretakers.

The Application of Internal Colonialism Model to the Black Experience

The experiences of blacks in relationship to the dominant white population in the Unites States are comparable to an internal colony in relation to a "mother country." Especially does this view seem supported if we look at the conditions and experiences of blacks from their arrival in America to the present time, and if we are not parochial in our observations of the conditions of blacks in northern and western ghettoes. There are, for instance, striking similarities between the conditions of blacks on slave plantations and the conditions of blacks in the concrete ghettos of the inner cities of America—whether North or South, East or West. In both cases, their administrators are white outsiders. Their power is limited by a dominant group that is external to their immediate residential area. They cannot depend upon an external power of respected nations in Africa to intervene in their behalf. Neither is it likely that the Arab oil barons will withhold oil from the United States in order to exact guarantees that the rights and privileges of the black ethnic Americans will be safeguarded.

How, then, are the administrative control, and control over scarce values, allocation of resources, means of production, and distribution of services and goods by the dominant white population evidence to support the view of an internally colonized condition or state? The following illustrations illuminate that evidence.

First, police administrators are more likely to be white than black. "Throughout the country, from city to city, the proportion of blacks on the police force is considerably lower than their proportion in the urban population. . . . In Washington, D.C., where blacks constitute 71.1 percent of the total population, only about 25 percent of its 4,409-member police force is black" (Blackwell, 1975b:257). (But they constitute less than 5 percent of all officers on the Washington police force) In Detroit, which has a black population of approximately 42 percent, only 20 percent of its 4,500-member police force is black; Atlanta is more than 51 percent black and 22 percent of its police force is black; New York City has a 22 percent black population but only 7 percent of its 30,000-member police force is black; and in Philadelphia, blacks comprise more than a third of the total population but only 17 percent of the police force (Blackwell, 1975b:257). Hence, across the nation, as Wilson (1973b:407) states, "barely 2 percent of the correctional officers are black or Spanish-speaking despite the fact that the urban nonwhite population constitutes more than 60 percent of the inmate population in the nation's jails and prisons. Most of the lower-ranking prison officials, such as guards, belong to the social class elements that are most resentful of, and antagonistic toward, blacks. . . ."

Similarly, data on various branches of the American military also show a pattern of rulership incumbency in authority positions by whites in relation to black members. For example, blacks constitute 15.1 percent of the Army's population, but only 3.9 percent of Army officers are black. Blacks comprise 12.5 percent of the Marines, but only 1.5 percent of officers in the Marines are black. The figures for the Air Force are 10.8 percent and 1.7 percent, respectively, while in the U.S. Navy, a mere 5.7 percent of its members are black and less than 1 percent of its officers are black. In other words, a disproportionate number of officers who command the decision-making processes in the American military are white (Blackwell, 1975:240–241).

Second, an examination of major structural elements of the society also reveal the scope of administration from the outside. In July 1975, the U.S. Census Bureau reported an unemployment rate among blacks that almost doubled that of the white population.[4] However, in some cities the national unemployment rate among blacks of 13.7 percent rises to more than 25 percent, and among black teenagers it reaches about 50 percent in some places (Detroit, for instance).

The 1975 census data also indicate that the median income of black families was about 58 percent of that of white families and reportedly remained stable between 1973 and 1974. Robert Hill, chief of the Urban League's research bureau, takes sharp exception to that interpretation following his analysis of census data. He indicates that the proportion of black middle-income families dropped sharply from one fourth to one fifth between 1973 and 1974 and, further, that the current economic crisis has affected the black population far more seriously than is currently reported in most areas. He points to the disproportionate number of layoffs of blacks and the less likelihood for unemployed black workers to receive unemployment compensation. At the same time, the proportion of white multiple wage earners increased, while that of black wage earners decreased. Further, Hill shows that the black unemployment rate has not been under 6 percent in the last two decades. Thus, it is easier to understand why blacks comprise about 30 percent of all poverty-stricken persons in the United States. (Cf. Delaney, 1975; Hill, 1975.)

Third, across the nation, school systems and school boards are likely to be controlled by nonblacks even in cities in which black children comprise a major proportion of the school population. Black teachers and school principals are underrepresented in the system, and one of the dysfunctional consequences of school desegregation in the South is the excessive number of black principals who have either lost their jobs entirely, been demoted to classroom teacher or, in some instances, offered jobs as janitors, having been replaced by white school principals, and administrators (Blackwell, 1975*b*:108–9). In the North, few black teachers and administrators were ever employed. The situation there seems to be improving only in those cities under court order to hire more black and other minority-group professionals.

The same situation applies to the level of college and universities. Perhaps the most significant problem now is one of differential access of blacks and other minority-group students to graduate and professional schools. In a recent study (Blackwell, 1975*b*), I have pointed to this problem and demonstrated the relationship between problems of

[4] The October 1975 issue of *Employment and Earnings,* published by the Bureau of Labor, reported a national unemployment rate of 14.9 percent for blacks and 8.1 percent for the nation as a whole.

access and the number of black professionals produced. The latest available evidence shows that only 1.4 percent of all engineers are black; one of every 456 American Ph.D.'s is black; 2.5 percent of all dentists, 1.5 percent of lawyers, 1 percent of historians, physicists, biologists, and chemists with doctorates are black; and only 2.2 percent of all allied health professionals are black. It is apparent that control over access to institutions of higher learning is a factor of primary salience affecting the supply of blacks with graduate and professional degrees.

Fourth, there is also considerable evidence to support my position that the greater share of property, the housing market in predominantly black areas and in areas into which blacks would like to move, as well as the ownership of stores and business establishments, and commercial radio and television stations which influence the $51 billion consumer market among blacks—all are controlled and manipulated by the dominant white power structure. In addition, residential segregation in all parts of the country facilitates that manipulation and control by the white power structure and enables blacks to be treated as an internal colony whose services redound to the benefit of the dominant group.

For example, the 163,000 businesses owned by blacks represent a mere 2 percent of all enterprises in the United States. Black businesses tend to be concentrated in retailing, selected services, burial establishments, insurance, contract construction, real estate, and small "Mom and Pop" stores. A further examination of ownership patterns among some of such enterprises shows that (1) blacks own less than 2 percent of all construction businesses, (2) 0.2 percent of wholesale trade establishments, (3) less than 2 percent of retail trade firms, and (4) 0.6 percent of all organizations combined which are involved in finance, insurance, and real estate. Moreover, all black businesses combined now receive not even 0.5 percent of the toal gross receipts of all businesses in the United States (Blackwell, 1975b: 166–77). Further, of the 300 black-oriented radio stations, blacks maintain a controlling interest in less than 10 percent of them. Only two of the 692 commercial television stations in the United States have a black manager. Thus, the control of blacks over the communications media intruding into black communities is at best limited. Similarly, blacks control approximately 2 percent of the $39 billion housing market in the United States (Blackwell, 1975b: 147).

Thus, blacks have neither the political power nor the economic power to control the decision-making process. And it may be necessary, as Chuck Stone (1968:24) has warned, for blacks to learn to manipulate the political process, as white ethnic groups have done in the past, "to satisfy their own selfish ends without regard for the best interest of the country."

Methods of Altering Power Relations: The Escalation of Conflict

One major function of the civil rights, black power and black liberation movements of the past two decades was to change power relations. These movements sought, in this process, to redistribute power more equitably between the dominant and subordinate groups in the pursuit of justice and equality before the law. We need very little to remind us of the fact that the violence encountered was not restricted to the South and its Bull Connors. For less than a decade ago, more than a hundred cities across the nation were seized by racial confrontations. Among the changes which followed these conflicts were some improvements in education, occupational distribution, wage and salary structure, access to better housing, and an increase in the number of black elected officials to approximately 3,503. However, it should be noted that black elected officials comprise less than one percent of all elected officials in the United States. It should also be stressed that although 120 black mayors have been elected, blacks are not necessarily in control of those cities nor of their patronage and their largesse. Most cities have an invisible power structure which controls the economic and political processes. That structure is almost always white.

Perhaps the most significant change in the black community since the 1950s was the rise of black ethnicity on a scale rarely witnessed before. It was a sense of ethnic pride, ethnic identity, cohesion, and solidarity, and self-acceptance in addition to a rejection of certain elements in the normative structure of the larger society that formed the core of this new ethnicity. The visibility of that ethnicity and its demands brought blacks into a competitive struggle with many white ethnic groups, particularly in the cities. This, in turn, gave rise to a neo-ethnicity among whites who claimed that blacks were treading on their prerogatives, "getting too much too soon" without working as hard as they had for their gains. The Nixon administration exploited that conflict and escalated it in the 1972 election to a kind of ethnic hysteria by the use of code words such as "welfare," "crime in the streets," "law and order," and, "let people work for what they get." The political implications of this strategy are clear, but a somewhat latent function of it was to subordinate the black population even more than it was at the time. The conflict generated is mounting and is likely to remain unabated until black and white ethnic groups realize that they are both losers in this form of struggle and unite for their common purposes.

However, black ethnicity is not without its internal struggle. Ideological distinctions persist between the integrationists/assimilationists, liberationists, cultural nationalists, separatists, and revolutionary nationalists. Since revolutionary nationalists have only the power to use civil disruptions, terror, and violence in guerilla warfare, they are not likely to win unless they can persuade a larger number of blacks to their position. However, the protracted struggle they envision, learned from experiences in Southeast Asia, may accelerate the process of change. In my view, some form of cultural nationalism, involving a recognition of the legitimacy of black culture and ethnic pluralism, is the more likely outcome. In either event, a change in the power relations between blacks and whites is not likely to occur without additional power struggles.

11

Ethnicity in Complex Societies: Structural, Cultural, and Characterological Factors

J. Milton Yinger

FEW DOUBT anymore that ethnic variation is a significant aspect of life in many societies. Even a casual reading of the newspapers turns up a steady stream of such headlines as these: "City's cultural mix called vital"; "The real boundaries in Africa are ethnic, not lines on a map"; "To the Basques it is their uniqueness that is on trial in Spain"; "New militancy emerges in Chinatown"; "Cubans in Miami stress heritage."

Anthropologists are beginning to give more attention to lines of division even in small and seemingly culturally homogeneous societies; ". . . most societies give evidence, mythological or otherwise, of some stubborn survival of alien traditions" (DeVos and Romanucci-Ross, 1975:v). Dominant ethnologies and histories, however, have often overlooked variations on the major cultural themes and in the lives of repressed minorities (for attempts to redress the balance, see Bricker, 1975). These accounts have also tended to minimize intergroup conflict. As DeVos puts it: "Like Freud's approach to personal history, a conflict approach to social history reveals the continuing influence of repressed forces—forces which do not disappear simply because they have been omitted from the official history written by the politically and socially dominant groups. . . . We have had in the past relatively little concern, for example, with reconstructing the internal crises faced by individual Gauls as they resisted or accepted Roman or Christian influence. Today, however, there is growing interest in those who resisted. It is a sign of the times that the most popular comic book hero in France today is Astérix, a counterculture Gaul whose Druidic potion gives him superhuman powers to help his tiny band of countrymen resist the establishment Romans" (DeVos and Romanucci-Ross, 1975:7).

Centers that specialize in the study of ethnicity, pluralism, and race relations now abound. In the United States we have, for example, the Center for Urban Ethnic Affairs (Washington), the Institute on Pluralism and Group Identity (New York), and the Center for the Study of American Pluralism (Chicago). Similar centers, often combining political or action interests with research, are found throughout the world. To mention only a few, we can list the Research Unit on Ethnic Relations (Bristol), the Foundation for the Study of Plural Societies (The Hague), L'Institute d'Etudes et de Recherches Interethniques et Interculturelles (Nice), the Institute of Race Relations (London), the Minority Rights Group (London), and the Nationalities Institute (Peking).

Although most of these centers have been founded only recently, the study of ethnic groups and ethnicity is by no means new. I do not share the view of some of my colleagues that interest in the ethnic factor has only just begun—the product, to an important degree, of the civil rights movement in the United States and of decolonization abroad. These have obviously heightened interest in ethnic groups, discrimination, and social conflict. In this field as in many others, however, we often hear what I call the "historical contortionist" critique: Why don't they—our predecessors—stand on our shoulders? I prefer Newton's formulation. There is also a tendency to forget that there are now about ten times as many sociologists (and probably other social scientists) as there were thirty-five years ago. Are we doing ten times as much good work on ethnicity, or most other topics, as was done by earlier generations?

Over half a century ago, Randolph Bourne (in *The History of a Literary Radical,* cited in Locke and Stern, 1946: 725) remarked that many of the immigrants to the United States were not simply those who missed the *Mayflower:* When they did come, they took a *Maiblume,* a *Fleur de Mai,* a *Fior di Maggio,* or a *Majblomst.* He was only one of many writers who were calling attention—from many different perspectives—to the importance of ethnicity in American life.

Despite the numerous studies, however, recognition of the significance of the ethnic factor in many societies has been forced on us more by events than by research. Scholarly work has often been dominated by insufficiently tested assumptions. An earlier tendency on the part of many writers to assume that in the long run, at least, ethnicity would fade as a decisive influence is now often replaced by an assumption that it is a persistent, perhaps permanent, aspect of social life. The earlier assumption surely led to hypotheses that could not be disconfirmed, for who can refute a statement that ethnic lines will eventually disappear?

Predictions based on arguments from "eventuality" are like the epitaph on the grave of the hypochondriac: "You see, I really was sick." Neither medical nor social diagnosis is advanced by arguments that something will "eventually" occur. On the other hand, I am made uncomfortable by the many contemporary assertions that ethnicity is a primordial fact, not simply tenacious but virtually indestructible. I do not disagree with those who affirm that ethnic groups can be as powerful a force in social processes as social classes. In some circumstances, at least, it would be easier to demonstrate, as Milton Esman says, "that class conflicts can be diverted into communal hostility and violence than that ethnic conflict can be transmuted into class struggle, except where class and communal cleavages coincide" (Esman in Glazer and Moynihan, 1975:415). There is a risk in contemporary statements, however, of assuming the inevitability of ethnicity—an assumption that affects definitions, observations, and interpretations. Ethnic groups have disappeared. Under some conditions they are minimally important. We will be wiser, in my judgment, to set aside both preconceptions and to ask: Under what conditions does the ethnic factor explain a large part of social process and human behavior? When is it of minor importance?

The moral and policy questions are as vital as the research questions. How and in what manner should we try to combine particularism and universalism as organizing principles of society? How do lines of division within a nation influence its international relations? A decade ago I wrote: "If we are to have international stability and peace, we shall have to learn to live with diversity; we shall have to extend the concept of pluralism beyond the frontiers of the nation. . . . It is my belief that the way in which the affiliation or rejection of racial, religious, and ethnic minorities is worked out within nations will strongly influence our ability to build a world order in which similarities are not coerced and differences do not divide. We are dealing here with one of the great intellectual and moral questions of the day" (Yinger, 1965*a*:xi).

I see no reason to change that statement today; but I am more concerned than I was then about the romanticism sometimes attached to the emphasis on ethnicity. (With Irving Babbitt I think of something as romantic if it is wonderful rather than probable.) Current romanticism matches that attached to earlier notions of the melting pot. There is something warm and supportive and rich about ethnic attachments, as there can be about national attachments. But there is also something small-minded, mean, and constricting. If we do not yet have a personalized noun to match on the ethnic-group level the use of the name of Chauvin on the national level, we do have some matching words and actions. I do not think that civilization will be advanced by listening to one's blood or by encouraging people to respond to the instincts of their flesh (see Novak, 1971). Lothrop Stoddard, Madison Grant, et al. (not to mention more vicious forms of ethnocentrism) are going to be no better the second time around.

The Definition and Measurement of Ethnicity

I shall not take much time defining ethnicity or in reviewing the numerous, and to some degree conflicting, definitions. An ethnic group, as I will use the term, is a segment of a larger society whose members are thought, by themselves and/or others, to have a common origin and to share important segments of a common culture and who, in addition, participate in shared activities in which the common origin and culture are significant ingredients. It is important to distinguish a sociologically and psychologically important ethnicity from one that is only administrative or classificatory. We clearly need to expand our behavioral measures of ethnic identity; we cannot be content with naming and counting. It has often been remarked that newspapers can create the appearance of a crime wave by the way the news is reported. Census makers and sociologists can create the appearance of an ethnicity wave by the way data are recorded. Our aim must be to strengthen a dynamic view of ethnicity that examines the ways in which it is involved in social life. Fortunately, current sociological and anthropological work is moving in that direction (see Andrew Greeley, 1974; and Gerald Berreman in DeVos and Romanucci-Ross, 1975:71–105).

The definition of an ethnic group that I have suggested has three ingredients: (1) The group is perceived by others in the society to be different in some combination of the following traits: language, religion, race, and ancestral homeland with its related culture; (2) the members also perceive themselves as different; and (3) they participate in shared activities built around their (real or mythical) common origin and culture. Each of these is a variable, of course; hence we need to work toward a scale of ethnicity. One can be fully ethnic or barely ethnic. Moreover, these factors vary independently of one another to some degree. If one transposes each of the three criteria into a question and answers it, for simplicity, either yes or no, there are eight possible combinations. Different forms of ethnicity have different causes and consequences. Putting them into a table, one gets a formal, and at this stage rather arid, typology of ethnic groups (see the following table). In particular times and places, several of the categories may be unimportant. Showing the full possible range, however, may help us to see ethnicity as a variable.

Some of the disagreements in the literature on ethnicity may be due to the fact that authors concentrate on different combinations of the three variables that together define the parameters of ethnicity. In my judgment, if even one of the three questions is answered "yes," there is an ethnic factor operating that deserves attention, in terms of its causes and consequences. Type 4, for example, which I have called Hidden Ethnicity, is not perceived as such either by the participants or by others. But if in fact there are activities built around a common origin and ancestral culture, perhaps hidden by a national ideology that obscures the presence of ethnic lines, the consequences may be quite significant. I need scarcely say that type 6, Stereotyped Ethnicity, can have important consequences, even in the absence of shared activities or perception by the individuals involved that they are ethnically distinct. Imagined Ethnicity, type 7, is only in the beliefs of the members, but it doubtless affects their behavior and is potentially more important if the situation within which they live changes.

Varieties of ethnic identity

	I. Are They Perceived by Others as Ethnically Distinct?			
	Yes		No	
	II. Do Individuals Perceive Themselves as Ethnically Distinct?		Do Individuals Perceive Themselves as Ethnically Distinct?	
III. Do they participate in shared activities?	Yes	No	Yes	No
Yes	1. Full	2. Unrecognized	3. Private	4. Hidden
No	5. Symbolic	6. Stereotyped	7. Imagined	8. Nonethnic

If the three criteria were seen as variables, rather than attributes, more subtle and refined distinctions among types and intensities of ethnicity could be drawn. We are a long way, however, from being able to measure and compare an 8-8-2 profile, let us say, with a 2-2-8 or a 5-5-5.

If we concentrate on the relationships of ethnic groups to the societies of which they are a part, a different way of looking at ethnic variation appears from the one that we see when attention is given to the three variables in the definition. At least four major types can be found among multi-ethnic societies in the contemporary world:

A. A society can be built out of formally equal ethnic groups.
B. A society can be characterized by a major national cultural

group, separated from one or more ethnic groups by a highly permeable boundary.

C. One or more ethnic groups can be strongly oriented toward an outside mother society.

D. One or more ethnic groups can be "imprisoned" as disprivileged minorities within the larger society.

These four types of societal patterns might be sketched in the following chart:

Varieties of Interethnic Societies

A. Society composed of several equal ethnic groups

B. Society with a core cultural group surrounded by ethnic groups

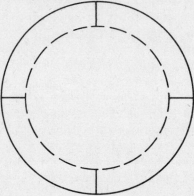

C. Society containing an ethnic group with outside orientation

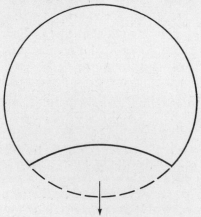

D. Society with an imprisoned ethnic minority

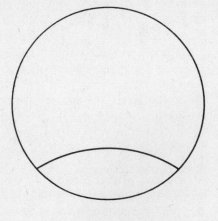

These types are not mutually exclusive. One can think of a society built up of two or more layers each of which exhibits, to a greater or lesser degree, the characteristics of one of the societal types. It can well be argued that the United States has elements of all four types, each limiting the full applicability of the others but not excluding them entirely.

Failure to distinguish among such different societal patterns as these would deprive us of many crucial observations regarding ethnicity. It is also important to recognize that these patterns are not fixed. Societies move from one to another—or more accurately, the mix of the four types changes: Boundaries become more or less permeable; equality among ethnic groups increases or decreases; orientation to outside societies grows stronger or weaker.

One further aspect of the question of definition requires comment. Among contemporary writers, there is some tendency to state that everyone belongs to an ethnic group. In this usage, ethnic group becomes nearly synonymous with culture group. In those rare instances where there is minimal ethnic variation, societies are simply described as ethnically homogeneous. The association of a theory of ethnicity with the study of social conflict, discrimination, minority and majority statuses—major connotations of the term, if not denotations, over a long period of time—is reduced or eliminated. Societal type B, in the chart, could not exist, since the inner core would itself be an ethnic group.

Such shifts of definition as this can often bring new insights; they can also blur important distinctions. They may come about, not because of major developments in theory or a flood of new data, but out of political or ideological needs. Obviously, one does not argue against action in service of those needs; but it is appropriate to distinguish such action from scientific efforts to understand the sources and consequences of emphasis on ethnicity. Does one understand England better, for example, by dividing the population into an English core group surrounded by English of Welsh, Irish, Scottish, Pakistani, Indian, Nigerian, Jamaican, and other descents, or by saying that the English population is made up of a multiplicity of ethnic groups, the largest of which is of Anglo-Saxon descent? To answer this question, I would want information on how the several groups perceive the situation and on the patterns of intragroup and intergroup behavior—that is, on the criteria of my definition of ethnicity.

In a similar way we can ask: Is there an American core group, surrounded by a series of "hyphenated Americans"—Mexican-Americans, Afro-Americans, Jewish-Americans, Italian-Americans, Native-Americans, and the like? Or are we all ethnics? We all have ancestors that came from other shores. Franklin D. Roosevelt once startled the D.A.R. by opening an address to them with the greeting, "fellow immigrants." Margaret Mead, with calculated exaggeration, has said that we are all "third generation." Most of us share the sentiments implicit in such statements. It seems much more democratic to affirm that nobody—or everybody—is a hyphenated American. It may not be wise, however, to affirm that everybody is equal if thereby we obscure the fact that some are more equal than others or make it more difficult to recognize the conflict and dissensus intrinsic to many multi-ethnic systems. Until I see research to the contrary, I believe that setting aside the idea that many large and heterogeneous societies have a core culture, however diverse in its origins, will weaken our analyses of social process.

This is not an evaluative statement. The core culture is not intrinsically better or worse than the ethnic cultures which surround it. It is an empirical estimate that many people in the United States place low salience on identity with their ancestral groups, that they are mainly identified by others simply as Americans, and that they participate in few activities in which shared ancestry is important as symbol or substance. In addition, extensive ethnic mixture in their backgrounds makes shifts in these facts—toward greater ethnic identification—unlikely.

Invention of an ethnic label for the core group may seem to make it into an ethnic group—and indeed words do both reflect and affect reality. But words can also deflect us from reality. Being a WASPish sort of fellow, I find no difficulty in being categorized as a WASP. It is purely a category, however; it has little or no social reality for me. Like tens of millions of Americans, my ancestry is so mixed that the Anglo-Saxon part of WASP has somehow to absorb a bit of Scotch, Irish, Dutch, German, and Swedish. I belong to no organizations in which WASPishness is, even informally, a criterion for membership (unless it is the A.S.A., in which case waspishness has a different meaning). If everyone is ethnic, then I am a WASP, but surely a poor one, a stingless one.

In renewing our attention to the important ethnic factor, we must not lose sight of earlier understandings. I would emphasize the point, made particularly by Linton, that many modern nations have as their core culture a great mélange on which most members draw and to which they have contributed. Indeed, the hybrid vigor from such mixtures has been crucial to their development.

Doubtless you all remember how Linton put it:

> [I]nsidious foreign ideas have . . . wormed their way into [the American's] civilization without his realizing what was going on. Thus dawn finds the unsuspecting patriot garbed in pajamas, a garment of East Indian origin; and lying in a bed built on a pattern which originated in either Persia or Asia Minor. He is muffled to the ears in un-American

materials: cotton, first domesticated in India; linen, domesticated in the Near East; wool from an animal native to Asia Minor; or silk whose uses were first discovered by the Chinese. . . .

On awakening he glances at the clock, a medieval European invention, uses one potent Latin word in abbreviated form, rises in haste, and goes to the bathroom. Here, if he stops to think about it, he must feel himself in the presence of a great American institution . . . and will know that in no other country does the average man perform his ablutions in the midst of such splendor. But the insidious foreign influence pursues him even here. Glass was invented by the ancient Egyptians, the use of glazed tile floors and walls in the Near East, porcelain in China, and the art of enameling on metal by Mediterranean artisans of the Bronze Age. Even his bathtub and toilet are but slightly modified copies of Roman originals.

In this bathroom the American washes with soap invented by the ancient Gauls. Next he cleans his teeth, a subversive European practice. . . . He then shaves, a masochistic rite first developed by the heathen priests of ancient Egypt and Sumer. The process is made less of a penance by the fact that his razor is of steel, an iron-carbon alloy discovered in either India or Turkestan. Lastly, he dries himself on a Turkish towel.

Breakfast over [and you can imagine what Linton did with that] . . . , as he scans the latest editorial pointing out the dire results to our institutions of accepting foreign ideas, he will not fail to thank a Hebrew God in an Indo-European language that he is a one hundred percent (decimal system invented by the Greeks) American (from Americus Vespucci, Italian geographer). [1937:427–29]

The cultural landscape would be seen as even more diverse if Linton had added attention to the influence of our indigenous population and of the many streams of migrants and refugees. I do not need to detail here the degree to which we all are Indian, Afro-American, Irish, Jewish, Italian, German, etc., etc. It is difficult to be much of a WASP in such a setting; and I suspect it is difficult, after two or three generations in the United States, to be closely bound into other groups, from the cultural point of view.

Ethnicity is a topic filled with so many assumptions, guided by such poorly defined terms, and evocative of such strong emotions that we often fail to see the culture-building process going on before our eyes. This is clearly not a one-way process; nor is there the least danger of producing dead-level homogeneity. A recent special issue of the *American Ethnologist* on "Intra-cultural Variation" (Bricker, 1975) demonstrates that the fear of narrow uniformity in the absence of ethnic differences is not well founded, even in small and superficially uniform societies. With reference to the United States, the evidence points against Novak's assertion that "the melting pot is a kind of homogenized soup" (1971:60). We're all aware of the great variety within our own groups (Blackwell, 1975*b*); failure to see it in others is a mark of our strong inclinations toward stereotypy. When I think of persons of Irish Catholic background, should I think of Eugene McCarthy or Joseph McCarthy? Is Adlai Stevenson or Richard Nixon the typical WASP? Is Rabbi Korff the standard for all American Jews? Ethnic differentiation can add strength to a society, but not because it protects us from bland homogeneity. The development of a complex core culture may make it possible, in Cooley's phrase, to move from differentiation based on isolation to differentiation based on choice.

The Sources of Persistence of Ethnicity

To many persons, the cultural aspects of ethnicity are not the important ones, at least in heterogeneous urban societies. The persistence of ethnic identity is strongly social psychological; it is, as Milton Gordon put it, "a special sense of both ancestral and future-oriented identification with the group. These are the 'people' of my ancestors, therefore they are my people, and they will be the people of my children and their children" (1964:29). Acculturation can go a long way, Gordon argues, without structural assimilation occurring.

There is a great deal of evidence to support this view. However, since ethnic groups are often defined, in the first instance, by their cultural distinctiveness, their persistence when that distinctiveness is greatly reduced is perhaps the major problem for a theory of ethnicity. This problem is dealt with in different ways. Three distinct answers are given to the question: Why do ethnic groups persist in spite of social and physical mobility, and acculturation?

1. Ethnicity is, under many conditions, a valuable identity. It can help to promote social mobility, protect status, serve economic and political interests. I will call this the structural argument.

2. Ethnicity is a primordial sentiment, with its sources deep in the socialization process. It is often attached to a distinctive religion or language, which are crucial sources of one's world view. Despite acculturation, deep layers of culture persist and are passed along within intimate family circles. This is the cultural argument.

3. In a period of rapid change and extensive mobility, many people feel cut loose from their moorings. They seem surrounded by anomie. Alienation is widespread. Unqualified gesellschaft, with its emphasis on universality, rationality, and instrumental values, creates a lonely crowd. Ethnicity is one of the ways some seek to escape from the freedom of that crowd. It gives us a "brand name," an identity (see Ries-

man, 1961; Fromm, 1941; Herberg, 1955). This is the characterological argument.

These explanations of the persistence of ethnicity are not mutually exclusive. In fact, without at least two of them, ethnic identity would tend to fade quite rapidly under many conditions. The analytic distinction among the three is important, however, because their comparative weight varies from setting to setting. Scholars differ significantly in the emphasis they give to one or another of these explanations, even when describing the same situation, because the variables are not well defined and are even less well measured. Nevertheless, we need to keep them clearly in our minds as analytic variables and to search for their various combinations.

A number of recent writers have emphasized the structural source of emphasis on ethnicity in their interpretations of the United States. Glazer and Moynihan write: "One of the striking characteristics of the present situation is indeed the extent to which we find the ethnic group defined in terms of interest, *as* an interest group" (1975:7). Talcott Parsons (in Glazer and Moynihan, 1975:63–67), using a term from David Schneider, emphasizes the "desocialization" of ethnic groups, the reduction of their cultural content, even though they remain important as interest groups. Hechter arrives at the same judgment in his study of the persistence of ethnic identities in England: ". . . ethnic solidarity in complex societies is best seen as a response to patterns of structural discrimination faced by certain groups in the society at large" (1974:1151). Daniel Bell argues that the shift of many decision-making processes from a relatively anonymous economic market to an open political arena has strongly supported the increase of communal and interest groups, "defensively to protect their places and privileges, or advantageously to gain place and privilege" (in Glazer and Moynihan, 1975:145).

In my judgment, this interest factor looms very large in the explanation of the importance of ethnicity in American society today. It may be easier in a society that tends to deny, or at least to obscure, class divisions, to fight for one's economic and political interests under an ethnic label. It seems less self-serving, less "radical." It may help to aggregate greater numbers behind some policy. Hence ethnocultural rather than class myths arise. If this is true, we are faced with a number of significant questions: Are ethnic group divisions an effective way for organizing conflicts, that is, for expressing them in such a way that individual and group wishes and needs are optimally fulfilled, compared with division by class, occupation, region, or some other distinction? Or, to put the question differently: Under what conditions are societal interests optimally served by organizing competition and conflict along ethnic group lines? Are blacks, for example, best served by fighting for their interests as blacks, or as labor unionists, residents of cities, persons of low income, or some other collectivity? Obviously one would need to take account, in attempting to answer this question, of many variables: the degree of intra-ethnic solidarity that can be maintained (and at what costs), the attitudes—including the prejudices—of possible allies, demographic facts, the nature of the interest being fought for, and other variables.

Under what conditions does ethnicity escape entanglement with the stratification system? That is, do some ethnic groups, in a society that emphasizes ethnicity, almost certainly gain or lose by that emphasis? Donald Noel (1968) thinks not, but he does not deal with urban, heterogeneous societies. John Porter (in Glazer and Moynihan, 1975:267–304) thinks that emphasis on ethnicity creates a high risk of ethnic stratification. In India, group mobility of at least a quasi-ethnic sort holds greater promise than individual mobility (see Gerald Berreman in Gelfand and Lee, 1973:33–47). From these diverse observations and judgments, it seems clear that sweeping generalizations about this problem are unlikely to be helpful.

One additional question looms large in the study of economic and political conflict organized along ethnic lines: Who *within* an ethnic group, if anyone, is most likely to profit by the use of ethnicity to fight for presumed shared interests? Such use obscures class lines, but it does not eliminate them. Is it most likely that the higher status groups will profit while their fellow ethnics of lower status will suffer? For decades the "poor whites" of the South were, and to some degree still are, paid off in the coin of "racial superiority." I doubt if a racial and quasicultural line of distinction was a good way for them to fight for their interests. In my judgment, the black power movement has helped the better-educated, higher-status blacks, but has scarcely touched the needs of those at the bottom of the ladder—in fact, it may have made them worse off.

I think it is apparent that the current emphasis on ethnicity involves the pursuit of interests to an important degree. We have a great deal to learn, however, about how well and for whom and under what conditions it does in fact promote interests.

What I have called the cultural interpretation of the persistence, or revival, of ethnicity in the United States is most likely to be expressed by those who are close to the communal centers of their ethnic groups. There is little doubt that where language and religion and other major cultural elements separate a group from others in a society, ethnic identity is likely to be maintained in all three of the senses of our definition: self-perception, the perception of others, and associational involvement. It is less evident that cultural factors are the basic ones in a situation where cultural differences are fading, language contrasts are minimal, and religious sentiments and attachments are weakening. The task, therefore, is to find reliable and valid measures of the extent to which cultural differences persist or are reduced, and to develop a theory of the conditions under which these occur. Undoubtedly demographic factors are involved, as are spacial mobility, the degree to which the occupational structure is open, the nature of political alignments, religious trends (ecumenicity versus denominationalizing as well as strength of attachments), and many other factors. We are dealing with a series of interdependent variables, not with simple cause-effect sequences.

We need researchable hypotheses that go beyond simple listing of variables. Greeley approaches such a hypothesis when he writes: ". . . we are not ready to assume that vast cultural differences do not persist. Our suspicion—and given the present state of the data, it is little more than suspicion—is that the core of these differences has to do with different expectations about close relatives; that is, in one ethnic group the expectations of how a husband or a wife, a father or a mother, a brother or a sister, a cousin, an aunt, or an uncle should behave are likely to be quite different than in another ethnic group" (1971:26).

Given the importance of family and kin groups for socialization and personality formation, although not all theories of "fathers and sons" emphasize the degree to which they are bound together, rates of intermarriage become decisive facts. I cannot discuss here the problems of measurement (see Yinger, 1968*a*, 1968*b*), but offer only a few suggestions and assertions:

In a society where one group is numerically dominant, most marriages are, of necessity, homogamous. In the United States, using religion for example, about 70 percent of the population is Protestant. If *all* non-Protestants were to marry Protestants, 40 percent of the majority group would remain, to marry among themselves. Or to make a slightly more meaningful assumption, if marriage choices were completely random so far as religion is concerned, religious homogamy would occur over 55 percent of the time (70 percent Protestant × 70%; 25 percent Catholic × 25%; 4 percent Jew × 4%). Most intermarriage data, moreover, do not take account of rates of conversion. But to examine such a question as that raised by Greeley, surely we need to know the religion of origin.

Taking account of such factors, I have reported elsewhere (Yinger, 1968*a*) a series of calculations which indicate that between 35 and 40 percent of the religious intermarriages that could occur, using the 1957 census data (no later census data are available), did occur. Most evidence shows that intermarriage rates—interreligious, interethnic, interracial—are increasing. To the extent that this is true, cultural factors in ethnic survival and revival will be modified.

High levels of anomie and alienation are used as a third explanation of the "new ethnicity" or of the continuing importance of ethnic identity in American society (see Greeley, 1971:chap. 13; Parsons in Glazer and Moynihan, 1975: 68–69; Kilson in Glazer and Moynihan, 1975: 260). Though I find the judgments to be too sweeping and unspecified (see Yinger, 1965b: chap. 9; Yinger in Knutson, 1973: chap. 7), almost everyone regards anomie and alienation as unhappy facts. Their varieties, sources, and consequences are described in a vast literature. Much of it is connected with discussions of identity, for it seems reasonable to assume that alienated individuals, living in societies with high levels of anomie, find it difficult to establish or maintain an identity. At this point, the argument goes, ethnicity is affirmed or reaffirmed as a cure: I do, in fact, know who I am—I am a Pole, a Jew, a WASP, a black. I have meaningful attachments; my ethnic group has standards and shared values and agreed-upon norms that reduce the burden of anomie in the larger society. Novak puts it particularly strongly: "The 'divisiveness' and free-floating 'rage' so prominent in America in the 1960s is one result of the shattering impact of 'forced nationalization' upon personality integration. People uncertain of their own identity are not wholly free. They are threatened not only by specific economic and social programs, but also at the very heart of their identity. The world is mediated to human persons through language and culture, that is, through ethnic belonging" (1971:229; see also DeVos and Romanucci-Ross, 1975:25).

It is quite easy to accept the idea that renewed ethnic attachments are a cure for overdoses of anomie and alienation. There are, however, logical and factual problems to be dealt with. If alienation and anomie are believed to be in part the *result* of loss of ethnic attachments, as is often affirmed, it isn't very helpful simply to say: Reverse the causal processes; strengthen ethnic attachments, and alienation and anomie will be reduced. This says nothing about the causal sequences which led to the original situation. There is also a tendency to overlook the question of alienation from one's ethnic group and the conditions that produce it; and little is said, at least in this context, about value disagreements and structural strains—tendencies toward anomie—within ethnic groups. It is not enough, therefore, simply to affirm that neo-ethnicity or the persistence of ethnicity is to be accounted for by its value in protecting one from a pervasive anomie and alienation. We need to ask: Under what conditions is this true and what are the side effects?

To make progress in the development of a theory that will explain most adequately the continuation and the renewal of ethnic identities in heterogeneous and mobile societies requires, in sum, attention to the interactions among three factors: the use of ethnicity in the pursuit of interests, the strength of subcultural continuity, and the effects of the experience of anomie and alienation. This is a formidable task. Until we have accomplished a large measure of it, the temptation will be strong to emphasize some part of an adequate theory, filling in the rest of the explanation with our predilections. This makes for good panels—particularly ones built around a theme of conflict and dissensus—but not for good sociology.

The Consequences of an Emphasis on Ethnicity in Heterogeneous, Rapidly Changing Societies

There is insufficient time to examine more than cursorily another basic aspect of a theory of ethnicity, namely, the consequences of an emphasis on ethnicity. Many factors condition those consequences—factors that may, in turn, be influenced by the resulting levels of ethnicity. These are among the critical factors:

1. History of the society. How did the ethnic mix come about—by the political and economic binding together of separate groups, by individual migration, by conquest?
2. Demographic and ecological facts. What are the comparative sizes, sex ratios, concentration or dispersal, and rates of growth of the various groups?
3. How equal are they in social status, educational attainment, occupational levels? And how open is the stratification system?
4. Prejudice and discrimination. These are correlated with the degree of equality, but are not identical with it.
5. How extensive are the contacts of the ethnic units with their ancestral homelands? It is one thing to fly by jet from southern Italy or Yugoslavia to Germany; it is another to take a boat from Europe to North America.
6. To what degree is ethnicity ascribed, to what degree chosen? Ascription may seem to be almost part of the definition of ethnic identity; yet there are times and places when people may, either individually or in groups, claim this or that ethnicity, identify with a group or stand aside. The strength of both external and internal pressures is involved (Donald Horowitz in Glazer and Moynihan, 1975:111–40).
7. How many factors are involved in tracing the lines among ethnic groups? If religion, language, national origin, race, and social class converge, the consequences of ethnic distinctions within a society are different from what they are when fewer lines of distinction mark the boundaries.

8. Closely related to this is the number of cross-cutting memberships and contacts. If the subsocieties are sharply separated in jobs, churches, schools, associations, and neighborhoods, the consequences of emphasis on ethnicity are different from what they are when contact is frequent across ethnic lines.

With such factors influencing the results, it is clear that any analysis of the consequences of an emphasis on ethnicity must be highly complex. I have time here only to state some of the basic issues, hoping to focus attention on them in such a way that you will think about them in the light of the theoretical guidelines I have suggested.

When ethnicity is an important principle of social organization, how are the speed and direction of social change affected? Many writers emphasize that ethnicity is inherently conservative; that it may re-enforce uncivilized practices (a lower status for women, for example); that under many conditions, ethnic groups lose their liberals, their marginals, to the larger society; that their leaders are most successful when they preserve a traditional way of life. This is a part truth. The other part notes that ethnic groups may become salient precisely to promote change, to fight discrimination, to help a group redefine its culture into a form better adapted to contemporary conditions. In terms borrowed from the sociology of religion, there are churchlike and sectarian ethnic groups. The task is to discover the conditions under which these types emerge and their varying effects on social change.

Does ethnicity promote or reduce social conflict? A cursory reading of current events leads to a quick answer. Malaysia, Pakistan, Uganda, Lebanon, Ethiopia, Canada, the United States, the Soviet Union, South Africa—it is probably easier to create a list of nations that have experienced severe ethnic conflict in the last decade than a list of ones that have not. But the question may be too simple. Are ethnic differences an independent cause of conflict, or only the form in which it is organized? Does conflict that has an ethnic color take on a peculiarly self-righteous quality on all sides, adding to its harshness, its irrationality, its permanence? Or is it organized around more important "real interests"—language, religion, cultural survival, and individual identity—than the usual list of "real interests"—income, jobs, political power? Whatever answer you give, or I give, makes sense only in the context of stated values. We will not get an adequate interpretation of the relationship of ethnicity to conflict until these values are made explicit.

A closely related question has to do with discrimination. Does an emphasis on ethnicity increase or reduce discrimination in a society? There is little doubt that ethnic lines are often used by those in power to exclude others, to deprive them of equal rights. There are other times when resurgent ethnicity becomes an instrument for aggregating resources among members of a minority group, boosting morale of its members, and organizing opposition to discriminatory practices. What we have to remember is that both of these processes are likely to be found in the same setting. If a deprived minority ethnic group organizes its ethnicity to fight discrimination, there is likely to be reciprocal organization by the dominant ethnic groups. The net gains are what count, and they should be measured against gains made possible by other modes of organizing opposition to discrimination. I am not impressed, for example, by claims that the black power movement has been the major force in making gains for black Americans. It followed by at least twenty years a thoroughly interethnic civil rights movement which, along with impersonal demographic and economic factors, had significantly altered the patterns of segregation and discrimination.

To what degree is emphasis on ethnic-group solidarity freedom-giving and identity-creating, to what degree is it coercive? Doubtless we all know people who seemed lost, directionless, poorly motivated until they "discovered their ethnicity." The opposite of this is the pressure from the group to conform to its standards, and to restrict contact with others. Powerful sanctions can be applied to those suspected of disloyalty. On college campuses, coercions against white students who date blacks are now matched by coercions against black students who date whites. Uncle Tom and Uncle Tomahawk are no less expressive of a social reality for having become clichés. Ethnic peer pressures in school can effectively cut off many academic and occupational options (DeVos and Romanucci-Ross, 1975:30–31). Are these necessary expressions of ethnic solidarity or unwarranted intrusions into personal affairs? Can these apparently contradictory effects of emphasis on ethnicity be reconciled or compromised? These questions urgently need study.

There is a vast literature dealing with the relationships of ethnicity to politics (e.g., Weed, 1973; Banfield and Wilson, 1963; Greeley, 1974: chaps. 6, 9). It would be foolish to try to understand American politics, not only on the city and state but also on the national level, without dealing with the ethnic factor. Studies of political behavior, particularly of voting, have documented the importance of ethnicity beyond question, even if they have not yet explored in depth the question of the conditions under which ethnicity explains a large or small part of the variance in political behavior. Less research deals with the effect of ethnicity on issues. Which problems get into the public debate, which ones are obscured in those situations where ethnic self-consciousness strongly influences the political process? If I can suggest an analogue for Muzafer Sherif's concept of "superordinate goals," I would ask: What are the superordinate problems faced by the nation and the world today—problems that can be dealt with only by total group participation? What energy sources will be available and safe twenty years

from now; can we maintain a decent level of oxygen in the air we
breathe; how many people can the planet sustain at what level of living;
can we keep from destroying all life? These are superordinate problems. Do we deal with them poorly in part because our interest is
deflected onto smaller and symbolic issues by the way politics is organized? To raise one further question dealing with ethnicity and politics:
What are the international consequences of strong ethnicity in the
United States, consequences in Ireland, Israel, the Soviet Union, and
various nations of Africa, for example? This is a complicated and deli-
cate question. Has the support of some Americans of Irish descent for
the I.R.A. helped sustain a gallant fight for equality, or has it helped
maintain a violent outlaw group and contributed to its intransigence?
Our values strongly infuse our efforts to answer such questions; yet our
values will not be well served until we learn to ask them with some de-
tachment and to follow the evidence with care.

Conclusion

I have only illustrated the consequences that may flow from an emphasis on ethnicity in the United States, or in heterogeneous, urban
societies generally. My aim has been to open up our thinking about ethnicity by asking questions from various points of view. These brief comments may help to indicate the distance we have to go to develop an adequate sociology of ethnicity. We have even further to go to develop an
adequate ethics; and since ethical questions infuse almost all discussions
of ethnicity, we should focus on them as well. Virtually everyone today
recognizes ethnicity as an important fact of American life. The question is, should we celebrate that fact as a source of great humanistic
strength, or lament it as an unfortunate necessity, or take a position
somewhere between those poles?

There is ample evidence "that strong networks of private associations, based on the ideal of pluralism, do not weaken the cohesion of a
democratic society but actually strengthen it. Such networks serve both
to relate an individual, through groups that are close and meaningful
to him, to the large, complex society, and also to protect him from excessive encroachments on his freedom by that society" (Yinger,
1962–63:398). The task is to keep identities derived from such networks in balance with individual and humanwide identities. Milosz is
speaking of Poland and Lithuania, but suggests a larger principle when
he writes: "Perhaps those sardines fighting each other in the mouth of
a whale are not untypical of the relations between humans when they
search for self-assertion through ethnic values magnified into abso-

lutes" (Milosz in DeVos and Romanucci-Ross, 1975:352). Will we be swallowed up by humanwide problems while identifying with parochial groups?

Devereux makes an opposite point—too strongly for my taste, but an essential point—when he calls attention to the strain between individual integrity and ethnicity: "Sane and mature persons do not hypercathect their ethnic identity or any other class identity. . . . The current tendency to stress one's ethnic or class identity, its use as a crutch, is prima facie evidence of the impending collapse of the only valid sense of identity: one's differentness, which is replaced by the most archaic pseudo-identity possible" (Devereux in DeVos and Romanucci-Ross, 1975:67–68).

In our research, we must strive to discover the causes and consequences of various mixes of individual, associational, and humanwide identities. And in our ethical analyses we need to assess the gains and costs. In an earlier paper I tried to distinguish between undesirable segregation and legitimate pluralism. Several criteria can be applied: A line of distinction—in this instance, an ethnic line—is undesirable if it is related in hidden ways to other lines of separation. "A men's club, justified on the grounds that one has a right to pick his friends, often has covert or even obvious significance in politics and the higher job market. . . . Housing segregation, often justified on much the same grounds, is frequently—one can almost say, I think, universally—related to segregation in schools, parks, and jobs. Above all, housing segregation separates the child from accessibility to the larger culture which he must master if he is to improve his situation" (Yinger, 1962–63:405). One person's ethnicity may be another person's tragedy.

There are other criteria. A line of distinction is not legitimate pluralism if it is systematic and total. A kind of lighthearted ethnicity contributes to individual freedom and societal flexibility. When it becomes an overpowering attachment, it is the source of social schism and interpersonal barriers. When a distinction is designed to keep certain individuals and groups out, rather than to keep persons with certain characteristics in, that is, when it is exclusive rather than inclusive, it is an undesirable separation. And when it is based on conveniently invented or superficially revived distinctions, not on deeply felt cultural and group attachments, an ethnic line is segregation, not pluralism.

I should like to make two points by way of summary. We need—but cannot even outline here—a parallel study of de-ethnicization. Movement of people into national populations and shifts of identity through religious, lingual, or other cultural changes and through intermarriage are greatly in need of further examination, to trace their causes and consequences. Finally, a society is wise, in my judgment, that creates an environment where the right to ethnicity is fully protected and mutual respect is strongly supported, while at the same time conditions tend to make ethnic identity a relatively small part of most persons' identities. That society is most fortunate where ethnicity continues as a minor melody, serving as counterpoint to major themes of individual identity on one hand and identity with the larger society and the world on the other.

VI

To Post the Limits of Labeling and Redirect the Study of Deviance

12

Deviant Behavior, Social Intervention, and Labeling Theory

Walter R. Gove

THE CITATION ANALYSIS done by Cole (1975) demonstrates that among sociologists concerned with deviance, labeling theory has become the dominant perspective. Perhaps more important, this theory has gained adherents among those members of society actually involved in processing deviance. Labeling theory provides part of the theoretical foundation for the antipsychiatry movement and was a major factor in the changing of the psychiatric commitment laws in California. Similarly, labeling theory was the key reason for changing the procedures for identifying the mentally retarded in California. It is behind many of the federal government's policies regarding the processing of criminals, particularly juvenile delinquents. It provides critical theoretical support for the movement to decriminalize the use of drugs, including heroin, and for such social movements as gay liberation.

When one wants to grasp the essence of a school of thought it is often useful to turn to the works of the originators of that school. However, in the case of labeling theory, the recent statements of some of the originators of the perspective reflect considerable dissatisfaction on their part with how the theory has evolved. For example, Lemert, who is probably labeling theory's most important theoretician, presents a devastating critique of the popularized version of labeling theory in his introductory chapter to the second edition of *Human Deviance, Social Problems, and Social Control* (Lemert, 1972), a critique which he subsequently elaborated upon in his presidential address to the Society for the Study of Social Problems (Lemert, 1974). Referring to the earlier essay, Manning (1973:124) states: "This essay marks an axial point in the development of deviance theory: It suggests the degree of moral, political and intellectual exhaustion that threatens to seize large segments of sociology and simultaneously signifies the beginning of the end of a creative period initiated by Lemert himself."

Becker, whose book *Outsiders* (1963) provided what was probably the most popular statement of labeling theory, has also attempted to disassociate himself from labeling theory. He argues (1973:178–79) that what he proposed was not a theory but simply that students of deviant behavior view deviant behavior as involving social interaction. Regarding what others have taken to be labeling theory, Becker states, "thus, some [persons] thought the theory attempted to explain deviance by the responses others made to it. After one was labeled a deviant, according to their paraphrase, then one began to do deviant things, but not before." Regarding this formulation, Becker states, "you can easily dispose of that theory by referring to the facts of everyday experience."

Goffman's work on stigma and mental illness provides much of the foundation for labeling theory; however, he is also critical of the theory. For example, in writing about the havoc created by the actions of the mentally ill he states:

> This havoc indicates that medical symptoms and mental symptoms are radically different in their social consequences and in their character. It is this havoc that the philosophy of containment must deal with. It is this havoc that psychiatrists have dismally failed to examine and that *sociologists ignore when they treat mental illness as a labeling process.* It is this havoc which we must explore. [Goffman, 1971:357; italics added]

As the above statements make obvious, many of the originators of labeling theory are currently dissatisfied with the thrust of the theory as popularly understood. It is unclear whether this is because their followers have misinterpreted their statements and inappropriately applied their formulations, or whether they saw the inaccuracy of their original formulations as the logical conclusions of their works were drawn and critically scrutinized. I tend to opt for the second explanation, while it is obvious they prefer the first. Which explanation is correct is perhaps unimportant; where we go from here is.

Lemert (1974) apparently feels labeling theorists should move away from the social-psychological aspects of deviance and turn to a macro-level of analysis, looking particularly at the institutionalized processes which classify and process deviants. Such a focus is suggested by some of Lemert's early work and seems to me to hold great promise. I, who have been a critic of the labeling explanation of mental illness, would welcome such a study in this area. In fact, as I am quite concerned about how mental illness is classified and processed, and as my point of view is not the one ascribed to me by the labeling theorists, let me digress on this point for a moment.

Scheff (1966, 1974) and others have argued that one's social attributes, particularly a marginal status, are the prime factors involved in entering the role of the mentally ill and that being officially labeled mentally ill is the prime cause of chronic mental illness. I have countered by arguing that the evidence indicates the prime reason for entering the role of the mentally ill is severe distress, disorganization and/or disruptive behavior ("havoc," to use Goffman's term). Furthermore, I have argued that psychiatric treatment, including hospitalization, does not typically have the negative consequences ascribed to it by labeling theorists and that, in fact, it often has positive consequences (Gove, 1970*a*, 1975*a*). Because of my response the labeling theorists (e.g., Scheff, 1975*a;* Anderson and Wilkinson, 1974) have characterized me as an apologist for the psychiatric perspective who accepts that model blindly. What the labeling theorists somehow have not noticed is that in my own work on mental illness I do not treat all persons in psychiatric treatment as mentally ill. In short, as I have emphasized elsewhere (Gove and Tudor, 1973; Gove and Clancy, 1975), I choose to limit the term "mental illness" to those with a functional (i.e., non-organic) disorder who are seriously distressed and/or disorganized. This category of disorders, which includes the neuroses, the functional psychoses, the transient situational disorders, and the psychophysiological disorders, are reactive to drug therapy and, to some extent, psychotherapy. Furthermore, it is possible to find theoretical links in the etiology of this category of disorders (e.g., Gove, 1970*b*). I would exclude from the category of "mental illness" the chronic brain syndromes, the drug and alcohol disorders, and the personality disorders. Patients in these last diagnostic categories do not respond to the same forms of intervention as those I would classify as mentally ill, nor do I see any theoretical link between the two groups. In my view those whom I would exclude are treated by the psychiatric profession (and thus labeled mentally ill) largely due to historical accident and psychiatric entrepreneurship. In short, with regard to those disorders I would exclude, while I think intervention is frequently called for, I do not think they should be categorized as mental illnesses.

Having made the point, following Lemert's suggestion, that it would be valuable to look at the institutional procedures for classifying and processing mental illness, let me shift back to the main point of this paper, the evaluation of labeling theory as it is understood. I will deal with two questions. First, why are some individuals and not others labeled deviant? Second, what are the consequences for the individual of being labeled a deviant? In my view these are the core questions of labeling theory, and labelling theory provides specific researchable answers to them. I would note, however, that not all persons in the labeling tradition would agree that these are the core questions. As has been frequently noted, labeling theory developed out of the symbolic interaction tradition which is concerned with—symbolic interaction. Under attack, some labeling theorists, notably Howard Becker (1973), Kitsuse (1975), and Schur (1975), have argued that the critical thrust of labeling is making social scientists aware that deviant behavior involves social interaction. As Becker (1973:179) states, the proponents of the perspective "wanted to enlarge the area taken into consideration in the study of deviant behavior by including in it of others than the deviant actor." I find this a very unsatisfactory argument. Sociologists have always known that social behavior involved social interaction. So have most other social scientists. In short, it is an exhortation to do something that is both obvious and already an intrinsic feature of the discipline. As such, it contributes virtually nothing. Furthermore, as is indicated by this session, a lot of us are concerned about labeling theory and I don't think we are concerned about a set of platitudes.

The Two Basic Questions

Before turning to what I feel are key propositions, three comments are in order. First, in attempting to evaluate the evidence bearing on the labeling perspective, the issue should not be whether there is *any* evidence supporting the labeling perspective, for I think we can all agree that there is at least some supportive evidence. Similarly, the question should not be whether there is *any* evidence supporting alternative explanations of the behavior in question, for I think we can also agree that there are other processes involved besides those described by the labeling theorists. Instead, the issue should be the importance of the labeling explanation *relative to* other explanations. At the crudest level, then, the issue is which explanation is the most powerful, that is, which accounts for the most variance. Hopefully, we will eventually be able to move beyond this either/or form of evaluation and specify with more precision the predictive power of the various perspectives and how the perspectives interact. We should be aware, however, that although some labeling theorists, such as Scheff (1974:445), agree that the weighing of the relative importance of the societal reaction explanation vis-à-vis its competitors is an extremely relevant question, this type of quantitative question lies outside the labeling tradition (e.g., see Back, 1975) and it has been held that it is not a particularly appropriate strategy (e.g., Schur, 1971:155, 1974:11). It is my position, however, that if a perspective which presumes to explain a particular phenomenon cannot be operationalized and tested, then that perspective does not provide a sociologically valid explanation of that phenomenon.

Second, it is extremely important to understand that the processes described by the labeling theorists have a particular thrust or direction. Thus, the labeling perspective specifies who is likely to be channeled into a deviant role, and this channeling process is viewed in a negative light. As suggested by the statements of Becker (1963; 1967), Lofland (1969), Lemert (1951), Sagarin (1975), Rubington and Weinberg (1971), N. Davis (1975), and Gibbs (1962), the labeling theorists side with the underdog, and they apparently equate the underdog with those on the margin of society who, because of their societal attributes, are ill equipped to prevent the imposition of a deviant label. Thus, the labeling perspective provides an explanation for why those on the margin, for example, the poor and the black, are particularly likely to be labeled as deviant. Furthermore, their explanation differs radically from the more traditional sociological explanations (e.g., Merton, 1968), which have attributed the higher rates of deviant behavior among marginal groups to characteristics of the social structure which increase the likelihood that persons in such groups will commit deviant acts.

Third, in evaluating the labeling perspective we should be aware that virtually all explanations of the development of deviant behavior involve a consideration of contingencies. Thus, the discovery that there are consequences to particular acts is consistent with most explanations and should not, by itself, be used as support for the labeling perspective. To constitute supporting evidence for the labeling perspective, the contingencies in question must work against those on the margin of society, and the imposition of a deviant label must work to promote the development of a deviant career. A finding that those who have the most power and the greatest number of resources were more likely to be labeled deviant, with the level of deviant behavior controlled, would not be consistent with the labeling perspective. Similarly, the discovery that controlling for the level of deviant behavior, those who were labeled by society as deviant were, over their lifetime, less likely to either commit deviant acts or to occupy a deviant role, would also be evidence against the labeling perspective.

WHO IS LABELED A DEVIANT?

The traditional view is that a person is labeled a deviant primarily because he either acts in a deviant manner or has characteristics that mark him as a deviant. For example, a person is labeled a criminal because he commits criminal acts, he is labeled mentally ill because he is mentally ill and behaves accordingly, or he is labeled physically disabled because he has a physical disability.

The societal reaction view is that a person is labeled a deviant primarily as a consequence of societal characteristics, particularly the lack of power and resources which marks him as an underdog and places him on the margin of society.

I recently chaired a conference where a number of scholars evaluated the evidence bearing on labeling theory. The conference participants and their topics were Lee Robins (1975), alcoholism; Robert Gordon (1975), mental retardation; Richard Smith (1975), physical disability; Charles Tittle (1975a), adult crime; Travis Hirschi (1975), juvenile delinquency; William McAuliffe (1975), drug use; Edward Sagarin and Robert Kelley (1975), sexual deviance; and myself (Gove, 1975a), mental illness. These papers have recently been published and I strongly recommend that you look at them. I think you will be impressed by the thoroughness of the reviews and the unanimity of the evidence. The evidence consistently indicates that it is the behavior or condition of the person that is the critical factor in causing someone to be labeled a deviant. Furthermore, the evidence indicates that with most forms of deviance the role played by social resources is relatively minor. Perhaps even more devastating to the labeling perspective is that with some forms of deviance, most clearly with mental illness and physical disability, the evidence indicates that the effect of individual resources is directly counter to that posited by labeling theory. For these forms of deviant behavior, and sometimes for other forms, social resources facilitate entrance into a deviant role. In summary, the role played by a lack of social resources has been greatly exaggerated by the labeling theorists, and the evidence provides more support for the traditional explanations than for the labeling perspective.

Even when, controlling for the level of deviant behavior, it is those without resources who are the most likely to be processed as deviant and who find it the most difficult to return to normal roles, it is not altogether clear that labeling theory adds valid information that was not already contained in the traditional perspective. For example, the medical profession has long recognized that persons who are senile are more likely to be placed in a nursing home if they lack family resources. Similarly, the psychiatric profession has always been aware that it is more difficult to place someone in the community who has a chronic mental illness if he or she lacks social and economic resources. Similarly, when the courts institutionalize a juvenile delinquent from a disturbed and broken home and put on probation a juvenile delinquent from an intact and supportive family, they apparently do this because they believe the juvenile with the intact family will receive more support and guidance in the community and is thus a better risk for probation. It is not clear that they are either unaware of the discriminatory nature of their acts or that their assessment is incorrect. In short, the traditional perspectives have long known that those without resources make up their most difficult and thus their more chronic cases. Simply pointing this out, while perhaps a useful reminder, is hardly a significant theoretical challenge to the traditional perspectives. It only becomes a real challenge when the effect of a lack of resources becomes an overriding factor, and, as I have already noted, the evidence consistently indicates that a lack of resources is rarely that important.

THE CONSEQUENCES OF BEING LABELED A DEVIANT

The labeling theorists argue that reacting to persons as if they were deviants is the major cause of deviant identities and life styles. It is assumed that without a societal reaction most deviant behavior would be transitory. In contrast, if the individual is reacted to as a deviant, it is assumed that his deviant status will become more or less permanent. It is argued that his deviant status will act as a master status which will determine how others will act toward him across the range of social interaction. It is argued that he will be cut off from interaction with normals and channeled into contact with deviants similar to himself. Furthermore, it is presumed that once this happens it becomes very difficult for the individual to return to a normal status (see Gove, 1975*b*). The most conservative formulation of the labeling perspective is that, over the person's lifetime, a deviant label produces more deviance than it prevents. This is a difficult proposition to test, for when we control the degree of deviant behavior we, in most instances, simply do not have comparable groups of unlabeled deviants. There are a number of reasons, however, to question this formulation. First, with many forms of deviance, stabilized deviant behavior occurs prior to labeling. Second, after labeling, most forms of deviance do not persist through a person's lifetime, that is, most deviance is transitory. Third, with most forms of deviant behavior a good case can be made that labeling results in a decrease rather than an increase in the amount of deviant behavior.

It has been a traditional view of society that for some forms of deviant behavior a punitive societal reaction will act as a deterrent which will prevent future deviant acts. In the area of crime, deterrence theory has recently received a great deal of attention and, by and large, the evidence supports the perspective (Tittle and Logan, 1973; Zimring and Hawkins, 1973; Geerken and Gove, 1975). Recently Tittle (1975*a*,

1975*b*) has carefully compared the relative empirical support for labeling and deterrence theory. Although be believes that the evidence is not conclusive because of the quality of the data, he indicates that it provides more support for the deterrence perspective. Most heroin addicts eventually give up their addiction, and McAuliffe (1975) has recently mounted a very compelling case that the major reason they give up their addiction is the deterrent effect of the societal reaction to their addiction. Similarly, a case can be readily made that the societal reactions to juvenile delinquency and alcoholism (for the case regarding alcoholism see Gove et al., 1974) will serve as a deterrent which will tend to minimize the manifestation of these forms of deviant behavior.

For many forms of deviance the traditional perspectives have argued that intervention, in the form of treatment, will have positive effects, reducing the amount of subsequent deviant behavior. In arguing for their own perspective, labeling theorists have frequently ignored the possibility that treatment may reduce deviance. However, in the case of physical disability, for example, there is ample evidence that treatment tends to minimize deviant behavior (R. Smith, 1975; Gove, 1975*b*). Similarly, in the area of mental illness, the efficacy of treatment has been well established. The evidence is particularly strong with regard to drug therapy, but even in the area of psychotherapy, which the labeling theorists have tended to disparage, the cumulative evidence is fairly impressive (Gove, 1975*a*). In the medical view, alcoholics and drug addicts should also receive treatment. As Robins (1975:27) notes, the evidence for the effectiveness of the treatment of alcoholics is modest, but on the other hand, there is no evidence that indicates that treatment results in an increase in heavy drinking. In the case of drug addiction, the evidence points to similar conclusions.

In short, when we look at the effects of labeling, the evidence consistently indicates that labeling is not the major cause of the development of stabilized deviant bevavior. Labeling, in fact, often appears to have the opposite effect.

Conclusion

Although labeling theory has been popular among social scientists and has played a significant role in how society reacts to various forms of deviant behavior, a careful scrutiny of the perspective suggests that it rests on a very tenuous base. Many of the originators of the perspective appear to have disassociated themselves from labeling theory in its present form, either calling for a very different focus, or backtracking and saying that all they wanted to do was call attention to the fact, already accepted by the social sciences, that deviant behavior involves social interaction. Furthermore, the evidence strongly suggests that the two most basic premises of labeling theory are substantially incorrect. Labeling theory argues that marginal social attributes play the major role in acquiring a deviant label; however, the evidence indicates that one acquires a deviant label primarily because of one's deviant behavior. Furthermore, at least with some forms of deviant behavior, individual resources, instead of preventing a deviant label, facilitate entrance into an official deviant status. Labeling theory's second major premise is that labeling is the prime cause of stabilized deviant behavior. However, the evidence not only indicates that this is not the case but also suggests that labeling, through treatment or deterrence, frequently prevents careers of deviance. In summary, although the issues with which labeling theory is concerned have theoretical and substantive importance, its answers tend to be inconsistent with the data.

13

A Reassessment of Labeling Theory:
A Constructive Response to Criticism

Patrick W. Conover

Introduction

LABELING THEORY has been recognized by friend and foe alike as one of the most significant developments in the sociology of deviance during the last two decades. At least four authors (N. Davis, 1972, 1975; Gove, 1970a; Manning 1973; Fabrega and Manning, 1972) have offered general critiques aimed at demolishing labeling theory as a prominent theory in the sociology of deviance. Twenty-four other authors (Gibbs, 1966, 1972; Akers, 1968; Bordua, 1967; Tittle, 1975b; Mankoff, 1971; Meade, 1974; Thorsell and Klemke, 1972; Goffman, 1969; Gove and Howell, 1974; Clancy and Gove, 1974; Turner, 1972; Lemert, 1967, 1974; Schur, 1971; Eaton, 1974; Llazos, 1972; Thio, 1973; Platt, 1973; Schervish, 1973; Rogers and Buffalo, 1974; Gibbons and Jones, 1975), at least, have offered specific critiques, some aimed at tearing down labeling theory, some as an introduction to suggested improvements, and some within the general context of creating or defending labeling theory. Many of the specific critiques overlap, and authors repeat each other, so that the response approach best suited to this plethora of criticism is to group the critiques logically. The procedure adopted here is to group the more than one hundred specific critiques into eight categories: bias, poor definition and lack of clarity, logical problems, incompleteness, relations to other theories, basic weaknesses, methodology, and evidence.

The sheer volume of the criticism could easily lead one to presume that labeling theory is dead and already buried. But when the criticisms are considered one at a time labeling theory emerges as a still lively and viable theory. Indeed, to the extent that the criticisms call for clarification and specification of the theory it may be fairly claimed that labeling theory is strengthened by going through the process of challenge and response. The volume of criticism may be seen as a tribute to the power of the theory.

There have been two stages in the history of the development of labeling theory. The first stage may be seen as Lemert's (1951) initial theoretical statement and some early exploratory research. A second stage includes attempts to expand the theorization and make it relevant to particular research areas, as seen in the work of Howard Becker (1963), Scheff (1966), and Schur (1971), among others. This second stage also included more than one hundred research efforts which bear upon one aspect or another of the issues at stake. In the second stage many of the efforts were limited in scope and no single statement of the theory was completely dominant, exactly the sort of circumstance that appropriately produces voluminous criticism. The question remains whether labeling theory will collapse under criticism or go forward to a third stage of clarity and powerful research. Perhaps the most important aspect of this question is whether labeling theory can be stated in a way which gives other theories of deviance their appropriate weight and place, in a general move toward a cumulative development of the sociology of deviance as a whole, since there is no possibility that labeling theory can serve as a complete theory of deviance in itself.

It is assumed that the reader is already familiar with the dominant conceptions of labeling theory as developed by Lemert (1951, 1967, 1974), Scheff (1966, 1975), H. Becker (1963), with additions by Lofland (1969) and Erikson (1962), among others. The basic idea is that audiences react to the behavior of the individual and present a label (image, picture, evaluation, etc.) to the person of himself or herself. The individual then takes account of this label in the construction of further action, sometimes developing a sense of identity around the content of the label and entering into a career of deviance as a result. This is a very complex theory in that it specifies a process which develops over several stages, with different causal elements having importance at the different stages. Labeling by the self (as audience), informal labeling by others, and formal labeling by social agencies, all can be important, and vary in importance depending upon the kind of deviance under consideration and the institutional and situational context of the audience response. One thing may be made clear at the beginning. Labeling theory does not seek to explain deviance as such but rather secondary deviance (Lemert), deviant careers (Becker), or the adoption of the role and self-image of mental illness (Scheff). The simple understanding that labeling theory has been trying to explain deviants rather than deviance will allow us to dispose of several critiques.

The Critique of Labeling Theory

BIAS

Three kinds of charges of bias have been raised against labeling theory. Nanette Davis (1975) has authored a broadcast smear. She has accused labeling theorists of everything from being unpublished to having unconventional sentimentality. There is no need to respond to the *argumentum ad hominen* fallacy, and attention can be directed to the more substantive critiques. When Davis charges that labeling theory is biased in favor of underdogs, Sagarin (1975) and Gove (1970c) agree. Because of this presumed bias, social control agents are presented as victimizing moral offenders, lower classes, and minorities, and society is indicted for its inhumane and arbitrary treatment accorded deviants. Labeling research has indeed found empirical evidence of discrimination, but it is not a central focus of labeling theory. The findings of discrimination are rather support for the assertion that agency processes are related to characteristics of the deviant other than the presumed kind of deviant act involved. Even Lemert (1974) is ready to admit an apparent underdog bias in some studies, but then quickly draws attention back to the important issues at stake. In contrast, Davis notes a significant amount of evidence showing arbitrariness in agency processing as if it were insignificant.

The opposite kind of bias, bias in favor of the ruling classes, has been charged by Llazos (1972), Thio (1973), and Platt (1973). This charge is based, not on what labeling theorists have done, but rather on what they have failed to do. Labeling theory has not analyzed deviance of economic and political elites and has not analyzed the role of power in the designation of deviance. Noticing the contrasting thrusts of these last two charges of ideological bias, it seems appropriate to argue that the scientific discussion can best be moved ahead by focusing on the empirical and theoretical issues in and of themselves. In contrast to the above, and as a partial rejoinder to the charges of bias that are in favor of the ruling class, Scheff (1970) analyzes the content of the label "schizophrenia," within the proper use of the sociology of knowledge, as embedded in the historical and cultural perspectives of the white middle class.

PROBLEMS OF CLARITY AND DEFINITION

At least eighteen authors have found fault with one aspect or another of the imagery or the definitions used in labeling theory. The most commonly attacked definition is that of Howard Becker (1963:9) that deviant behavior "is behavior that people so label." This definition is found wanting in contrast to the more typical kind of definition which emphasizes the violation of rules, norms, or expectations, as the key feature. Davis (1975) and Sagarin (1975) argue that this definition doesn't include "secret" deviance—deviance which is known only by the self and not others. Schur (1971) answers this charge by pointing out that in the case of "secret" deviance self-labeling is at work. Lemert's (1974) response to the critique of the reaction type of definition is that unless a "violation" is validated by some kind of significant response, there is doubt as to the salience of the norm in the first place. The best way out of the dilemma presented here seems to me to be simply to recognize that some may wish to study behavior which violates norms, while others may wish to study the effects of social reactions. Labeling theory, in its specific empirical concern, is focused on the impact of social reactions and can be satisfied with a reaction-based definition. Indeed, when Becker (1963:25) addresses the issue of "secret" deviance he considers the importance of "nonconforming"—he later says "deviant"—behavior, and discusses deviance as being of three kinds: secret, reacted against, and falsely asserted.

The charges of vagueness, imprecision, and subjectivity are difficult to respond to. On the one hand, there are plenty of examples of empirical research with tight operational definitions, such as adjudicated incompetency, but interview and observational studies may not be as clear. At the nominal level, however, it seems hard to be confused about the sensitizing concepts, particularly if we remember to distinguish between self, other (group), and formal (societal) labeling, distinctions made, for example, by Becker (1963) and Schur (1971). Scheff (1975b) points out that a great deal of sociology has trouble with producing completely denotative concepts.

Because labeling theory has to deal with subjective issues, such as normalization and self identity, it is intrinsically difficult to ground definitions on an objective base. Were such objectivity attempted, the serious charge of reification could be brought. Lemert (1974) may be correct in asserting that the contributions of ethnomethodology to this conversation carry subjectivity too far, but his own insistence on the processual and interactive shape of labeling theory requires that sociologists must continue with the difficult work of making judgments about subjective states. Because there are some objective reference points, especially in formal labeling, labeling theory has the advantage of being able to use both verstehen-based and category-based definitions. While this has posed some difficulty in theoretical integration, much is gained in empirical richness.

Lemert (1974) joins Davis (1975) in arguing that use of the dramatistic metaphor makes label-appliers seem overly arbitrary and inflexible. Two rejoinders seem appropriate here. One is that Goffman, primary proponent of the metaphor, has also been careful to argue (1969) for basing the reality of concepts such as "mental symptoms" on actual rule breaking. Then, use of the metaphor may be kept in perspective as a metaphor. As a metaphor, it is intrinsically highly flexible and any faults of inflexibility lie in the user. It may be noted here that analyzing only one half of the interaction process, treating one side for the moment as given, is not so much a signal of inflexibility as of emphasizing the virtue of clarity gained from limited focus.

Much of the criticism of definitions seems to be because there is no single author or research that completely establishes labeling theory by itself. Critiques of one author are answered by another from within the labeling position. When it is realized that there are several definitions at stake, which must be specified and operationalized, relative to their place within overall labeling theory, no basic difficulty remains beyond the carelessness and lack of rigor that afflicts us all.

LOGICAL PROBLEMS

Five different logical problems in labeling theory have been asserted.

Davis (1975) charges that labeling theory is microsociological in that it features analysis of local groups rather than differentially ranked participants. It is not clear that being microsociological is a fault. Not many sociologists would consider the differential rankings of participants as a distinguishing feature of sociological scale. Studies of agency processing do deal with differentially ranked participants. Large-scale records studies have compared the distributions of labels in populations.

Labeling theory is tautological, says Tittle (1975b), because it takes the position that when recidivism occurs it is due to the label and that when it does not the label didn't stick. The correct charge here should be that labeling theory analysis is *post hoc* or that labeling theorems are untestable because there is no possibility of negative evidence. But labeling research has proceeded in *pre hoc* designs, and the finding that a label doesn't stick is evidence against the concept of the labeling act as an overwhelming causal force. Further, there is labeling-theory-based research which holds the act constant and can then compare the effect of adding or not adding labels. Further yet, there is research which examines the mechanisms by which a label comes to have salience for an individual. To be tautological, it would be necessary that the outcome of secondary deviance be present in the definition of the cause, labeling. This is clearly not the case since not all people who are labeled become secondary deviants. Merely to assert that a cause has an effect, even if a one-to-one relationship is asserted, is not tautological anyhow. In the probabilistic form of labeling theory it is appropriate to examine the conditions under which the labeling act has efficacy in promoting deviant careers.

Davis (1975) argues that labeling should not be seen as the only causal force producing deviance and that other forces should be considered. None of the proponents of labeling theory have argued that it is a complete unicausal theory. It has been argued (Schur, 1971) that it is an important theory that may be seen as complementary to other theories as part of a general theory of deviance.

Davis and Sagarin (1975), among others, have charged that labeling theory is relativistic. This charge, in part, focuses on the issue, previously discussed, of whether the key definition should focus on norm violation or social reaction. The charge by Davis is muted by the fact that in the same sentence (1975:172) she accuses labeling theory of being normative. Later (p. 185) she attacks labeling theory for *not* recognizing that deviance is a relative concept. Schur (1971) argues that the relativism of labeling theory is a strength rather than a weakness. Not to recognize the fact that our research and theoretical efforts must be specified relative to the culture and society within which our subject matter obtains would be the serious fault.

It is sometimes asserted that labeling theory must reject the content of societal labels. Rogers and Buffalo (1974), following Fabrega and Manning (1972), hold to a softer version of this criticism by claiming that labeling theory equivocates about the "location" or substance of deviance. Is deviance merely "fictive," or is it based on a real state of being or action? This problem also seems to go back to the issue of definition which has already been discussed. However, an additional dimension presents itself when labeling theorists attack "mental illness" as a myth. In this case it is clear that the assertion is that the societal label is baseless relative to its own putative grounding. It still exists as a social fact, as an orientation for social actors and reactors, and it is in this sense, as a social reality, that sociological study is appropriate. This orientation is appropriate whatever the stance taken toward the putative grounding of the label.

INCOMPLETION

Labeling theory has been attacked for (1) not examining the economic and political relationships which perpetuate the ranking system behind labeling (Davis, 1975); (2) not recommending policies to alleviate deviance (Davis) and for directing concern away from rehabilitation (Sagarin, 1975); (3) not explaining primary deviance (Akers, 1968; Bordua, 1967; Gibbs, 1972; Davis; Sagarin, 1975); (4) not paying sufficient attention to how rules are formed or changed (Davis; Gibbs, 1972; Gibbons and Jones, 1975); (5) being insensitive to the positive or negative functional impacts of deviance on society (Davis); (6) not accounting for deviance which is merely situational adjustment (Davis); (7) failure to analyze organizational deviance (Davis); (8) inadequacy as a theory of social control (Davis).

In each of the above charges labeling theory is being attacked for not doing something it didn't set out to do. These charges may be taken as a partial list of issues which need attention from complementary theories in the establishment of a general theory of deviance. It should also be noted that some authors associated with labeling theory have addressed some of these other issues. Lemert (1974) and Becker (1963) have analyzed historical, cultural, and structural sources of change in legal structures. Lemert (1974) has been concerned with the diversion movement in criminal justice which developed in response to labeling theory. Labeling theory has not been presented by its primary authors as a general theory of deviance. We would be further along if the misdirected energy put into criticizing labeling theory as a general theory had been put into integrative theorization. Such lack of care and combativeness makes it difficult for sociology to function as a cumulative discipline.

RELATIONS TO OTHER THEORIES

Labeling theory has been criticized by Davis (1975) for being opposed to major theoretical stances such as formalism (functional theory) and positivism. To the extent that labeling theory is seen as a part of symbolic interactionist theory (Schur, 1971) it is at least fair to note that such theory differs from other alternatives. Schur goes on to add that labeling theory is not fairly seen as drawing only from the symbolic interactionist perspective. The issue of positivism will be dealt with under the section on methodology. With regard to functional theory, while it is clear that labeling theory did not originate from a functionalist perspective, it is also easy to state some of the basic labeling theory assertions in functionalist terms. For example: The promotion on secondary deviance is an unanticipated consequence (hidden functional impact) of social control efforts involving labeling. Sometimes labeling is part of the scapegoating function. Because labeling theory is sequentially designated, a cause at one stage has functional implications at another. Tittle (1975*b*), Schur (1971), and Petroni (1972) also see labeling theory as congruent with, or complementary to, functional theory.

Other deviance theories have been advanced as opposed to, or as being better than, labeling theory. Tittle (1975*b*) has tried to argue that control theory and labeling theory have much agreement but can be tested against each other at the point of hypothesized effects of negative sanctions. Control theory predicts that the imposition of a label as a negative sanction should deter deviance, whereas Tittle holds that labeling theory predicts an increase in deviance. But labeling theory is not opposed to control theory. The key is in clarification of the dependent variable. Labeling theory sets out to explain the stabilization of secondary deviance. Control theory seeks to explain rates of primary deviant acts. It can easily be the case that negative sanctions may deter many from acting in a particular deviant way and also, for those for whom the label becomes an important referent for self-identity, a cause of stabilized secondary deviance. Indeed, one of the most important issues needing additional attention is the specification of the conditions, by kind of deviance, and other factors, under which labeling leads to deterrence or stabilization. To assert that labeling is an important cause of secondary deviance is not to assert that the causal force cannot be overcome. After all, we have now built rockets which can overcome Earth's gravity.

Mechanic (1972) and Gove (1970*a*), among others, have held that mental illness can be explained by some mixture of physiological, psychological, and sociological causes without reference to labeling theory. The generalization of these assertions is that secondary deviance can be explained by the continued action of the causes of the primary deviance. This kind of charge is best answered with reference to the relevant data. It will be handled in the later section on evidence. One thing may be clarified at this point, however. For many forms of primary deviance, suicide and abortion for example, there is no corresponding secondary deviance. It may be an insignificant consideration for other forms of deviance as well, such as murder. But to hold that powerful social reactions have little or no impact on role-taking or identity change, not only challenges labeling theory, but a great mass of conventional sociology as well.

INTERNAL THEORETICAL PROBLEMS

Labeling theory has been accused (Schervish, 1973; Rogers and Buffalo, 1974; Davis, 1975) of placing too much emphasis on the deviant as actor, instead of seeing the individual in terms of group membership, organizational positions, statuses and roles, and so on. The basic point asserted here is that in sociological studies it is not appropriate to treat the individual as an isolated unit. An extension of this charge is that labeling theory treats the individual as passive, as able only to react to the force of social labeling. This assertion is made by Gibbs (1966), Davis (1975), Lemert (1974), Schur (1971), Sagarin (1975), Gibbons and Jones (1975) following Akers (1968) and Bordua (1967), Rogers and Buffalo (1974), and Schervish (1973).

Part of an appropriate rejoinder is to note with Turner (1972) that labeling theory has also considered the side of the labelers and their procedures. In fact it is this kind of study, focusing on the labelers rather than upon the deviant as actor, which is the reference for the charge of passivity. Turner goes on to argue that Lemert's (1951) theory does not posit a passive actor, and he then tries to work out a more active concept of the actor based on the concept of role and role taking. Rogers and Buffalo (1974) offer the criticism of passivity as the introduction to an effort to correct the situation. Schur (1971) and Gibbons and Jones (1975) also treat the problem of passivity as one which can be handled by highlighting the parts of labeling theory which do emphasize an active conception of the actor. Scheff (1968) makes a contribution in this direction by a study on the process by which patients "negotiate reality." Lemert (1974) provides the wisest counsel on this issue by noting that the treating of actors as passive is a perennial problem in sociology, and then setting forth theory and research (Lemert, 1960) which seeks to correct this problem. However, as long as labeling theory makes significant use of records studies, a caution on this issue is appropriate. By distinguishing the analysis of *process* from the analysis of *states,* it is possible to place research which is in a static framework, with an emphasis on the analysis of the impact of social forces, in relationship to processual studies highlighting dynamic features of individuals and groups. Rogers and Buffalo offer a typology as a solution, though they admit typologies are useful only as transitional theoretical efforts. What is needed is to specify causal paths and contingencies in time sequence.

The charge that labeling theory rarely studies the interactive process, made by Davis (1975), Sagarin (1975), and Rogers and Buffalo (1974), is closely related to the previous charge and is largely answered in rejoinder to that charge. Lemert (1974), Schur (1971), and Gibbons and Jones (1975), among others, have all presented labeling theory as highly interactive. The problem remains that some research considers only one aspect of process and thereby may be misunderstood as suggesting a static bias to the theory. This misimpression may be countered by the careful placing of particular research efforts within the larger theoretical picture which is processual.

The next set of charges is lengthy and significant. They all deal with some failure to specify fully the conditions, contexts, alternate paths of causation, and alternate sequences in the deviant career. All of these charges may be taken as internal or perfecting critiques. A restatement of labeling theory should include these refinements.

The general charge of failure to specify conditions is made by Davis (1975) and Tittle (1975*b*). Tittle then goes on to correct this fault by indicating nine groups of specifying conditions: the character of the violated norm, characteristics of offenders, characteristics of sanctions, kinds of behavior involved, whether sanctioning produces general or specific alienation, the position of the sanctioned act in series of actions, the nature of the community in which the deviant act is committed, the nature of the community in which the sanction is applied, and the role of perception (of rejection, opportunity, etc.) in contrast to the "real situation." Many specific critiques are handled by the recognition that labeling theory needs this sort of specification. Davis admits that many conditions have been specified. Important work in specification has been done by: Lemert (1974), Fein and Miller (1972), Ageton and Elliott (1974), Short and Strodtbeck (1965), Steadman (1972), Williams and Gold (1972), Marshall and Purdy (1972), Eaton (1974), Schur (1971), Rogers and Buffalo (1974), Greenley (1972*a*; 1972*b*), Miller, Simons, and Fein (1974). Thus it is hardly fair to claim that people working in a labeling theory perspective have been entirely lax in this matter. Work on specification comes in the second generation of research effort, and it was well enough launched so that contributions had been made in each of Tittle's classes of specification before he wrote.

The concern about specifying the historical context of labeling theory (Davis, 1975) is useful for noting the limits to the generalization of research findings. Turner's point (1972) that the historical setting has changed with the emergence of quasipublic voluntary associations of deviants should be considered in future research, particularly for certain kinds of deviance.

Davis (1975) argues that membership in a deviant group doesn't lead to the crystallization of a deviant identity for all members. Gove (1970*a*), Lemert (1974), and Davis argue that Goffman's conception of total institutions is too totalistic and rigid, though Gove concedes that Goffman's conception may be more accurately applied to old-style public mental hospitals. Sagarin (1975), Mankoff (1971), Thorsell and Klemke (1972), and Davis argue that negative labeling may lead to conformity when the labelee has a commitment to labelers and desires to retain a relationship. Self-help groups such as Alcoholics Anonymous are relevant at this point. Even after adoption of a deviant role, an individual may avoid a deviant career in that role by focusing his activity in a counter social movement, by suicide, or by involvement in distracting deviance. At this point, cycles of abstinence and relapse should also be considered. All of the specifications developed here deal with *exits* from the primary path theorized by those in the labeling perspectives. The issues at stake here are empirical ones. Under what conditions, for which kinds of deviance, do what proportion of people who enter the deviant process follow variant paths? By conceiving of labeling theory as one path through the complex of causes studied in the sociology of deviance, one can then approach this work in a cumulative and cooperative spirit. This conception of alternate paths and exits is also offered as the appropriate rejoinder to the charge that labeling theorists overemphasize the effect of labeling on self-conceptions (Davis, 1975; Sagarin, 1975; Mankoff, 1971; Thorsell and Klemke, 1972; Gove, 1970a, on appeal to Angrist et al., 1968; and Gibbons and Jones, 1975). Self-conception is one node or state in the general processes of deviance. It is a node that must be considered as critical to the development of a deviant career but is not important for the answering of other questions in the sociology of deviance.

The remaining critique in this category is that individuals may develop deviant careers without formal labeling. It is offered by Davis (1975), Klein (1974) following Clinard (1963), Lemert (1967), and Sutherland (1940); and by Tittle (1975b). This critique may be handled by specification of a separate path and empirical investigation which emphasizes self- and other (nonformal) labeling plus factors such as positive labeling by deviant groups.

METHODOLOGY

One easily handled charge, by Davis (1975), is that labeling theory uses small-scale research. Some of the examples to the contrary include Jensen (1972), Fein and Miller (1972), Ageton and Elliott (1974), Chiricos and Jackson (1972), Steadman (1972), Williams and Gold (1972), Miller et al. (1974), Eaton (1974), and Greenley (1972a).

A more serious charge by Davis (1975) is that labeling theory rejects positivistic doctrines and has provoked an "epistemological crisis," a breakdown of the normal assumptions of the discipline, by introducing human biases (subconscious impulses, cultural values, class biases, and political positions) and assumptions into the research process. She particularly attacks symbolic interactionist methodology for seeking "understanding of the phenomena" rather than "confirming or contradicting theoretical hypotheses."

The bias charge has already been answered. The "epistemological crisis" charge is silly, since sociology has been able to carry on for several decades with continual dialogue between positivistic and verstehen perspectives. In addition, there are quite a few positivistic studies in the labeling tradition (Williams and Gold, 1972; Caetano, 1974; Greenley, 1972a; Weiner and Willie, 1971; Meade, 1974; Serban and Gidynski, 1974; Fein and Miller, 1972; Chiricos and Jackson, 1972; Steadman, 1972; Marshall and Purdy, 1972; Levinson and York, 1974; Miller et al., 1974; Ageton and Elliott, 1974; Petroni, 1973; Steffensmeir and Terry, 1973). The above recent studies include the following kinds of data collection procedures: cross-sectional survey research, experimental, field experimental, observational, records analysis, interview, and longitudinal following of a population cohort with annual interviews. In fact, the recent years have seen more positivistic than verstehen studies. The broad spread of data collection procedures also stands as an answer to the Davis charge that labeling theory has a weak methodology because it relies on personal testimonies and case histories for data. These studies also serve as an additional rejoinder to the charges that labeling theory is overly subjective. If anything, the current generation of research might be characterized as broad, varied, imaginative, and in some cases (Greenley, 1972a; Williams and Gold, 1972; Steadman, 1972; Ageton and Elliott, 1974) careful and sophisticated.

More limited methodological charges such as problems with the Langner scale (Clancy and Gove, 1974), some failures to distinguish incidence from prevalence (Tittle, 1975b), bias in the Hollingshead and Redlich class index (Mechanic, 1972), for examples, are the kind of perfecting criticisms appropriate to a maturing subdiscipline.

But there is no need to be defensive about the virtues of a verstehen approach. As Meade (1974) points out, since labeling theory involves such processes as neutralization and self-definition, it follows that subjective research is required for clarification. When labeling theory is seen as dealing with a long and complex process which passes through several individual states and social locations, it becomes immediately apparent that both research traditions are necessary.

EVIDENCE

All of the previous criticisms might be met and we would still find it appropriate to discard the labeling theory if the evidence available pointed to rejection. There are plenty of assertions that rejection is the appropriate response.

Sagarin (1975) makes a case against labeling theory for juvenile delinquency. In an independent review of the most recent relevant articles in the major journals, I found two articles (Fisher, 1972; J. Foster et al., 1972) which could be counted as negative evidence. Foster et al. and Fisher both did small-scale studies with weak conceptions of the dependent variable. Definitely mixed or positive evidence has been provided by Weiner and Willie (1971), Meade (1974), Ageton and Elliott (1974), Short and Strodtbeck (1965), Williams and Gold (1972), Gold and Williams (1969), and Arnold (1971). However, these researches also suffer from data or methods limitations, or in the cases of the few excellent studies, produce findings which are mixed or equivocal. We have already dealt with Tittle's false contrast of deterrence and labeling theory. His contention that recidivism rates in one set of studies of between 33 and 40 percent count as negative evidence in themselves is misconstrued, because labeling theory does not require that most people who are labeled should develop deviant careers but that, of those who do develop deviant careers, many were significantly propelled toward a stabilized deviant role by the application of labels. The four studies which he chose for review have weaknesses and are open to alternate interpretation, but even his own evaluations are equivocal. As in many research traditions, we seem left with the conclusion that more research is needed.

The relevance of labeling theory for criminology has recently been reviewed by Wellford (1975). The quality of the review work is very high, as far as it goes. Unfortunately, Wellford takes his view of what labeling theory is from Schrag (1971), who produced a list of nine assumptions. Eight of the issues raised by Schrag are disposed of by Wellford or have been resolved in earlier sections of this chapter. Then Wellford focuses in on the critical issue. He notes that the heart of labeling theory is Schrag's ninth "hypothesis," that labeling produces identification with a deviant image and subculture and leads to the rejecting of rejectors. Schrag's form of this crucial hypothesis leaves a lot to be desired, but we can proceed to the substantive issues. Wellford notes that a lot of the impact of labeling comes from secondary impacts on employment, education, and community acceptance. He notes the study by Schwartz and Skolnick (1964) in favor of the hypothesis. He attacks the hypothesis by arguing that one cannot assume simple consistency between the concepts of self-concept, attitudes, and behavior, and must include important situational factors in the causal chain. But this is hardly an attack! The very same point was made by Schwartz and Skolnick. Wellford himself noted that the important effects of labeling may be through secondary impacts. Following Lemert, Becker, and

Scheff, labeling theory has no difficulty in including situational factors. Thus it would appear that labeling theory may still have a future in the area of criminology and that better research is needed here.

The primary critique of labeling theory has come from Gove and associates (1970*a*, 1970*b*, 1970*c*, 1972, 1975 with Clancy, 1974 with Howell, 1975 with Fain). Their attack has been focused on the work of Scheff (1963, 1964*a*, 1964*b*, 1966, 1967, 1968, 1970, 1975*b*). Objections to labeling theory of a nonevidential nature have been dealt with in earlier parts of this chapter.

In his most famous critique (1970*a*), Gove makes six charges. His first is that there is a great deal of resistance to defining behavior as mentally ill. This charge is in support of Scheff's assertion that there is a high rate of unrecorded to recorded acts of residual deviance. His second charge is that since there is a great deal of difference between the behavior that leads to labeling and the public stereotypes held, then stereotyping cannot be treated as a cause of labeling. Of course. Scheff doesn't assert that they are. It is only *after* the label has been attached that the salience of the stereotype for group reaction occurs.

A third charge is that not all who are screened are admitted to mental hospitals. This is certainly true for some studies, primarily studies of voluntary admissions. Other studies, particularly for large public hospitals, show a low rate of screening. In any case this is not a serious attack, since labeling theory is only seeking to consider how those who adopt the mentally ill role come to do so. Institutionalization is merely one factor in specifying the impact of the label on labelees. It is easy to argue that the more significant the impact of the label on the person, including whether or not it leads to institutionalization, the more likely it is to be a cause of secondary deviance.

As a fourth charge, Gove argues that hospitalization may have positive, though often unintended, effects and that new hospitalization practices may decrease the negative effects. This is simply to say that if the negative effects of labeling decrease, then there should be less secondary deviance, a finding that would be in support of labeling theory.

In a fifth charge, Gove follows a study by Angrist and associates (1968), which held that poor functioning rather than stigma was the cause of recidivism among mental patients. This charge is seriously weakened by his own admission that when Angrist and associates controlled for singleness, education, and household arrangement, differences in level of functioning disappear. More importantly, in this study there is no variation of the important independent variable of stigma, since all concerned were former mental patients. Since two thirds of Angrist's population did not recidivate, it is clear that neither stigma nor poor functioning taken together can account for most of the results. Again, it is crucial to keep in mind just what labeling theory is trying to explain. At each point in the deviance process, labeling theory is only trying to account for the factors that lead toward the stabilization of secondary deviance.

As a final critique, Gove simply reasserts the medical model, that people are hospitalized because they have active psychiatric disorders. Thus none of his charges *against* labeling theory are sustained and we are left with the initial issue of arguing labeling theory against the medical model. As far as Gove's challenge to labeling theory is concerned, it is most instructive to consider the positive attempt at explanatory theory which he seeks to develop as an alternative. In his article on the relation of sleep deprivation to mental illness (1970*b*), his formulations look a great deal like labeling theory. His theory has twelve sequential points. The first four points compose an assertion that the process begins with a crisis or disruption of life leading to acute disturbance or distress, which causes sleeping loss and symptoms, such as hallucinations, associated with sleep loss. Scheff would have no trouble accepting this presentation as part of his first proposition about the diverse sources of mental illness. The next three points are that poor behavioral functioning which results from sleep loss leads to the alienation of others and the disruption of interpersonal relations in a snowballing process. These points fit with the assertion by Scheff that most residual deviance is denied and transitory and that it is only when the act contingencies of seriousness, duration, and visibility come into play that labeling is initiated. It should be noted that Gove has introduced the principle of social reaction into his explanatory scheme. The next two points, that the individual lacks a ready self-explanation and is therefore suggestible, is much like Scheff's assertion that suggestibility is a crucial feature in the labeling crisis. When Gove further argues that it is at this point that interpretation by others has impact and leads to reorganization into deviant roles, it is again easy to see the close similarity to Scheff's position regarding the significance of stereotyping and the reward features of the deviant role. Gove is left with a closing assertion that after this long process physiological change occurs. It seems theoretically gratuitous and it is hard to image what kind of evidence could be found to support it.

The medical model dies hard. The most recent reviews in the *Annual Review of Psychology* (Cromwell, 1975; Zubin et al., 1975) show what the older reviews show. After decades of effort no one has found a physiological, biochemical, hormonal, or neurological basis for schizophrenia or the other "functional" mental disorders. Two good sociologists, Mechanic and Kohn, have been impressed by genetic findings, though they disagree about the process by which they have effect. But a careful sympathetic review by Millon (1969) notes that there are grave methodological weaknesses in the genetic studies, particularly the failure to control for confounding factors, which he admits may completely destroy the role of the genetic factor and also the problem of using the courrente classification system to define the independent variable. In any case, all that anyone is contesting for with the genetic theory is for some kind of vague predisposing factor, exactly the kind of causation of primary deviance which Scheff posits. Why did we ever forget that Kraepelin, who invented schizophrenia, considered it an arbitrary generic grouping of disorders which did not constitute a clinical syndrome or entity? Decades of research have proved him right.

By contrast, there is evidence in support of labeling theory. In his most recent review, Scheff (1975*b*) considers eighteen studies which meet minimum methodological conditions. He found thirteen to favor labeling theory and five to oppose his operative assertion about the importance of labeling. There is also support for his foundation propositions. The Dohrenwends (1965, 1969) review twenty-five epidemiological studies which show a great deal of "mental illness symptomatology" in the population compared to that which comes to attention. Similar findings may be found for delinquency (Murphy et al., 1946), felonious behavior (Wallerstein and Wyle, 1947), and homosexuality (Kinsey et al., 1948). Nunnaly (1961), among others, has found that the population does have stereotypic conceptions of mental illness. Two studies of the reward features of the mental illness role by Smith and Thrasher (1963) and by Rosenham (1973) support a labeling position. Greenley (1972*a*) has shown that psychiatrists adjust their diagnoses to mesh with family attitudes, and a rebuttal attempt by Gove and Fain (1975) is unsatisfying, since their research uses the methodologically inferior technique of path analysis, compared to Greenley's time-ordered measurements, on a subject where time ordering is clearly crucial. Thus, labeling theory must still be judged to be a viable guide to research and practice.

Summary of Critique

Many critiques were rejected on logical grounds. Some were rejected by showing the strength of one labeling theorist to fill in gaps not handled by others. Most importantly, some new procedures for indicating labeling theory and for showing relationships to other theory were developed. Strong evidence in favor of the labeling theory of "mental illness" was discussed along with the equivocal evidence for other kinds of deviance. Important limits to the scope of labeling theory were indicated.

14

Response to Critics: Feedback and Choice

Edwin M. Lemert

I HAVE OBSERVED to some of my colleagues that labeling theory seems to be largely an invention of its critics. By this I mean that with a few commendable exceptions critics tend to impute common ideas to a number of authors, including myself, whose writings in reality are quite diverse. Critics even derive hypotheses for us or enumerate our underlying assumptions, most recently reaching an impressive total of nine. Having done this, they proceed to demonstrate the logical, methodological, and empirical insufficiencies of the theory. When confronted, those who have been identified with the theory or "school," so called, must deny or refute that which they haven't said or defend ideas they don't necessarily share, or accept only with qualifications.

Recently the tone of criticism has grown more militant and aggressive. A kind of *delenda est*—Carthage must be destroyed—attitude prevails. Critics seem less interested in careful assessment than in attack and destruction (e.g., Gove, 1975a). Alleged disregard for the "traditional" approach to deviance by labeling theorists presumably decrees that he who lives by the sword shall die by the sword. Up the counter-revolution!

Unhappily the revolutionary mood abets if not encourages carelessness and misrepresentation. Consider, for example, recent exchanges between Scheff and Gove concerning the pertinence of labeling theory for the study of mental disorders. When I first read Scheff's demurrer that Gove misrepresented his writings, I thought that he—Scheff—was being normally testy about his cherished ideas or showing some mild academic paranoia (Scheff, 1974). My impression changed when in a recent paper Gove stated that in my 1951 book I said:

"Those labeled as mentally ill do not differ markedly from those who are not labeled and it is those on the margin of society who are most readily labeled" (Lemert, 1951).* Curious after twenty-four years to see again what I had said, I reread the designated pages not once but four times. I found no such statements in them.

Lest I too was being only testy, I read carefully a 1969 article by Mendel and Rapport cited by Gove to show that the mentally ill in Los Angeles county are prescreened before commitment and not routinely hospitalized. This turned out to be true and it questions some of Scheff's conclusions, but what Gove doesn't tell us is that commitments varied consistently by day of the week and time of day, and by the professional background of the admitting officials. More importantly it showed that there was no relationship between professionally rated seriousness of mental symptoms and decisions to hospitalize.

Gove's net even brings up a statement by Goffman that labeling theorists fail to examine the "organizational havoc" done to families by mental symptoms, citing this to support the "psychiatric perspective" that persons in mental hospitals are truly sick in a medical sense. Again, what Gove leaves out is that psychiatrists don't examine the havoc either, and further, to quote Goffman, "claims and actions of the ill person are not necessarily bizarre in themselves, merely bizarre when coming from a particular person addressing himself to a particular family. . . . And bizarreness itself is not the issue" (Goffman, 1969).

Years ago the Institute for Propaganda Analysis had a name for Gove's citing practices: It was called card stacking.

Hirschi's recent indictment of labeling theory is less chargeable with misrepresentation; obviously he is a man who reads carefully what others say before he speaks, and he sticks to the text (Hirschi, 1975). I must, however, object to his choice of targets. Tannenbaum strikes me as a sitting duck for a man with as much methodological expertise as Hirschi. Alas, poor Tannenbaum, he wrote thirty-seven years ago, at a time when there was little beyond Shaw and McKay to draw on (Tannenbaum, 1938). Further, he was a historian, most at home with labor problems and foreign policy. Moreover he was not really trying to go beyond presentation of a point of view. And he *did* have a new idea, something attested to by the men who urged its publication: John Dewey, Walton Hamilton, and Thorstein Veblen.

I prefer to think that Hirschi is fighting on ground not of his own choosing against opponents who to him obstinately refuse to follow the rules of the scientific method. This surfaces in his recent assessment of the evidence for and against the application of labeling theory to juve-

---

* The pages in question are 392–98 and are cited in the paper read by Gove at the Vanderbilt deviancy conference.

nile delinquency. Hirschi takes labeling simply as a variable in the traditional positivist sense to see whether it causes delinquency. In passing he acknowledges that interaction exists, but to him it is nothing more than the interaction of variables: If X, then Y.

Like the early determinists, Hirschi ignores or denies the existence of choice in human action lest this make us slip back into murky supernatural thinking officially tabooed by science. Our task is to find invariate orders between factors; X causes Y and that's that!

But the process of choice is *not* invariate. Unfortunately the mechanical model of cause and effect has been in use for so long in our culture that it is very difficult to advocate models which take teleology into account. Perhaps, though, as W. F. Cottrell says, now that we can build missiles that hunt missiles we can accept the purposeful behavior that invented them. The idea that human beings respond selectively to symbolic feedback on their actions can give us a model that may contribute to better understanding of what takes place without compelling us to leave what we regard as scientific ground.

A beginning was made with George Herbert Mead's conception of symbolic interaction. This becomes more precise when we include evaluation and groups as well as individuals in the process. To me interaction means that acts and events do not have fixed meanings or consequences when feedback and choice intervene. This does not deny that such things as anxiety exist, or that boys break windows or take automobiles without permission, or that heroin users have withdrawal symptoms. It means rather that human beings exercise choice in responding to these—organizing events into "cases," making judgments as to their seriousness, applying administrative categories, and opting for one among different lines of action.

The issue is whether agents of social control make choices in doing these things and, if they do, what factors influence their choice. If I understand Hirschi correctly, he says that police make simple choices between arresting and not arresting juveniles based on legal criteria, namely seriousness and frequency of the offense. Presumably there is no need to study police to predict the volume and nature of delinquency; delinquency already exists; police passively acknowledge its existence and certify it.

A number of studies are cited to support this conclusion. However, in addition to seriousness of offense, arrest record, age, demeanor, probation status, department, and officer emerge in varying degrees as influences on dispositions. Black and Reiss (1970) discovered that when interaction occurred between police and complainants, arrests of juveniles were more likely, and interaction with black complainants was more apt to produce arrests than with white complainants.

In J. Q. Wilson's study (1968) comparing police control of juveniles in eastern and western cities, either overlooked or ignored by Hirschi, large differences came to light in police discretion. Arrest and processing rates for juveniles ran 50 percent higher for western over eastern police, although crimes rates did not differ markedly. The greater normalization of juvenile conduct in the East was influenced by different conceptions of the seriousness of offenses, what constituted a record, racial attitudes, local area recruitment of police, location of juvenile officers and their records, patrolling practices, interaction with other officers, and time costs involved in presentation of cases in court—English style by the police themselves.

Similar findings emerged in a study of cautioning juvenile offenders by police in England, mainly done in northern cities (Steer, 1970). Factors influencing choice were age, sex, and nature of the offense but not necessarily its seriousness. Prior offenses were not important unless they were similar to the one in question. Differences between rates of juveniles cautioned rather than arrested varied substantially from one police force to another.

Still another study in Toronto (Gandy, 1970) revealed that differences in the nature and outcome of police discretion in dispositions of juvenile cases varied with the administrative unit to which officers were assigned. Significant differences lay in the emphasis and weight given to similar criteria for choosing dispositions, in perception of the relative seriousness of certain types of behavior, and in the frequency with which certain courses of action were chosen.

When I examine juvenile arrest figures for the State of California I am puzzled, to say the least, by the insistence that police arrest mainly juveniles committing serious offenses. In the 1973 report of the Bureau of Criminal Statistics of 362,000 arrests, 32 percent were felony-level violations, 39 percent misdemeanor-level, and 29 percent delinquent tendencies, such as truancy, runaways, and beyond control. In Sacramento County in 1974 only 40 percent of minors placed in the juvenile hall were for law violations, as opposed to 60 percent for delinquent tendencies and "various other reasons." This, of course, doesn't reflect cases processed by probation and court without being placed in detention, more likely less serious.

These data are consistent with the 1963 Erickson-Empey study in southern California dealing with seriousness of self-reported, undetected delinquency in samples of those never in court, those there once, those on probation, and those in institutions. Court records were found not to reflect the seriousness and frequency of offenses, nor did the latter differentiate or account for those in institutions when measured by undetected offenses. This is supported by Sheridan's 1966 survey of fifteen correctional institutions showing that 30 percent of the child in-mates had committed no law violations. Other studies have put this fig-ure as high as 48 percent.

In general I have found that studies of police and juvenile court processing of minors do not contradict the societal reaction view of delinquency, that is, that choice-making by agents of social control, in-fluenced by values, interactions with others, social organization, avail-ability of means and their costs, affect the designation of minors as delinquent and the overall volume and rate of delinquency. The loose definition of delinquency—not even defined in eight states—plus the ambiguous image of the juvenile court have meant that a large number of diverse problems, some of them not even problems, get redefined or rationalized as delinquency and processed because there seems no other way to deal with them.

The number of studies which have been specifically designed to test propositions drawn from societal reaction theory is not large. Many of them are short-term, synchronous in nature, which may show interac-tion of variables but not how outcomes are produced by symbolic in-teraction and feedback. They may postdict but not predict, because findings at one point in a process are not those at another point.

Denther and Erikson (1959), for example, some years ago found that recruits in army camps tended to normalize, accommodate, and even protect ineffective, "schizoid" soldiers. But a similar, more ex-tended study by David Schneider (1947) showed that while new recruits accommodated psychosomatic complainers in much the same way, over time, as soldiers assimilated masculinity values of the military, they rejected the complainers, forcing them either to shape up or seek of-ficial validation of their sick role through the medical department. The five-year study of schizophrenic women by Sampson, Towne, and Mes-singer (1962) reached a roughly similar conclusion, that is, that accom-modations to deviance may change and break down through time, resulting in hospitalization.

A more impressive demonstration of the effects of feedback based on the discovery of new facts from research came out of the 1969 Mendel-Rapport study. When directors of the admitting center discov-ered that time of day and day of week were affecting staff recommen-dations for hospitalization of mental cases, they changed procedure so that weekend cases were held over for review by the Monday staff. Commitments dropped and came more in line with instituted purposes to discover resources and alternative to avoid hospitalization.

It may be that there is reason to use traditional methodology to study the causes of actions I will cautiously call primary deviance. But I don't think that search for abstract or timeless and spaceless attributes like seriousness of the offense or of symptoms will ever prove fruitful.

The best we can hope for is to discover the costs of certain kinds of actions—of the controllers as well as the controlled—and the conditions under which such knowledge will enter into evaluation and policy formation, and, of course, if and how they influence creation and change of definitions of deviance.

VII

To Disentangle and Reassemble the Links Between Knowledge and Policy

15

The Emergence of Sociology as a Policy Science

James S. Coleman

OVER TWENTY YEARS AGO, Harold Lasswell coined the term "the policy sciences," referring to those aspects of the social sciences that had explicit implications for social policy.

For a long time, the "policy sciences," at least sociology and political science, showed few signs of becoming policy sciences, and few outside these disciplines saw them in this way. Economics was something different; it had been a policy science for some years before Lasswell coined the term. But in the past few years, sociology has shown signs of becoming a policy science in fact as well as name. This is not necessarily good for sociology, nor is it necessarily good for society; so in remarking on this development, I am not harkening the dawning of a great new era for sociology and society. I am rather suggesting that it constitutes an extensive change both for the discipline and for society.

First, it is important to recognize that sociology's emergence as a policy science is not a total transformation of the discipline. The sociological enterprise takes us, and should take us, in many directions, and most of these bear no direct relation to social policy of any kind. So the development of sociology as a policy science is not a transformation but a *proliferation* of sociology. Nor is the development something that has had no precursors. In the applied social research beginning in the late 1930s and 1940s, sociology has acted as a policy science for business firms, trade unions, and other organizations. And there were some early uses of social research for governmental social policy. But the extensive use of social research in governmental policy is a phenomenon of the last decade.

Causes of the Emergence of Sociology as a Policy Science

Until the 1960s, explicitly social policies of the federal government were (with the exception of the period of the Great Depression, which I will mention again) principally marked by their absence. The federal government made economic policy; it even has come to have a Council of Economic Advisors. But it largely refrained from making social policy in areas of health, education, crime, poverty, delinquency, and even housing.

With the 1960s came a rapid growth of social policies on the part of the federal government. Many of these policies had as their announced goal—whatever the consequences later turned out to be—the alleviation of problems afflicting the least well off in the society, and the alleviation of problems experienced by minorities—first blacks, then others.

One might say that the "cause" of these social policies was a growing social consciousness on the part of the American population. While that is true, the complacency of the 1950s being replaced by the activism of the 1960s, I think it is useful to look for the cause at a somewhat deeper level. By 1960, there had taken place a great shift of a disadvantaged black population from obscurity and impotence in the rural South to visibility and emerging political strength in the cities of the North. For the first time in recent history, disadvantaged blacks came to have some political strength, both through the social consciousness their presence instilled in many whites and, directly, through their emerging political strength. Now one generalization that can be made, true not only in the United States but in other countries as well, is that disadvantaged or oppressed minorities will use national instruments for fighting local elites. In this country, that is the federal government and U.S. circuit courts. Thus in the conflict that develops, there are three parties: local elites, attempting to maintain the status quo; an underclass or disadvantaged group which has little power at the local level, but more at a national level; and the national government, which then becomes the instrument acting on behalf of the underclass in opposition to the local elites (although of course not uniformly so, and not without political opposition at the national level).

But one characteristic of national governments, when they begin to devise and execute social policy, is that the policy makers are at a great distance from those whom the policy affects. Another characteristic is that their policies must be general, not particular, not designed afresh for each local situation. The first of these characteristics leads to a need for some sort of systematic, noncasual information as feedback concerning the consequences of policies it institutes. The second characteristic requires that such information, and in fact all the information it uses in the formation of policy, be in the form of generalizations useful for general policy, not in the form of specific items about specific events to be treated individually.

Still another difference between a national government and a local government in the design of social policy is that it is economically efficient for the national government to institute research and development to aid the design of that policy, while it seldom is for the local government. For the national government, the costs of research and development are spread across the many local instances where their results will be applied; for the local government, these costs must be justified in terms of their benefits in that single application. Thus much social research, in the form of evaluation of social programs or in the form of social experiments, is economically efficient when social policy is at a national level, inefficient when the same policy problems are addressed at the local level.

For these three reasons, the entrance of the federal government into social policy creates a potential *demand* for the products of sociology for social policy. There has been another development, this time in the discipline, that provided the *supply*. This was the growth of systematic applied social research and its techniques, beginning with the work of Paul Lazarsfeld and others in the 1940s, and enormously expanded by the advent of computers and the mass data processing and sophisticated analytical methods they made possible. This apparatus did not exist in the 1930s, so that the potential demand for the products of sociology in the social programs of the Roosevelt era was not matched by a potential supply. Instead, commonsense approaches and commonsense modifications of policy were used. They may have been better, they may have been worse, but they, rather than systematic social research, were for the most part used.

Thus, as I see the cause of the growth of sociology as a policy science, it lies in a demand created by the emergence of social policy at a national level (which in turn was spurred by the movement of blacks to northern cities and the consequent actions of the federal government on their behalf against local elites), and in a potential supply created by the developments of systematic social research and mass data processing.

I will turn to consequences for sociology of its growth as a policy science.

The growth of sociology as a policy science has had important consequences for the discipline and, I believe, will come to have even more important ones. Sociology has, as befits a discipline that is an academic enterprise in every sense, consisted largely of teachers of sociology. But the growth of social research related to social programs has begun to expand an occupation that has until now been rather small: full-time social researchers, either in evaluation research, in social experimentation, in research management, or in other policy research. At present, people filling these jobs are drawn from a number of disciplines: economics, statistics, operations research, psychology, education, and sociology. As the activity takes more differentiated form, and comes to provide nonacademic career lines for policy-related social research, it will take some sort of professional form, probably as a specialization within an academic discipline. The most likely home for such a specialty is sociology, though it is certainly too early to say that the ultimate resting place of this specialty *will* be sociology. For it to lodge itself in sociology, several requirements are necessary: The training for this kind of activity must exist in graduate departments, both at the M.A. level and at the Ph.D. level; and there must come to be within the Sociological Association enough of a nucleus of full-time social researchers such that there is a comfortable home within the discipline for this specialty. If this does happen, the shape of sociology as a professional association will come to resemble that of psychology, with large numbers of professionals who are not academics. If this change does come about, the "old" sociological profession will appear in recollection as an informal club engaged in the leisurely pursuits of academia.

A second consequence of this growth of sociology as a policy science is one that is already evident: increased attention, scrutiny, and care concerning the correctness of results. When research results in sociology have no social consequences beyond their possible value in contributing to the discipline's store of conjectures, partial findings, apparent relationships, and verified results, the cost of an incorrect result is relatively small, to the researcher and to anyone else. The cost is small to the researcher since his research is seldom replicated on the same sample or system, so his results are seldom challenged. The cost is small to anyone else since the evolutionary processes of the discipline discard research results in time if they are inconsistent with other results in related areas, or if they are of little use.

The matter changes drastically when research results are used for policy. The cost of incorrect results is high, both to the researcher and to society. It is high to the researcher because, since the results will affect social policy and since they are likely to be harmful to some interests, there *will* very likely be reanalysis and attempts at replication of results. It is high to the society because of the incorrect social policies that may be guided by these results.

This shift has already become evident. The Russell Sage Foundation has initiated a program in secondary analyses of social experiments and social evaluations, providing some confrontations unusual for social research. The continuing controversies over the effects of school integration, which I know firsthand, have involved many reanalyses of data, and much closer examinations of methods and results than one finds in "ordinary" research in the discipline.

These increasingly stringent standards for what qualifies as a result in policy-related social research will, I believe, be valuable for social research in general. Less rigid standards are appropriate for "findings" or apparent relationships that merely enter the discipline's memory; but the more stringent requirements of policy research will force—and to some degree have already forced—the development of more powerful analytical tools that will benefit other research in the discipline. Already more sophisticated methods of multivariate analysis and experimental design are being used in the discipline, partly as a result of borrowing from economists and psychologists when they have addressed policy problems in common with sociologists.

The increased scrutiny and reanalysis that policy-relevant results in sociology receive is an indicator of a further difference between this research and "ordinary" research in the discipline. This research receives such scrutiny because the results affect some interests in society adversely. This forces us to recognize that policy-relevant research always impinges on various *interests* in differing ways, and further, that such research is often initiated under the sponsorship of an interested party. This means that the research results will often be inattentive to questions of interest to other parties, and in the worst case, will state results and implications wholly from the perspective of one interested party. What does not exist in the discipline, and what has had no need to exist until now is an institutional structure within the discipline that assures that information provided by social research will be equitable, in the questions asked and the implications drawn, to the various interests involved. There is nothing in the initiation and reporting of social research to provide that assurance; the two dominant modes of initiation are the interest or curiosity of the investigator and the sponsorship of a client. Both of these are likely to view a policy question from the point of view of a single interest only. This is often reinforced on issues of social importance by the development of a dominant norm or value among sociologists, which is allied with one set of interests.

In legal proceedings, such an institutional structure does exist: the adversary procedure. Now, this procedure is not appropriate for social science, and anyone who has observed the use of social science research in legal proceedings has been the incompatibility between the disciplinary ethic of scientific or scholarly inquiry and the legal ethic of adversary contests. I should mention an interesting paper by Eleanor Wolf

(1976) which shows this in the Detroit school segregation case. But the inapplicability of adversary proceedings to social science does not relieve the discipline of the responsibility to develop a structure for policy research that insures attention to the various interests involved. One possible procedure is the simultaneous commissioning of research by two sets of investigators attentive to the interests of two differently interested parties. But this is not a sufficient change. At this point, all I can say is that in the long run, there will come to exist some equity-insuring structure in policy-relevant social research; but it would be helpful if sufficient thought were given to the matter so that the structure developed in the short run rather than the long run.

Still another consequence for sociology of its growth as a policy science is a spur to the development of quantitative macrosociology. Quantitative macrosociology depends upon estimates of parameters characterizing a well-defined population, whether a nation as a whole or a portion of it. Demography has until recently been the only branch of sociology engaged in this kind of activity, in its work on population, migration flows, and distributional parameters such as measures of segregation; but recent work in occupation, income, educational attainment and achievement, and various black-white differentials has extended the domain of this work.

Consequences for Society

The change in the way society makes and modifies policies—the use of sociological theory in policy design and the use of social research in policy modification—is of course only a part of the more fundamental shift from local to national policy making in social areas. This shift, however, is partial, and its partial nature can lead to serious anomalies. An example is in a series of semi-experiments, or "planned variations" as they were called, for "Follow Through" (that is, post–Head Start) programs. These planned variations were special programs of instruction initiated and funded by the U.S. Office of Education, and acquiesced in by a number of local school systems. The idea was that evaluative research on the effects of these programs would be carried out, comparatively, and then the local systems themselves would pick up those programs which were most successful. The mistake lay in the design of the research: Because the Office of Education felt that achievement in reading and arithmetic were the most important consequences of the programs—that is, what *they* wanted out of them—the research was designed primarily to examine those achievement consequences. But the consequences most important to the local school systems were neglected, in many cases not even measured: how acceptable the program was to the teachers; how much it would add to per pupil cost; how it affected absenteeism of students; and its holding power in keeping middle-class families from leaving the city and lower-class children from leaving the school. Consequently, though the research was initiated at the federal level, the final policy decisions would be made at the local level, and the research as designed was largely irrelevant to their decisions. (This research is examined in Rivlin and Timpane, 1975.)

Another example illustrates the same mismatch in the federal-local "partnership" that has developed in many areas of policy. The federal government has initiated and helped fund a public transportation system for isolated rural areas to aid persons without cars or who cannot drive. In one isolated area of West Virginia, the State hired a New York–based research firm to provide the research and design work for the network. Their initial design called for a "Dial-a-ride" system, in which the vehicle comes when telephoned, like a taxi. Trials of such a system have proved promising in some suburban areas. What the research organization failed to note is something that would lead anyone with local and particular knowledge, rather than national and general knowledge, to immediately reject such a system: Many persons, including those most needing transportation, had no telephone. In this example as in the other, the federal initiation led to use of research which disregarded the local: in the first case the local school policy makers, and in the second case the specific needs of the local users.

There is a more general point: The shift from local policy making using common sense and detailed local knowledge to national policy making involves a fundamental change in the structure of information surrounding the decision. The decision maker is at a distance from the object of the decision, and the policy-informing research is intended to close that distance. But social research has not developed the appropriate combination of methods to insure that the results provide both the specific detail and the general knowledge. There is an increasing tendency, as the scale of the research increases, for the researcher *himself* to be at a distance from the subjects of the research, who are the objects of the policy. Thus he's not effective in closing the distance for those making policy, because he himself remains distant from the object of the decision. Remaining at a distance, the imperatives of the concrete and particular never impress themselves upon him. He never can experience, even vicariously, the absurdities of an absurd policy, because he remains distant from those who do. Because his research is on such a wide scale, he cannot contact all or even a reasonable sample of those who are the subjects of his research, so he contacts none. He remains two or three levels removed even from those who do contact the subjects of the research. Just as survey research is a social invention for helping to close the distance from objects of policy to policy maker, what is needed, as social research grows in scale, is a comparable social invention for closing the distance from the subjects of research to the researcher.

Another consequence for society of the use of systematic research in social policy is the bias introduced by a new set of interests. As sociologists, we know that with the task differentiation which leads to a set of researchers distinct from those who make policy, a new set of interests arises, the interests of the researchers. These may be career interests, they may derive from the values of the researchers that favor a particular outcome, they may be interests in power. Whatever they are, they impose a systematic distortion upon the policy-relevant information. The distortion is probably most often in the direction of transforming the policy problem into a question of academic interest, and thus the researcher's career interest—thus making it irrelevant to the policy problem to which it was initially addressed. In addition, there is the bias that depends on the researcher's occupational location—who his client is, and what the client's interests are. These clients and their interests range widely, but there are two rather large classes: the clients who are themselves the policy makers, and who want the research to determine how their goals can be realized given the constraints imposed by the persons who are the objects of policy; and the third-party clients who are acting on behalf of a disadvantaged or oppressed group, and who want the research results to force policy changes to benefit the disadvantaged or oppressed. (Foundations often fall into this latter category, as does the federal government when it does not have policy control in an area but wants to use research results to force local policy changes.) In an examination I recently carried out of policy research in sociology (Coleman, 1973), the biases corresponding to both these types of client were apparent in the research results.

In this discussion of the consequences to society of the emergent use of social research on social policy, I have pointed principally to negative consequences—to the policy defects that stem from this changed structure of decision making.

This was deliberate—I wanted to show the very immature state of our techniques for informing social policy that must be made at a distance from its object. This is not to say that we must go back to local policy making in these areas, for local policy making unconstrained by outside forces often favors local elites and neglects the local disadvantaged or outcasts. But if the policies made at the national level, or made locally under nationally imposed constraints, are to be effective, then this immaturity must be quickly overcome. This requires more than merely more powerful statistical techniques or better data. It requires intensive analysis of just what kind of information is necessary if policy decisions made at a distance are to be responsive to the specific needs of the local objects of policy. It requires also development within the discipline of structures which will insure attention to various interests.

Altogether, then, I see the emergence of sociology as a policy science first as a consequence of a changed structure of decision making in social policy in this country—from local to national—and this change itself a consequence of the increased visibility and national power of disadvantaged minorities, especially blacks.

The consequences for sociology of this development lie in a spur to quantitative macrosociology, in the development of methods that are more powerful in testing the correctness of results, in the possible emergence of a large new set of sociologists who are engaged in full-time research over their whole career, and in the development of new institutions that lie somewhere between detached scientific inquiry and adversary procedure.

The consequences for society of this change are so far some good and some bad. They evidence the growing pains of this new decision-making structure in society, and already suggest some ways in which the informational aspects of that structure can be improved. This new structure involves sociologists in two ways: in one, as the researchers who provide the information that is increasingly used in social policy; in the second, as analysts of society and its structural changes, to gain an understanding of these changes sufficient to aid in the improvement not only of the information basis for policy decisions, but also in the policy decisions themselves. In both of these respects, we have a long way to go. Sociology as a policy science still has a long way to go; and the increasingly frequent national modes of policy making which use social science information still have a long way to go.

16

Competent Authority: Reality and Legitimating Model

Dennis H. Wrong

I SHALL DISCUSS "the expert society" from the standpoint of the ancient question of the relation between knowledge and power. Both Plato and Aristotle compared the relation of a ruler to his subjects to that of a helmsman to the crew of a ship and a physician to the human body. Hannah Arendt observes of Plato's political philosophy: "Here the concept of the expert enters the realm of political action for the first time, and the statesman is understood to be competent to deal with human affairs in the same sense as the carpenter is competent to make furniture or the physician to heal the sick" (1961:111). Plato in *The Republic* and Aristotle in *Politics* identified as a defining trait of the authority exercised by the helmsman, the physician, and "the arts in general" that, in Aristotle's words, it "is exercised in the first instance for the good of the governed or for the common good of both parties, but essentially for the good of the governed" (book 3, chap. 6). Socrates, addressing Thrasymachus in the first book of *The Republic,* concluded that "there is no one in any rule who, insofar as he is a ruler, considers or enjoins what is for his own interest, but always what is for the interest of his subject or suitable to his art."

Let us beg for the moment the issue of the validity of the comparison between the authority of the pilot or physician and political rule, which I shall consider later on. In their descriptions of the former, Plato and Aristotle clearly had in mind what I shall call *competent authority.* They were also well aware that it was far from being the only type of authority or power in human society. Aristotle specifically distinguished it from the master-slave relationship in which "the rule of a master . . . is . . . exercised primarily with a view to the interest of the master" (*Politics,* book 3, chap. 6).

Competent authority is a power relation in which the subject obeys the directives of the authority out of belief in the authority's superior competence or expertise to decide which actions will best serve the subject's interests and goals. The phrase "competent authority," however, is often used to refer to authority that is exercised in accordance with public or private statutory law. Such a usage makes it merely a special case of legitimate authority, notably Weber's rational-legal type. But, as Talcott Parsons has pointed out, "competent authority" in this sense is not at all the same thing as authority based on "technical" competence, that is, on knowledge or expertise. In Parsons' example (1947:58–59), the treasurer of a corporation authorized to sign checks is not necessarily a better check-signer than the secretaries and clerks who work in his office. I mean by competent authority, the authority exercised by the "expert," authority that rests solely on the subject's belief in the superior knowledge or skill of the exerciser rather than on formal position in an established hierarchy of authority.

The authority of "doctor's orders" may be taken as the prototype of competent authority. The doctor who says, "Stop drinking or you'll be dead within a year," is not threatening to kill the patient should the patient refuse to comply; the doctor's authority does not rest on the ability to impose any coercive sanctions. Nor is the doctor appealing to a duty or moral obligation to obey that is incumbent upon the patient; he may greet the patient's refusal with a shrugged "Do what you want, it's your life." Legitimate authority therefore is not at issue. Competent authority resembles persuasion, which is why it has been seen since the time of the Greeks as the most benign and desirable form of authority.

In common speech the term "authority" is used as a synonym for possessor of special knowledge or expertise, as when we describe someone as an authority on tax law or the philosophy of Hegel. Such a usage does not refer to a social relationship at all, let alone a power relation, although it at least implies that we are disposed to act on the advice of such authorities in practical matters, recognizing that their directives possess, in Carl Friedrich's phrase (1958:35), the "potentiality of reasoned elaboration." But there is nothing compulsory or mandatory about such authority, which is why it appears to be close to, if not identical with, persuasion. Yet we are not speaking loosely or obliquely when we refer to doctor's *orders* rather than "suggestions" or "arguments." Successful persuasion involves the acceptance by the persuaded of the *content* of the persuader's communications on the basis of his or her independent assessment of them, whereas authority involves the subject's compliance with a directive because of its *source* rather than its content. The subject's belief in the superior competence of another provides therefore a basis for authority that is not reducible to, or a special case of, persuasion. The patient may understand nothing of the rationale for the doctor's directives; he complies with them out of trust in the doctor's superior competence to judge what will cure him of his ailment. The doctor may even become annoyed if the patient presses for a detailed explanation of the connection between the symptoms and the proposed cure, thereby attempting to convert a relationship of competent authority into one of persuasion. As Freidson (1968:30) has argued, when competence has been granted professional status, "[What] is desired—even demanded—by the profession is that the client obeys because he has faith in the competence of the consultant without evaluating the grounds of the consultant's advice."

Despite the apparent specificity of competent authority, it tends to shade into legitimate authority when it is vested in professional roles. Freidson's previously cited paper is entitled "The Impurity of Professional Authority" and his major conclusion is that "the authority of the professional is . . . in everyday practice, more like that of an office-holder than conventional characterizations would have us believe" (p. 34). The professional practitioner possesses no sanctions over the client, but he has achieved through state recognition a virtual monopoly of the service he supplies. His formal credentials function like insignia of office in permitting him to avoid the burden of having to persuade the client to follow his advice. The client, moreover, is not free to prescribe drugs for himself or to decide which academic courses should entitle him to a degree, in two of Freidson's examples. In addition, a large part of professional work does not consist of applied technical and objective knowledge but of moral judgments and often self-serving occupational customs. In a later work, Freidson (1972:337) concludes that "the professional has gained a status which protects him more than other experts from outside scrutiny and criticism and which grants him extraordinary autonomy in controlling both the definition of the problem he works on and the way he performs his work."

Organizations of experts providing a service to the public strive to prescribe the technical and ethical standards of practice, required training, and certification procedures. Their success in winning state recognition of their exclusive control over these defines an occupation as a full-fledged profession. Professional associations, therefore, depend upon, and in a sense exercise, political power, a power that supports the competent authority of the individual practitioner dealing with a client: The power of the collective organization of experts and ultimately of the state plays a significant role in establishing the competent authority of the expert.

If competent authorities sometimes take on some of the attributes of legitimate and even coercive authorities, it is also true that the latter may lay claim to certifiable competence in leadership and administration. This is typically the case in modern bureaucratic organization, as was recognized by Max Weber. "Bureaucratic administration," he wrote in a famous statement, "means fundamentally the exercise of control on the basis of knowledge. . . . The decisive reason for the advance of bureaucratic organization has always been its purely technical superiority over any other form or organization." [1] Weber's stress on the *expertise* of the bureaucrat, an expertise based not only on administrative experience but on educational certification as well, has been insufficiently recognized, according to Charles Perrow (1972:56–58), by contemporary sociologists, who have exaggerated the difference between professionals and administrators, or between "staff" and "line" positions within formal organizations. Increasingly, administrators present themselves as experts in management and exhibit graduate degrees from schools of business or public administration. Perrow, however, overlooks the fact that these very fields of applied knowledge, or would-be "professions," presuppose that the practitioner has the power to impose sanctions and to enjoin compliance as a duty. His control over both coercive and normative resources, in Etzioni's terminology (1968:357–59), derives from his incumbency in office. The bureaucratic manager may lay claim to special competence in management, and the possession of educational credentials may even be a requirement for, or a mode of access to, holding office. But in contrast to the expert or professional whose authority rests primarily on his certified competence, the manager has other resources at his disposal to obtain compliance, and these are clearly the chief basis of his authority. His claim to superior competence in administration amounts to an additional legitimating argument invoked to buttress the authority of his office, although his academic knowledge may indeed help him to exercise authority more efficiently.

In summary, the professional, who possesses power based on knowledge, also possesses, according to Freidson, some of the attributes of power based on legally ratified status, and this status depends on the power of the collective organization of his fellow experts. The bureaucrat with degrees in management has acquired knowledge that supplements the authority of office and the sanctions and resources it controls. Both, though not to the same degree, represent adulterations of an ideal-typically "pure" competent authority.

Neither Plato nor Aristotle considered the comparison between the authority of the helmsman or physician and that of the statesman as no

---

[1] I have actually combined two famous statements in the quotation. The first sentence is from Weber, 1947:339; the second is from Gerth and Mills, 1946:214.

more than a metaphor, nor even as a lofty ideal rarely if ever achieved in practice (though Plato's conception was closer to this than Aristotle's). The Greek philosophers believed in the reality of "wisdom" or knowledge of "the Good" and regarded their application in ethics and politics as in no way different in kind from the application of knowledge of the winds and tides in navigation or of the workings of the human body in medicine. We owe such common expressions as the "ship of state" and the "body politic" to these Platonic analogies.[2] Later thinkers, however, have viewed the possibility of a rational political authority comparable to that of the skilled craftsman or professional with skepticism. Bertrand Russell (1945:106–7) remarked that belief in a generalized gift of "wisdom" the possession of which "is supposed to make a man capable of governing wisely" is a view that "to us . . . seems remote from reality."

Although Plato and Aristotle were well acquainted with tyranny in the experience of the Greek city-states, later thinkers have not only doubted the existence of political "wisdom" as a special ability to govern and dispense justice, but have expressed a deep suspicion and mistrust of *all* political power, not merely of that wielded by the "wrong people," that is, by tyrants and demagogues. This attitude, of course, is deeply rooted in Christianity and persisted among leading thinkers of the Enlightenment. Immanuel Kant wrote: "That kings should philosophize or philosophers become kings is not to be expected, nor is it to be wished, since the possession of power inevitably corrupts the untrammeled judgment of reason" (*Perpetual Peace,* second supplement). In doubting that political power can exemplify the rule of disinterested reason, we are disposed to interpret the physician-statesman comparison as a "mere" metaphor, one, moreover, which serves the interests of the powerful as a spurious legitimating argument or ideological rationale justifying their rule.

The birth of modern science led to a revival of the Platonic dream of the union of knowledge and power. In the early nineteenth century, the "prophets of Paris," Fourier, Saint-Simon, and Comte, foresaw and advocated a new society directed by social scientists who had acquired basic knowledge of the laws of social stability and change by applying to

---

[2] See Bambrough, 1956. This is a valuable analytical critique of the cogency of Plato's analogies. See also Weldon, 1953:138–43. In contemporary China, Mao is regularly described as "the Great Helmsman." I do not know whether the metaphor was borrowed from Western Marxism and thus ultimately may derive from Plato, or whether it is also indigenous to traditional Chinese culture. Stalin, from whom Mao imitated what Stalin's heirs later anathematized as "the cult of personality," used to prefer more modern, industrial metaphors such as "the Great Driver of the Locomotive of History." Incidentally, Richard Nixon, after his visit to China in early 1972, was frequently described in 1972 campaign literature as "the helmsman of the American ship of state," so there may have been a three-step West to East and back again diffusion of this ancient metaphor.

the study of human affairs the methods which had proved so successful in the study of nature. Living in an age in which science has become the ultimate cognitive authority, the vision of a society designed and controlled by "social engineers" survives to the present day as the core of "technocratic" theories and ideologies. But such conceptions have scarcely escaped corrosive doubt and criticism. The metaphor of the policy maker as a social engineer has been debunked and unmasked as ideology with the same arguments employed against Plato's prescientific and preindustrial analogies between the statesman and the skilled craftsman. Few of us may share William F. Buckley's political views, but most of us are likely to respond with an initial twitch of amused sympathy to his remark that he would rather be ruled by the first one hundred names in the Boston telephone directory than by the faculty of Harvard College.

Freidson (1972:337) has argued that the extraordinary prestige and high degree of organization of professionals carries the risk that "expertise is more and more in danger of being used as a mask for privilege and power rather than, as it claims, as a mode of advancing the public interest." Freidson is referring primarily to the autonomy won by professionals to control the conditions under which they supply a vital service to the public. Professional organizations also engage in collective bargaining and political lobbying to advance the economic interests of their members in ways that do not differ from trade unions and other occupational associations. Although the "halo" of their professional status may for a time result in their demands being granted greater legitimacy than those of most groups, they are increasingly perceived as not essentially different in kind from other special-interest associations competing in the political and economic arenas. One is surprised to discover that in the early 1920s Thorstein Veblen believed that so prosaic an organization as the American Society of Mechanical Engineers could become a "class-conscious" political force promoting the "Soviet of Technicians" that he favored as an alternative to proletarian revolution (Bell, 1963). (One of Veblen's admirers at this time was Howard Scott, a self-described engineer who later popularized the term "technocracy" as the founder of the movement by that name which flourished for a few years in the early 1930s.)

This brings us to the numerous "new class" theories that have cast experts or men of knowledge, variously defined, in the role of builders of a new rationally designed social order. Such theories, most notably that of Saint-Simon, actually antedated Marx's baptism of the proletariat as the revolutionary class, although since Marx they have usually, like Veblen's theory, been put forward as alternatives to the predicted ascendancy of the working class. Saint-Simon's "producers," Comte's priests of "positivism," Waclaw Machajski's "intellectual workers," Veb-

len's "engineers," James Burnham's "managers," J. K. Galbraith's
"techno-structure," George Lichtheim's "scientific and technical intelligentsia," Robert Heilbroner's "scientific elites," Alain Touraine's
"technocrats," Richard Flacks' "young intelligentsia in revolt"—all have
been designated in the course of a century and a half as carriers of a
movement toward a planned society in which social rationality prevails.
Discussions of their role are central to the current debate over the nature of the "postindustrial," "knowledgeable," or, as the organizers of
this session have more modestly chosen to call it, "expert" society.

Some new class theorists have favored the groups and tendencies
they discerned and predicted, others have opposed them, treating technocratic visions of the future as ideologies making universalistic claims
while actually, like all ideologies, promoting the particular interests of a
limited group. If technicians and experts have often been welcomed as
heirs to the failed mission of the proletariat, they have also been as-
sailed as an actual or prospective new ruling class frustrating the dream
of a classless society. Some writers have assigned to the "new class" the
parts of both the bourgeoisie and the proletariat in the Marxist drama,
seeing it as an outgrowth of the "old middle class" that is nevertheless
destined to be the carrier of an anticapitalist ethos stemming from its
antagonism to the planlessness and waste of the market and the
vulgarities of commercialism. New class theorists include writers who
can be loosely classified as on the left as well as on the right, but even
among those who identify themselves as leftists one finds diametrically
opposed views: Some, particularly those sympathetic to the so-called
counterculture, see professionals and technocrats as a new class enemy,
whereas others, buoyed by the student revolt of the late sixties, have
regarded the university as the seedbed of a vastly expanded and
radicalized intelligentsia equipped with skills that are functionally indispensable to modern society and capable therefore of transforming it.

The empirical and conceptual issues raised by new class theories are
well known. There is, first of all, the ambiguity with which the alleged
new class is defined. Does it include only technical and professional occupations in the strict sense, or does it also embrace administrators who
wield an institutionalized bureaucratic authority that is based neither
on property ownership nor solely on trained expertise? Are "pure" scientists who "do not have clients" (Hughes, 1958:139) included, or is the
new class confined to applied scientists and professionals claiming to
exercise competent authority over a lay public? Failure to delimit
clearly the boundaries of the group in question raises a second major
issue: To what extent can social cohesion, a common ethos, and at least
nascent political aims be attributed to it? Is it, at least potentially, a full-
fledged class with a distinctive class-consciousness, or is it no more than
a stratum, scarcely even a *Klasse an sich* in Marx's sense? Or is it an elite

rather than a class or stratum, or merely a congerie of different "strategic elites" [3] possessing little or no unity of outlook?

These unsettled empirical and definitional problems lead to the central issue of whether the knowledgeable have become, or merged inseparably with, the powerful, or whether the powerful have enlisted more and more of the knowledgeable in their service in the face of growing technical complexity of advanced industrial societies, while retaining an individual and collective identity distinct from that of their servants. In short, do "the knowledgeable have power," or is it rather that increasingly "the powerful have knowledge," that is, access to the services of a growing number of trained experts? [4]

There is by now a huge literature, much of it ideologically motivated, debating these issues. It is not my purpose here to make another contribution to it. I want merely to note that in all technocratic theories the ultimate legitimation of the power of the experts or technocrats is seen as resting on the model of competent authority. Both the attractiveness to some of a society run by experts and the fears of others that technocratic visions possess a special seductiveness and capability of masking the self-interested elitism or class rule of a new intelligentsia, stem from a recognition of the apparently benign character of competent authority. As Habermas (1970:111) has remarked, "technocratic consciousness is . . . 'less ideological' than all previous ideologies" and yet at the same time "more irresistible and farther-reaching than ideologies of the old type." Moreover, the group invoking and destined to benefit from technocratic legitimations of power contains professionals and consulting experts who are used to exercising competent authority in their relations with clients.

Describing the views of Saint-Simon, the first "technocratic visionary," Daniel Bell (1973:263) writes: "In a technocratic society politics would disappear since all problems would be decided by the expert. One would obey the competence of a superior just as one obeys the instructions of a doctor or an orchestra conductor or a ship's captain." We encounter once again awareness of the legitimating use of the ancient Platonic analogies. Lewis Coser (1965:238) has similarly observed of Comte's utopia that "freedom of conscience would no longer play a progressive part because it would be absurd to oppose a scientifically managed society, just as it would be absurd to oppose a scientifically established law of nature." The equation of subjection to scientifically established laws of nature with obedience to scientist-rulers nicely demonstrates how a technocratic ideology obscures the difference between the cognitive authority of science and legitimation of the authority of

[3] The term is from Keller, 1963.
[4] See Sartori, 1971. For a valuable discussion, see also Giddens, 1973:255–64.

rulers who claim to be social and political experts. Competent authority, linked today to theoretical science insofar as it is "knowledge-based," may appear to be the ideal and minimally necessary form of authority in human society. However, as critics of Plato's philosopher-kings have long argued, people are unlikely unanimously to acknowledge the superior competence of political and institutional leaders with the result that manipulation, esoteric appeals to "miracle, mystery, and authority," in the words of Dostoevsky's Grand Inquisitor, and, ultimately, coercion are required to buttress the esoteric legitimations accepted by the leaders themselves, in contrast to the more ready acceptance of the competent authority of the engineer or the physician within their restricted spheres. Plato recognized this, which is why, since he abhorred the direct use of force and violence, his utopian republic relies so heavily on manipulation and intensive educational indoctrination (see the discussion by Arendt, 1961:104–15).

The new class and postindustrial theorists, whatever the differences among them, regard technocratic consciousness as the distinctive ethos of scientific and professional workers. But there have been a number of ideological movements in the past century that have capitalized on the prestige of science without seeking their primary social base in the technical and scientific intelligentsia itself: Social Darwinism, various racist creeds, and, most notably, Marxism, a doctrine that has proved to be as protean in the adaptability of its appeals to diverse groups as any Oriental religion. In the 1930s a Marxism with a technocratic accent was attractive to many Western scientists, who thought of the Soviet Union as a "great experiment" and persuaded themselves that communism gave scientific experts a free hand at social planning unrestrained by base political and commercial considerations (see N. Wood, 1959:121–51). Yet Marxism, even when claiming to be itself a science, has usually directed its appeals to groups other than experts and professionals.

Political ideologies such as Social Darwinism, racism, and Marxism are characterized by what Hannah Arendt (1951:336–40) has called "scientificality." "Scientificality" stands in roughly the same relation to science as an institution as "religiosity" stands to religious institutions. Far from expressing a technocratic consciousness, such creeds have usually been opposed by scientists and professionals, attracting primarily the charlatans, quacks, and failures within their ranks. They have by and large appealed to a half-educated public by claiming privileged insight into the laws of nature from which laws of history and politics can be inferred just as religious prophets claimed unique access to the will of God.

Arendt attributed scientificality to creeds reflecting the apparent victory of science over traditional religion, which evolved into the totalitarian ideologies of the twentieth century. More recently, scientificality *and* religiosity have been combined in the doctrines of a variety of movements, some of them defining themselves as religious rather than political, others advertising themselves as psychotherapies, and a few sharing aspects of all three. Maoism and Taoism, Marxist jargon and charismatic hero cults, "scientologies" appealing both to laws of nature and to occult spiritual forces, therapies starting with a medical model and ending in the celebration of mystical rituals of group communion, chemical knowledge of drugs and magical practices—syncretistic permutations and combinations of all of these have become common features of a host of cults and sects that have flourished in the past decade. Each of the polarities exists in pure strains as well, pitting Establishment against counterculture, science against gnosis, computer analysts and behavior controllers against swamis and gurus, technocrats against humanists. The blends may indeed reflect a healthy impulse, lurid and ludicrous though they presently appear. Not only do they bridge conflict between polarized outlooks, but they reduce the likelihood of static symbiosis between them, of a world in which, as Max Weber foresaw, "specialists without vision and sensualists without heart" might peacefully coexist, or where, in the foreboding of Saul Bellow's Mr. Sammler, "An oligarchy of technicians, engineers, the men who ran the grand machines . . . would come to govern vast slums filled with bohemian adolescents, narcotized, beflowered, and 'whole'" (Bellow, 1971:166–67).

We have come a long way from the simple model of competent authority with which I started. I have moved along a continuum from cases of actual competent authority to analogical generalizations from them put forward in order to legitimate the exercise of power in contexts where it is far from obvious that the superior knowledge of some and the self-interested need of others unite to create a distinctive, noncoercive power relation. The use of competent authority as a model for political rule had its beginnings in Western thought with Plato. The birth of modern science and its increasing application to human needs has since widened the gap between the knowledge and skill of experts and the innocence and ignorance of laymen. The vesting of competent authority in institutionalized professions, however, has led to its adulteration as a result of the collective power wielded by professional associations with the support of the state over the conditions of their work.

Still further along the continuum, technocratic theories and ideologies treat the habits of mind of professionals and technicians as applicable to the organization of society as a whole. Such theories have regarded the scientific and technical intelligentsia as the agency *par ex-*

cellence aiming at institutional innovation and planned social change. Ideologies that are still further removed from the actual exercise of competent authority in expert-client relationships have drawn on the popular cognitive authority of science to make totalistic claims to the understanding of reality which have sometimes served to legitimate actual totalitarian rule. More recently, curious blends of scientific and religio-magical beliefs have formed the basis of a variety of new movements.

It would be as great an error to deny the reality of the competent authority of the expert within his sphere as it is to make analogical use of it to legitimate power that inevitably and necessarily rests on the control of resources other than expert knowledge. Populist mistrust of the inherent "elitism" of all competent authority, giving rise to what might be called "technophobia," distorts reality as much as the most "nonreflexive" technocratic consciousness. It is an illusion to suppose that we can do away with experts by becoming jacks-of-all-trades, that we can "hunt in the morning, fish in the afternoon, rear cattle in the evening, criticize after dinner, just as [we] have in mind, without ever becoming hunter, fisherman, shepherd, or critic." As has often been pointed out, Marx and Engels actually here describe the occupational activities of an agrarian, pre-industrial society rather than those of a developed technological order.[5] Yet however great our inescapable dependence on experts, the late George Lichtheim (1971:199) was surely correct in maintaining that "in the end the technocrats themselves may discover to their surprise that they cannot function unless someone tells them what the whole expenditure of energy is supposed to be *for*. And that someone won't be another technocrat."

[5] A valuable recent discussion is Avineri, 1973.

17

Law and the Distribution of Power

Laura Nader and David Serber

Introduction

LAW HAS BEEN ANALYZED by scholars as a mechanism which maintains order in society. Whose order, however, is a question that is rarely asked. One observation that we illustrate in this paper is that powerful classes and groups shape the legal structure so that it serves their own narrow interests.

National law is a mechanism and a process which may be used to distribute or centralize power, or it may be used to legitimate and maintain power groups. In this paper our general concern is to improve our understanding of the direction and nature of controlling processes. This concern relates directly to the debate over the respective roles of formal government apparatus and informal controlling groups in ruling nation-states, and as well to the debate as to how change is best accomplished. Informal processes are often more important than formal processes in the shaping of the legal system. Knowledge of the formal and informal processes by which the powerful maintain control could enable the powerless to more effectively mobilize their resources to force a redistribution of power. Social scientists have an important role to play in obtaining and disseminating this information.

In the sociological literature on power attention has been paid to legal structures and the way in which such structures have been used to

□ The authors would like to thank William Domhoff, Allen Grimshaw, Klaus Koch, Claire Nader, and unmentioned others for their critical evaluations of our materials.

maintain incipient or entrenched social stratification (see, e.g., Carlin et al., 1967; Sutherland, 1968). In the United States today there is a striking imbalance of power, if power is to be measured by accumulated capital and income.[1] Yet we still know relatively little about the structures and processes which function either to equalize or redistribute power on the one hand, or to further increase and maintain an imbalance of power on the other. Nor is there any comprehensive understanding of law and the distribution of power in other parts of the world and in other kinds of societies which would help us to develop a model for legal development. We need to know whether national legal systems are performing similar functions independent of cultural differences, and whether these similar functions may be related to the larger framework of the world's economy.

In the first part of this essay we discuss how the legal structure affects the distribution of power in relatively simple societies. In the second part of the paper we discuss how the distribution of power affects the legal structure in the United States. On the one hand we are concerned with law as it functions to maintain and legitimize the distribution of power; on the other hand we are concerned with how the powerful control legal mechanisms.

The recent body of literature on the corporate and state sectors of modern societies and their interrelationships (e.g., Domhoff, 1970; O'Connor, 1973) tends to be largely structural and directed toward describing the composition and integration of these sectors. The network approach, as for example in studies of ruling class kinship (Zeitlin, 1974), or in studies of the corporate-based policy-making bodies like the Committee for Economic Development (e.g., Domhoff, 1975; Schriftgiesser, 1974; Shoup, 1975) have been for the most part studies "at a distance." The significance of these studies is inadequate without full understanding of both the formal and informal processes, and without relating the sociology of the powerful to the sociology of the powerless (L. Nader, 1969).

Legal Structures in Comparative Perspective

The function of law in the economically simple preliterate societies is not necessarily that of power equalization. We have studied small-scale societies from New Guinea to Turkey and Sweden and found situa-

---

[1] According to the Statistical Abstract of the United States, U.S. Department of Commerce, Bureau of the Census, 1968, in 1968 only 14.7% of American families had an income of $15,000+ annually (pp. 322), while only 19.7% of individuals had earned more than $10,000 in that year. During the same year 22% of the American population in

tions where local law tends to favor dominant parties. There is, however, a pervasive theme that keeps cropping up which suggests that with the development of the nation-state and the concomitant economic interdependence accompanying industrialization, the law of the nation has become less and less used as a tool which would equalize or redistribute power.[2] For the moment we will assumed that a model for legal development would need to concern itself with economics and stratification.

In this section we explore the types of variables that one needs to examine in order to understand the context within which law reflects a particular system of power. Among the Ifugao of the northern Philippines for example (R. F. Barton, 1919), each class is fined according to its ability to pay. In Mexico there are a number of Indian communities as yet relatively isolated from the effects of the larger society, such as the Zapotec, among whom there is a strong ideology that power should be widely shared. Laura Nader (1964, 1976) has described the diffuse system of power that characterizes these Zapotec communities.

Zapotec settlements number from three hundred to several thousand individuals and each settlement maintains a court which is used as a forum for the hearing of grievances. The pattern of outcome in cases which deal with unequal parties is a reflection of the distribution of power. If the case is specific—for example, dealing with a grievance that is localized, such as a landowner not allowing neighbors access to his land for water—the court can exhort the fairness principle, but the landowner can as well threaten to take his case to the state district court where he can use his influence to manipulate the outcome of the case regardless of the facts. This usage of the state district court in turn sabotages the traditional power of the local court. On the other hand, when the cases are generalized—for example, dealing with an issue that affects the welfare of the whole town—there is no hesitation on the part of the court to take action, regardless of threats to use the district court, because the ultimate sanction, that of exile by the village town meeting, would back local court action. There was such a case a few years back when during a summer of flood and ruination of harvest, corn had to be imported from the capital of the state. One rich property owner bought up three truckloads of corn in Oaxaca and as they arrived into the mountains began to sell the corn at very high cost to the depressed populace. After the first truckload was thus sold and many grievances began to flow into the court, the court officials went

---

1968 had an income, "below the poverty level" (pp. 329). During the same period one percent of the American people earned 25–30% of the total yearly income for all Americans, and those same one percent held 60–70% of the privately owned corporate wealth and 25–30% of all the privately held wealth in the country (Domhoff 1975:82).

[2] For an interesting discussion of law, power, and social structure see Friedman, 1975.

out to meet the second and third carload and simply took the corn over and sold to the people at an equitable price. If the rich man had objected, he would have been ejected from the town, through the use of force if necessary.

While the state would like to fully integrate these Indians, the Zapotec maintain their own legal separateness for their own corporate welfare. Such communities have found a way of protecting themselves in the face of centuries of powerlessness and exploitation vis-à-vis the outside world. It is, as Eric Wolf would have it, a "defensive corporativism" that until recently has allowed them to use the law to the advantage of the community. Perhaps the maintainance of mono-ethnic boundaries has enabled the Zapotec to respond to injustice in ways unavailable to multi-ethnic areas or even to individualized Americans not organized along ethnic lines. Structural networks exist in closed or isolated societies for recovering grievances and responding to wrong. The network breaks down however, as the market place becomes the sole structural network within which people act.

Mono-ethnic communities such as the Zapotec may also be part of multi-ethnic societies, and in the latter context the law operates in strikingly different ways. In Chiapas, Mexico, Duane Metzger (1960) found that the relative power of different participants in the court varied with their place of residence and also with their respective ethnicities. When both plaintiff and defendant live in the same village and the case is tried in their community, all parties, including the courts, have about equal influence and power with regard to case outcome. But when, for example, this community tries a case in which both plaintiff and defendant are from another village, the litigants are treated as equal in power but the court is more powerful than either. Metzger also found that where one of the parties is ethnically classified as a Ladino or non-Indian, a different set of relationships holds. The difference seems to be largely a function of the higher caste status which enables Ladinos to have access to other courts in the district and elsewhere in the state to which they may appeal if given cause. The resulting relationship, whether the Ladino is plaintiff or defendant, is that the Ladino has greater power than the court or the other litigant. If the Ladino chooses to present the case in a non-Indian court, the chances of convicting an Indian are nearly or equally as great, regardless of evidence, but he is unlikely to receive damages in his own courts, which prefer fines. It is not surprising that Indians prefer not to use Ladino courts. In Metzger's examples we see that the courts function as "power equalizers" only when dealing with members of the same Indian community. At the same time courts function to legitimize the power position of Indians in home territory when dealing with other Indians, and supports the power of Ladinos when the latter are in dispute with Indians regardless of whether the Ladino is on home ground or not.

Rarely is more than one legal system recognized in the area of state justice,[3] for to recognize the legitimacy of "other" ideas of justice is thought to cast in doubt one's own ideas. Yet conflicting systems of law are found everywhere, and everywhere decrease the likelihood that state law will function to redistribute power, because one of the legal systems represents the interests of the dominant element in the social structure. In Sardinia, for example, the vendetta is a system of laws in competition with the state. The traditional system does not incorporate laws of the state that are not coherent with its system, and see state law as something alien and oppressive (Ruffini, 1974). The compliment is returned by the Italian state, which sees the Sardinians as violent and lawless, and uses its greater power to coerce them. As Lawrence Friedman notes (1975:106), "Cultural pluralism is extremely common and a classic source of unenforceability of laws."

In some definitions of law, such as that by E. A. Hoebel (1954), is found the assumption that in a society some individual or group is socially recognized, that is, by the society as a whole, as having the privilege of applying physical force. Barnes (1961), in his discussions about pluralism among the African Ngoni, questions whether in discussions about law in Western society we should assume a single nucleus of legitimate authority. As Barnes points out, in many societies some individuals are recognized as legitimate only by one segment of the population and not by the rest. If we regard legality as a relative term, we no longer speak of the legal system of a society, but of the various legal systems that are possibly found within it. This is a point that has, in another context, been made as well by Pospisil (1967). The notion, then, that legality depends on social recognition by the whole community is based on an erroneous assumption that law always arises from some kind of consensus of opinion.

There is a clear similarity between the plural or multi-ethnic societies described above and the colonial situation. Barnes is correct in noting that mere diversity is not the important characteristic of plural societies. Rather, what is important is, as with Metzger's materials, that usually one segment of the population imposes or endeavors to impose its norms on other segments that do not accept it but that are coerced to conform. In Africa colonialists tried to claim for themselves a monopoly to dispense law not only to their own people, but to all those they had conquered. There followed a struggle for legal power

[3] A known example of a government that did allow pluralism in law was the Ottoman Empire. By means of the millet system, religious communities were allowed to govern social life by means of their own formally recognized legal system.

whereby rival courts were used as instruments in the wider struggle for power of all kinds. The situation that Barnes describes for the colonial period in Africa is not too different from the situation found in parts of Mexico, or more recently the situation that Richard Canter (1973) describes for Zambia, six years after independence. In his analysis of cattle rustling cases among the Lenje in Zambia, Canter describes how communities deal at the local level with events which are imposed upon them from urban centers. For over twenty years the people of Mungule have taken their cattle cases to urban magistrates courts which follow a form dictated by the unified criminal code originally imposed by the British. The magistrates courts are punitive sanctions. The local system is primarily based on compensation. The way the local peoples measured the success or failure of magistrates courts was simple. If cattle rustling decreased in frequency, the national court could be considered a success; since it did not, it was a failure. The tensions between the local peoples and the national officials that escalated over the issues of compensation and of competence in handling cattle-rustling cases encouraged self-help solutions that were locally damaging and disruptive.

While under colonialism law was used to administer and control, the motivation of the new states is more elaborate. The leadership in many of these new states deeply believes that national success, meaning economic development, depends on creating a homogeneous people, and that the best way to do this is by means of the law, usually law imported from the West. These elites seem to be functioning as if the seeds of progress and modernity are somehow linked to the importation of a legal system or code from a more developed country, often a country where they had received their formal education. Furthermore, in these new nations new loci of power are developing and consolidating, and the law is often used as a means to consolidate power positions.

Legal development abroad has long rested on the assumption that some legal systems are best for facilitating economic development. The specific case of Korea, as described by the Korean legal scholar Pyongchoon Hahm (1968), illustrates the impact of colonialist strategies based on this assumption.

In an article entitled "Korea's Initial Encounter with the Western Law: 1866–1910 A.D." Hahm tells the vivid story of the use of Western law as a technique to gain power, first by the Japanese and then by the Americans. He describes how Japan justified its military conquest of Asia by the terms of international law, and cites the 1882 Treaty of Peace, Amity, Commerce, and Navigation between Korea and the United States. He quotes to us the fourth paragraph of article 4 which states:

It is, however, mutually agreed and understood between the high contracting powers, that whenever the king of Chosen shall have so far modified and reformed the statutes and judicial procedure of his kingdom that, in the judgment of the United States, they conform to the laws and course of justice in the United States, the right of extraterritorial jurisdiction over U.S. citizens in Chosen shall be abandoned, and thereafter United States citizens, when within the limits of the Kingdom of Chosen, shall be subject to the jurisdiction of the native authorities.

Hahm also goes on to note:

What was implied by this paragraph of the treaty was a clear recognition on the part of the United States that the traditional legal system was plainly not civilized enough under the prevailing standards of international law. . . . The paragraph . . . amounted to a demand on the part of the United States that Korea had to Americanize or Westernize its legal system in order for it to escape the onus of extraterritoriality.

It was by means of the law that economic transactions related to industrialization were facilitated in the United States and it was by means of law that the power of United States economic interests in the industrialization process would be facilitated in other countries. We would provide them with our language for developing contracts and rights over property, thus imposing a Western value system transmitted through laws which would weaken local power bases.

The creation of a Westernized legal system in Korea was part of a larger process of change. The reaction was violent and the repression employed by their national elite was harsh. "Reform and modernization" were during this century accompanied by a progressive loss of national political and economic independence. Even the loss of judicial sovereignty was justified in the name of modernizing the judiciary or making possible the extermination of extraterritoriality.

The "modernization" process in rapidly industrializing countries is further explored in Witty's recent study (1975) of legal pluralism in Lebanon. Witty analyzes local use of national law as a power mechanism to restructure relations or to maintain the status quo in the village and regional power networks. At the same time, she reports on the role of law at the national level by reporting the case of the injured laborer who worked in a foundry in the capital until he was injured, was hospitalized, and died. The foundry did not report the accident; the insurance administration refused to pay the family any compensation. When an individual cannot recruit an effective group of village supporters because the opponent is distant and unknown, he is very effectively isolated from legal representation. The case requires a lawyer who is willing to fight a lengthy debate in the courts for little remuneration. This case is as yet unusual for the villagers, but it does illustrate a dilemma which will become more frequent as family members become dispersed, due to the need for employment outside the village, into the metropolitan areas. The projected implications here are straight-forward. If the state can effectively replace local legal forums, and then control the access patterns for the use of courts, only the state and cer-tain power groups will be able to use the national legal system effec-tively (Nader and Witty, 1975). As elsewhere, in Lebanon villagers' access to law has been steadily lost with nationalization of law. There seems to be some rough correlation between "economic modernization" (or imperialist penetration by modern nations, as in the Korean case) and the development of legal structures which drastically lessen the control of individuals and communities over and by means of the legal system.

In an article on the legal explosion in the United States, John Bar-ton (1975) of the Stanford Law School has lamented the growing in-trusion of law on every aspect of American society. What is of particu-lar interest about this expansion of the legal domain is the correlative pattern—a change in user pattern and access to law. According to legal historian Lawrence Friedman (1971) we have over the past three hundred years shifted from a time of relatively easy access to courts in the colonial period to a rather striking absence of access to courts for purposes of dispute resolution in the latter part of the twentieth cen-tury. Studies of dispute resolution during the colonial period indicate that forums such as courts were regularly used by people to solve dis-putes ranging from the religious to the economic. The change in the function of the courts and therefore in access evolved during the mid-dle of the last century. This change coincided with a period of great economic development and with the beginnings of industrialization in the United States, and as well with the appearance of large waves of im-migrant families.

Elsewhere Nader (1976) has written on the consequences of limited public access to law in the political, economic, and health fields. The ab-sence of access to law is seen in this country as mainly due to cost, lack of know-how, delay, and so forth. However, we do not yet have any good evidence that the change in the use and function of the courts in any broad way affected the use of law to equalize power in this country. Much of the analyses of case material from the colonial period indicate that courts were then, as now, used to the detriment of the poor and powerless. However, decreased access for what euphemistically came to be called the small claim caused concern about developing dissatis-faction with the law (Pound, 1906). There have been several govern-mental responses to this dissatisfaction: small-claims courts, regulatory agencies, and government-funded legal services for the poor. Of these three solutions, regulation was the prime response by the state to the need to equalize the power of the consumer vis-à-vis big business. The effectiveness of this response and the ways in which the ideology of equalization has been subverted will be dealt with in the following section.

Power as Process in Regulation

Much of the recent research on social structure in the United States concludes that the government tends to function in the interest of the corporate rather than the public sector (see Domhoff, 1970: chaps. 5, 6; Miliband, 1969; O'Connor, 1973). Power structure researchers have attempted to demonstrate "ruling class" control of various state institutions through network studies revealing consistent patterns of cross-cutting linkages between personnel in the monopoly segment of the economy and the government (see Domhoff, 1975). What we still have not documented, however, are the processes by which state policy and its administration is controlled or what the nature of that control is. However, researchers imply that the formal processes of courts, government agencies, and elected bodies may not be the loci of this control and that increased access by powerless people to the formal processes of the state is unlikely to affect power equalization (Galanter, 1973). For example, the formal process of selection of public officeholders in the United States is structured to equalize power. Theoretically, every citizen has equal access to the ballot box and no person's vote is weighted more than another's. Yet the informal process by which individuals are selected to seek public office tends to be dominated by those who either control the capital or have access to the capital necessary to run a successful election campaign.

State and federal regulatory agencies are the classic examples of state institutions which have been organized to function as "power equalizers," that is, their stated role is to protect consumer interests by regulating various aspects of big business. Yet, as with the legal system, this goal is merely rhetorical, as their practice serves the interests in the industry they are intended to regulate. It is common knowledge in the fields of political economy and public policy that regulatory agencies are substantially captured by the regulated.[4] But, as M. Bernstein has

[4] See Bernstein, 1972, for an excellent summary of some of the academic literature concerning regulatory agencies. See Kolko, 1963, for a discussion of the development of economic regulation by the state; and Kolko, 1965. Also see Mark Green, 1973, which contains numerous references to the political science, law, and economics literature in the extensive footnotes, pp. 347–89.

pointed out (1972:21), "Our thinking about the regulatory process and the independent commissions, as much of our thinking about the state, remains impressionistic, and the need for empirical research is largely unfulfilled." In order to understand effective and ineffective responses to access and equalization we must understand the processes by which these agencies are captured.

The type of research Bernstein is discussing here goes beyond studying formal procedures, tracing complex linkages, or analyzing policy; he is implicitly proposing the study of informal process by which regulatory policy and practice are developed and carried out. It is a study of the processes of power in action, not simply the structure of power and the results of its influence. This type of research would involve not only firsthand field work among those who are active in the government agency and legislatures, but also field work among those industry representatives who are actually involved in persistently undermining the potential "power equalization" function of regulation.

Insurance regulation in California [5] epitomizes the actual and ideological patterns of the relationship between the industry, the state, and the public. The law originally mandating insurance regulation in California embodies the fundamental contradiction of government regulation. On the one hand, it outlines the duties of the insurance commissioner on behalf of the consuming public, and on the other hand, the duties of the commissioner on behalf of the private industry in adequately supervising and maintaining "the financial stability" of the insurance companies licensed in California (see State of Calif., 1940:36–37). In terms of the actual regulatory practice the term "financial stability" has become a euphemism for industry profit maximization. Despite the fact that more often than not public interests tend to be in conflict with the interests of maintaining "industry stability," the practice of the department is to "safeguard" consumer interests by promoting continued industry growth and profits.

Given this statutory mandate, let us examine examples of the actual

[5] Unlike most national industries, there is little federal regulation of the insurance industry; rather, each state regulates independently of every other state. The U.S. Supreme Court in *United States* v. *Southeastern Underwriters* held that insurance companies conducting their activities across state lines are subject to federal antimonopoly legislation within the regulatory power of Congress under the Commerce Clause. Soon thereafter the Congress passed the McCarran-Ferguson Act, declaring "the continued regulation and taxation of insurance by the several states. . . . No act of Congress shall be construed to invalidate, impair, or supersede any law enacted by any state for the purpose of regulating the business of insurance. [*United States* v. *Southeastern Underwriters Association* (Ga. 1944) 64s. Ct. 1162, 322 U.S. 533, 88 L.Ed. 1440, rehearing denied 65, S. Ct. 26, 323 U.S. 811 L.Ed. 646 ; McCarran-Ferguson Act 2, ch. 20, 59 Stat. 34 (1945), as amended, 15 U.S.C. 1012(b) (1964). For legislative history, see congressional debate, 91 Cong. Rec. 499–509, 1112–22, 1470–73, 1548–59 (1945). As introduced, the bill was based upon a draft by the legislative committee of the National Association of Insurance Commissioners. See 91 Cong. Rec. 504 (1945).]

process of insurance regulation in California and Pennsylvania. In both states there are two primary types of influence by which the industry becomes an active participant in the regulatory process (Serber, 1975). One consists of the building of long-term informal relationships with both the regulators and the legislators at all levels throughout the legislative and regulatory hierarchies. The effect of this type of influence is operative in the day-to-day regulatory and legislative activities. The relationship desired by industry is achieved through various types of collegial interaction and gift-giving by the industry. Many of the regulators are recruited from industry and/or have a promise of positions in industry—the delayed bribe, this is sometimes called.

On the level of the regulatory agency the regulators, excepting isolated instances, are not being "bought off" by the industry in the way that police may be by narcotics dealers or underworld syndicates. The mechanisms are more subtle and complex. The process by which this type of influence is established centers around making the regulators feel a privileged and personal part of the social milieu of industry rather than a part of the public, thereby negating the motivation to make the agency function as a power-equalizing institution working in the interests of the people.

Normal regulatory activities frequently involve industry representatives meeting with middle-level regulators. The social status of these civil servants is relatively low, and not only does their work tend to be boring and routinized, but there is little room for any type of professional autonomy, just as the hierarchy leaves little room for personal autonomy.[6]

> They [the higher-level bureaucrats] are always looking for ways to make you do things their way. You are treated like a super-clerk with an overly close supervision of your work.
>
> Most of our work autonomy and all of our personal autonomy has been taken. [California Department of Insurance Attorneys]

The industry representatives who deal with the departments, on the other hand, are of a relatively high status. The company presidents, vice-presidents, successful corporate attorneys, or professional lobbyists who come into the department consciously interact with the civil servants in a friendly, cordial, and respectful fashion, unlike the way these civil servants are so often treated by those higher up on the bureaucratic ladder. When a lobbyist and a few company vice-presidents take a supervisor, assistant supervisor, and an insurance officer out to lunch at an elegant restaurant they are not necessarily bribing them, they are attempting to make them feel important and to reaffirm their continu-

---

[6] For a detailed discussion of workers within the California regulatory system see Serber, forthcoming.

ing relations. Many regulators come to measure their success as civil servants by the quality of their relationships with higher-status industry representatives:

> Formally I was quite successful in the Department of Insurance. I advanced quite quickly. But the real measure of success is informal. Informally, Jesus! I had a list of references, I mean fifteen company presidents. I'd say I was pretty successful. [A former attorney for the California Department of Insurance]

It is through this process that the industry is successfully transformed from an adversary to an esteemed reference group or a client in the consciousness of many regulators.

The establishment of long-term influence of an informal nature involves the general adoption of a set of expectations and attitudes by the regulators which are the basis for behavior in everyday regulatory practice. Despite the civil service system, acceptance of industry's sets of ideas and behaviors governs advancement of individuals within the bureaucracy. We can show how people lose their jobs when they do not follow this pattern (Nader, Petkaf, and Blackwell, 1972).

> Knowledge of the insurance code . . . is never tested in any exam administered to us. They pick out who they want and they put on a little show and pretend there is some authenticity and fairness. The criterion is being close to the Commissioner and his immediate assistants. And that always reflects their interpretation of the law and policy of regulation. Those people who know what companies and issues not to touch and do what the Commissioner and his assistants would like them to with a smile are those who advance. If you don't go along with their decisions with a smile you can forget it. The kind of people they want to advance are those who know the line. I mean this on many levels: socially, politically and regulatory. [California Department of Insurance Attorneys]

In this sense the rigid hierarchy and spurious meritocracy of the bureaucratic structure perpetuates informal industry influence within the regulatory agency.

This type of long-term influence establishes a firm social base for the second type of influence, which is instrumental in nature and involves the manipulation of specific regulatory activities and policies, and usually operates at the top levels of the agency. Without the access provided by the long-term yet nonspecific influence, direct instrumental control over the individual cases would be far more problematic for the industry. In this sense the establishment and maintenance of long-term informal influence is more critical for the industry than their effectiveness in determining the substance and direction any one particular piece of legislation or agency regulation.

The maintenance of the staff-industry relationship may also function as an important protective barrier to change if the traditional network connections are severed at the top levels of the agency. In both California and Pennsylvania, as network-oriented research would suggest, the commissioner of insurance is either drafted from industry or is actively involved with industry representatives in social clubs or other informal settings. Yet occasionally a maverick who does not see himself as a member of that community is appointed and attempts to establish and maintain an adversarial relationship with the industry. This occurred in Pennsylvania between 1971 and early 1974. The commissioner, Herbert S. Denenberg, actively attempted to regulate in the interest of the public in order to end industry influence in the regulatory process. In effect Denenberg was attempting to transform the Department of Insurance into the power-equalizing institution the ideology would suggest it should be.

Denenberg's strategy to reform regulation was primarily composed of three aspects. The thrust of his approach was to publicize, through an extensive media campaign, the abuses of consumers by the insurance industry. The goals of this strategy were to bring public pressure on the insurance industry to reform some of its practices, to gain public support for Denenberg's regulatory policies, and to raise the level of public awareness of exploitation by industry. The second aspect was to increase public awareness of the problems of the Department of Insurance. The third aspect of the strategy was to sever the relationships previously existing between the regulators and the industry.

Denenberg maintained his extreme adversarial position throughout his term and increased public access to the formal insurance complaint remedies of the agency. However, he was unable to transform the agency itself. The relationship of the industry with the regulatory staff successfully functioned to maintain the perspective of industry in day-to-day regulation. Furthermore, civil service staff members successfully undermined attempts by the commissioner to implement proconsumer policies potentially damaging to the industry. Many of these programs had to be abandoned because of staff sabotage (Serber, forthcoming). The locus of the industry's instrumental influence in the regulatory agency was shifted from the commissioner to the civil service staff. New regulations specifically aimed at severing the informal relationships between the civil service staff and the industry were proposed by Denenberg, but were never implemented. The proposal to draft a formal regulation forbidding staff members to meet industry representatives for lunch (paid or unpaid) or to accept gifts encountered so much resistance by staff that Denenberg was forced to abandon the idea.

Not all civil service workers were unsympathetic to the attempted reforms of the administration, though the cynicism and passivity of

these bureaucrats made them easily susceptible to the pressure which
was exerted by the industry and those regulators closest to the industry.
Furthermore, the staff was aware that Denenberg would not be reap-
pointed (as industry promised) and that the next commissioner would
seek to maintain a "better," more amicable relationship with industry.
Fearing reprisals from industry and those higher up in the bureaucracy
even proreform civil service staff continued to work closely with industry:

> Part of the problem of reorganizing the Department of Insurance is
> that the staff fights you. When you try to regulate the industry they
> have an instinctive feeling that one way or another this is the only thing
> that could eventually cost them their job and any career possibilities in
> insurance they might have. And in most cases they are right. [An assis-
> tant to Commissioner Denenberg]

Not only did Denenberg's own staff function to negate the attempts
at reform but the legislature, where industry long-term and instrumental influence is strong, actively prevented any legal institutionalization
of the attempted reforms. Not a single bill which was sponsored by
Denenberg and strongly opposed by industry was passed by the Pennsylvania State Legislature during Denenberg's entire administration.

Denenberg's highly visible anti-insurance industry public relations
program to gain public support may have created the illusion for vast
numbers of people that the industry was now being regulated in the
public interest, and that Denenberg had made the ideology of power
equalization a reality. In effect Denenberg's attempted reform of insurance regulation in Pennsylvania may have strengthened the power relationships previously existing rather than equalizing power, and may
also have strengthened the ideology of regulation, while industry's informal influence continued and continues to dominate insurance regulation in Pennsylvania.

In both the California and Pennsylvania cases we discover that the
insurance industry does not dictate regulation in an instrumental fashion, except upon occasion. Rather industry's techniques of informal influence and the structure and subculture of the bureaucracy integrate
the regulator into the industry, and as well integrate the industry into
the regulatory process. Informal influence increases industry power
which already exists in terms of the wealth and resources it commands
as the second largest industry in the world.[7] However, such informal

---

[7] The insurance industry and individual insurance companies transacting business in California are the institutions involved in disputes with one individual consumer. The
assets of insurance companies operating in California were $226,262,231,000 in 1969.
This figure is larger than the 1969 Gross National Product of any nation in the world
except the U.S.A. Just the premiums collected by these companies in California
($6,079,416,000) are greater than the G.N.P. of any nation in Africa with the exception

influence or control of an institution ideologically dedicated to power equalization permits the industry to continue its expansion while appearing to be regulated. Furthermore, such informal control has the built-in feature of *nearly* being reform-proof.

Despite the apparent impermeability of industry influence, there is at least one potential conflict within the system of regulation itself which becomes apparent when studying the informal processes of regulation. The conflict lies in the experiences of workers in the regulatory agency. Being a public servant, yet not serving the public interest, but in fact having material success determined by how effectively the worker undermines the public interest, is a contradiction. A growing portion of employees are sensitive to this situation and would welcome a chance to work creatively in the interests of the public.

In the case presented here we have found that an analysis which focuses on leadership alone, or which concentrates on models of change which are uninformed of informal regulatory processes, is inadequate for understanding industry control of a regulatory agency. One must examine the social organization and subculture of the regulatory process. Such analyses have important implications in developing models of change or reform of such state institutions. Policy studies of administrative agencies and state regulatory commissions such as those produced by the Brookings Institution (Knolls, 1974) and the Ash Commission [8] have developed models of change which are uninformed of informal regulatory process. As a result the model of change generated by these studies focuses on leadership, formal procedures, and public access rather than informal relationships between the state and industry which are a result of both the wealth and organization of the industry and the structure and subculture of the state bureaucracies.

There is a qualitative aspect to this process which can only be achieved through the qualitative type of research summarized above. It is inadequate to look at the question of power manipulation simply as a mechanical process. One cannot get at the actual social organization of the process by just looking at legal structures or formal relationships between legal structures, because, in fact, the social organization functions through sets of informal relationships based on individuals and

---

of South Africa. The total premiums collected by these companies from consumers nation-wide ($61,816,513,000.00) is larger than the combined GNP of all Near Eastern nations or all African nations, and over half that of the combined GNP of all Latin American countries. (From State of California, 1970:53–72; and *The Official Associated Press Almanac* [New York: Almanac Publishing Company, 1973], p. 568.)

[8] President's Advisory Council on Executive Organization, 1971. Also there have been four other major governmental studies of problems and possible reforms of agencies: the President's Committee on Administrative Management (1937), the First Hoover Commission (see U.S. Commission on Organization of the Executive Branch of Government, 1949*a*, 1949*b*), the Second Hoover Commission (1955), the Landis Report (1960).

their perception of their life chances. We cannot, either empirically or theoretically, entirely separate the actual power relations from how people feel about these relations. Without looking at how people interpret their own life chances, whether they are working in the courts, in Congress, in regulatory agencies, or in industry, we cannot adequately understand or demonstrate how power functions.

In the setting of the regulatory processes described above it is clear that people interpret their life chances in terms of their own private individual advancement and profit.

> Ultimately, all you have to look forward to in Civil Service is promotion to the next job; incompetence won't bar you from that next job, but getting somebody in the industry really angry at you, getting involved in a real furor, will. And a civil servant knows that, you train a man, it's like training a puppy—you can tell him what you want him to do, but he knows that's not what you want him to do. He has gotten his nose spanked with a newspaper or has seen somebody else being spanked.
>
> . . . there's the savagery of the inner office struggle in the Department to get that next job, which results in more and more Machiavellian and Byzantine type people at each level up. The competition for the next job is murderous. They're jockeying for attention and developing techniques for bypassing your next superior and down-grading him if he's weak and getting the men above him and brown-nosing him if he's strong. . . .
>
> You look at the illness records for Department of Insurance Personnel, and in this nice calm spot where nobody ever bugs them, and they don't have to put in a full day's work most of their life. They have got ulcers, heart attacks, and a series of diseases that you normally associate with high stress. They have those diseases because they are in a situation of high stress. You put a man in a situation where he is not competing for anything but the next job up and for more power, he is insecure and the people he is competing with are all at approximately the same level, and when there are no objective ways of getting at that next step up, then you are gonna create a situation that is demoralizing. Then you compound that and make certain that nothing will ever get done because you structure it so that if he is incompetent he will get promoted or so that will not bar him from being promoted. [A former high-level employee, California Department of Insurance]

In this cultural milieu the idea of power equalization is not taken seriously by people at all levels. Returning to the question of models of reform, the kind of data discussed here is indispensable in developing a model which may bring the ideology of power equalization in line with practice. The current conceptual model of the state and its regulatory agencies is based on the attempt to represent a collective public by individual bureaucrats who are looking for private gains, and is a contradiction which impedes reform of the sort based solely on leadership, access, and formal procedures.

Discussion

The degree to which law functions as a power equalizer will depend on a number of factors, such as who controls the courts, or who controls the civil servants, or whether there is easy access to adversarial representatives such as lawyers. There is in all societies some contradiction between the ideology governing legal structures and how such structures operate in reality. However, gross contradictions are most likely to appear in communities characterized by social and cultural diversity. Scholars who theorize about the function of law (see Nader, 1965) speak to the function of the ideology of law rather than to the functions of the law in action. Clearly, law functions to equalize power, to insure fairness, and also to legitimize the dominance relations of some cultures or subcultures over others. One needs only to scan the cases decided on merit, to examine the subject matter of public-interest litigation, or to see who it is that sits in our jails to document these functions. In the examples given in this chapter, however, the suggestion is being made that in isolated indigenous societies a variety of functions may appear, but in industrialized and highly stratified countries characterized also by cultural diversity the weight of law as equalizer appears light in comparison to the power derived from the routine actions of law. There is public-interest litigation that is addressing problems that result from an imbalance in power. Nevertheless, unless government provides plaintiffs as well as defendants with lawyers, unless the legislatures focus more on prevention, it is likely that increased industrialization and class stratification will make it improbable that legal structures will in the main be used for purposes of power distribution.

In isolated, homogeneous societies there is a kind of social control that stems from the fact that people in conflict know each other and share a broad range of interpersonal ties and consensus about power relations. Individuals are dependent on each other for their social welfare. In the United States there is a general absence of the kind of community social control so usual in isolated societies. Economics is crucial here. When individuals are no longer dependent on each other for their economic welfare the tendency is for the powerful to manipulate available legal means for exclusive advantage. The case of the United States illustrates the relation between economic conditions, the relative distribution of power, and the kinds of legal mechanisms used and outcome sought. Without community social control the lack of access to individual and class legal action is all the more striking. In the absence of the main avenues by which order is traditionally maintained in society, power is likely to be abused by the powerful and the response is likely to be self-help. Self-help can be negative, as with increased incidence of theft, or positive, as with the work of such groups as California Citizen Action Groups.

For many reasons Americans today tend to bypass the courts, which theoretically could be functioning as power equalizers. There are two different strategies used by people to deal positively with the lack of state responsiveness to their needs. The first is to mobilize their resources to obtain the influence of those occupying formal positions sufficiently high in the system to at least attempt to equalize power. Political machines such as that of Daley are built on such demands. Our analyses of consumer complaint letters show that increasingly people use strategies such as the carbon-copy strategy—sending letters of complaint, then building up a support group by sending copies of the complaint letter to individuals thought to be of the same or higher level of power as the person being complained about. Problems with government bureaucracies such as social security, workmen's compensation, taxation are taken increasingly to Congressmen. Other problems go to Action Lines, to volunteer consumer action groups, to consumer advocates, to attorney-generals' offices. The alternative strategy is to deal collectively with conflict, rather than individually with complaints. As people discover the difference between making a specific complaint and a general complaint that is preventative in orientation, People's Lobbies, tenants' unions, rank-and-file union caucuses, and other groups are organized.

Americans since 1960 are responding to their powerlessness and inventing mechanisms which are not embedded either in formal or codified law; rather, these extrajudicial mechanisms are part of a developing American customary law which is independent of but affected by our national law. We are in the early stages of building support groups to function as power equalizers, much in the way that the small isolated communities such as the Zapotec have done over the centuries. Such support groups need to be informed of the informal processes by which private interests manipulate institutions of the state if they are to be more effective than previous government responses to the need for reform, responses which accept as a norm industry power and the subculture of bureaucratic society. These developing efforts at community or consumer control, based on group rather than individual advancement, could provide a common focus for those currently isolated workers within the state bureaucracy whose role as public servant has become meaningless in the face of industry control of their work place.

Studies of power processes are extremely important in developing directions for change. For example, if rank-and-file workers wanted to make critical changes in established labor unions, it would be essential to understand not only who the leadership of the union was and their relationship to the bosses, but also what the conflicts and weak points of the system were and the process by which the needs of the rank and file are subjected to the demands of the company and the union bureaucracy. If citizens were organizing a controlling voice in a comprehensive national health care program, it would be critical to know not only what powerful interests are seeking to profit from the control of such a program (such as the insurance industry or the medical profession), but also the processes by which such control is sought. As anthropologists we believe our contribution in the study of power is not only in demonstrating that the public interest *is* undermined, but in laying out in detail *how* it is undermined, in order to help the understanding of those citizen groups who are working to transform vastly unequal power relations.

In 1969 Nader argued for a reordering of the academic priorities of anthropologists, and suggested that a study of the power bases of society would improve our science and as well improve our contributions as citizens. The need today is even more urgent because we are being forced to realize that as professionals we must work and participate in the changing process of our society as conscious rather than unconscious participants. For changes to be meaningful and not subjected to the demands and needs of the few powerful people we must have knowledge of the powerful groups in this society, and how that power is held and used for private aggrandizement. Furthermore, this knowledge and its methodology must not be privately held, it must be public. In the smaller societies such knowledge is passed by word of mouth and used as part of the system of community control. Such a social science effort will be geared toward informing a broad range of citizens about how their society actually operates, rather than simply informing the powerful, as we have done, that they may change and manipulate the lives of citizens.

In the past most social scientists who have been concerned with social policy have looked to those in power to make reforms. Yet it has been shown that reforms made by and through this homogeneous class of people, without the input of varied citizen groups, do not function in the public interest.

18

Local Control of Community Services

Albert K. Cohen

INSTEAD OF WORKING my way into my subject and then digressing, as I usually do, I shall start right out with my digression. The "communities" we are talking about are neighborhoods or some other areal subdivisions of the city. We are not talking about universities, but I would like to say a few words about the experience of the universities during the sixties and seventies because, first, it is an experience that all or almost all of us know intimately and painfully at first hand and, second, it contains some lessons for our main subject.

The university is a community of a sort and one in which the desirability of local control, here called university autonomy, is taken for granted. Autonomy refers to self-determination of the university as against determination of university policy and activities by legislatures or other outsiders. But the university in turn has several components—trustees, administration, faculty, and students—and this gives rise to questions of local control in at least two other senses: first, the question of the extent to which any one of these segments is to participate in the shaping of the decisions of the university and, second, the extent to which faculty, on the one hand, and students, on the other, are to be free to operate autonomously within the university. I shall be mainly concerned with student participation in decision making and student autonomy, but I will have to touch upon local control in all these senses.

In the 1960s students, who, after all, are supposed to be the main beneficiaries of the services of the university, were demanding a much larger voice in the formulation of university policy and in making the decisions that affected their lives. It was, as you know, a period of great

292

contention, militancy, strife, and confrontation. There was resistance but, despite the resistance, there was considerable success, and some of the successes have endured, although many of them have melted away. It was a period of experimentation, variety, new structures, and new programs in response to student demands and pressures. On most university campuses students were given an increased voice in university governance and on some the responsiveness to student demands went as far as the establishment of little sheltered enclaves, communities within the community, where students established their own goals, worked out their own arrangements for services, were their own and one another's teachers, collectively made the collectivity's decisions, and administered their own budget—in short, assumed responsibility for defining what education was to mean and for accomplishing their education.

Now these incessant, boisterous, impassioned demands and confrontations, and the motivation to work and sacrifice in their behalf, were premised on certain assumptions: that the university was the repository of a certain amount of authority to make decisions and dispose of resources; that this authority and these resources were a fixed or expanding quantity; that how the authority and resources would be used would be decided inside the university; and that, by militant and heroic effort and organization, students could wrest power from the board, the faculty, and the administration. The most important of the assumptions was that the university's resources, very much like the physical plant, were always there or would be more or less automatically renewed. Therefore, the existence and availability of resources was not an issue; what was at issue was the question of who was to be served, in what way, and who, within the university, was to decide.

Things have changed greatly and for many reasons. Chief among these, however, was the transition from a climate of abundance to a climate of scarcity on the state and national level; a corresponding decline in resources available to funding agencies; a problem, on the part of the agencies, of how to adjudicate among competing claims on their resources; a consequent demand by the agencies for detailed and persuasive justification—persuasive, that is to say, in the light of *the agencies'* notions of what is right, necessary, or expedient; denial of discretion to recipients; and continued agency surveillance in the expenditure of funds after they had been granted.

In short, it turned out that the power that the students were trying to wrest from faculty, the administration, and even the board was now lodged in the state house and other places outside the university. The resources whose renewal was as certain as the spring thaw turned out to be variable, contingent, precarious, and scarce; it required great, concerted, and often humiliating effort to obtain them; and in exchange one had to surrender much of one's control over the goods and services they purchased. On the campus the scene has been transformed: from conflict over innovation and change to protest against dismantling; from demands for autonomous power to requests to be informed, consulted, considered; from "Who shall design the stained-glass windows of the Cathedral of Learning?" to "How shall we patch the roof?"; from a dispersal of power on the campus to concentration of power in the hands of the board and the administration; on the part of the administration, from attentiveness to their faculty and student constituencies to deference to the broader constituency of taxpayers and others who pay the piper; in spite of this centralization, a sense that the enemy or opposition is somebody outside the campus rather than "one of us"; a redirection, on the part of all concerned, of pressure and persuasion from other members of the university family to the governor, legislature, foundations, alumni, and the like; and finally, a mood of depression, apathy, despair, bitterness, and reluctant resignation.

I will not burden you with a detailed translation of this drama into the language of municipal politics. Anybody who has been following in the newspapers the agonies of New York City—its efforts to avoid bankruptcy, the transfer of the power to govern from City Hall to the state house and the financial community, the muting of demands for local control, the redirection of energies to the prevention of radical curtailment of centrally directed and administered municipal services, and the abject and humiliating acceptance, on every level of municipal government, of accountability not to the population served but to some hierarchically superior level of government—can make the necessary substitutions. However, I would remind you that one element of the university situation needs no translation: The most deprived element of the student population and the one most sensitive to the inadequacy of university services to their needs was the blacks and other racial and ethnic minorities, and there is no element that feels more abandoned, frustrated, and helpless in the new situation. *Mutatis mutandis,* we are speaking of the ghetto populations of all of our cities, even those with black mayors. I shall, however, try to draw some inferences, not all of them equally obvious, from what I concede is an imperfect but nonetheless relevant paradigm.

The inference is sometimes drawn that the sixties revealed where power "really" resided "all along"—that is, in the resource environment—and that this was brutally unmasked in the seventies. My point, however, is that there really *was* power on the campus and even in the student body in the sixties that was not there in the seventies. Under the conditions of the sixties it was possible, through organization, effort, and leadership, to wage conflict with other elements of the university and to get tangible and significant results. Students could and did make things happen then that they cannot make happen today. It does not follow, then, that efforts to achieve local control, and the aggregation of power and its concentration on the local scene are always and inevitably futile. The proper inference is that the returns from confrontation at the local level depend on properties of the resource environment *at the time*. This is especially true where, as in the case of public universities and impoverished areas of our cities, resources generated internally and not derived from external sources are meager relative to needs. This is not equally true of all universities, of all cities, or of all communities within cities.

Since the properties of the resource environment are subject to change over time, the strategies and tactics that are most likely to achieve a given result—the composition of coalitions, the scope and level of organization, and the points at which pressure is applied—will vary accordingly. If black students today want more scholarship funds and more special services, it is not enough to persuade or coerce the administration. They must make their power felt in the state house, and they cannot do this by themselves. It is not for black students at, say, the University of Connecticut, or for black students generally; it is a job for the black people, with whatever allies they can find, and organized in a manner and on a level appropriate to the theater on which the struggle must be waged.

Nor is it a proper inference that it is necessary to abandon the goal of local control and participation. I am not going to expand on the question of the desirability of local control. I take it for granted that however fully it may be realized, it cannot solve all the problems of the people in the locality, and that some services, by their nature, cannot be planned and administered on a local basis. But it seems to me that after we get through totaling up all the costs, benefits, and residual needs that local control cannot satisfy, the quality and quantity of services in the inner city are so miserable, so unresponsive to the needs of the citizenry, and so resistant to improvement except through active participation of the affected populations in the formulation and administration of policy, that unremitting pressure for greater local control is both necessary and inevitable. But local control must mean something more than occupying or sharing the driver's seat when there is no gas in the tank. Furthermore, the tank that is full today may be empty tomorrow. A strategy for filling the tank and keeping it full calls for participation and power on a level that transcends the local neighborhood or community. (The language of petrol may be more than a figure of speech. If we take the national state as a "locality" in the international system, events of the last two years impress upon us that it makes literal as well as figurative sense.)

A further conclusion—although this is hardly an inference from the university paradigm—looks like a paradox: In order to think small about jurisdictions for the administration of services, one must first think big. One must think about the ways in which resources flow in the larger society and the legal and governmental arrangements that condition this flow; and one must consider changes in these arrangements that would provide a more stable and dependable resource base for local control. Specifically, wealth is increasingly generated outside the core cities where suburbs tax themselves to provide the services that support their life styles while the cities try desperately to provide high-cost services from a shrinking tax base. The small town and the incorporated suburbs of our metropolitan areas are prime examples of the local control that our inner-city neighborhoods are crying for. What is apple pie in the suburbs is often considered subversive and un-American in the ghettos. To put it bluntly, in a complex and interdependent society, maximal local control for some means impoverishment and dependency for others. (The fact that local control is no solution to all the problems of the small town and the suburb is no argument against local control; it merely emphasizes the point alluded to earlier: that whatever the scale of the community in question, there are always problems that cannot be successfully dealt with at that level.) There is no way, it seems to me, that the flow of resources necessary to make increased participation and local control effective in the inner-city neighborhoods can be accomplished without changes in the formal, legal arrangements for the gathering and redistribution of resources. Proposals for accomplishing this and their respective merits and pitfalls have been discussed endlessly. Conspicuous among these are the assignment of revenues to school districts on the basis of need, which means the transfer of moneys from affluent communities to poor communities, and the creation of new governmental units, larger than our cities and comprehending their satellites, with powers to tax and spend. To the latter, in particular, the objection may be raised that it creates new centers of power even more remote from the consumers of service than our city halls and even less responsive. The argument has merit, but I am not sure that the consequence always and inevitably follows, that the creation of larger taxing jurisdictions *necessarily* means the creation of correspondingly larger and more inflexible bureaucracies, that the centralization of control over fiscal resources is not possible without a devolution of administration and increased opportunities for meaningful local participation.

Be that as it may, any change in the legal structure of taxation and the distribution of revenues itself requires effective aggregation and concentration of power at strategic points, and of course this is the heart of the dilemma. To a large extent, although not altogether, the demand for local control is a reflex of failure and frustration in trying to act politically on a larger scale. For the poor, there is hardly any less promising way of effecting change than through the American party system, and taking to the streets has not greatly changed the conditions of life for most of them. Some changes have occurred that have made it easier for some of the poor to become nonpoor, but those who remain are not better off. Indeed, there is probably less hope and more despair in the inner city today than there was ten years ago. It is understandable that people should turn to local control, not as a panacea but as a way of making capital of the meager political resources that they have in their numbers, propinquity, common race or ethnicity, and whatever indigenous structures of association they have on the neighborhood level. Furthermore, one objective of community control is to provide experience in political participation so that poor people, black people, Puerto Rican people can develop competence and confidence to act more effectively in the larger arena where the major payoffs lie. However, where community control is so hamstrung by lack of resources that it cannot produce striking and gratifying accomplishments, the incentive to participate itself languishes and dies.

I cannot point the way out of the dilemma. To tell poor people not to seek local control of community services is like telling people who cannot afford to go to the doctor not to experiment with patent medicines. You can't tell people to do nothing. My point is that, however bleak the prospects, one must seek, by whatever means possible, political or economic, inside or outside the traditional system of electoral politics, to find ways of being effective on a level that transcends the local community, not as an alternative to local control but to make it possible of realization.

VIII

To Spur the Development of the
Discipline by Pinpointing Theoretical
and Methodological Deficiencies

19

Marxist Theories of Power and Empirical Research

Arthur L. Stinchcombe

I WOULD LIKE to make two assumptions in this chapter that are, I believe, somewhat unusual in the discussion of the Marxist theory of the organization of power. The first is a positivist assumption, that the principal interesting question about the Marxist approach to power is whether or not it is true. The second is the assumption of arrogance, that what the Marxists need is a course in elementary empirical methods.

Given these assumptions, I want to address three principal questions about how to do Marxist research on the ruling class. The first has to do with variations in the mode of production. My argument will be that, just as the Marxist study of the response of workers (say, worker alienation or the strike rate) depends on an analysis of the mode of production (that mode's political and ideological requirements, its authority system, its property system, and its technical organization), so also rulers derive their ideology from their work life, and different modes of production produce different kinds of rulers. This is, of course, a belief that Marx expressed at great length. My proposal is that we find out whether it is true, instead of mixing up all capitalist thought into a gray dough of "monopoly capitalism."

The second question appears in two forms in the Marxist literature, that of the role of the vanguard party in Lenin and that of the notion of hegemony of bourgeois ideology. The problem Lenin posed was that in order to win, the working class had to consider its collective interest rather than its individual interests, or its "trade union consciousness."

As I understand Althusser, his point about hegemony of bourgeois ideology is a mirror image of Lenin's analysis of Social Democracy and trade unionism. The notion is that like the vanguard party, the capitalist class collectively so organizes itself to give in easily on the particular, disaggregated interests of individual capitalists, but becomes increasingly hard to deal with as the collective interests of capitalism as a system are threatened. The result is that they easily tolerate professorial vaporings over the dialectic or the crisis of Western sociology, or Social Democratic speeches about the rights of the working man, but are careful that the ideology *actually operating* in work relations, in collective bargaining, in curricular organization of the university, or in foreign policy, is a bourgeois ideology. That is, the hypothesis is that the capitalists, by being the ruling class, have *naturally* the advantages that the proletariat can only achieve by a vanguard party. This inequality means that compromise on the workers' side, that is, Social Democracy, is almost always compromise of basic principles for concrete advantages, while capitalist compromise is almost always an expedient to save the basic features of the system by bargaining away some concrete advantages. My argument will be that there are empirical variations in the preconditions of Lenin's "trade union consciousness" and Althusser's "bourgeois ideological hegemony," and that these variations allow an empirical test of the relevant theory.

The first of these hypotheses has to do with the bases of differentiation of the ruling class, that it should typically be on the basis of involvement in different modes of production. Althusser's hegemony and Lenin's vanguard party have to do with the capacity of the ruling class, because it is ruling, to work out an authoritative definition of its collective interest which can overcome its internal diversity, in a way that can only be done by the poor through an agency like a vanguard party. This organization of the ruling class is an empirical variable that ought to have causes and effects that are measurable, and the hypotheses ought to be judged as true or false, rather than as radical or conservative.

The third question has to do with historical processes, specifically with revolution. The core question, as I see it, is: What determines whether socialist governments act differently from capitalist ones? Marxist theory maintains that unless the power of the bourgeoisie is destroyed, socialist governments act like bourgeois governments, but with a different rhetoric. A revolution destroys the power, hence indirectly the property, of the bourgeoisie, since property is basically a political phenomenon. Without a revolution, the power remains behind a socialist façade; hence one way or another property remains. I put it to you that a systematic and empirically responsible comparison of socialism with capitalism, and within each, a comparison of different styles and power constellations, has never been carried out. Instead socialist states are compared with the socialist ideal, and are found to fall short. Capitalist states are also compared to the socialist ideal, and also fall short. The failure of capitalism to achieve socialist ideals is, of course, to be expected. The explanation of the failure of socialist states is usually that people are evil, perhaps because they are bureaucrats, perhaps because they are, like Stalin, insane paranoids, perhaps because of capitalist encirclement.

My argument is terribly naive empiricism, that things alleged to be due to monopoly capitalism should not be true of the Soviet Union and China. Further, it is that the difference between revolutionary Social Democrats such as Allende or the early Swedish socialist governments and the tame socialism of the English Labor Party or the hollow populism of the average African or South American socialist, must have an explanation. To point out that each is equally distant from revolutionary purity does not advance the analysis. The question is, then, what determines the different degrees of distance of socialist governments from the practice of capitalist governments, and is this distance related to the depth and character of the revolutionary process?

Let me illustrate these major questions with the example of the Marxist theory of race relations, specifically the "internal colonialism" theory. I rely heavily on Robert Blauner. The first question is whether the economic, enterprise authority and political requirements of different industries lead to different ideologies and practices of race relations, and specifically whether the colonial character of an industry affects capitalist ideology and practice. By the colonial character of a mode of production, we mean three things: (1) does the enterprise produce raw materials shipped to a national or world market from a distinct region, raw materials requiring a large input of relatively unskilled labor, as opposed to producing services for a local market, manufacturing goods out of the raw materials, or providing government services? (2) Do the labor relations in these regional enterprises depend on the political suppression of class conflict, in such a way that they would be undermined by independent local self-government of a bourgeois-democratic kind, allowing workers' representation—or more briefly, does the labor relations system depend on disenfranchised workers? (3) Are the other middle classes and the governmental leadership of the region in question dependent on the colonial enterprises, so as to constitute a dependent comprador class, and so that the conflict of capitalist interests that Marx argued produced bourgeois-democratic pressures does not take place? For example, the plantation mode of production of cotton in the American South or vegetable farming in the irrigated Southwest or Hawaii has had a colonial character to a high degree, by all three criteria, while government services in the industrial

North and West are at the opposite extreme. The question is, do upper-class ideologies and institutional practice show a more racist character, the more colonial the mode of production?

The question of hegemony, and its mirror-image problem of Social Democracy and trade-union consciousness, has two components for the colonialism model. First, it urges that as the role of blacks or Chicanos in the mode of production changes in the aggregate from colonial to bourgeois, the centers of organizing power in the capitalist class (the banks, the peak associations of business, the conservative parties) manage the change of the class as a whole from a colonial model of race relations to a free labor market, bourgeois-democratic model. This movement by the bourgeoisie toward Social Democracy is predicted to show changes relatively rapidly on the trade-union type of issues, but to be very sticky on all sorts of questions having to do with the rights of property in the market, and specifically to be against paying minority people more than their productive value in the market. That is, capitalist ideology should move in a "liberal" direction much faster on questions of improving the market value of black or Chicano productivity, for example, by educational reforms, and much slower on questions of redistributing income and wealth. Conversely, without a vanguard party, the Social Democratic part of the thesis would be that the protest ideology and practice of minority groups should tend to move over time, and to move especially in concrete bargaining and legislative arenas as opposed to speechmaking, in a direction compatible with capitalist hegemony. That is, in practice such movements will more and more accept the improvement of minority market position and participation in limited bourgeois democratic politics as evidence of the advance of collective ethnic interests, replacing or playing down the objectives of redistribution of income and wealth, challenge to capitalist authority in the enterprise, and so on.

The third major question is whether, say, the treatment of Chicanos and blacks in the United States differs in a significant way from the treatment of Muslim, Caucasian, and Ukrainian minorities by Russians in the Soviet Union; the treatment of Macedonians or Bosnians by the Serbe or Croats in Yugoslavia; the treatment of Tibetans by the Chinese in China; the treatment of blacks in Cuba. If inequality of races is produced by colonial capitalism, it ought not be regularly produced by revolutionary socialism.

My general impression from a casual acquaintance with the facts is that the Marxist theory of race relations stands up pretty well. But the fact that at this late date I am giving my impressions is an indictment of the empirical quality of Marxist scholarship on how the power networks of capitalist and socialist societies work, and of the lack of theoretical imagination of the positivist opponents of the Marxist view.

These are empirical propositions derived from the theory of internal colonialism by straightforward applications of conventional Marxist reasoning. I put it to you again that the interesting question about them is whether or not they are true, not whether some fact-free version of the Marxist "approach" is better because it is dialectical, or useful for identifying oneself as radical, or in some other nonempirical way a superior philosophy.

Elementary Methods Applied

The first thing we learn in elementary methods, starting with a quotation from John Stuart Mill if we like, is that causal inference depends on comparisons. We have to so choose our units of analysis that the causal variable of interest varies over these units. The usual practice in power studies in America is to show that people with power are rich. What that shows is, whatever the mode of production of their business, they are good at it, they know how to make it go. It requires a considerable gift to read Marx's long discussions of the stages of evolution of factory enterprises, or variations in bourgeois political behavior in France, Germany, and England, and completely miss the point of the comparisons. As Marx observed repeatedly, it is branches of industry that have distinct technical, enterprise government, and economic requirements. Thus they produce different types of upper classes, different kinds of the rich.

There are three main units of analysis that vary in their mode of production: individuals, firms or government organizations, and countries. If the oil business has a monopoly, capital-intensive, skilled-labor mode of production, for example, Standard Oil capitalists are capitalists in such a mode of production; Standard Oil as a firm should show the characteristic labor relations of such a mode of production; and the Arab oil-exporting nations should be distinctive in having their capitalist parts be monopolistic, capital-intensive, and high-skill. All three kinds of units of analysis vary in their mode of production both over time and cross-sectionally. It is true both that Arab countries now have more monopolistic capitalism than the United States, and that their capitalism is more monopolistic now than fifty years ago; a capitalist in food retailing fifty years ago was in a petty bourgeois mode of production; now he is liable to be either in petty bourgeois or oligopolistic corporate competitive modes of production; a firm in cotton culture fifty years ago needed a labor relations system to manage black cotton pickers, which wheat farmers did not need, while now it needs one to manage cotton-picking machines.

That is, history should be disaggregated by industrial modes of production, into separate industry evolutions of the ideology and practice of individual capitalists, separate industry evolutions of the practice of firms, and separate comparative histories of countries with different modes of production. The prediction would be, for example, that the king of Saudi Arabia, as Rockefeller's successor to the oil monopoly, should act pretty much like Rockefeller, except perhaps for being cleverer and more powerful, and should act in quite a different way from a sheik based on nomadic subsistence camel herding, pilgrimage services, and petty trading by camel caravans.

But further, the Saudi king should act differently than Sra. Perón, who is based on a competitive agricultural export sector and a nationalist, protected industrial base. That is, besides the historical continuity of the types of upper classes produced by a given mode of production, and historical change as the mode of production changes, individuals, firms, and countries should have different ideologies and practices at a given time, depending on their industrial base.

The main units of analysis that vary with respect to the hegemony variables are social and political protest movements, and upper-class establishments. Here we have three aspects of variation: I will call one the "class organizational health" aspect, the second the "linking" aspect, and the third the "oppositional arena" aspect. First, social movements or establishments *as a whole* vary in the degree to which they are so set up as to be able to make the class collective interest dominate the individual, sectoral, or trade-union, particular interests. Second, given any degree of collective organizational health, particular segments of the class may be tightly or loosely linked to the organizational center. Thirdly, the process of class negotiation may be so set up that what is hegemonic or central among capitalists is what Social Democrats and trade unions give up first, and conversely that what is peripheral to the capitalists is easily won by the Social Democratic workers. Or it may be the case that capitalists foolishly fight on irrelevancies, and Social Democrats can find no one to compromise with and so lose out to a vanguard party for the constituency of the poor.

So what we have, then, are again three types of units of analysis. The first are collective organizations of the contending classes, which vary over history and between countries, and are to be classified by their degree of capacity to make class interests dominate particular interests. The second are segments of the contending classes, classified by the tightness of their links to the center. The third are oppositional arenas, like industry-specific collective bargaining, or legislatures, or riots, which are to be classified by the degree to which hegemonic content gets into the practical deals made in those arenas.

Since this is pretty abstract, let me specify the interrelations among these types of variation a bit more, using our example of internal colonialism. The argument would be that as a society moves from a mode of production that uses black people and Chicanos in a colonial mode of production, effective bourgeois hegemony would be reflected in a movement, *including* dominant Southern capitalists in places like Atlanta and Dallas, toward a bourgeois democratic incorporation of blacks and Chicanos. Effective ethnic vanguard organization would be reflected in continuing insistence that black and Chicano incomes have to go up, regardless of whether their market value as laborers in capitalist enterprise goes up.

Now, if we classify parts of the internal colony by its degree of linkage with the hegemonic capitalist organization—say, for instance, by the involvement of national banks in the investment in the colonial section, the degree of incorporation of blacks and Chicanos into less colonial modes of production, and so on—we should find that the closer the linkage, the more dominant the hegemonic (progressively more bourgeois democratic) ideology and practice becomes. The stronger the hegemony the less rapidly, however, this falloff toward the periphery takes place. That is, if New York banking already controls cotton plantations, then plantation counties will be as easy to move toward modern race relations as Atlanta. Further the *content* of the hegemonic ideology can be diagnosed by those aspects of bourgeois opinion and practice that slope most sharply with the strength of the links. So, for example, capitalist support (or at least tolerance) for voting rights, collective bargaining rights, and schooling should slope from black reaction among peripheral capitalists to enlightened conservatism among Atlanta bankers, while opposition to improving black and Chicano situations by taxing the wealth being made off their backs should not slope toward the peak, with Chase Manhattan being just as defensive of property rights as a rural Alabama cotton grower on a family plantation.

On the other side we have two predictions about protest ethnic movements. The first is that, in the absence (or weakness) of a vanguard party, over time there will be increasing demands for programs compatible with bourgeois democratic hegemony, that is, demands for educational equality, individual promotion opportunities for ethnic minorities rather than collective redistribution, voting participation rather than national self-determination, and the like. The second is that among countries, those with stronger collective organization of oppressed ethnic groups should evolve in the direction of trade union consciousness more slowly than they do in the United States.

Finally, arenas of conflict vary in the degree to which they are dominated by the hegemonic organizing center for capitalists, and the older, compromising, Social Democratic movements for the poor. For ex-

ample, national collective bargaining as an arena has least participation
of primitive Southern racists, Congress has somewhat more, Southern
state politics has more yet, and labor relations in plantation agriculture
most of all. What we should find is that the more the dominance of
hegemonic institutions in an arena of conflict, and the less the dominance of loosely linked peripheral sectors of the Establishment, the
more rapid the drift of the protest movement in a bourgeois democratic or trade union direction.

A second source of variation is in the substantive content of the
issues in an arena, with questions of taxation, expropriation, property
rights, and revolution being central to the system; education, promotion policy in the civil service or the military, collective bargaining over
the price of labor, social security paid for by a tax on workers, being
more peripheral. The argument implies, for example, that the Ways
and Means Committee will underrepresent the interests of the poor,
while the Health, Education and Labor Committee will overrepresent
them (relatively). Further it argues that bourgeois courts will not decide
to bus black people into Wall Street, but will be much more open to
busing them to a white school, or to giving them membership in a trade
union. It further argues that as time goes on, Social Democratic movements will focus more on the arenas with open competition, and will
count their victories in Health, Education, and Labor rather than their
defeats in Ways and Means.

So much for hegemony and Social Democracy.

For the third variable, the revolutionary process, the primary unit
of analysis is the political system, that is, nowadays, the nation, and
within nations, different historical times. The variable we want to classify political systems by is the degree of destruction of the special access
of bourgeois interests to those parts of the system that are crucial for
bourgeois rule, specifically the property system. The general argument
is that the more integrated the working-class movement around an
ideologically organized party, and the more that party controls the state
apparatus, the less influence bourgeois interests will have in those parts
of the system having to do with taxes, expropriation, property rights.
Further, the argument implies that the greater the development of
Social Democratic or trade unionist trends in the left movement, the
more its coming to power will leave the channels of access open to
bourgeois interests in these crucial sectors, and the more they will open
channels for workers only on the trade union, education, and welfare
aspects of the system.

For example, with respect to internal colonialism and race relations,
the argument implies that a revolutionary socialist regime (or a Social
Democratic regime less penetrated by hegemonic bourgeois ideology) is
more likely to expropriate properties in businesses with a colonial

mode of production and rebuild them on a noncolonial basis, to intervene directly in the labor market decisions of firms to achieve fair
employment goals, to organize equally strong worker protest organizations in the colonial periphery as in the metropolitan center, to intervene in the process of appointment of general managers of firms when
goals of ethnic equality are undermined, and for all these reasons to
move the income and wealth of oppressed minorities more rapidly
toward equality than do capitalist or tame Social Democratic regimes.

Thus it should be the case both that Uzbeks and Ukrainians have
moved faster toward Russian standards of income than blacks or Chicanos have moved toward whites in the United States, and also that
they have moved faster since the Revolution of 1917 than under the
Russian Empire.

To summarize the application of John Stuart Mill to the comparison
problem, the units of analysis that have to be compared for different
parts of the Marxist analysis of power are:

1. For the mode of production
   a) capitalists as individuals
   b) firms as organizations
   c) countries
   (each compared cross-sectionally and historically, by industrial
   types)
2. For hegemony–Social Democracy
   a) class organizations, cross-culturally and historically
   b) sectors with different linkages to hegemonic or vanguard
   class centers
   c) arenas of conflict, by the participation of hegemonic centers
   and by substantive centrality to capitalist viability
3. For revolutionary process
   a) countries, comparative and historical, by degree of control by
   worker interests of the property system

For the internal colonialism model of race relations, the variables
we have to evaluate for these units of analysis are:

1. For the mode of production
   a) labor-intensive raw material production for capitalist markets
   b) labor relations systems depending on a disenfranchised labor
   c) dependence of other regional middle classes on the colonial
   enterprises
   d) as the dependent variable, racist ideology and institutional
   racism, measured for individuals, firms, and political systems
2. For hegemony–Social Democracy
   a) the variation over time from black reaction to enlightened

bourgeois conservatism (as the role of blacks and Chicanos changes from colonial labor) in the centers of banking, corporate management, and peak associations
  b) the same variation within the colony as we move from family plantations to corporate plantations to nationally oriented manufacturing to regional banking and investment centers to local representatives of the national bourgeoisie
  c) the content of protest programs as the protest movement ages or becomes more involved with hegemonic centers, varying from redistribution to improving the market value of black or Chicano labor through education
  d) the degree of representation of the interests of the poor as we move from arenas peripheral to capitalism such as Health, Education, and Labor to arenas that are central such as Ways and Means
3. For revolutionary process
  a) special access of capitalists in the political system at points where policy touches on the property system, presumably from high access in capitalist and tame Social Democratic regimes to low access in revolutionary socialist regimes
  b) the speed of movement toward racial equality, supposed to be especially marked in the former colonial areas in revolutionary regimes

Sources and Types of Data

Now we turn from the point that one has to have comparisons, and units of analysis and variables that yield comparisons, in order to make causal inferences, to the point that one has to have observations on those variables for those units in order to test the causal ideas.

The first point to note about the units of analysis above is that they are mostly *collective, cross-cultural or cross-industry,* and *historical.* As long as positivist observation in race relations insists on studying the social psychology of prejudice in the mass public of *individuals,* in one country, ignoring people's location in the productive order except for a loose social class variable, at one point in time, there is not much chance that they will speak to the issues. As long as Domhoff shows again that the people who run things tend, as individuals, to be rich and to live their lives with other rich people, and forgets that the king of Saudi Arabia is also rich, we are not likely to see any advance. As long as the pluralists insist on counting a black speechmaker on the Health, Education and Labor Committee as equal to a friend of oil depletion allowances on Ways and Means, we have no hope of studying variations in arenas. The individualist illusion, ethnocentric parochialism, and historical shortsightedness of the positivist tradition in sociology tend to make its observations irrelevant to any sophisticated theory of the power system.

The second point is that one has to observe at least two values of the variable in order to get anywhere. If internal colonialist theorists insist on calling New York equally colonialist as Mississippi, which rather strains one's credibility but seems to be respectable nowadays, then they will have to observe what happens in Soviet Central Asia to the Muslims. If "monopoly capitalism" means anything observable in the world, some modes of production such as the oil industry must be more monopolistic than some others such as retail trade; some countries such as Saudi Arabia must have more monopolistic capitalism than others such as the United States; socialist countries must have less monopoly capitalism than capitalist countries. The careful absence of comparative study among students of internal colonialism suggests an overwhelming desire to be ignorant about whether what they say is true or not.

The third point is that there are a lot of things to count and measure in the variables above. There is no reason that the column inches of capitalist testimony to the Ways and Means Committee cannot be compared to column inches on Health, Education, and Labor. The evolution over time of the demands of social movements ought to be codable by criteria of redistributiveness versus improvement of labor market position, and the rates of change of the ratio of Social Democratic or trade union consciousness types of demands to challenges to central capitalist institutions compared in the different situations where Marxists predict different rates of change. The rate of approach to income equality by Uzbeks in Uzbekistan as compared to blacks in the South is theoretically observable, although the Soviet government does not go out of its way to facilitate bourgeois sociological analysis. If the racial employment of firms classified by monopoly position can be calculated by Gary Becker (1971) for his neoclassical economic purposes, it is hard to see why Marxists cannot do the same thing. Incidentally, in every relevant respect Becker's results support the Marxist analysis of race relations given above, whenever they are relevant to the issues. Firm policies in race relations are measured both by contract compliance officials and by Parsonian investigators like Leon Mayhew. There is no particular reason for a Marxist to be less competent than a routine civil servant or than a Parsonian. The race relations ideology that pervades different industries can be easily calculated, even for the self-employed and managerial personnel alone, by simply coding the industry questions asked in every respectable academic national survey study. The industry code is now used for the purpose of coding occupation, but this bourgeois shortsightedness of survey researchers need not hinder its use to study the impact of the mode of production. Southern states can be statistically described by the dependence of their middle classes on peculiarly colonial modes of production with little difficulty. The distinction in closeness to national capitalist banking centers between Atlanta or Dallas on the one hand, and Birmingham or Tallahassee on the other, can be found in a half dozen statistical sources available for metropolitan areas.

In short, Marxist variables are variables in this world; variables in this world can be observed; things that can be observed can be counted or measured or both, with a little bit of scientific ingenuity. If Marxist studies cripple themselves by not observing comparatively, they double their disability by refusing to use the inherently quantitative and countable nature of their variables for precision of empirical analysis.

Now we turn to the analytical technology necessary to turn the raw facts into facts or parameters relevant to the theory. Marxist theory is about comparative rates of change in different circumstances: For example, rates of change of the mode of production in which blacks and Chicanos are involved are supposed to determine rates of change of hegemonic institutions toward bourgeois democratic types of reforms; or, for example, sectors closely linked to capitalist centers are supposed to respond to this change faster than loosely linked peripheral sectors. The ordinary analytical technology for studying causes of rates of change is differential equations. In my most intransigent moments, I sometimes urge that people without the calculus should not be allowed to study social change, because their comments on the value of quantitative and mathematical theories are necessarily incompetent. But even in reasonable periods, I would urge that Marxists need the calculus more than Parsonians, because they have theories of the causes of different rates of change, while Parsonians usually have theories of the form that eventually change will happen by social differentiation.

It is not much wonder that the positivists have not made much contribution to the study of Marxist theory, because their analytical technology has been peculiarly inappropriate to the questions at hand. Cross tabulations, or a panel at time one and time two, are hardly adequate to the empirical issues. The statistical problems are those of relating time series data to differential equations models of the social process.

The fifth point has to do with interaction, or as Lazarfeld called it, "specification." The prediction of the theory of hegemony, for example, is that as we go closer to capitalist centers, the slope of consent to racial reform of a bourgeois sort (education, voting rights, collective bargaining) is steep, while the slope of consent to redistributive programs (collective contributions to black income out of taxes on wealth, self-determination by blacks governing central economic institutions such as property) is essentially flat. The analytical technology for studying interaction effects or differences in slope is analysis of covariance, or its analogue in the log-linear model for cross tabulations. Elementary multiple regression without interaction, or path analysis, simply are not adequate to the question. The average level of statistical ingenuity required for studying Marxist theory is going to have to be *above* the competence necessary to be an ordinary social-psychological kind of positivist, in order to turn a set of raw facts into a fact about a statistical parameter that speaks to Marxist theory.

How Did We Get into Such a Mess?

Let me suppose for the sake of argument (what I don't suppose for a minute in reality) that I have convinced the reader that Marxism is an empirical theory, testable by the methods of quantitative investigation, when these methods are suitably improved over the present dismaying state. How does it come about that investigation in this area is so far below what is required—in fact, so far below the level of empirical investigation of Marx and Trotsky? I want to offer three hypotheses to account for this situation. The first is that we allow people to be theorists in the discipline. The second is that we have turned over the development of methodology to the social psychologists. The third is the ethnocentrism of the American ideological left, the audience to which many Marxists hope to speak.

When I compare the travesty of Marxism I learned in a theory course to the sophistication of Marx's empirical analyses of nineteenth-century English capitalism and of French politics, I am persuaded that the central cause of theoretical disability is to pose as, and aspire to be, a theorist. This empirically empty schematism that generates no investigable results is only possible because we provide sociologists a social role as theorist. Furthermore, a Marxist is not a specialist in a subject, so he has to be a theorist, and is shaped by the tradition of empirical emptiness by which we sociologists recognize something as theoretical. If there were no specialists in nonempirical investigations of ideas in the discipline, we would not channel Marxists into such nonempirical activities.

The overdevelopment of quantitative methods for social-psychological studies, and their underdevelopment for structural and historical units of analysis, is primarily due to the fact that only survey researchers specialize in methods. This has two effects. The first is that most of what we learn in methods courses is irrelevant to the study of

structural problems, especially structural change. The second is that a
Marxist has to show that he can hardly count in order to show he is not
a social psychologist. Usually the demonstration is convincing, if not
very fruitful for testing Marxist ideas.

The third problem comes from the peculiarly untheoretical nature
of the American left ideological public. It is very hard to get the *New
York Review* interested in race relations outside the United States, or in
the oil monopoly when it passes from Rockefeller, Governor of New
York, to the king of Saudi Arabia. What use is it to find out who in abstract terms is responsible for racial oppression or oil prices ten times
the cost of production, if you cannot, respectively, keep him from becoming chairman of the Judiciary Committee or vice-president? This
ethnocentric view is, perhaps, appropriate for a general intelligentsia,
for intellectual consultants to American left politicians. It is radically inappropriate for the scientific investigation of Marxist ideas.

The general practice of Marxist investigations results in their not
having much to say to the profession. Their orientation to a particularly parochial ideological community, as an alternative audience, confirms them in a kind of research strategy that keeps them from making
causal inferences, which keeps them from having much to say to the
profession, and so the sterile circle is closed.

20

Hermeneutics, Ethnomethodology, and Problems of Interpretative Analysis

Anthony Giddens

I

THIS CHAPTER WAS PROMPTED by some of the remarks contained in Lewis Coser's address to the meetings of the A.S.A. in San Francisco. It is not a defense of ethnomethodology as such, but rather an attempt to connect up some of the themes found in the writings of Garfinkel and others influenced by him with some relatively recent developments in European social philosophy. I believe these ideas to be of fundamental importance to sociological theory, although they have as yet made little impact upon it. By submitting them to a constructive critique, I shall try to show how their contributions can be integrated with an appraisal of their shortcomings.

The developments in European social thought to which I wish to call attention involve a revitalization of the notion of *Verstehen* in the context of the latter-day evolution of the *Geisteswissenschaften*. In Germany, this centers above all upon the work of Hans-Georg Gadamer, which in turn draws extensively upon Heidegger's "hermeneutic phenomenology." But Gadamer's writings demonstrate clear connections and overlaps with the work of such authors as Winch in Britain and Ricoeur in France (see Gadamer, 1960; Winch, 1958; Ricoeur, 1965). In this brief chapter I shall not attempt to single out the distinctive views of such authors, but only to characterize certain notions arising from them—ones that contrast rather radically with those embodied in Max Weber's version of interpretative sociology, which more than any other has served to introduce the concept of *Verstehen* into English-speaking sociology. More qualifications are in order, with respect to "ethnomethodology"—already a term, of course, that embraces a number of mutually dissident views. What I have to say is not directed at Garfinkel's program of practical studies of "everyday accomplishments," which seems to me at once deeply interesting and poorly elucidated philosophically. All I want to do is to take hold of a few ideas that I find expressed in the writings of Garfinkel and others which seem to me parallel to those emanating from the very much more abstract traditions of European social philosophy.[1]

I shall argue that a grasp of these themes, and an appreciation of their significance, signals a major break with the erstwhile dominant schools in sociology (and with at least certain versions of Marxism), according to whom the social sciences can be narrowly modeled upon natural science. An important emphasis of these schools is that sociology is (or can hope to be) *revelatory* in respect of the confusions or misapprehensions of "common sense." That is to say, just as the natural sciences seem to have stood in opposition to commonsense views of the physical world, to have penetrated the mystifications of ordinary lay thought, so sociology can aspire to stripping away the musty errors of everyday beliefs about society. The claimed "findings" of social research, like the findings of natural science, are frequently resisted or disclaimed by laymen on the basis of what "common sense shows." As far as natural science is concerned, such resistance normally takes the form of the refusal to abandon a commonsense belief in the face of findings that contravene it: for example, the clinging to the belief that the Earth is flat rather than spherical. I don't want to deny that something like this occurs in respect of the claims generated by sociology, but I do want to suggest that another—almost diametrically opposed— response is common. This is not that social science reports conclusions that laymen cannot accept because they go against trusted beliefs, but rather that it merely *repeats the familiar*—that it tells us what we already know, albeit perhaps wrapped up in a technical language. Sociologists are prone to dismiss this sort of rejoinder to their work rather cursorily, holding that it is the business of social research to check up on the convictions of common sense, which may be right or wrong. But to regard lay beliefs as in principle corrigible in this sense is to treat them as if they were merely adjuncts to human action, rather than integral to it. Lay beliefs are not merely *descriptions* of the social world, but are the very basis of the *constitution* of that world, as the organized product of human acts. Recognition of this point, I shall seek to demonstrate, makes us aware that sociology stands in more complex relation to its "subject matter"—human social conduct—than natural science does. The natural world is *transformed* by human activity, but it is not consti-

---

[1] Most of the views in this chapter are discussed in more detail in Giddens, 1976.

tuted as an object-world by human beings. The social world, on the other hand, is constituted and reproduced through and in human action; the concepts of common sense, and the everyday language in which they are expressed, are drawn upon by lay actors to make social life happen.

II

Let me distinguish five themes that I discover in at least some of the writings of those involved with, or close to, ethnomethodology. These by no means exhaust the interest of such writings, but I consider them to be particularly important. First, the theme of the significance of the notion of human *action* or *agency* in sociological theory. I suggest that most of the leading schools of sociology, with the partial exception of symbolic interactionism, lack a concept of action. Now this initially seems an odd thing to say, because perhaps the leading figure in English-speaking sociology, Talcott Parsons, has explicitly based his scheme of sociological theory upon an "action frame of reference," and in his first major work, *The Structure of Social Action,* attempted to incorporate "voluntarism" as a core component of it. It is sometimes argued that, whereas Parsons began his intellectual career as a voluntarist, his theories become more and more deterministic. I think it more accurate to claim that Parsons did not successfully embody such a perspective within his system of theory in the first place. What Parsons did was to treat voluntarism as equivalent to the internalization of values in personality, thereby attempting to relate motivation to the *consensus universel* upon which social solidarity is held to depend. But this has the consequence that the creative element in human action becomes translated into a causal outcome of "need-dispositions," and the adoption of "voluntarism" merely a plea for complementing sociology with psychology. Here the actor does indeed appear as a "cultural dope," rather than as a knowing agent at least in some part the master of his own fate. As against the determinism inherent in the sort of approach favored by Parsons, it is fruitful to place in the forefront the thesis that society is a skilled accomplishment of actors; this is true even of the most trivial social encounter.

Second, the theme of reflexivity. The notion of action, as the writings of philosophers have made clear, is integrally bound up with the capacity of human agents for self-reflection, for the rational "monitoring" of their own conduct. In most orthodox forms of sociology (including Parsonian functionalism), but not in ethnomethodology, reflexivity is treated as a "nuisance" whose effects are to be minimized as far as possible, and which is only recognized in various marginal forms, as "bandwaggon effect," "self-fulfilling prophecies," and so on. Moreover, these tend to compress together two aspects of reflexivity: that of the sociologist in relation to the theories he formulates, and that of the actors whose behavior he seeks to analyze or explain. There is an irony here that ties together these two aspects of reflexivity, or rather the neglect of them, in positivistically-minded forms of social thought. For what is denied, or obscured, on the level of theory—namely, that human agents act for reasons and are, in some sense, responsible for their actions—is implicitly assumed on the level of sociological discourse: That is to say, it is accepted that one has to provide "reasoned grounds" for the adoption of a particular theory in the face of the critical evaluations offered by others in the sociological community.

Symbolic interactionism is perhaps the only leading school of thought in English-speaking sociology that comes near assigning a central place to agency and reflexivity. G. H. Mead's philosophy hinges upon the relation of "I" and "me" in social interaction and the development of personality. But even in Mead's own writings, the "I" appears as a more shadowy element than the socially determined self, which is elaborately discussed. In the works of most of Mead's followers, the social self displaces the "I" altogether, thus foreclosing the option that Mead took out on the possibility of incorporating reflexivity into the theory of action (cf. Winter, 1966:9 ff.). Where this happens, symbolic interactionism is readily assimilated within the mainstream of sociological thought, as a sort of sociological social psychology concentrated upon face-to-face interaction. The differentiation between the two is represented only as one between "macro-" and "microsociology."

Third, the theme of language. Now, language, in the form of the symbol, is obviously stressed within symbolic interactionism, as the term itself indicates. But this is distinct from the standpoint of ethnomethodology, in which language is conceived, not simply as a set of symbols or signs, as a mode of representing things, but as a medium of practical activity, a mode of doing things. Language, to use Wittgensteinian terminology, operates within definite "forms of life," and is routinely used by lay actors as the medium of organizing their day-to-day social conduct. The "meanings" of utterances thus have to be understood in relation to the whole variety of uses to which language is put by social actors—not just those of "describing," but also those of "arguing," "persuading," "joking," "evaluating," and so on. I have alluded briefly to the significance of this above. One of its consequences is that ordinary language cannot be ignored by sociological investigators in favor of a wholly separate technical metalanguage which clears up the "fuzziness" or the "ambiguity" of everyday speech. Ordinary language is the medium whereby social life is organized *as* meaningful by its constituent actors: To study a form of life involves grasping lay modes of talk which express that form of life. Ordinary language is not therefore just a topic that can be made available for analysis, but is a resource that every sociological or anthropological observer must use to gain access to his researchable subject matter."

Fourth, the theme of the temporal and contextual locating of action. I think it would be plausible to say that it is only in respect of societal evolution that orthodox sociological theory has attempted to build temporality into its analyses. In ethnomethodology, on the other hand, the locating of interaction in time becomes of central interest. In the conduct of a conversation, for example, it is pointed out that participants typically use the conversation reflexively to characterize "what has been said," and also anticipate its future course to characterize "what is being said." The context-dependence or indexical character of meanings in interaction, of course, involves other elements besides that of time. Garfinkel is undoubtedly correct in emphasizing the indexical character of ordinary language communication—and also in seeing this as an intractable source of difficulty for orthodox views of the nature of sociological metalanguages.

Fifth, and finally, the theme of tacit or taken-for-granted understandings. In the active constitution of interaction as a skilled performance, the "silences" are as important as the words that are uttered, and indeed make up the necessary background of mutual knowledge in terms of which utterances make sense or, rather, sense is made of them. Tacit understandings are drawn upon by actors as ordinary, but unexplicated, conditions of social interaction. The emphasis upon this in ethnomethodology is one of the direct points of connection between it and the forms of European social philosophy I shall turn to in the next section, reflecting Garfinkel's indebtedness to Schutz, thereby linking the former's work to the great traditions of phenomenology such as exemplified, for example, in Husserl's *Crisis of the European Sciences* (1970) (and also, incidentally, indirectly to the "newer philosophy of science" of Kuhn, whose "normal science" is science that proceeds within an agreed-upon framework of tacit understandings).

III

Insofar as ethnomethodology shares certain common origins, in "existentialist phenomenology," with the developments in European social thought that I shall now go on to mention, it is not particularly surprising that we should be able to discern similarities between them. If these are not immediately apparent it is because the styles of writing in which they are couched are so different, ethnomethodology being mainly oriented to generating an empirical research program, the other being expressed in the style of abstract philosophy. In approaching the traditions of thought that have breathed new life into the notion of *Verstehen,* it is important to appreciate the contrast which they offer to the earlier phases of development of the *Geisteswissenschaften,* as represented by Dilthey and (in spite of many reservations) Max Weber.[2] In the older tradition, *Verstehen* was regarded above all as a *method,* to be applied to the "human sciences," in contrast to the sorts of methods of external observation employed in the natural sciences. For Dilthey, especially in his earlier writings, the process of understanding was conceived to depend upon the re-experiencing or re-enactment of the thoughts and feelings of those whose conduct was to be understood. That is to say, in some sense or another—which Dilthey increasingly found difficult to specify—in understanding the action of others one mentally "puts oneself in the other's shoes." Weber adopted much the same stance, although suspicious of notions such as re-experiencing and empathy, and rejecting the idea that there is a logical gulf between the methods of the social and natural sciences. Weber's version of interpretative sociology meshed closely with his commitment to what has subsequently come to be called "methodological individualism": the thesis that statements that refer to collectivities can always in principle be expressed as the behavior of concrete individuals.

Both Dilthey and Weber wished to claim that their particular understandings of "understanding" could be reconciled with the achievement of objective sciences of history (Dilthey) or sociology (Weber). Their views have been sharply attacked by critics (Abel, 1948; Hempel, 1953) writing from a positivistic standpoint, on the basis that *Verstehen* cannot yield the sort of evidence that would seem to be necessary to objective science. According to such critics, the process of interpretation can be useful as a source of hypotheses about conduct, but cannot be used to test hypotheses thus derived. It is difficult to resist the force of such criticism, I think, within the context of Weber's endeavor to make the idea of *Verstehen* compatible with criteria of evidence that are supposed to have the same logical form as those characteristic of natural sciences. Moreover, there are a series of other difficulties with Weber's views, of which I shall mention here only two. One is to do with empathy, the other with Weber's formulation of "social action." Weber wished to distance himself from the view that empathic identification plays a major part in understanding the meaning of actions; but that he was unable to do so is illustrated by certain puzzles to which his position

[2] For a good, short discussion in English see Outhwaite, 1975. A longer account appears in Radnitzky, 1970.

gives rise. Thus he supposes that mysticism is "on the margins of mean-ingful action," since the behavior of mystics can only be understood by those who are "religiously musical." Let us suppose that some, and only some, social scientists are "religiously musical": how could they ever communicate their understanding to those who are not? To admit that they could not seems once more to compromise Weber's views upon the possibility of achieving an intersubjectively agreed-upon set of cri-teria in terms of which an objective "observation language" can be es-tablished in the social sciences. As against Weber's view, I would want to claim that to call conduct "mystical" is already in a certain sense to have understood it meaningfully: and that understanding is tied to the capacity to describe actions linguistically—to typify them in Schutz's term. There are a series of problems relating to what Schutz calls, rather unhappily, "objective meaning," that Weber's analysis, con-cerned only with "subjective meaning," fails to come to terms with.

Weber's preoccupation with subjective meaning was closely bound up with his methodological individualism, since meaning only comes into being through the subjective consciousness of actors. It is against this backdrop that Weber distinguished between "meaningful action" and "social action," the latter being the main interest of interpretative sociology, defined as action which is oriented toward others and thereby influenced in its course. In Weber's famous example, if two cyclists who do not see each other coming bump into one another, this is not a case of social action, since the behavior of the one did not fig-ure in the subjective orientation of the other. If, having collided, they start quarreling about who was responsible for the accident, this then becomes social action. But this formulation, which specifies what is social only in terms of the subjective standpoint of actors, does not seem at all satisfactory: It is neither easy to apply, nor does it en-compass the range of elements that I would wish to claim are "social." It is not easy to apply to actual conduct because there are many cases of behavior in which the "other," to whom the action may be said to be oriented, is not present on the scene. What are we to make, for in-stance, of a man shaving prior to going out for the evening? Is he orienting his action toward another particular person he anticipates meeting later on? The answer is that he may or may not have another's possible responses clearly in mind while he carries on the activity; and this is in fact not particularly relevant to the "social" character of what he is doing, which is likely to reside more in conventions or norms of cleanliness, etc. Similarly, I want to say that the action of a cyclist pedal-ing along the road is already social, regardless of whether others are in sight or not, insofar as what the cyclist does is oriented toward, and "in-terpretable" in terms of, the social rules governing traffic behavior.

IV

In the more recent series of writings to which I have referred previously, *Verstehen* is treated, not as a *method* of investigation peculiar to the social sciences, but as an *ontological condition* of life in society as such; it is regarded, not as depending upon a psychological process of re-enactment or something similar, but as primarily a *linguistic* matter of grasping the content of familiar and unfamiliar forms of life; to understand others, it is held, is in an important sense to enter into *dialogue* with them; such understanding cannot be "objective" in any single sense, since all knowledge moves in a circle, and there can be no knowledge free from presuppositions; and, finally, *Verstehen* is linked to norms or rules of meaning in such a way as to break free from methodological individualism.

There can be no question of pursuing these very complex ideas in any sort of detail within the purvey of a short chapter, and all I shall try to do is to spell out a few of their implications in such a way as to help clarify what they share with the points of interest in ethnomethodology that I have distinguished earlier.

To argue that *Verstehen* should be regarded as an ontological condition of human society, rather than as a special method of the sociologist or historian, is to hold that it is the means whereby social life is constituted by lay actors. That is to say understanding the meaning of the actions and communications of others, as a skilled accomplishment, is an integral element of the routine capabilities of "competent" social actors. Hermeneutics is not simply the privileged reserve of the professional social investigator, but is practiced by everyone; mastery of such practice is the only avenue whereby professional social scientists, like lay actors themselves, are able to generate the descriptions of social life they use in their analyses. One of the consequences of this, of course, is to reduce the distance between what sociologists do in their researches, and what lay actors do in their day-to-day activities. To revert to the terminology of ethnomethodology, not only is it the case that every sociologist is a member of society, and draws upon the skills associated with such membership as a resource in his investigations: It is equally important that every member of society is a "practical social theorist." The "predictability" of the social world does not just happen, it is made to happen by lay actors.

The centrality of language as the organizing medium of the "lived-in world" is stressed alike in the "hermeneutic phenomenology" of Heidegger, Gadamer, and Ricoeur, and in the writings of those following the later Wittgenstein in English-speaking sociology. Garfinkel has of course drawn directly upon Wittgenstein's writings. It is particularly interesting to see, however, that Continental philosophers have begun to emphasize the relevance of Wittgenstein's writings to their own concerns. For while Wittgenstein gave no special technical meaning to *Verstehen,* his later philosophy certainly moves toward recommending that the understanding of actions and communications can only be approached within the practical involvements of definite language games. Gadamer emphasises that man "lives in and through language," and that to understand a language is to understand the mode of life which that language expresses. In focusing upon the importance of dialogue *between* different forms of life, however, Gadamer goes beyond Wittgenstein. The characteristic problem that Wittgenstein's philosophy seems to lead to is: How does one ever get out of one language game into another? For language games appear as closed universes of meaning. In Gadamer, on the other hand, the mediation of language games through dialogue is placed as a beginning point rather than as a conclusion; the emphasis is upon what is involved in grasping the meaning of long-distant historical texts, understanding alien forms of life, and so on. It is perhaps not too fanciful to suppose that the prominence of "dialogue" in Gadamer's philosophy finds something of a parallel, on a much more modest scale, with the prominence of "conversation" in Garfinkel's work.

The circle in which all knowledge moves is a preoccupation of many different modern philosophies. If one breaks—as in the philosophy of science Popper, Kuhn, and others have broken—with the idea of a "first philosophy," founded upon a bedrock of certainty, one becomes committed to the notion that it is the business of epistemology to make the circle of knowledge a fruitful rather than a vicious one. That is, for example, what Popper tries to do for science by means of his philosophy of conjecture and refutation; and what, from what is in most respects a very different standpoint, the modern phenomenological philosophers seek to do via the notion of the hermeneutic circle. I don't want to suggest that in Garfinkel's writings, or in those of others immediately influenced by him, one can find a sophisticated discussion of such matters of epistemology. Such a concern would appear to be foreign to the style of work characteristic of ethnomethodology. Nonetheless, the theme of "indexicality" is certainly directly relevant to the sorts of issues raised by philosophies that stress the inherent circularity of knowledge—although again on a minor scale. Some of the similarities are quite easy to see. One of the notions associated with the hermeneutic circle is that in, say, understanding a text, the reader grasps each part through an initial appreciation of the whole; there is thus a constant process of moving from part to whole and back again, whereby an enriched understanding of the whole illuminates each part and vice versa. A similar idea appears in Garfinkel's discussion of indexicality in conversations, where it is pointed out that a conversation is constantly drawn upon by participants both as a mode of characterizing itself and so as to "gloss" the meaning of each particular contribution to that conversation. Garfinkel (cf. also Cicourel on "indefinite triangulation") seems to present a version of the idea that the circularity of knowledge can be fruitfully explored, but does not feel any need to elucidate this on any kind of abstract level; in fact, this idea seems to go along with a defined strain of naturalism in Garfinkel's writing, as expressed, for example, in the claim that it is the task of ethnomethodology to describe indexical expressions "free of any thought of remedy." Such unresolved perplexities seem to underlie the very different directions which the work of those originally influenced in some part by Garfinkel has taken: On the one hand, in the writings of Schegloff and Sacks (1973), toward a naturalistic form of "conversational analysis"; on the other, in the writings of Blum (1974) and McHugh et al. (1974), toward a concern with the abstract ramifications of the hermeneutic circle.

The newer version of *Verstehen* depends upon the thesis that understanding the meaning of either actions or communications involves the application of "publicly accessible" linguistic categories connected to tacitly known norms or rules. In tracing out some of the connections between this and ethnomethodology, we return to the origins that each partly shares in the development of phenomenology after Husserl, in Schutz and in Heidegger. It is highly important to appreciate the degree to which this development, as culminating in hermeneutic phenomenology and linking up to the largely independent evolution of post-Wittgensteinian philosophy, marks a movement away from the original impetus to phenomenology. Hermeneutic phenomenology in the hands of Heidegger and Gadamer breaks with the subjectivism characteristic of the earlier phase of development of phenomenology (Schutz never managed to complete this break). From this perspective, as from that of the later Wittgenstein, language is essentially a social or "public" phenomenon grounded in forms of life: The self-understanding of the individual can only occur in terms of "publicly available" concepts. A person can only refer to his "private" sensations in the same framework of language as he refers to those of others. This is very different from the philosophical schema within which Weber worked, and cuts across the assumptions of methodological individualism, since the locus of the creation of meaning is taken to be the standards or rules of the collectivity rather than the subjective consciousness of the individual actor, the latter in fact presupposing the former. Garfinkel's writings certainly assume the same stance as this, and it is thus quite misleading to identify ethnomethodology, as many critics have been prone to do, with subjectivism.

V

I believe that most of the ideas I have mentioned in the foregoing sections are of basic significance to the social sciences, and will have to be built into the reconstruction of sociological theory that the current phase of uncertainty in sociology poses as an urgent task. But they cannot be accepted as they stand, within the traditions of thought that have given rise to them: It is as vital to recognize the shortcomings of these traditions as it is to appreciate the signal value of their contributions. I think the limitations of certain versions of ethnomethodology bear definite similarities to those apparent in the *Verstehen* tradition. In identifying some such shortcomings, however, I shall for purposes of remaining concise refer directly only to ethnomethodology, rather than to the much broader and more complex European schools of social philosophy.

First, in Garfinkel's writings—and in the work of most of those who have made use of them at all extensively in seeking to do the sort of "remedying of constructive analysis" that Garfinkel himself disclaims a concern with—"accountability" is severed from the pursuance of practical motives or interests. Everyday practical activities, as I would use such a phrase, refers to much more than the sustaining of an intelligible world. The achievement of an "ordered" social world has to refer not only to its meaningful or intelligible character, but to the meshings—and conflicts—of interests that actors bring to accounting processes and which they endeavor to pursue as part and parcel of those processes. This is one reason, I think, why the reports of conversations that figure in ethnomethodological writings have a peculiarly empty character: Conversations are not described in relation to the goals or motives of speakers, and appear as disembodied verbal interchange. Terms such as "practical accomplishment" that loom learge in ethnomethodological discourse are in this sense not used appropriately. "Doing bureaucracy," "doing science," and so on, involve more than merely making such phenomena "accountable."

Second, to recognize the force of these comments is to accept that every relation of meaning is also a relation of power—a matter of what makes some accounts *count*. In the most transient forms of everyday conversation there are elements of power, which may exist in a direct sense as differential resources that participants bring to the interaction, such as the possession of superior verbal skills, but which may also reflect much more generalized imbalances of power (e.g., class relations) structured into the society as a totality. The creation of an accountable world cannot be explicated apart from such imbalances of resources that actors bring to encounters.

Third, acknowledgment of the central importance of the notion of human agency to sociological theory has to be complemented with something akin to orthodox structural analysis in sociology. I would express this by saying that ethnomethodological studies are concerned with the production of society as a skilled accomplishment of lay actors, but much less with its *reproduction* as a series of structures. However, the problem of the social reproduction of structures is also dealt with quite inadequately, I believe, in orthodox functionalist theory, where it appears in the guise of the "internalization of values." To reconcile the notions of agency and structure, I think, it is necessary to refer to what I call the *duality of structure*. The essence of this idea is quite readily explicated in terms of the relation between speech acts and the existence of a language. When a speaker utters a sentence, he draws upon a structure of syntactical rules in producing the speech act. The rules in this sense generate what the speaker says. But the act of speaking grammatically also *reproduces* the rules which generate the utterance, and which only "exist" in this way (cf. Giddens, 1976).

Fourth, the term "common sense" has to be elucidated more carefully than is characteristic of commonsense thought itself. The "incorrigibility" of common sense as a necessary *resource* for social analysis should not blind us to its status as a *topic*. To understand a form of life is to be able in principle (not necessarily, of course, in practice) to participate in it as a "competent member." From this angle, common sense—that is to say, the forms of mutual knowledge shared by the members of a common culture—is a resource that sociologists and anthropologists have to make use of. As a resource, such "mutual knowledge" is not corrigible for the social scientist. The mistake of many of those influenced by ethnomethodological writings is to suppose that there is not another sense of common sense represented as beliefs that are corrigible in the light of the findings of social science. If common sense is itself set up as a "topic," the beliefs that are involved, whether about society itself or about nature, are in principle open to rational examination. To study, say, the practice of sorcery in an unfamiliar culture, an anthropologist has to master the categories of meaning whereby sorcery is organized as an activity in that culture. But it does not follow from this that he has to accept as valid the belief, say, that sickness can be induced in a victim by means of magical ritual.

VI

At this point we can return to the problem, introduced in the early part of the paper, of the conditions under which sociology can aspire to be revelatory with regard to common sense. In one respect, this becomes easy to deal with. What we can hope to do in sociological analysis is to offer explanations of the unacknowledged grounds of action whereby society is produced and reproduced by its constituent actors as a skilled accomplishment. But the matter cannot be left there, since I have so far not mentioned a key respect in which one of the themes of ethnomethodology conjoin to those of the new *Verstehen* tradition: that of reflexivity. The notion of self-reflection enters ethnomethodology only in respect of the "members" whose "ethnomethods" are subjected to study. The reflexivity of the ethnomethodological observer, on the other hand, is rarely mentioned at all. This helps conceal the unresolved character of the two strains in Garfinkel's writings I noted earlier: a recognition of the hermeneutic circle on the one hand, and a tendency toward naturalism on the other. For if it is the case that we should treat lay actors as knowledgeable agents, who reflexively monitor their own behavior, surely the same has to be said of the self-reference of the ethnomethodologist? That is to say, the providing of ethnomethodological accounts of lay actions is itself a reflexively monitored skilled accomplishment. At this point, the circle threatens to become a vicious one: for any ethnomethodological account must display the same characteristics as it claims to discern in the accounts of lay actors; it could in turn be subjected to ethnomethodological analysis, and so could *that* account, and so on. Garfinkel obviously accepts this fact of infinite potential elaboration, and indeed in one way wants to point it up as a feature of all "accounting procedures." I don't believe that one should remain satisfied with this, however, and I think it reflects a failure to explicate the problems involved in the relation between observers' and lay actors' accounts of their connected forms of "practical activity."

The importance of the European schools of social philosophy to which I have referred is that they do seek to confront reflexivity on these two levels—that of the observing social scientist and that of lay actors. In this respect, however, I think some of the critics of hermeneutic phenomenology have more interesting things to say than those who have remained within its confines. Although I have strong reservations about some of their work, I would single out such authors as Apel (1967), Habermas (1971), and Lorenzer (1970) as having provided outstandingly important analyses of some of these issues. It is a principal emphasis of their writings that the relations between the elements that actors, within definite forms of society, reflexively apply as "reasons" for actions, and the grounds of those actions that operate independently of their awareness, is a shifting one. The greater the range of knowledge that is made available to actors, the more previously unacknowledged grounds of action become available to their reflexive "monitoring," thus extending the sphere of rational autonomy of action. The social scientist is in principle able to contribute to extending the compass of such knowledge; it follows, for such authors, that *his* reflexivity should be tied to an awareness of the potentialities of sociological theory as *critical* theory.

21

Two Methods in Search of a Substance

Lewis A. Coser

IN TUNE with the overall theme of this book, this chapter is an exercise in the uses of controversy. I am perturbed about present developments in American sociology which seem to foster the growth of both narrow, routine activities, and of sectlike, esoteric ruminations. While on the surface these two trends are dissimilar, together they are an expression of crisis and fatigue within the discipline and its theoretical underpinnings. I shall eschew statesmanlike weighing of the pros and cons of the issues to be considered and shall attempt instead to express bluntly certain of my misgivings and alarms about these recent trends in our common enterprise; let the chips fall where they may.

Building on other students of science, Diana Crane (1972) has argued that scientific disciplines typically go through various stages of growth accompanied by a series of changes in the characteristics of scientific knowledge and of the scientific community involved in the study of the area. In stage one, important discoveries provide models for future work and attract new enthusiastic scientists. In the next stage, a few highly productive scientists recruit and train students, set priorities for research, and maintain informal contacts with one another. All this leads to rapid growth in both membership and publications. But in later stages the seminal ideas become exhausted and the original theories no longer seem sufficient. At this point a gradual decline in both membership and publication sets in, and those who remain develop increasingly narrow, specialized, though often methodologically

☐ Presidential Address delivered at the Annual Meeting of The American Sociological Association in San Francisco, August, 1975.

highly refined, interests. Unless fresh theoretical leads are produced at this point to inspire new growth, the field gradually declines.

Such stages of growth and decline are, of course, not limited to the sciences. In other spheres of culture, religion and the arts for example, similar phenomena have been observed (cf. Thomas O'Dea, 1966; Max Weber, 1963; Alfred Kroeber, 1957). One need only think of the creative effervescence in the communities of Christ's immediate disciples and their direct successors in contrast to quotidian routines and ritualized devotions of the later stages in what had now become the Church of Rome. Or consider the art of Byzantine icon painting where, after the early creative period, the same motives, even techniques, were endlessly repeated so that it takes a specialist to distinguish between paintings executed not just decades but even centuries apart. In religion and the arts, however, innovation is not a necessary condition for flowering and appeal, but in the sciences, when no innovation is forthcoming, rigor mortis is not far away.

The findings of Crane and others in the sociology of science typically refer not to a whole branch of knowledge but only to sub-fields within such branches. It would therefore be wrong to apply these findings to sociology as a whole, composed as it is of a wide variety of subareas each with its own pattern and rhythm of growth. Yet permit me nevertheless roughly, and perhaps rashly, to sketch what I consider the present condition of sociology as a whole.

By and large, we are still in the second stage of growth, the stage of lively development, of creative ability and innovative effervescence. Yet there now appear a number of danger signs suggesting that the fat years of the past may be followed by lean years, by years of normal science with a vengeance, in which not only the mediocre minds but even the minds of the best are hitched to quotidian endeavors and routine activities. This seems portended by the recent insistence among many sociologists on the primacy of precise measurement over substantive issues.

The germ of the idea for this chapter came to me earlier this year when a friend of mine, the editor of a major sociological journal, explained with some pride that, no matter what the substantive merits of the paper might be, he would refuse to accept contributions using old-fashioned tabular methods rather than modern techniques of regression and path analysis. I gather, for I have respect for his opinion, that he meant that he would not accept articles requiring modern methods of data analysis that do not make use of such techniques. Yet, though his intentions are undoubtedly excellent, I submit that such an orientation is likely to have a dynamic of its own and that, inadvertently perhaps, it will lead to a situation where the methodological tail wags the substantive dog, where, as Robert Bierstedt (1974:316) once put it, methods would be considered the independent and substantive issues the dependent variable.

My friend's voice is, of course, not a lonely one. In fact, he expressed what is tacitly assumed or openly asserted by a growing number of our colleagues. Fascinated by new tools of research, such as computers, that have come to be available in the last decades, and spellbound by the apparently irresistible appeal of techniques that allow measures of a precision hitherto unattainable, many of our colleagues are in danger of forgetting that measurements are, after all, but a means toward better analysis and explanation. If concepts and theoretical notions are weak, no measurement, however precise, will advance an explanatory science.

The fallacy of misplaced precision consists in believing that one can compensate for theoretical weakness by methodological strength. Concern with precision in measurement before theoretical clarification of what is worth measuring and what is not, and before one clearly knows what one is measuring, is a roadblock to progress in sociological analysis. Too many ethusiastic researchers seem to be in the same situation as Saint Augustine when he wrote, on the concept of time, "For so it is Oh Lord, My God, I measure it but what it is I measure I do not know" (Saint Augustine 1953:35).[1]

No doubt, modern methods of research have immeasurably advanced sociological inquiry. Only sociological Luddites would argue that computers be smashed and path diagrams outlawed. What I am concerned with is not the uses but rather the abuses of these instruments of research. They serve us well in certain areas of inquiry, but they can become Frankenstein monsters when they are applied indiscriminately and, above all, when their availability dictates the problem choices of the investigator so that trivial problems are treated with the utmost refinement.

The sheer availability of new methods encourages their use and seems to release the user from the obligation to decide whether his problem or findings are worthy of attention. By way of illustrating this let me quote from the summary of a recent paper by Oksanen and Spencer (1975) in one of the official journals of the A.S.A., *The American Sociologist:* "A rather large degree of explanatory power has been achieved by our regression model, in terms of overall goodness of fit and in terms of significant variables. It is of considerable interest to learn that high school performance is an invariably significant indicator of 'success' in the [college] courses examined." Abraham Kaplan's

---

[1] In fairness to St. Augustine, modern physics tends to agree with his position. "Time is a primitive element in the logical structure of physics," state W. H. Cannon and O. G. Jensen (1975), "consequently physics does not explicitly define time but rather specifies operational procedures for its measurement in units of seconds."

(1964:28) delightful formulation of the Law of the Instrument comes to mind here: "Give a small boy a hammer, and he will find that everything he encounters needs pounding."

The fact is that, though in principle these new methods and technologies could help us achieve greater theoretical sophistication, they are used as "magic helpers," as a shortcut to, or even replacement for, theoretical analysis rather than as a means for furthering it. An insistence on the use of these refined methods, no matter what, makes it fall prey to Kaplan's law.

It would be easy, and perhaps entertaining, to go on quoting similar instances, but each of us can easily supply other examples. Let me instead return to the serious problems now faced by our discipline, many of which have been created, or at least accentuated, by the revolution in methodology and research technology.

Our new methodological tools may well be adaptable to deal with a great variety of topics and problems, and I hope they are. However, the data needed for path or regression analyses are much harder to come by in some areas than in others, and in many of them it would take a great deal of sophistication to discover and handle usable indicators. Consequently, under the pressure to publish to avoid perishing, or to gain promotion, or simply to obtain the narcissistic gratification that comes from seeing one's name in print, it is more attractive to do what is quick and easy. This is so in every scholarly field and even in the healing arts. In psychiatry, for example, it leads to prescribing drugs instead of psychotherapy, often not as a result of deliberate choice between alternative diagnoses and prognoses, but simply because drug therapy is easy to administer and promises quick results, superficial though they may be. In the world of scholarship, moreover, not only the choice of technique but even the choice of the problem tends to be determined by what is quick and easy rather than by theoretical considerations or an evaluation of the importance of the questions that are raised. Moreover, the uses of a sophisticated technological and methodological apparatus gives assurance, but often deceptive assurance, to the researcher.

Sociology is not advanced enough solely to rely on precisely measured variables. Qualitative observations on a small universe can provide theoretical leads that may at a later stage become amenable to more refined statistical treatment. To refrain from using descriptive data because they may lend themselves only to tabular presentation will not only diminish our theoretical powers but will retard the refinement of statistical analysis as well.

Training the new generation of sociologists not to bother with problems about which data are hard to come by, and to concentrate on areas in which data can be easily gathered, will result, in the worst of cases, in the piling up of useless information and, in the best of cases, in a kind of tunnel vision in which some problems are explored exhaustively while others are not even perceived.

There is at least some evidence that we tend to produce young sociologists with superior research skills but with a trained incapacity to think in theoretically innovative ways. Much of our present way of training as well as our system of rewards for scientific contributions encourages our students to eschew the risks of theoretical work and to search instead for the security that comes with proceeding along a well-traveled course, chartered though it may be by ever more refined instruments of navigation. J. E. McGrath and I. Altman (1966) have shown this in instructive detail for small-group research, but it applies in other areas as well.

Careers, especially those of people with modest ambitions, can be more easily advanced through quantity rather than quality of publication. This leads to an emphasis on methodological rigor, not on theoretical substance. One way to publish rapidly is to apply "the [same] procedure, task, or piece of equipment over and over, introducing new variables or slight modification of old variables, and thereby generate a host of studies rather quickly" (McGrath and Altman, 1966:87). The formulation of theories, moreover, is time-consuming, and may not lend itself easily to publication in journals increasingly geared to publishing empirical research, and to reject "soft" theoretical papers. There exist, then, a number of factors in our present systems of training and of rewards that exercise pressures on incoming generations of sociologists to refine their methods at the expense of developing innovative lines.

This is not inherent in methods per se, but it is, let me emphasize again at the risk of repetition, a temptation for lesser minds. And here as elsewhere inflation has set in. However, it is important to note that even the better minds, those who have been able to use the new methods innovatively, are *nolens volens* geared to deal with problems, important as they may be, for which these methods promise quick results. Even in the serious work that is being done with the help of the new statistical techniques there lurks the danger of one-sided emphasis.

Stratification studies of recent years will illustrate this point. This field has benefited a great deal from modern path analytical methods whose power is perhaps shown at its best in Blau and Duncan's *The American Occupational Structure* (1967). Path analysis allows these authors systematically to trace the impact of such factors as father's occupation, father's educational attainments, and son's education and first job on the son's placement in the occupational hierarchy. It allows for the first time the assessment in precise detail of the ways in which occupational status in a modern industrial society is based on a combination of achieved and ascribed characteristics. It permits, in fact, the assessment of the contributions of social inheritance and individual effort in the attainment of socioeconomic status.

Yet, to use an important distinction by John Goldthorpe (1972), this research contributes to the understanding of the *distributive,* not to the *relational* aspects of social class. The focus is predominantly on the impact on individual careers of differences in parental resources, access to educational institutions and the like, or they center attention upon individual characteristics of people variously placed in the class structure. There is no concern here with the ways in which differential class power and social advantage operate in predictable and routine ways, through specifiable social interactions between classes or interest groups, to give shape to determinate social structures and to create differential life chances. The first and only entry under path analysis in the 1966–1970 Index to *The American Sociological Review* (vols. 31–35) refers to a paper by Hodge and Treiman (1968) tracing the effects of the social participation of parents on that of their offspring. There were only two papers analyzing problems in social stratification with the aid of path analytical methods in the 1973 (vol. 38) volume of *The American Sociological Review,* and both (Kelley, 1973; Jackman and Jackman, 1973) deal with the *distributional* aspects of social stratification or with the characteristics of individuals in the class hierarchy.

The 1974 volume of *The American Sociological Review* published three papers on stratification using path analysis, two of which (James N. Porter, 1974; Alexander and Eckland, 1974) deal again with distributional aspects. The *Rose Monograph Series* published by the A.S.A. had issued twelve titles up to the end of 1974. Of these, four, that is one third, deal with problems of stratification and use highly sophisticated research methods. Their titles speak for themselves: "Socioeconomic Background and Educational Performance" (Hauser, 1972); "Attitudes and Facilitation in the Attainment of Status" (Gasson et al., 1972); "Looking Ahead: Self-conceptions, Race and Family as Determinants of Adolescent Orientation to Achievement" (Chad Gordon, 1972); and "Ambition and Attainment: A Study of Four Samples of American Boys" (Kerckhoff, 1974). It would appear as if authors and editors of the series are fixated on the problems of making it.

Yet a class system is not only a distributive system, in which individuals are assigned to their respective niches in terms of background and training, nor is its analytical significance exhausted by individual characteristics of people who make their way within it; it is also a system that is shaped by the interaction between various classes and interest groups differentially located within the social structure. It is a system, moreover, in which command and coercion play major parts. Classes and other socio-economic groups use their resources so as effectively to maintain or advance their positions and to maximize the distribution of material and social benefits to their advantage. Exclusive concern with the distributive aspects of stratification directs attention away from the sociopolitical mechanisms through which members of different strata monopolize chances by reducing the chances of others. Max Weber (Gerth and Mills, 1947), building on Karl Marx, saw this with exemplary clarity when he stated that "It is the most elemental economic fact that the way in which disposition over material property is distributed among a plurality of people . . . in itself creates specific life chances. According to the law of marginal utility this mode of distribution excludes the nonowners from competing for highly valued goods. . . . It increases . . . the power [of the propertied] in price wars with those who, being propertyless, have nothing to offer but their labor. . . ."

One need not accept Marx's dichotomous scheme of class analysis in order to agree that classes are linked in asymmetrical relationships. The notion of a class of owners of means of production is dialectically bound to the notion of a class of nonowners. Just as in the classical Indian caste system, as Louis Dumont (1970) has shown, the purity of the Brahmans is inseparable from the impurity of the Untouchables, so the central characteristics of the class systems is not that there are propertied and the propertyless but that they are mutually interdependent. Randall Collins, arguing against a narrowly defined sociology of poverty, puts the matter well when he writes, "Why some people are poor is only one aspect of the same question as to why some people are rich: A generalized explanation of the distribution of wealth is called for if one is to have a testable explanation of either particular" (Collins, 1975:17).

A system of stratification consists in relationships between groups or categories of men and women which sustain, or alter, their respective access to life chances. It is one thing to investigate the ways in which, for example, people manage to attain the status position of medical practitioners in American society; it is quite another to analyze the institutions that help the American Medical Association to monopolize the market for health care by restricting access. What needs analysis is not merely the ladder to medical success but those institutional factors that contribute to the maintenance of a system of medical service that effectively minimizes the life chances of the poor (Kelman, 1974).

Analysis of the distributional aspects of stratification systems can dispense with considerations of social and political power; concern with the relational aspects, however, directs attention to the power contentions that make for the relationships which establish differential class privileges, and create patterned conflicts between unequally benefited contenders. When no question is asked about two benefits from existing social and political arrangements, stratification research, no matter how sophisticated its methodological tools, presents a "bowdlerized" version of social reality. When the causes and consequences of differential location in the class structure remain unanalyzed, the whole area of research so brilliantly opened up by Robert K. Merton's (1968: chaps. 6, 7) seminal anomie paradigm remains unexplored.

I am not arguing, let this be clearly understood, that concern with the structures of power and exploitation is necessarily better than preoccupation with the pathways to individual mobility. There is surely a need for both types of studies. I believe, however, that the methodological tools that are available help focus on the latter. It must be added—lest I be accused of technological determinism—that such restrictions are also rooted in the prevailing American ideology of individual achievement. But taken together, the ideology combined with the use of statistical methods in limited areas, prevents the growth of our discipline and curtails our ability to strive for a full accounting and explanation of the major societal forces that shape our common destiny and determine our life chances. If the computer and the new methodological tools we possess now are not yet adequate for handling some of the issues I have raised, then let us at least press forward with theoretical explorations even if they should later have to be refined or modified by more precise empirical research. Let us not continue on a path about which one may say with the poet Roy Campbell (1955:198): "They use the snaffle and the curb all right. But where is the bloody horse?"

Another symptom of the decline of a discipline, as Diana Crane (1972) indicates, is exclusive insistence on one particular dimension of reality and one particular mode of analysis by cliques or sects who fail to communicate with the larger body, or with one another. Under such conditions, a community of scholars will gradually dissolve through splitting up into a variety of camps of ever more restricted esoteric and specialized sects, jealously fighting each other and proclaiming that they alone possess the keys to the kingdom, while others are not just in error, but in sin. Under such conditions the only dialogue between antagonistic camps is a dialogue of the deaf. Such tendencies have also become apparent in the last few years of the history of our discipline. This brings me to my second topic of examination, the assessment of ethnomethodology.

If I understand correctly, ethnomethodology aims at a descriptive reconstruction of the cognitive map in people's minds which enables them to make sense of their everyday activities and encounters. It is a method that endeavors to penetrate to the deeper layers of the categorical and perceptual apparatus that is used in the construction of diverse realities. The method also aims at a rigorous description of ordinary linguistic usage and speech acts. As such it seems aggressively and programmatically devoid of theoretical content of sociological relevance. Limiting itself by a self-denying ordinance to the concrete observation of communicative codes, subjective categorizations, and conversational gestures, it underplays the behavioral aspects of goal-directed social interaction. It focuses instead on descriptions of definitions of the situation, meaning structures, conversational exchanges and the mutual modifications of images of self in such interchanges. Ignoring institutional factors in general, and the centrality of power in social interaction in particular, it is restricted to the descriptive tracing of the ways in which both individual actors and students of their activities account for their actions.

Ethnomethodologists put particular stress on the contextuality of accounts and meanings, their imbeddedness in the interactive context, their "situated" nature. Given the constitutive situatedness of any act, it is asserted that no objective generalizing approach is possible in the social sciences which by their very nature can only provide ideographic description. In some versions of ethnomethodology, intersubjectivity is consciously neglected so that one ends up with a view of individual actors as monads without windows enclosed in their private and unsharable universes of meaning.

As distinct from path analysis and similar methods, ethnomethodology has not found ready acceptance within our discipline, in fact it has never sought such acceptance. It has consciously limited its appeal to devoted followers united in the knowledge that they possess a special kind of insight denied to outsiders.

Ethnomethodology claims access to types of knowledge not accessible to the sociological *vulgus*. Write Zimmermann and Pollner (1970), for example, on the ethnomethodological reduction, one of the mainstays of the method: "The reduction does not generate research that may be regarded as an extension, refinement, or correction of extant sociological inquiry. . . . The reduction constitutes as its phenomenon an order of affairs that has no identifiable counterpart in contemporary social science." More typically still than the oft-repeated insistence that ethnomethodology has a unique subject matter is the esoteric and particularistic nature of the pronouncements of its practitioners. Consider, for example, a paper by David Sudnow (1972) entitled "Temporal Parameters of Interpersonal Observation," which turns out to deal with the glances people exchange with one another or direct at the passing scene. It is concerned, as the author elegantly puts it, with "the issue of glance timing importance" (1972:273). "Let us consider," he states, "the situation of 'walking across the street,' where an orientation to be clearly so seen is held by virtue of the noted presence of a rapidly approaching vehicle. Here a familiar traffic situation may be regularly imagined where a mere and single glance is expected, where the sufficiency of the mere and single glance is criterial for bringing off safe passage . . . and where, as a consequence, the concern for a correspondence between the 'details' of what we are doing and what we are seen at a single glance to be doing, may be of paramount concern" (p. 269). When I try to explain to my four-year-old grandson that he should always be careful when crossing a street, I say to him, "Always watch for passing cars." I do not think that Sudnow's jargon conveys anything more. Each field, to be sure, must construct its own defined terms, but what is developed here is a restricted code of communications rather than open scientific vocabulary (B. Bernstein, 1971).

It is much too facile simply to poke fun at a group of people who profess central concern with linguistic aspects of interactive processes and yet seem unable to handle the vernacular. But the fact is that such language diseases have sociological significance in the development of particularistic communities of True Believers. To begin with, esoteric language erects barriers against outsiders and confirms to the insiders that they have indeed a hold on some special truth. But there is more: Such jargon, as the philosopher Susanne Langer puts it, "is language which is more technical than the ideas it serves to express" (1967:36), so that it can successfully camouflage relatively trivial ideas. Moreover, esoteric jargon may serve to bind the neophyte to his new-found anchorage. People tend to value highly those activities in which they have invested a great deal. Having invested considerable time and energy in mastering an esoteric vocabulary, people are loath, even when some disillusionment has already set in, to admit to themselves that what has cost them so much, might, after all, be devoid of genuine value. Hence the particularistic vocabulary is not due to happenstance; it serves significant functions in marking boundaries and holding members.

Yet another characteristic with obvious functional value that ethnomethodologists share with similar close groupings in other scholarly areas, is the characteristic habit to limit their footnote references almost exclusively to members of the in-group or to nonsociologists, while quoting other sociologists mainly in order to show the errors of their way. There is, in addition, a peculiar propensity to refer to as yet unpublished manuscripts, to lecture notes and research notebooks.

It will be recognized that the characteristics I have outlined are those of a sect rather than of a field of specialization. I here define a sect as a group that has separated in protest from a larger body and emphasizes an esoteric and "pure" doctrine that is said to have been abandoned or ignored by the wider body. Sects are typically closed systems, usually led by charismatic leaders and their immediate followers. They attempt to reduce communication with the outside world to a minimum while engaging in highly intense interactions between the

True Believers (Coser, 1974). Sects develop a special particularistic language, distinctive norms of relevance, and specialized behavior patterns
that effectively set off the believers from the unconverted, serve as a
badge of special status, and highlight their members' differentiation
from the larger body of which they once formed a part.[2]

Yet what is functional for the sect is, by the same token, dysfunctional for those who are not among the elect. Blockage of the flow of
communication is among the most serious impediments of scientific developments. A science is utterly dependent on the free exchange of information between its practitioners. Preciseness and economy in information flow make for growth, and blockages lead to decline (cf. Crane,
1972). But the language of ethnomethodology, as James Coleman
(1968:130) once put it, makes for "an extraordinarily high ratio of
reading time to information transfer." More generally, an esoteric language can only serve to dissociate a body of people who were once
united in common pursuits. As in the story of Babel in Genesis, "And
the Lord said, 'Behold they are one people, and they have one language; and this is only the beginning of what they will do. . . . Come,
let us go down, and there confuse their language, that they may not
understand one another's speech.' "

Even though the sect is still quite young, the splits and fissions that
typically beset sectarian developments have already set in. I do not
profess to be knowledgeable about the detailed grounds of these developments (see Attewell, 1974, for an excellent mapping and critique),
but shall only sketch some of them very roughly. At present, the ethnomethodology of Garfinkel differs significantly from that of Sacks,
which, in turn, is far removed from the concerns of Blum or the researches of Cicourel. Some versions are, in fact, solipsistic, others attend to intersubjective meanings, some admit the existence of invariant
rules and procedures that transcend situations, others deny the possibility of any analysis that is not situation-specific. Some find philosophical anchorage in the German idealistic tradition and its Husserlian
offshoots, others make use of British linguistic philosophy and seem to
have replaced the guidance of Alfred Schuetz by that of Ludwig
Wittgenstein. Some concentrate on the analysis of unique events, others
attend to invariant properties of situated actions. The only thing all of
them still seem to hold in common is the rejection of the possibility of
an objective study and explanation of society and history, and a celebration of that long-dead warhorse of German idealistic philosophy,
the transcendental ego.

Concern with the hypertrophy of wordage among ethnomethodologists and their other sectarian characteristics should, however, not

---

[2] For an earlier analysis of sectlike characteristics in sociology cf. Coser, 1955.

preempt all of our attention. It is axiomatic among sociologists of knowledge that the origin of ideas does not prejudice their validity. It is possible that important and fruitful ideas may indeed develop in sectarian milieus. This has, in fact, often been the case, from the inception of puritanism to the emergence of psychoanalysis in the Viennese sect of Freud's immediate disciples.

Yet, when one turns to the problems that ethnomethodology tries to illuminate one is struck, for the most part, by their embarrassing triviality. We have already encountered Sudnow's "glancing research." Schegloff (1968) has spent productive years studying the ways in which people manage to begin and end their telephone conversations. I am not denying that "Studies of the Routine Grounds of Everyday Activities" (Garfinkel, 1967) may uncover significant and valuable matters, but in my considered judgment what has so far been dug up is mostly dross or interminable methodological disquisitions and polemics. Bittner's (1967) fine studies of the police or Cicourel's (1968) analysis of juvenile justice and a very few other good studies are not enough to justify the enormous ballyhoo surrounding ethnomethodology.

In general, it would seem to me that we deal here with a massive cop-out, a determined refusal to undertake research that would indicate the extent to which our lives are affected by the socio-economic context in which they are embedded. It amounts to an orgy of subjectivism, a self-indulgent enterprise in which perpetual methodological analysis and self-analysis leads to infinite regress, where the discovery of the ineffable qualities of the mind of analyst and analysand and their private construction of reality serves to obscure the tangible qualities of the world "out there." By limiting itself to trying to discover what is in the actors' minds, it blocks the way to an investigation of those central aspects of their lives about which they know very little. By attempting to describe the manifest content of people's experiences, ethnomethodologists neglect that central area of sociological analysis which deals with latent structures. The analysis of ever more refined minutiae of reality construction, and the assertion that one cannot possibly understand larger social structures before all these minutiae have been exhaustively mapped, irresistibly brings to mind Dr. Johnson's pregnant observation that "You don't have to eat the whole ox to know that the meat is tough."

Path analysis, as has been shown, is a method that found quick acceptance among wide circles in the sociological discipline because it provided technical means for more precise measurements hitherto unavailable; ethnomethodology, in contrast, found acceptance only among a small number of practitioners huddled around a charismatic leader and his apostles. The first was widely communicated through the various informational networks, both personal and impersonal, available to sociologists; the second developed particularistic codes of communication that effectively restricted access to all but the insiders. Yet what both have in common is a hypertrophy of method at the expense of substantive theory. The first has been used as an encouragement to neglect important areas of inquiry even while it has brought about greater precision of measurement in other areas, some important, some trivial. The second lends itself at best to atheoretical mappings of cognitive categories, and deliberately eschews concern with most of the matters that sociology has been centrally interested in ever since Auguste Comte. In both cases, I submit, preoccupation with method largely has led to neglect of significance and substance. And yet, our discipline will be judged in the last analysis on the basis of the substantive enlightenment which it is able to supply about the social structures in which we are enmeshed and which largely condition the course of our lives. If we neglect that major task, if we refuse the challenge to answer these questions, we shall forfeit our birthright and degenerate into congeries of rival sects and specialized researchers who will learn more and more about less and less.

References

ABEL, THEODORE
1948   "The operation called Verstehen." American Journal of
          Sociology 54 (November): 211–18.

ADAM, H.
1971   Modernizing Racial Domination: South Africa's Political
          Dynamics. Berkeley and Los Angeles: University of California
          Press.

ADELMAN, IRMA, AND CYNTHIA T. MORRIS
1971   Society, Politics, and Economic Development. Baltimore: Johns
          Hopkins University Press.

1973   Economic Growth and Social Equity in Developing Countries.
          Stanford: Stanford University Press.

AGETON, SUZANNE S., AND DELBERT S. ELLIOTT
1974   "The effects of legal processing on delinquent orientations."
          Social Problems 22 (October):87–100.

AKERS, RONALD L.
1968   "Problems in the sociology of deviance: Social definitions and
          behavior." Social Forces 46 (June):455–65.

ALEXANDER, KARL, AND BRUCE ECKLAND
1974   "Sex differences in the educational attainment process."
          American Sociological Review 39:668–82.

ALMOND, GABRIEL A., AND SIDNEY VERBA
1963   The Civic Culture: Political Attitudes and Democracy in Five
          Nations. Princeton: Princeton University Press.

ANDERSON, JOHN,, AND GREGG WILKINSON
1974   "Psychiatric illness and labeling theory: An analysis of Gove's
          critique." Paper presented at the meeting of the A.S.A.,
          Montreal.

343

ANGRIST, SHIRLEY, MARK LEFTON, SIMON DINITZ, AND BENJAMIN PASAMANICK
1968   Women After Treatment. New York: Appleton-Century-
          Crofts.

APEL, KARL-OTTO
1967   Analytic Philosophy of Language and the
          Geisteswissenschaften. Dordrecht: D. Reidel.

ARCHER, MARGARET SCOTFORD, AND SALVADOR GINER (EDS.)
1971   Contemporary Europe: Class, Status, and Power. New York:
          St. Martin's Press.

ARENDT, HANNAH
1951   The Origins of Totalitarianism. New York: Harcourt, Brace.
1961   Between Past and Future. New York: Viking Press.
1965   On Revolution. New York: Viking Press.

ARMBRUSTER, FRANK E.
1972   The Forgotten Americans: A Survey of the Values, Beliefs,
          and Concerns of the Majority. New York: Hudson Institute.

ARMER, MICHAEL, AND ALLAN SCHNAIBERG
1972   "Measuring individual modernity: A near myth." American
          Sociological Review 37:301–16.

ARMER, MICHAEL, AND ROBERT YOUTZ
1971   "Formal education and individual modernity in an African
          society." American Journal of Sociology 76 (4):604–26.

ARNOLD, WILLIAM R.
1971   "Race and ethnicity relative to other factors in juvenile court
          dispositions." American Journal of Sociology 77
          (September):211–27.

ARONOWITZ, STANLEY
1974   False Promises: The Making of American Working-Class
          Consciousness. New York: McGraw-Hill.

ATTEWELL, PAUL
1974   "Ethnomethodology since Garfinkel." Theory and Society I.

AVINERI, SHLOMO
1973   "Marx's vision of future society." Dissent 20 (Summer):323–31.

AVRICH, PAUL H.
1963   "Russian factory committees in 1917." Jahrbücher für
          Geschichte Osteuropas 11:161–82.

BACK, KURT
1975   "Labeling and mental illness." Pp. 135–47 in J. Demerath, O.
          Larsen, and K. Schuessler (eds.), Social Policy and Sociology.
          New York: Academic Press.

BAKER, ELIZABETH FAULKNER
1925   Protestive Legislation. New York: Privately published.

BAMBROUGH, RENFORD
1956   "Plato's political analogies." Pp. 98–115 in Peter Laslett (ed.),
          Philosophy, Politics and Society. New York: Macmillan.

BANFIELD, EDWARD, AND JAMES Q. WILSON
1963   City Politics. Cambridge: Harvard University Press.

BARNES, J. A.
1961   "Law as politically active: An anthropological view." Pp.
167–96 in G. Sawer (ed.), Studies in the Sociology of Law.
Canberra: Australian National University.

BARTH, FREDRIK
1969   Ethnic Groups and Boundaries. Boston: Little, Brown.

BARTON, JOHN
1975   "Behind the legal explosion." Stanford Law Review 27:567–84.

BARTON, R. F.
1919   "Ifugao law." University of California Publications in
American Archaeology and Ethnology 15(1):1–186.

BAUER, RAYMOND A.
1952   The New Man in Soviet Psychology. Cambridge: Harvard
University Press.

BAUMAN, ZYGMUNT
1972   Between Class and Elite. Manchester: Manchester University
Press.

BECKER, GARY S.
1964   Human Capital. New York: Columbia University Press.
1971   The Economics of Discrimination. 2nd ed. Chicago: University
of Chicago Press.

BECKER, HOWARD S.
1963   Outsiders: Studies in the Sociology of Deviance. New York:
Free Press.
1967   "Whose side are we on?" Social Problems 14 (Winter):239–47.
1973   "Labelling theory reconsidered." In H. Becker (ed.),
Outsiders. 2d ed. New York: Free Press.

BELL, DANIEL
1949   "America's un-Marxist revolution." Commentary 12 (March):
207–15.
1960   "Work and its discontents: The cult of efficiency in America."
Pp. 249–51 in The End of Ideology. Glencoe, Ill.: Free Press.
1963   "Veblen and the new class." The American Scholar 32
(Autumn):628–29.
1973   The Coming of Post-Industrial Society. New York: Basic
Books.
1975   "The revolution of rising entitlements." Fortune 91:99 et seq.

BELL, DAVID V. J.
1974   Resistance and Revolution. Boston: Houghton Mifflin.

BELLAH, ROBERT N.
Forthcoming   "A new religious consciousness." In Glock and Bellah (eds.),
The New Consciousness. Berkeley: University of California
Press.

BELLOW, SAUL
1971   Mr. Sammler's Planet. New York: Fawcett World Library.

BENGSTON, VERN L., JAMES DOUD, DAVID H. SMITH, AND ALEX INKELES
1975   "Modernization, modernity, and perceptions of aging: A cross-
            cultural study." Journal of Gerontology 30 (6):688–95.

BERG, IVAR
1971   Education and Jobs: The Great Training Robbery. Boston:
            Praeger.

BERK, RICHARD A.
1974   Collective Behavior. Dubuque, Iowa: Brown.

BERNSTEIN, BASIL
1971   Class, Codes and Control. London: Routledge and K. Paul.

BERNSTEIN, MARVER
1972   "Independent regulatory agencies: A perspective on their
            reform." In Marver Bernstein (ed.), The Government as
            Regulator. Annals of The American Academy of Political and
            Social Sciences, vol. 400 (March).

BERQUIST, VIRGINIA A.
1974   "Women's participation in labor organizations." Monthly
            Labor Review 97 (October):3–9.

BERRY, JOHN W.
Forthcoming "The psychology of social change." In Harry Triandis (ed.),
            Handbook of Cross-Cultural Psychology. Rockleigh, N.J.:
            Allyn and Bacon.

BIBB, ROBERT C., AND WILLIAM H. FORM
1975   "The effects of industrial, occupational, and sex stratification
            on wages in blue collar markets." PASS Working Paper #75-
            10. Sociology Department, University of Illinois at Urbana-
            Champaign.

BIERSTEDT, ROBERT
1951   "An analysis of social power." American Sociological Review
            15 (December):730–38.

1974   Power and Progress. New York: McGraw-Hill.

BITTNER, EGON
1967   "The police on skid-row." American Sociological Review
            32:699–715.

BLACK, C. E.
1966   The Dynamics of Modernization: A Study in Comparative
            History. New York: Harper & Row.

BLACK, DONALD L., AND ALBERT J. REISS
1970   "Police control of juveniles." American Sociological Review 35
            (February):63–77.

BLACKMORE, DONALD J.
1968   "Occupational wage relationships in metropolitan areas."
            Monthly Labor Review 91 (December):29–36.

BLACKWELL, JAMES E.
1975a   Access of Black Students to Graduate and Professional
         Schools. Atlanta: Southern Education Foundation.
1975b   The Black Community: Diversity and Unity. New York:
         Dodd, Mead.

BLALOCK, H. M., JR.
1960   "A power analysis of racial discrimination." Social Forces
         39:53–69.
1967   Toward a General Theory of Intergroup Relations. New
         York: Wiley.

BLAU, PETER, AND OTIS D. DUNCAN
1967   The American Occupational Structure. New York: Wiley.

BLAUNER, ROBERT
1964   Alienation and Freedom: The Factory Worker and His
         Industry. Chicago: University of Chicago Press.
1969   "Internal colonialism and ghetto revolt." Social Problems 16
         (Spring):393–408.

BLUESTONE, BARRY
1970   "The tripartite economy: Labor markets and the working
         poor." Poverty and Human Relations Abstracts
         (July–August):15–35.

BLUM, ALAN F.
1974   Theorising. London: Heinemann.

BOK, DEREK C., AND JOHN T. DUNLOP
1970   Labor and the American Community. New York: Simon and
         Schuster.

BORDUA, DAVID J.
1967   "Recent trends: Deviant behavior and social control." Annals
         of the American Academy of Political and Social Science 359
         (January):149–163.

BRICKER, VICTORIA REIFLER (ED.)
1975   "Intra-cultural variation." American Ethnologist 2 (February).

BRILL, HARRY
1973   "The uses and abuses of legal assistance." The Public Interest
         31:38–55.
1975   Why Organizers Fail. Berkeley: University of California Press.

BRINTON, CRANE
1938   The Anatomy of Revolution. New York: Norton.

BRISLIN, RICHARD W., WALTER LONNER, AND ROBERT M. THORNDIKE
1973   Cross-Cultural Research Methods. New York: Wiley.

BRODE, JOHN
1969   The Process of Modernization: An Annotated Bibliography of
         the Sociocultural Aspects of Development. Cambridge:
         Harvard University Press.

BROWN, STANLEY H.
1967   "Walter Reuther: 'He's got to walk that last mile.' " Fortune
            76 (July):87–89, 141–49.

BUREAU OF CRIMINAL STATISTICS
1973   Crime and Delinquency in California, p. 27, table 14.
            Sacramento.

BURKE, DONALD R., AND LESTER RUBIN
1973   "Is contract rejection a major collective bargaining problem?"
            Industrial and Labor Relations Review 26 (January):820–33.

BUSS, ARNOLD H., AND ROBERT PLOMIN
1975   Temperament Theory of Personality Development. New York:
            Wiley.

BUTLER, D. E., AND RICHARD ROSE
1960   The British General Election of 1959. London: Macmillan.

CAETANO, DONALD F.
1974   "Labeling theory and the presumption of mental illness in
            diagnosis: An experimental design." Journal of Health and
            Social Behavior 15 (September):253–60.

CAMPBELL, ROY
1955   Selected Poems, Chicago: Regnery.

CANNON, W. H., AND O. G. JENSEN
1975   "Terrestrial timekeeping and general relativity—a discovery."
            Science 188 (April 25).

CANTER, R.
1973   "Consequences of legal engineering: A case from Zambia."
            Paper presented at the meeting of the American
            Anthropological Association, New Orleans, November.

CARLIN, JEROME E.
1962   Lawyers on Their Own. New Brunswick: Rutgers University
            Press.

CARLIN, J. E., J. HOWARD, AND S. L. MESSINGER
1967   Civil justice and the poor; Issues for Sociological Research.
            New York: Russell Sage.

CARR-SAUNDERS, A. M., AND D. C. JONES.
1937   A Survey of the Social Structure of England and Wales.
            Oxford: Oxford University Press.

CASE, JOHN
1973   "Workers' control: Toward a North-American movement." Pp.
            438–68 in Gerry Hunnius, G. David Garson, and John Case
            (eds.), Workers' Control. New York: Vintage.

CENTRAL INTELLIGENCE AGENCY
1963   Average Annual Money Earnings of Wage Workers in Soviet
            Industry, 1928–1961. Washington, D.C.: U.S. Government
            Printing Office (July).

CHAMBERLIN, WILLIAM HENRY
1935   The Russian Revolution, 1917–1921. New York: Grosset and Dunlap, 1965.

CHIRICOS, THEODORE C., AND PHILLIP D. JACKSON
1972   "Inequality in the imposition of a criminal label." Social Problems 19 (Spring):553–72.

CICOUREL, AARON V.
1968   The Social Organization of Juvenile Justice. New York: Wiley.

CLANCY, KEVIN, AND WALTER GOVE
1974   "Sex differences in mental illness: An analysis of response bias." American Journal of Sociology 80 (July):205–16.

CLINARD, M.
1963   Sociology of Deviant Behavior. New York: Holt, Rinehart and Winston.

COLE, STEPHEN
1975   "The growth of scientific knowledge: Theories of deviance as a case study." In L. Coser (ed.), The Idea of Social Structure: Papers in Honor of Robert K. Merton. New York: Harcourt, Brace and Jovanovich.

COLEMAN, JAMES S.
1968   Review of H. Garfinkel, Studies in Ethnomethodology. American Sociological Review 33:126–30.
1973   "Utilization of policy research and the social location of the researcher." Unpublished manuscript.

COLLINS, RANDALL
1975   Conflict Sociology: Toward an Explanatory Science. New York: Academic Press.

COMMONS, JOHN R., et al.
1918   A History of Labor in the United States. 2 vols. New York: Macmillan.

COOK, ALICE
1968   "Women and American trade unions." Annals of the American Academy of Political and Social Science 375 (January):124–32.

CORNELIUS, WAYNE A.
1975   Politics and the Migrant Poor in Mexico City. Stanford: Stanford University Press.

COSER, LEWIS A.
1955   "The functions of small-group research." Social Problems: 1–6.
1965   Men of Ideas. New York: Free Press.
1974   Greedy Institutions. New York: Free Press.

CRANE, DIANA
1972   Invisible Colleges: Diffusion of Knowledge in Scientific Communities. Chicago: University of Chicago Press.

CROMWELL, RUE L.
1975   "Assessment of schizophrenia." In Mark R. Rosenzweig and
            Lyman W. Porter (eds.), Annual Review of Psychology
            26:593–619.

CUNNINGHAM, INEKE
1972   Modernity and Academic Performance: A Study of Students
            in a Puerto Rican High School. Puerto Rico: University of
            Puerto Rico Press.

CUTRIGHT, PHILIP
1965   "Negro subordination and white gains." American Sociological
            Review 30:110–12.

DAHRENDORF, RALF
1959   Class and Class Conflict in Industrial Society. Stanford: Stanford
            University Press.

DANIELS, DAVID N., ET AL. (EDS.)
1970   Violence and the Struggle for Existence. Boston: Little, Brown.

DAVIES, JAMES C.
1962   "Toward a theory of revolution." American Sociological Review
            27:5–19.

1969   "The J-curve of rising and declining satisfactions as a cause of
            some great revolutions and a contained rebellion." Pp. 671–709
            in Hugh Davis Graham and Ted Robert Gurr (eds.), Violence in
            America. New York: Signet Books.

DAVIS, FRED
1971   On Youth Subcultures: The Hippie Variant. New York: General
            Learning.

DAVIS, KINGSLEY, AND WILBERT E. MOORE
1945   "Some principles of stratification." American Sociological Re-
            view 10 (2):242–49.

DAVIS, NANNETTE J.
1972   "Labeling theory in deviance research: A critique and recon-
            sideration." Sociological Quarterly 13 (Autumn):447–74.

1975   Sociological Constructions of Deviance: Perspectives and Issues
            in the Field. Dubuque, Iowa: William C. Brown.

DAWSON, J. L. M.
1967   "Traditional versus Western attitudes in West Africa: The con-
            struction, validation and application of a measuring device."
            British Journal of Social and Clinical Psychology 6:81–96.

DAWSON, J. L. M., H. LAW, A. LEUNG, AND R. E. WHITNEY
1971   "Scaling Chinese traditional-modern attitudes and the GSR mea-
            surement of 'important' versus 'unimportant' Chinese concepts."
            Journal of Cross-Cultural Psychology 2:1–27.

DEFRONZO, JAMES
1973   "Embourgeoisement in Indianapolis?" Social Problems 21
            (Fall):269–83.

DELANEY, PAUL
1975   "Economic survey cites black loss." New York Times (July 29).

DENTLER, ROBERT, AND KAI ERIKSON
1959   "The functions of deviance in groups." Social Problems 7 (Fall):98–107.

DEVOS, GEORGE, AND LOLA ROMANUCCI-ROSS (EDS.)
1975   Ethnic Identity. Palo Alto, Calif.: Mayfield Publishing Co.

DOERINGER, PETER, AND MICHAEL PIORE
1971   Internal Labor Markets and Manpower Analysis. Lexington, Mass.: D. C. Heath.

DOHRENWEND, BRUCE P., AND BARBARA INELL DOHRENWEND
1965   "The problems of validity in field studies of psychological disorders." Journal of Abnormal Psychology 70:52–69.

1969   Social Status and Psychological Inquiry. New York: Wiley.

DOMHOFF, G. WILLIAM
1970   The Higher Circles. New York, Random House.

DOMHOFF, G. WILLIAM (ED.)
1975   "New directions in power structure research." Special issue of the Insurgent Sociologist 5, no. 3 (Spring).

DOOB, LEONARD W.
1960   Becoming More Civilized. New Haven: Yale University Press.

DOUTY, H. M.
1953   "Union impact on wage structures." Vol. 12, pp. 61–76 in Proceedings of the Industrial Relations Research Association.

DUMONT, LOUIS
1970   Homo Hierarchicus. Chicago: Chicago University Press.

DUNCAN, OTIS D., DAVID L. FEATHERMAN, AND BEVERLY DUNCAN
1972   Socio-economic Background and Achievement. New York: Academic Press.

DUNLOP, JOHN T.
1944   Wage Determination under Trade Unions. New York: Macmillan.

DUVALL, RAYMOND
1976   "An appraisal of the methodological and statistical procedures of the correlates of war project." In Dina Zinnes and Francis Hoole (eds.), Quantitative International Politics: An Appraisal. New York: Praeger.

EATON, WILLIAM W., JR.
1974a   "Mental hospitalization as a reinforcement process." American Sociological Review 39 (April):252–60.

1974b   "Residence, social class and schizophrenia." Journal of Health and Social Behavior 15 (December):289–99.

ECKSTEIN, HARRY
1965   "On the etiology of internal wars." History and Theory 4:133–63.

1973   "Patterns of authority: A structural basis for political inquiry."
                    American Political Science Review 67 (December):1142–61.

EDWARDS, LYFORD P.
1927   The Natural History of Revolution. Chicago: University of Chicago Press.

EISENSTADT, S. N.
1973   Tradition, Change, and Modernity. New York: Wiley.

EISENSTADT, S. N., AND STEIN ROKKAN (EDS.)
1973   Building States and Nations. Beverly Hills: Sage Publications.

ELLIOTT, GEORGE P.
1974   "Buried envy: The last dirty little secret." Harper's 249:12–18.

ERICKSON, MAYNARD L., AND LAMAR EMPEY
1963   "Court records, undetected delinquency and decision-making."
                    Journal of Criminal Law, Criminology and Police Science 54
                    (December):456–69.

ERIKSON, KAI T.
1962   "Notes on the sociology of deviance." Social Problems 9:307–14.

ETZIONI, AMITAI
1968   The Active Society. New York: Free Press.

FABREGA, HORATIO, AND PETER K. MANNING
1972   "Disease, illness and deviant careers." Pp. 93–116 in Robert A.
                    Scott and Jack D. Douglas (eds.), Theoretical Perspectives in
                    Deviance. New York: Basic Books.

FARIS, R. E. L.
1954   "The alleged class system of the United States." Research Studies of the State College of Washington 22 (June):77–83.

FEIERABEND, IVO K., AND ROSALIND L. FEIERABEND
1972   "Systemic conditions of political aggression: An application of
                    frustration-aggression theory." Pp. 136–83 in Ivo K. and Rosalind L. Feierabend and Ted Robert Gurr (eds.), Anger, Violence, and Politics. Englewood Cliffs, N.J.: Prentice-Hall.

FEIERABEND, IVO K., ROSALIND L. FEIERABEND, AND TED ROBERT GURR (EDS.)
1972   Anger, Violence, and Politics. Englewood Cliffs, N.J.: Prentice-Hall.

FEIERABEND, IVO K., ROSALIND L. FEIERABEND, AND BETTY A. NESVOLD
1969   "Social change and political violence: Cross-national patterns."
                    Pp. 606–68 in Hugh Davis Graham and Ted Robert Gurr (eds.), Violence in America. New York: Signet Books.
1973   "The comparative study of revolution and violence." Comparative Politics 5:393–424.

FEIN, SARA, AND KENT S. MILLER
1972   "Legal processes and adjudication in mental incompetency proceedings." Social Problems 20 (Summer):57–64.

References   353

FEUER, LEWIS S. (ED.)
1959   Marx and Engels: Basic Writings on Politics and Philosophy.
         Garden City, N.Y.: Doubleday Anchor.

FISHER, SETHARD
1972   "Stigma and deviant careers in school." Social Problems 20
         (Summer):78–83.

FORM, WILLIAM H.
1972   "Technology and social behavior of workers in four countries: A
         sociotechnical perspective." American Sociological Review 37
         (December):727–38.

1973   "The internal stratification of the working class: System involve-
         ments of autoworkers in four countries." American Sociological
         Review 38 (December):697–711.

FOSTER, GEORGE M.
1972   "The anatomy of envy: A study in symbolic behavior." Current
         Anthropology 13:165–203.

FOSTER, JACK D., SIMON DINITZ, AND WALTER C. RECKLESS
1972   "Perceptions of stigma following public intervention for delin-
         quent behavior." Social Problems 20 (Fall):202–9.

FREEMAN, JO
1972   "The tyranny of structurelessness." Berkeley Journal of Sociol-
         ogy 17:151–64.

1975   The Politics of Women's Liberation: A Case Study of an Emerg-
         ing Social Movement and Its Relation to the Policy Process. New
         York: McKay.

FREIDSON, ELIOT
1968   "The impurity of professional authority." In Howard S. Becker
         et al. (eds.), Institutions and the Person. Chicago: Aldine.

1972   Profession of Medicine. New York: Dodd, Mead.

FRIED, MARK
1973   The World of the Urban Working Class. Cambridge: Harvard
         University Press.

FRIEDMAN, LAWRENCE
1973   "Some historical aspects of law and social change in the United
         States." Working paper, Law and Society Program, University of
         California, Berkeley.

1975   The Legal System: A Social Science Perspective. New York: Rus-
         sell Sage Foundation.

FRIEDMAN, MURRAY
1973   "The Jews." In Peter I. Rose et al. (eds.), Through Different
         Eyes. New York: Oxford University Press.

FRIEDMANN, GEORGES
1955   Industrial Society: The Emergence of the Human Problems of
         Automation. Ed. by Harold L. Sheppard. Glencoe: Free Press.

FRIEDRICH, CARL J.
   1958   "Authority, reason, and discretion." In C. J. Friedrich (ed.), Au-
               thority, Nomos I. Cambridge: Harvard University Press.

FROMM, ERICH
   1941   Escape from Freedom. New York: Holt, Rinehart and Winston.

FUSFELD, DANIEL R.
   1973   The Basic Economics of the Urban Racial Crisis. New York:
               Holt, Rinehart and Winston.

GADAMER, HANS-GEORG
   1960   Wahrheit und Methode. Tubingen: Mohr.

GALANTER, M.
   1974   "Why the 'haves' come out ahead." Law and Society Review 9,
               no. 1 (Fall):95–160.

GALBRAITH, JOHN KENNETH
   1958   The Affluent Society. Boston: Houghton-Mifflin.

GALTUNG, JOHAN
   1971   Members of Two Worlds. New York: Columbia University
               Press.

GANDY, JOHN M.
   1970   "The exercise of discretion by the police as a decision-making
               process in the disposition of juvenile offenders." Osgoode Hall
               Law Journal 8 (November):329–44.

GANS, HERBERT J.
   1962   The Urban Villagers. New York: Free Press.
   1974   Popular Culture and High Culture: An Analysis and Evaluation
               of Taste. New York: Basic Books.

GARFINKEL, HERBERT
   1967   Studies in Ethnomethodology. Englewood Cliffs, N.J.: Prentice-
               Hall.

GASSON, RUTH M., ARCHIBALD O. HALLER, AND WILLIAM H. SEWELL
   1972   Attitudes and Facilitation in the Attainment of Status. Rose
               Monograph Series, American Sociological Association.

GAY, PETER
   1952   The Dilemma of Democratic Socialism. New York: Columbia
               University Press.

GEERKEN, MICHAEL, AND WALTER GOVE
   1975   "Deterrence: Some theoretical considerations" Law and Society
               Review 9, no. 3 (Spring):497–513.

GEIGER, H. KENT
   1969a   National Development 1776–1966: A Selective and Annotated
               Guide to the Most Important Articles in English. Metuchen,
               N.J.: Scarecrow Press.
   1969b   "Social class differences in family life in the U.S.S.R." Pp.
               284–96 in Celia S. Heller (ed.), Socially Structured Inequality.
               New York: Macmillan.

GELFAND, DONALD E., AND RUSSELL D. LEE (EDS.)
1973   Ethnic Conflicts and Power: A Cross-National Perspective. New York: Wiley.

GERTH, HANS, AND C. WRIGHT MILLS (EDS.)
1946   From Max Weber: Essays in Sociology. New York: Oxford University Press.

GESCHWENDER, JAMES A.
1968   "Explorations in the theory of social movements and revolutions." Social Forces 42:127–35.

GIBBONS, DON C., AND JOSEPH F. JONES
1975   The Study of Deviance: Perspectives and Problems. Englewood Cliffs, N.J.: Prentice-Hall.

GIBBS, JACK P.
1962   "Rates of mental hospitalization: A study of societal reaction to deviant behavior." American Sociological Review 27 (December):782–92.

1966   "Conceptions of deviant behavior: The old and the new." Pacific Sociological Review 9 (Spring):9–14.

1972   Issues in defining deviant behavior." In Robert A. Scott and Jack D. Douglas (eds.), Theoretical Perspectives on Deviance. New York: Basic Books.

GIDDENS, ANTHONY
1973   The Class Structure of the Advanced Societies. London: Hutchinson.

1976   New Rules of Sociological Method. New York: Basic Books.

GILES, WILLIAM E.
1975   "Managers: China's Achilles heel?" Wall Street Journal (July 21).

GITLIN, TODD, AND NANCI HOLLANDER
1970   Uptown: Poor Whites in Chicago. New York: Harper Colophon.

GLAZER, NATHAN
1971   "Blacks and ethnic groups: The difference, and the political difference it makes." Social Problems 18, no. 4 (Spring):444–61.

1975   "Towards an imperial judiciary?" The Public Interest no. 41:104–23.

GLAZER, NATHAN, AND DANIEL P. MOYNIHAN
1963   Beyond the Melting Pot. Cambridge: M.I.T. Press.

GLAZER, NATHAN, AND DANIEL P. MOYNIHAN (EDS.)
1975   Ethnicity: Theory and Experience. Cambridge: Harvard University Press.

GLENN, NORVAL
1963   "Occupational benefits to whites from the subordination of Negroes." American Sociological Review 28:443–48.

GLENN, NORVAL D., AND JON P. ALSTON
1968   "Cultural distances among occupational categories." American Sociological Review 33 (June):365–82.

GOFFMAN, ERVING
1969   "The insanity of place." Psychiatry 32 (November):357–88.
1971   Relations in Public: Mircostudies of the Public Orders. New York: Basic Books.

GOLD, M., AND J. R. WILLIAMS
1969   "The effect of getting caught: Apprehension of the juvenile offender as a cause of subsequent delinquencies." Prospectus 3 (December):1–12.

GOLDSCHEIDER, CALVIN
1971   Population, Modernization and Social Structure. Boston: Little, Brown.

GOLDSMITH, JEFF
1973   "Youth and the public sector: Institutional paths to social membership." Unpublished doctoral dissertation. Department of Sociology, University of Chicago.

GOLDTHORPE, JOHN H.
1972   "Class, status and party in modern Britain." European Journal of Sociology 13:342–72.

GOLDTHORPE, JOHN H., DAVID LOCKWOOD, FRANK BECHHOFER, AND JENNIFER PLATT
1969   The Affluent Worker and the Class Structure. Cambridge: At the University Press.

GOODE, WILLIAM H., AND IRVING FOWLER
1949   "Incentive factors in a low morale plant." American Sociological Review 14 (October):618–23.

GOODENOUGH, WARD H.
1963   An Anthropological Approach to Community Development. New York: Russell Sage Foundation.

GOODMAN, PAUL
1960   Growing Up Absurd. New York: Random House.

GORDON, CHAD
1972   Looking Ahead: Self-conceptions, Race and Family as Determinants of Adolescent Orientation to Achievement. Rose Monograph Series, American Sociological Association.

GORDON, MILTON M.
1964   Assimilation in American Life: The Role of Religion, Race and National Origin. New York: Oxford University Press.
1975   "Toward a general theory of racial and ethnic group relations." Chap. 8 in Nathan Glazer and Daniel P. Moynihan (eds.), Ethnicity: Theory and Experience. Cambridge: Harvard University Press.

GORDON, ROBERT
1975   "Examining labelling theory: the case of the mental retardate." Pp. 83–146 in Walter R. Gove (ed.), Labelling Deviant Behavior: The Evaluation of a Perspective. New York: Sage/Halstead.

Gorz, André
1973   "Workers' control is more than just that." Pp. 325–43 in Gerry Hunnius, G. David Garson, and John Case (eds.), Workers' Control. New York: Vintage.

Gove, Walter R.
1970a   "Societal reaction as an explanation of mental illness: An evaluation." American Sociological Review 35 (October):873–84.

1970b   "Sleep deprivation: a cause of psychotic disorganization." American Journal of Sociology 75 (March):782–99.

1970c   "Who is hospitalized: A critical review of some sociological studies of mental illness." Journal of Health and Social Behavior 11 (December):294–304.

1972   "The relationship between sex roles, marital status, and mental illness." Social Forces 51 (September):34–44.

1975a   "Labelling and mental illness: A critique." Pp. 35–81 in Gove (ed.), Labelling Deviant Behavior: The Evaluation of a Perspective. New York: Sage/Halstead.

1975b   "The labelling perspective: An overview." Pp. 3–20 in Gove (ed.), Labelling Deviant Behavior: The Evaluation of a Perspective. New York: Sage/Halstead.

Gove, Walter, and Kevin Clancy
1975   "Response bias, sex differences and mental illness: A rejoinder." Unpublished manuscript.

Gove, Walter R., and Terry Fain
1975   "The length of psychiatric hospitalization." Social Problems 22 (February):407–9.

Gove, Walter, Omer Galle, John McCarthy, and Michael Hughes
1974   "Living circumstances and social pathology: The effect of population density, overcrowding and isolation on suicide, homicide and alcoholism." Paper presented at the meeting of the Population Society of America, New York.

Gove, Walter, and Patrick Howell
1974   "Individual resources and mental hospitalization: A comparison and evaluation of the societal reaction and psychiatric perspectives." American Sociological Review 39:86–100.

Gove, Walter, and Jeanette Tudor
1973   "Adult sex roles and mental illness." American Journal of Sociology 78 (January):812–35.

Greeley, Andrew M.
1971   Why Can't They Be Like Us? New York: Dutton.

1972   "The new ethnicity and blue collars." Dissent 19 (Winter):270–77.

1973   "The Irish." Pp. 126–47 in Peter I. Rose et al. (eds.), Through Different Eyes. New York: Oxford University Press.

1974   Ethnicity in the United States. New York: Wiley.

1975a   "Review of Ivan Light's Ethnic Enterprise in America: Business
            and Welfare among Chinese, Japanese and Blacks." American
            Journal of Sociology 80, no. 5 (March):1264–66.

1975b   "TV's Italian cops—trapped in old stereotypes." New York
            Times (July 27):sec. 2.

GREELEY, ANDREW M., AND WILLIAM C. McCREADY
1975   "The transmission of cultural heritages." Chap. 7 in Nathan
            Glazer and Daniel P. Moynihan (eds.), Ethnicity: Theory and
            Experience. Cambridge: Harvard University Press.

GREEN, JAMES
1975   "Labor militancy, union democracy." The Nation (September
            6):183.

GREEN, MARK (ED.)
1973   The Monopoly Makers. New York: Grossman.

GREENLEY, JAMES R.
1972a   "Psychiatric patient's family and length of hospitalization." Jour-
            nal of Health and Social Behavior 13 (March):25–37.

1972b   "Alternative views of the psychiatrist's role." Social Problems 20
            (Fall):252–62.

GRIEWANK, KARL
1971   "Emergence of the concept of revolution." Pp. 13–17 in Bruce
            Mazlish, Arthur D. Kaledin, and David B. Ralston (eds.), Revo-
            lution: A Reader. New York: Macmillan.

GURR, TED ROBERT
1968a   "A causal model of civil strife: A comparative analysis using new
            indices." American Political Science Review 27:1104–24.

1968b   "Psychological factors in civil violence." World Politics
            20:245–78.

1969   "A comparative survey of civil strife." In Hugh Davis Graham
            and Ted Robert Gurr (eds.), Violence in America: Historical
            and Comparative Perspectives. Washington, D.C.: U.S. Govern-
            ment Printing Office for the National Commission on the
            Causes and Prevention of Violence.

1970   Why Men Rebel. Princeton, N.J.: Princeton University Press.

1973   "The revolution-social-change nexus." Comparative Politics
            5:359–92.

1974   "The Neo-Alexandrians: a review essay on data handbooks in
            political inquiry." American Political Science Review 68
            (March):243–52.

GURR, TED ROBERT, AND RAYMOND DUVALL
1973   "Civil conflict in the 1960's: A reciprocal theoretical system with
            parameter estimates." Comparative Political Studies 6 (July):
            135–69.

GUSFIELD, JOSEPH
1964   Symbolic Crusade. Urbana: University of Illinois Press.
1967   "Tradition and modernity: Misplaced polarities in the study of social change." American Journal of Sociology 72:351–62.

GUSTMAN, ALAN L., AND MARTIN SEGAL
1974   "The skilled-unskilled wage differential in construction." Industrial and Labor Relations Review (January):261–75.

GUTHRIE, GEORGE M.
1970   The Psychology of Modernization in the Rural Philippines. Quezon City: Ateneo de Manila University Press.

HABERMAS, JÜRGEN
1970   Toward a Rational Society. Boston: Beacon Press.
1971   Knowledge and Human Interests. Tr. by Jeremy J. Shapiro. Boston: Beacon Press.
1973   Theory and Practice. Tr. by John Viertel. Boston: Beacon Press.

HAGEN, EVERETT E.
1962   On the Theory of Social Change. Homewood, Ill: Dorsey Press.
1975   "Becoming modern: The dangers of research governed by preconceptions." History of Childhood Quarterly (Winter).

HAHM, PYONG-CHOON
1968   "Korea's initial encounter with western law:1866–1910, A.D." Korea Observer 1:80–93.

HALPERN, BEN
1971   Jews and Blacks: The Classic American Minorities. New York: Herder and Herder.

HALPERN, JOEL
1967   The Changing Village Community. Englewood Cliffs, N.J.: Prentice-Hall.

HAMILTON, RICHARD F.
1963   "The income difference between skilled and white collar workers." British Journal of Sociology 14 (December):363–73.
1964   "The behavior and values of skilled workers." Pp. 43–57 in Arthur B. Shostak and William Gomberg (eds.), Blue-Collar World. Englewood Cliffs, N.J.: Prentice-Hall.
1965a   "Affluence and the worker: The West German case." American Journal of Sociology 71 (September):144–52.
1965b   "Skill level and politics." Public Opinion Quarterly 31 (Winter):390–99.
1966   "The marginal middle class: A reconsideration." American Sociological Review 31 (April):192–99.
1967   Affluence and the French Worker in the Fourth Republic. Princeton: Princeton University Press.
1972   Class and Politics in the United States. New York: Wiley.
1975   Restraining Myths: Critical Studies of U.S. Social Structure and Politics. Beverly Hills, Calif.: Sage Publications.

HARBISON, FRED, AND CHARLES A. MYERS
  1964   Education, Manpower and Economic Growth: Strategies of
             Human Resource Development. New York: McGraw-Hill.

HARDMAN, J. B. S.
  1959   "An emerging synthesis." Pp. 36–39 in Jack Barbash (ed.),
             Unions and Union Leadership. New York: Harper.

HATTO, ARTHUR
  1949   " 'Revolution': An inquiry into the usefulness of an historical
             term." Mind 58:495–517.

HAUSER, ROBERT M.
  1972   Socioeconomic Background and Educational Performance. Rose
             Monograph Series, American Sociological Association.

HECHTER, MICHAEL
  1974   "The political economy of ethnic change." American Journal of
             Sociology 79, (March):1151–78.

HEDGES, J. N., AND S. E. BEMIS
  1974   "Sex stereotyping: Its decline in skilled trades." Monthly Labor
             Review 97 (May):14–22.

HEILBRONER, ROBERT
  1974   An Inquiry into the Human Prospect. New York: Norton.

HEMPEL, CARL
  1953   "On the method of verstehen as the sole method of philosophy."
             The Journal of Philosophy 50.

HERBERG, WILL
  1955   Protestant-Catholic-Jew. Garden City. N.Y.: Doubleday.

HILL, ROBERT
  1975   "A report on the economic condition of black Americans."
             Address given at the Convention of the National Urban League,
             Atlanta, Georgia, July 28.

HIRSCHI, TRAVIS
  1975   "Labelling theory and juvenile delinquency: An assessment of
             the evidence." Pp. 181–203 in Walter Gove (ed.), Labelling De-
             viant Behavior: The Evaluation of a Perspective. New York:
             Sage/Halstead.

HOCHSCHILD, ARLIE RUSSELL
  1975   "Inside the clockwork of male careers." Pp. 47–80 in Florence
             Howe (ed.), Women and the Power to Change. New York: Mc-
             Graw-Hill.

HODGE, ROBERT W., PAUL M. SIEGEL, AND PETER H. ROSSI
  1964   "Occupational prestige in the United States: 1925–1963." Amer-
             ican Journal of Sociology 70 (November):286–302.

HODGE, ROBERT W., AND DONALD J. TREIMAN
  1968   "Social participation and social status." American Sociological
             Review 33:722–40.

HODGE, ROBERT W., DONALD J. TREIMAN, AND PETER H. ROSSI
1966   "A comparative study of occupational prestige." In R. Bencis and S. M. Lipset (eds.), Class, Status and Power. New York: Free Press.

HOEBEL, E. A.
1954   The Law of Primitive Man: A Study in Comparative Legal Dynamics. Cambridge: Harvard University Press.

HOFSTADTER, RICHARD
1965   The Paranoid Style in American Politics. New York: Knopf.

HOLLINGSHEAD, AUGUST B.
1949   Elmtown's Youth. New York: Wiley.

HOLSINGER, DONALD B.
1973   "The elementary school as a modernizer: A Brazilian study." International Journal of Comparative Sociology 14:180–202.

HOPE, KEITH (ed.)
1972   The Analysis of Social Mobility. Oxford: Clarendon Press.

HOPKINS, TERENCE K., AND IMMANUEL WALLERSTEIN
1967   "The comparative study of national societies." Social Science Information 6:25–58.

HOROWITZ, IRVING LOUIS
1972   "The Jewish vote." Commonweal 97 (October 13):30–33.

HOWE, IRVING
1971   "Review of Jews and Blacks." Commentary 52 (October):112–16.

HOWELL, JOSEPH T.
1973   Hard Living on Clay Street: Portraits of Blue Collar Families. New York: Anchor.

HUGHES, EVERETT C.
1958   Men and Their Work. Glencoe, Ill.: Free Press.

HUNTER, L. C., AND D. J. ROBERTSON
1969   Economics of Wages and Labor. New York: August M. Kelley.

HUNTINGTON, SAMUEL P.
1968   Political Order in Changing Societies. New Haven: Yale University Press.

1975   "The governability of democracy: The American case." In Samuel P. Huntington, Michel Crozier, and Joji Watanuki (eds.), The Governability of Democracies. New York: New York University Press.

HUSSERL, EDMUND
1970   The Crisis of Europeon Sciences and Transcendental Phenomenology. Tr. with an Introduction, by David Carr. Chicago: Northwestern University Press.

INKELES, ALEX
1960   "Industrial man: The relation of status to experience, perception, and value." American Journal of Sociology 66:1–31.

1969   "Participant citizenship in six developing countries." American
            Political Science Review 58:1120–41.

1971   "Continuity and change in the interaction of the personal and
            the socio-cultural system." In Bernard Barber and Alex Inkeles
            (eds.), Stability and Social Change. Boston: Little, Brown.

1974   "National differences in individual modernity." Paper presented
            at the 69th annual meeting of the A.S.A., Montreal, August.

1975   "Remaining orthodox: A rejoinder to Everett Hagen's review-es-
            say of Becoming Modern." History of Childhood Quarterly
            (Winter).

1976a   "The modernization of man in socialist and non-socialist coun-
            tries." In Mark G. Field (ed.), Social Consequences of Moderni-
            zation in Communist Societies. Baltimore: Johns Hopkins Uni-
            versity Press.

1976b   "Individual modernity in different ethnic and religious groups:
            Data from a six-nation study." Annals of the New York State
            Academy of Science.

INKELES, ALEX, EUGENIA HANFMANN, AND HELEN BEIER
1958   "Modal personality and adjustment to the Soviet socio-political
            system." Human Relations 11:3–22.

INKELES, ALEX, AND KAREN MILLER
1974   "Construction and validation of a cross-national scale of family
            modernism." International Journal of Sociology of the Family 4
            (no. 2).

INKELES, ALEX, AND DAVID H. SMITH
1970   "The fate of personal adjustment in the process of moderniza-
            tion." International Journal of Comparative Sociology 11, no. 2
            (June):81–114.

1974   Becoming Modern. Cambridge: Harvard University Press.

INTERNATIONAL LABOUR OFFICE
1956   Problems of Wage Policy in Asian Countries. Studies and Re-
            ports, New Series, no. 43. Geneva, Switzerland.

1958   Statistical Supplement, International Labour Review (July).
            Geneva, Switzerland.

1974   Yearbook of Labour Statistics. Geneva, Switzerland.

JACKMAN, MARY R., AND ROBERT W. JACKMAN
1973   "An interpretation of the relation between objective and subjec-
            tive social status." American Sociological Review 38:569–82.

JEHLIN, ELIZABETH
1974   "The concept of working-class embourgeoisement." Studies in
            Comparative International Development 9 (Spring):1–19.

JENCKS, CHRISTOPHER, et al.
1972   Inequality: A Reassessment of the Effects of Family and School-
            ing in America. New York: Basic Books.

JENKINS, ROBIN
 1971 "Why *do* men rebel?" Race 13 (July):90–92.

JOHNSON, CHALMERS
 1964 Revolution and the Social System. Stanford, Calif.: Hoover Institution on War, Revolution, and Peace.
 1966 Revolutionary Change. Boston: Little, Brown.

JUSTER, THOMAS M.
 1975 Education, Income and Human Behavior. New York: McGraw-
 Hill.

KAHL, JOSEPH A.
 1968 The Measurement of Modernism: A Study of Values in Brazil
 and Mexico. Austin: University of Texas Press.

KAHN, KATHY
 1972 Hillbilly Women. New York: Doubleday.

KAPLAN, ABRAHAM
 1964 The Conduct of Inquiry, San Francisco: Chandler.

KASSCHAU, PATRICIA L., H. EDWARD RANSFORD, AND VERN L. BENGTSON
 1974 "Generational consciousness and youth participation: Contrasts
 in blue collar and white collar youth." Journal of Social Issues
 30(3):69–94.

KATONA, GEORGE F., CHARLES A. LININGER, AND EVA MUELLER
 1964 Survey of Consumer Finances. Monograph 34. Institute for Social Research. University of Michigan, Ann Arbor.

KELLER, SUZANNE
 1963 Beyond the Ruling Class. New York: Random House.

KELLEY, JONATHAN
 1973 "Causal chain models for socioeconomic career." American Sociological Review 38:481–93.

KELMAN, MARK
 1974 "The social cost of inequality." Pp. 151–64 in Lewis A. Coser
 (ed.), The New Conservatives. New York: Quadrangle.

KERCKHOFF, ALAN C.
 1974 Ambition and Attainment: A Study of Four Samples of American Boys. Rose Monograph Series, American Sociological Association.

KERR, CLARK, JOHN T. DUNLOP, FREDERICK H. HARBISON, AND CHARLES A.
MYERS
 1960 Industrialism and Industrial Man. Cambridge: Harvard University Press.

KILSON, MARTIN
 1975 "Blacks and neo-ethnicity in American political life." Chap. 8 in
 Nathan Glazer and Daniel Moynihan (eds.), Ethnicity: Theory
 and Experience. Cambridge: Harvard University Press.

KINSEY, A., ET AL.,
1948   Sexual Behavior in the American Male. Philadelphia: W. B. Saunders Company.

KIRSCHT, JOHN P., AND RONALD C. DILLEHAY
1967   Dimensions of Authoritarianism: A Review of Research and Theory. Lexington: University of Kentucky Press.

KITSUSE, JOHN
1975   "The 'new conception of deviance' and its critics." Pp. 273–84 in Walter Gove (ed.), Labelling Deviant Behavior: The Evaluation of a Perspective. New York: Sage/Halstead.

KLINEBERG, STEPHEN L.
1973   "Parents, schools, and modernity: An exploratory investigation of sex differences in the attitudinal development of Tunisian adolescents." International Journal of Comparative Sociology 14:221–44.

KNOLLS, ROGER
1974   Reforming Regulation. Washington, D.C.: Brookings Institution.

KNUTSON, JEANNE N. (ED.)
1973   Handbook of Political Psychology. San Francisco: Jossey-Bass.

KOHN, MELVIN L., AND CARMI SCHOOLER
1973   "Occupational experience and psychological functioning: An assessment of reciprocal effects." American Sociological Review 38:97–118.

KOLAJA, JIRI
1965   Workers' Councils: The Yugoslav Experience. London: Tavistock Publications.

KOLKO, GABRIEL
1963   The Triumph of Conservatism. New York: Free Press.
1965   Railroads and Regulation. Princeton: Princeton University Press.

KORNHAUSER, ARTHUR
1965   Mental Health of the Industrial Worker. New York: Wiley.

KORNHAUSER, WILLIAM
1959   The Politics of Mass Society. Glencoe, Ill.: Free Press.

KREPS, JUANITA
1971   Sex and the Marketplace. Baltimore: Johns Hopkins Press.

KRIESBERG, LOUIS
1973   The Sociology of Social Conflicts. Englewood Cliffs, N.J.: Prentice-Hall.

KRISTOL, IRVING
1966   "The Negro of today is the immigrant of yesterday." The New York Times Magazine (September 11).

KROEBER, A. L.
1957   Style and Civilizations. Ithaca, N.Y.: Cornell University Press.

References   **365**

KUHN, THOMAS S.
  1961   "The function of measurement in modern physical science."
             In Harry Woolf (ed.), Quantification. Indianapolis: Bobbs-
             Merrill.

KÜSTERMEIER, RUDOLF
  1933   Die Mittelschichten und ihr politischer Weg. Potsdam: Alfred
             Protte.

KUZNETS, SIMON
  1966   Modern Economic Growth: Rate, Structure, and Spread. New
             Haven: Yale University Press.

LAMBERT, RICHARD
  1963   Workers, Factories, and Social Change in India. Princeton:
             Princeton University Press.

LANDIS, JAMES M.
  1960   Report on Regulatory Agencies to the President-Elect. Washing-
             ton, D.C.: U.S. Government Printing Office.

LANGER, SUSANNE K.
  1967   Mind: An Essay on Human Feeling. Baltimore: Johns Hopkins
             Press.

LEFEVRE, GEORGES
  1932   The Great Fear of 1789. New York: Pantheon, 1973.

LEMASTERS, E. E.
  1975   Blue-Collar Aristocrats. Ann Arbor: University of Michigan
             Press.

LEMERT, EDWIN M.
  1951   Social Pathology. New York: McGraw-Hill.

  1960   "Paranoia and the dynamics of exclusion." Sociometry 25:2–20.

  1967   Human Deviance, Social Problems, and Social Control. Engle-
             wood Cliffs, N.J.: Prentice-Hall.

  1972   "Social problems and the sociology of deviance." Pp. 3–25 in E.
             Lemert (ed.), Human Deviance, Social Problems, and Social
             Control. 2d ed. Englewood Cliffs, N.J.: Prentice-Hall.

  1974   "Beyond Mead: The societal reaction to deviance." Social Prob-
             lems 21 (April):457–68.

LENIN, NIKOLAI
  1943   Selected Works. Vol. 10. New York: International Publishers.

LENSKI, GERHARD
  1961   The Religious Factor. Garden City, N.Y.: Doubleday.

LERNER, DANIEL
  1958   The Passing of Traditional Society: Modernizing the Middle
             East. Glencoe, Ill.: Free Press.

LEVIN, HENRY M.
  1975   "A decade of policy developments in improving education and
             training for low income populations." Mimeographed. Stanford
             University School of Education.

LeVine, Robert A.
    1966   Dreams and Deeds: Achievement Motivation in Nigeria. Chi-
                cago: University of Chicago Press.

Levinson, Andrew
    1974   Working-Class Majority. New York: Coward, McCann and
                Geoghegan, Inc.

Levinson, Richard M., and M. Zan York
    1974   "The attribution of 'dangerousness' in mental health evalua-
                tions." Journal of Health and Social Behavior 15 (Decem-
                ber):328–35.

Lichtheim, George
    1971   From Marx to Hegel. New York: Herder and Herder.

Lifton, Robert J.
    1968   Death in Life: Survivors of Hiroshima. New York: Random
                House.

Lijphart, Arend
    1971   "Comparative politics and the comparative method." American
                Political Science Review 65:682–93.

Linton, Ralph
    1937   "One hundred per cent American." The American Mercury 40
                (April): 427–29.

Lipset, Seymour Martin
    1960   Political Man: The Social Bases of Politics. Garden City, N.Y.:
                Doubleday.

    1961   "A changing American character?" In Lipset and Leo Lowenthal
                (eds.), Culture and Social Character: The Work of David Ries-
                man Reviewed. Glencoe, Ill.: Free Press.

    1963   "Three decades of the radical right: Coughlinites, McCarthyites,
                and Birchers—1962." Pp. 340–41 in Daniel Bell (ed.), The Radi-
                cal Right. Garden City, N.Y.: Doubleday.

    1967   The First New Nation: The United States in Historical and
                Comparative Perspective. New York: Doubleday Anchor.

Lipset, Seymour Martin, and Reinhard Bendix
    1959   Social Mobility in Industrial Society. Berkeley: University of Cal-
                ifornia Press.

Llazos, Alexander
    1972   "The poverty of the sociology of deviance: Nuts, sluts, and per-
                verts." Social Problems 20 (Summer):103–20.

Locke, Alain, and Bernhard J. Stern (eds.)
    1946   When Peoples Meet: A Study in Race and Culture Contacts.
                Rev. ed. New York: Hinds, Hayden and Eldredge.

Lofland, John
    1969   Deviance and Identity. Englewood Cliffs, N.J.: Prentice-Hall.

Lorenzer, A.
    1970   Sprachzerstorung und Rellonstruction. Frankfurt: Suhrkamp.

LUBELL, SAMUEL
   1973   The Future While It Happened. New York: Norton.

LUPSHA, PETER A.
   1971   "Explanation of political violence: Some psychological theories versus indignation." Politics and Society 2:89–104.

LYND, ROBERT S., AND HELEN M. LYND
   1929   Middletown. New York: Harcourt Brace.

LYND, STAUGHTON
   1975   "Why labor?" Win (August 14):4–6.

McAULIFFE, WILLIAM
   1975   "Beyond secondary deviance: Negative labelling and its effect on heroin addiction." Pp. 205–42 in Walter Gove (ed.), Labelling Deviant Behavior: The Evaluation of a Perspective. New York: Sage/Halstead.

McCLELLAND, DAVID
   1961   The Achieving Society. Princeton: Van Nostrand.

McGRATH, J. E., AND I. ALTMAN
   1966   Small Group Research: A Synthesis and Critique of the Field. New York: Holt, Rinehart and Winston.

McHUGH, PETER, et al.
   1974   On the Beginning of Social Enquiry. London: Routledge and Kegan Paul.

MACKENZIE, GAVIN
   1973   The Aristocracy of Labor. Cambridge: Cambridge University Press.

MACINTYRE, ALASDAIR
   1973   "Ideology, social science, and revolution." Comparative Politics 5 (April):321–42.

McNAMEE, STEPHEN J.
   1975   "Skill level and politics: A replication." PASS Working Paper, #122. Sociology Department, University of Illinois, Urbana–Champaign.

MAHLER, JOHN E.
   1961   "The wage pattern in the United States." Industrial and Labor Relations Review 15 (October):3–20.

MANKOFF, MILTON
   1971   "Societal reaction and career deviance: A critical analysis." Sociological Quarterly 12:204–18.

MANKOFF, MILTON, AND RICHARD FLACKS
   1971   "The changing social basis of the American student movement." Annals of the American Academy of Political and Social Science 371:54–67.

MANNING, PETER K.
   1973   "On deviance." Contemporary Sociology 2 (March):123–28.

MARGLIN, STEVE
1974   "What do bosses do?" Review of Radical Economics 6 (Summer).

MARSHALL, HARVEY, AND ROSS PURDY
1972   "Hidden deviance and the labeling approach." Social Problems
            19 (Spring):541–53.

MARSHALL, RAY
1968   "Racial practices of unions." Pp. 277–98 in Louis A. Ferman,
            Joyce A. Kornbluh, and J. A. Miller (eds.), Negroes and Jobs.
            Ann Arbor: University of Michigan Press.
1972   "Black workers and the union." Dissent 19 (Winter):295–302.

MARTIĆ, MILOŠ
1975   Insurrection: Five Schools of Revolutionary Thought. New
            York: Dunellen.

MASON, KAREN OPPENHEIM, JOHN CZAJKA, AND SARA ARBER
1975   "Change in U.S. women's sex-role attitudes, 1964–74." Un-
            published paper, University of Michigan Population Studies
            Center.

MAYER, KURT B., AND WALTER BUCKLEY
1955   Class and Society. New York: Random House.

MEAD, MARGARET
1956   New Lives for Old. New York: Morrow.

MEADE, ANTHONY C.
1974   "The labeling approach to delinquency: State of the theory as a
            function to method." Social Forces 53 (September):83–91.

MECHANIC, DAVID
1972   "Social class and schizophrenia: Some requirements for a plausi-
            ble theory of social influence." Social Forces 50 (March):305–9.

MENDEL, WERNER, AND SAMUEL RAPPORT
1969   "Determinants in the decision for psychiatric hospitalization."
            Archives of General Psychiatry 20 (March):321–28.

MERTON, ROBERT K.
1968   Social Theory and Social Structure. New York: Free Press.

METZGER, DUANE
1960   "Conflict in Chulsanto: A village in Chiapas." Alpha Kappa Del-
            tan 30:35–48.

MEYER, JOHN, MICHAEL HANNAN, AND RICHARD RUBINSON
1973   "National economic development 1950–1965: Educational and
            political factors." Paper presented at a Southeast Asian Develop-
            ment Advisory Group (Seadag) Seminar on Ecucation and De-
            velopment, Singapore.

MEYERSOHN, ROLF, AND ELIHU KATZ
1957   "Notes on the natural history of fads." American Journal of So-
            ciology 62:594–601. (Reprinted in Eric Larrabee and Rolf
            Meyersohn, Mass Leisure. Glencoe, Ill.: Free Press, 1958.)

MICHELS, ROBERT
1959 Political Parties. Translated by Eden and Cedar Paul. New York: Dover.

MILIBAND, RALPH
1969 The State in Capitalist Society. New York: Basic Books.

MILLER, HERMAN P.
1966 Income Distribution in the United States. Washington, D.C.: U.S. Bureau of the Census, U.S. Government Printing Office.

MILLER, KENT S., RONALD L. SIMONS, AND SARA B. FEIN
1974 "Compulsory mental hospitalization in England and Wales." Journal of Health and Social Behavior 15 (June):151–56.

MILLER, S. M., AND MARTIN REIN
1966 "Poverty, inequality, and policy." Pp. 426–576 in Howard S. Becker (ed.), Social Problems. New York: Wiley.

MILLON, THEODORE
1969 Modern Psychopathology: A Biosocial Approach to Maladaptive Learning and Functioning. Philadelphia: Saunders.

MILLS, C. WRIGHT
1956 The Power Elite. New York: Oxford.

MOORE, BARRINGTON, JR.
1966 Social Origins of Dictatorship and Democracy: Lord and Peasant in the Making of the Modern World. Boston: Beacon.

MORRISON, DONALD G., AND HUGH MICHAEL STEVENSON
1971 "Political instability in independent black Africa: More dimensions of conflict behavior within nations." Journal of Conflict Resolution 15 (September):347–68.

MULLER, EDWARD N.
1972 "A test for a partial theory of potential for political violence." American Political Science Review 66:928–59.

MURPHY, FRED J., MARY M. SHIRLEY, AND HELEN L. WITNER
1946 "The incidence of hidden delinquency." American Journal of Orthopsychiatry 16:686–96.

MURPHY, H. B. M.
1961 "Social change and mental health." Milbank Memorial Fund Quarterly 39:385–445.

NADER, L.
1964 "Talea and Juquila: A comparison of Zapotec social organization." University of California Publications in American Archaeology and Ethnology 48(3):195–296.

1965 "The anthropological study of law." In The Ethnography of Law. Special issue of American Anthropologist 67:3–32.

1969 "Up the anthropologist." In D. Hymes (ed.), Reinventing Anthropology. New York: Pantheon Books.

1975   "Forums for justice: A cross-cultural perspective." Journal of
          Social Issues 31 (Summer):151–70.

1976   "Powerlessness in Zapotec and American societies." In R. Adams
          and R. Fogelson (eds.), The Anthropology of Power. New York:
          Academic Press.

NADER, L., AND C. WITTY
1975   "Legal development and administration." Paper prepared for a
          round table on administrative law and its role in development in
          the Arab countries. National Institute of Administration and
          Development, Beirut.

NADER, RALPH, P. PETKAF, AND K. BLACKWELL
1972   Whistle Blowing: The Report of the Conference on Professional
          Responsibility. New York: Grossman.

NAGEL, ERNEST (ED.)
1950   John Stuart Mill's Philosophy of Scientific Method. New York:
          Hafner.

NARDIN, TERRY
1971   Violence and the State: A Critique of Empirical Political Theory.
          Beverly Hills, Calif.: Sage Publications.

NELSON, JOAN M.
1969   Migrants, Urban Poverty, and Instability in Developing Nations.
          Occasional Papers in International Affairs, no. 22 (September),
          Harvard University Center for International Affairs.

NILL, MICHAEL
1975   "Workplace organizing." Liberation (May):16–18.

NOEL, DONALD L.
1968   "A theory of the origin of ethnic stratification." Social Problems
          16 (Fall):157–72.

NOLAN, RICHARD L., AND RODNEY E. SCHNECK
1969   "Small businessmen, branch managers, and their relative suscep-
          tibility to right-wing extremism: An empirical test." Canadian
          Journal of Political Science 2 (March):89–102.

NOVAK, MICHAEL
1971   The Rise of the Unmeltable Ethnics: Politics and Culture in the
          Seventies. New York: Macmillan.

NUNNALY, JUNE
1961   Popular Conceptions of Mental Health. New York: Holt, Rine-
          hart and Winston.

OBER, HARRY
1948   "Occupational wage differentials, 1907–47." Monthly Labor Re-
          view 67 (August):127–34.

OBERSCHALL, ANTHONY
1969   "Rising expectations and political turmoil." Journal of Develop-
          ment Studies 6:5–22.

1973 Social Conflict and Social Movements. Englewood Cliffs, N.J.: Prentice-Hall.

O'CONNOR, JAMES
1973 The Fiscal Crisis of the State. New York: St. Martin's Press.

O'DEA, THOMAS
1966 The Sociology of Religion. Englewood Cliffs, N.J.: Prentice-Hall.

O'DONNELL, LAURENCE G.
1974 "UAW internal battle looms as unit says skilled workers can't veto new contracts." Wall Street Journal (April 15).

OKSANAN, ERNEST H., AND BYRON G. SPENCER
1975 "On the determinants of student performance in introductory courses in the social sciences." The American Sociologist 10:103–9.

OUTHWAITE, WILLIAM
1975 Understanding Social Life. London: Allen and Unwin.

OVERHOLT, WILLIAM
1972 "Revolution." In The Sociology of Political Organization. Croton-on-Hudson, N.Y.: Hudson Institute.

OZANNE, ROBERT A.
1962 "A century of occupational differentiation in manufacturing." Review of Economics and Statistics 44 (August):292–99.

PACKARD, STEVE
1975 "Steelmill blues." Liberation (May):7–15.

PANDEY, RAMA S.
1971 "Socialization and social policy in modernizing society." Unpublished Ph.D. Thesis presented to The Florence Heller Graduate School for Advanced Studies in Social Welfare, Brandeis University.

PANEL ON YOUTH
1974 Youth: Transition to Adulthood. Report of the Panel on Youth of the President's Science Advisory Committee. Chicago: University of Chicago Press.

PARKER, RICHARD
1972 The Myth of the Middle Class. New York: Harper & Row.

PARSONS, TALCOTT
1947 "Introduction" to Max Weber, The Theory of Social and Economic Organization. New York: Oxford University Press.

1951 The Social System. New York: Free Press.

PARSONS, TALCOTT, AND WINSTON WHITE
1961 "The link between character and society." Chap. 6 in Seymour Lipset and Leo Lowenthal (eds.), Culture and Social Character: The Work of David Riesman Reviewed. Glencoe, Ill.: Free Press.

PERLMAN, RICHARD
1958   "Forces widening occupational wage differentials." Review of
            Economics and Statistics 40 (May):107–15.

PERLMAN, SELIG, AND PHILIP TAFT
1935   History of Labor in the United States, 1896–1932. New York:
            Macmillan.

PERROW, CHARLES
1972   Complex Organization: A Critical Essay. Glenview, Ill.: Scott,
            Foresman.

PETRONI, FRANK A.
1972   "Correlates of the psychiatric sick role." Journal of Health and
            Social Behavior 13 (March):47–54.

PHELPS, ORME W.
1957   "A structural model of the U.S. labor market." Industrial and
            Labor Relations Review 10 (April):402–23.

PLATT, TONY
1973   "Toward a new crimonology." Paper presented at the meetings
            of the Pacific Sociological Association, Scottsdale, Arizona.

PORTER, JACK NUSAN
1972   "Jewish conservative backlash?" Commonweal 97 (October
            13):33–37.

PORTER, JAMES N.
1974   "Race, socialization, and mobility." American Sociological Re-
            view 39:303–16.

PORTES, ALEJANDRO
1971   "On the logic of post-factum explanations: The hypothesis of
            lower-class frustrations as the cause of leftist radicalism." Social
            Forces 50:26–44.

1973   "The factorial structure of modernity: Empirical replication and
            a critique." American Journal of Sociology 79:15–36.

POSPISIL, L.
1967   "Legal levels and multiplicity of legal systems in human socie-
            ties." Journal of Conflict Resolution 11:2–26.

POUND, R.
1906   "The causes of popular dissatisfaction with the administration of
            justice." Reports of the American Bar Association 29, pt.
            1:294–417.

PRATT, SAMUEL A.
1948   "The social basis of Nazism and Communism in urban Ger-
            many." Unpublished master's thesis, Michigan State College,
            East Lansing.

THE PRESIDENT'S ADVISORY COUNCIL ON EXECUTIVE ORGANIZATION
1971   A New Regulatory Framework: Report on Selected Indepen-
            dent Regulatory Agencies. Washington, D.C.: U.S. Government
            Printing Office.

THE PRESIDENT'S COMMITTEE ON ADMINISTRATIVE MANAGEMENT
1937   Report of the President's Committee on Administrative Management. Washington, D.C.: U.S. Government Printing Office.

QUINN, ROBERT P., AND LINDA J. SHEPERD
1973   The 1972–1973 Quality of Employment Survey. Ann Arbor, Mich.: Institute of Social Research.

RABB, EARL
1969   "The Black revolution and the Jewish question." Commentary 47 (January):23–33.

RADNITZKY, GERARD
1970   Contemporary Schools of Metascience. Vol. 2. Göteborg: Akademiförlaget/Gumpert.

RAINWATER, LEE
1971   "Making the good life: Working-class family and life styles." Pp. 204–29 in Sar A. Levitan (ed.), Blue-Collar Workers: A Symposium on Middle America. New York: McGraw-Hill.

1975   What Money Buys: Inequality and the Social Meanings of Income. New York: Basic Books.

RAINWATER, LEE (ED.)
1974   Social Problems and Public Policy: Inequality and Justice. Chicago: Aldine.

RAPHAEL, EDNA E.
1974   "Working women and their membership in labor unions." Monthly Labor Review 97 (May):27–33.

REDER, MELVIN
1955   "The theory of occupational wage differentials." American Economic Review 45 (December):833–52.

REISS, ALBERT J.
1961   Occupations and Social Status. New York: Free Press.

RICOEUR, PAUL
1965   De l'interpretation: Essai sur Freud. Paris: Editions du Seuil.

RIESMAN, DAVID
1963   "Containment and initiatives." Council for Correspondence Newsletter 23:21–30.

1968a   "America moves to the right." New York Times Magazine (October 27): 34–35, 69–70, 74, 76, 79, 82, 84.

1968b   "Review of Robert J. Lifton, Death in Life: Survivors of Hiroshima." Dissent (April).

1969   "The lonely crowd, twenty years after." Encounter 33 (October):36–41.

1975   "The future of diversity in a time of retrenchment." Higher Education 4:461–82.

RIESMAN, DAVID, AND NATHAN GLAZER
1950   "Criteria for political apathy." In Alvin Gouldner (ed.), Studies in Leadership. New York: Harper.

1961   "The lonely crowd: A reconsideration." Pp. 419–58 in Seymour
            Lipset and Leo Lowenthal (eds.), Culture and Social Character:
            The Work of David Riesman Reviewed. Glencoe, Ill.: Free
            Press.

RIESMAN, DAVID, WITH NATHAN GLAZER AND REUEL DENNEY
1961   The Lonely Crowd. Rev. ed. New Haven: Yale University Press.

RIESSMAN, FRANK
1972   "Backward vanguard." Society 10:104–6.

RIVLIN, ALICE, AND MICHAEL TIMPANE (EDS.)
1975   Planned Variation in Education. Washington: Brookings.

ROBINS, LEE
1975   "Alcoholism and labelling theory." Pp. 21–33 in Walter Gove
            (ed.), Labelling Deviant Behavior: The Evaluation of a Perspec-
            tive. New York: Sage/Halstead.

ROGERS, EVERETT, IN ASSOCIATION WITH LYNNE SVENNING
1969   Modernization Among Peasants. New York: Holt, Rinehart and
            Winston.

ROGERS, JOSEPH W., AND M. D. BUFFALO
1974   "Fighting back: Nine modes of adaptation to a deviant label."
            Social Problems 22 (October):101–18.

ROSENHAM, D. L.
1973   "On being sane in insane places." Science 179 (January):250–58.

ROSENTHAL, NEAL, AND H. DILLON
1974   "Occupational outlook for the mid-1980's." Occupational Out-
            look Quarterly 18 (Winter):3–11.

ROSSI, ALICE
1965   "A modest proposal." In Robert J. Lifton (ed.), Woman in
            America. Boston: Houghton Mifflin.

ROSSI, PETER H., RICHARD BERK, AND BETTYE EIDSON
1974   The Roots of Urban Discontent. New York: Wiley-Interscience.

ROSSI, PETER H., AND KATHARINE LYALL
Forthcoming Social Policy and Social Experiments. New York: Russell Sage
            Foundation.

ROTHBAUM, MELVIN
1957   "National wage structure comparisons." Pp. 299–327 in George
            W. Taylor and Frank C. Pierson (eds.), New Concepts in Wage
            Determination. New York: McGraw-Hill.

RUBINGTON, EARL, AND MARTIN WEINBERG
1971   "Labeling." Pp. 163–71 in E. Rubington and M. Weinberg (eds.),
            The Study of Social Problems. New York: Oxford University
            Press.

RUDÉ, GEORGE
1959   The Crowd in the French Revolution. New York: Oxford Uni-
            versity Press.

RUDOLPH, LLOYD I., AND SUZANNE H. RUDOLPH
1967   The Modernity of Tradition. Chicago: University of Chicago
Press.

RUFFINI, J.
1974   "Alternative systems of conflict management in Sardinia." Unpublished doctoral dissertation. University of California, Berkeley.

RUMMEL, RUDOLPH J.
1963   "Dimensions of conflict behavior within and between nations."
General Systems 8:1–50.

RUSSELL, BERTRAND
1945   A History of Western Philosophy. New York: Simon & Schuster.

RUSSELL, D. E. H.
1974   Rebellion, Revolution, and Armed Force. New York: Academic
Press.

RUSSETT, BRUCE M., et al.
1964   World Handbook of Political and Social Indicators. New Haven,
Conn.: Yale University Press.

SACK, RICHARD
1973   "The impact of education on individual modernity in Tunisia."
International Journal of Comparative Sociology 14:245–72.

SACRAMENTO COUNTY PROBATION DEPARTMENT
1974   General Report. P. 33.

SAGARIN, EDWARD
1975   Deviants and Deviance: An Introduction to the Study of Dis-
valued People and Behavior. New York: Praeger.

SAGARIN, EDWARD, AND ROBERT KELLEY
1975   "Sexual deviance and labelling perspectives." Pp. 243–71 in
Walter Gove (ed.), Labelling Deviant Behavior: The Evaluation
of a Perspective. New York: Sage/Halstead.

SAINT AUGUSTINE
1953   [401] Confessions. New York: Fathers of the Church.

SAMPSON, HAROLD, SHELDON MESSINGER, AND ROBERT TOWNE
1962   "Family processes and becoming a mental patient." American
Journal of Sociology 68 (July):88–96.

SARTORI, GIOVANNI
1971   "Technological forecasting and politics." Survey 16 (Winter):66–
68.

SCHEFF, THOMAS J.
1963   "The role of the mentally ill and the dynamics of mental disorder." Sociometry 26:436–53.

1964a   "The societal reaction to deviance: Ascriptive elements in the
psychiatric screening of mental patients in a midwestern state."
Social Problems 11:401–13.

1964b   "Social conditions for rationality: How urban and rural courts deal with the mentally ill." American Behavioral Scientist (March):21–24.

1966   Being Mentally Ill: A Sociological Theory. Chicago: Aldine.

1967   Mental Illness and Social Processes. New York: Harper & Row.

1968   "Negotiating reality: Notes on power in the assessment of responsibility." Social Problems 16 (Summer):1–17.

1970   "Schizophrenia as ideology." Schizophrenia Bulletin 2:15–19.

1974   "The labelling theory of mental illness." American Sociological Review 39 (June):444–52.

1975a   "Reply to Chauncey and Gove." American Sociological Review 40 (April):252–57.

SCHEFF, THOMAS (ED.)
1975b   Labeling Madness. Englewood Cliffs, N.J.: Prentice-Hall.

SCHEGLOFF, EMMANUEL
1968   "Sequencing in conversational openings." American Anthropologist 70:1075–95.

SCHEGLOFF, EMMANUEL A., AND HARVEY SACKS
1973   "Opening up closings." Semiotica 8.

SCHELLING, THOMAS C.
1971   "The Ecology of micromotives." The Public Interest no. 25:59–98.

SCHERER, KLAUS R., et al.
1975   Human Aggression and Conflict: Interdisciplinary Perspectives. Englewood Cliffs, N.J.: Prentice-Hall.

SCHERMERHORN, RICHARD A.
1970   Comparative Ethnic Relations: A Framework for Theory and Research. New York: Random House.

SCHERVISH, PAUL G.
1973   "The labeling perspective: Its bias and potential in the study of political science." American Sociologist 8 (May):45–57.

SCHNAIBERG, ALLAN
1970   "Measuring modernism: Theoretical and empirical exploration." American Journal of Sociology 76:399–425.

SCHNEIDER, DAVID
1947   "The social dynamics of physical disability in army basic training." Psychiatry 10 (August):323–33.

SCHNEIDER, WILLIAM
1974   "Public opinion: The beginning of ideology?" Foreign Policy no. 17:88–120.

SCHOEPLEIN, ROBERT
1975   "The impact of recent inflation on labor skill differentials." Faculty Working Paper #244. College of Commerce and Business Administration, University of Illinois at Urbana-Champaign.

SCHRAG, CLARENCE
1971   Crime and Justice: American Style. Washington, D.C.: U.S. Government Printing Office.

SCHRIFTGIESSER, KARL
1974   The Commission on Money and Credit. Englewood Cliffs, N.J.: Prentice-Hall.

SCHUR, EDWIN M.
1971   Labeling Deviant Behavior: Its Sociological Implications. New York: Harper & Row.

1974   "The concept of secondary deviation: Its theoretical significance and empirical elusiveness." Unpublished manuscript.

1975   "Comments." Pp. 285–94 in Walter Gove (ed.), Labelling Deviant Behavior: The Evaluation of a Perspective. New York: Sage/Halstead.

SCHWARTZ, DAVID C.
1971   "A theory of revolutionary behavior." Pp. 109–32 in James C. Davies (ed.), When Men Revolt and Why. New York: Free Press.

1972   "Political alienation: The psychology of revolution's first stage." Pp. 58–66 in Ivo K. and Rosalind L. Feierabend and Ted Robert Gurr (eds.), Anger, Violence, and Politics. Englewood Cliffs, N.J.: Prentice-Hall.

1973   Political Alienation and Political Behavior. Chicago: Aldine.

SCHWARTZ, GARY, PAUL TURNER, AND EMIL PELUSO.
1973   "Neither heads nor freaks: Working-class drug subculture." Urban Life and Culture 2 (3) (October):288–313.

SCHWARTZ, RICHARD, AND JEROME SKOLNICK
1964   "Two studies of legal stigma." In H. Becker (ed.), The Other Side. Glencoe, Ill.: Free Press.

SCOVILLE, JAMES G.
1972   Manpower and Occupational Analysis: Concepts and Measurements. Lexington, Mass.: D. C. Heath.

SENNETT, RICHARD, AND JONATHAN COBB
1972   The Hidden Injuries of Class. New York: Knopf.

SERBAN, GEORGE, AND CHRISTINA B. GIDYNSKI
1974   "Significance of social demographic data for rehospitalization of schizophrenia patients." Journal of Health and Social Behavior 15 (June):117–26.

SERBER, DAVID
1975   "Regulating reform: The social organization of insurance regulation." In G. W. Domhoff (ed.), New Directions in Power Structure Research. Special issue of The Insurgent Sociologist 5, no. 3 (Spring).

Forthcoming "Assemblyline lawyers: The proletarianization of legal professionals in the California Department of Insurance." In Karen Michaelson (ed.), The Anthropology of the Middle Class.

SEWELL, WILLIAM H. JR.
1967   "Marc Bloch and the logic of comparative history." History and Theory 6:208–18.

SEWELL, WILLIAM H., AND HAUSER, R. M.
1975   Education, Occupation and Earnings: Achievement in the Early Career. New York: Academic Press.

SHARP, GENE
1971   Exploring Nonviolent Alternatives. Boston: Porter Sargent.
1973   The Politics of Nonviolent Action. Boston: Porter Sargent.

SHERIDAN, WILLIAM H.
1967   Juveniles who commit non-criminal acts: Why treat them in a correctional system? Federal Probation XXXI:26–30.

SHIBUTANI, TAMOTSU, AND KIAN M. KWAN
1972   Ethnic Stratification: A Comparative Approach. New York: Macmillan.

SHORT, JAMES F. JR., AND FRED L. STRODTBECK
1965   Group Processes and Gang Delinquency. Chicago: University of Chicago Press.

SHOSTAK, ARTHUR B.
1969   Blue Collar Life. New York: Random House.

SHOUP, LAURENCE
1968   Statistical Abstract of the United States. U. S. Department of Commerce, Bureau of the Census.
1975   "Shaping the postwar world: The council on Foreign Relations and United States war aims during World War Two." In G. W. Domhoff (ed), New directions in power structure research. Special issue of The Insurgent Sociologist 5, no. 3 (Spring).

SIEGEL, PAUL M.
Forthcoming Prestige of Occupations. New York: Academic Press.

SIMKIN, WILLIAM E.
1968   "Refusals to ratify contracts." Industrial and Labor Relations Review (July):518–40.

SIMON, WILLIAM, et al.
1971   "Son of Joe: Continuity and change among white working-class adolescents." Journal of Youth and Adolescence 1:13–34.

SKOCPOL, THEDA
1976   "France, Russia, and China: A structural analysis of social revolutions." Comparative Studies in Society and History 18.

SLATER, PHILIP E.
1968   The Glory of Hera: Greek Mythology and the Greek Family. Boston: Beacon Press.

SMELSER, NEIL J.
1963   Theory of Collective Behavior. New York: Free Press.
1966   "The methodology of comparative anlaysis." Unpublished.

1971   "Alexis de Tocqueville as a comparative analyst." Pp. 19–47 in Ivan Vallier (ed.), Comparative Methods in Sociology. Berkeley and Los Angeles: University of California Press.

SMITH, DAVID, AND ALEX INKELES
1966   "The OM scale: A comparative socio-psychological measure of individual modernity." Sociometry 29:353–77.

1975   "Individual modernizing experiences and psycho-social modernity: Validation of the OM scales in six developing countries." Journal of Comparative Sociology 16 (nos. 3–4):157–73.

SMITH, HARVEY L., AND THRASHER, JEAN
1963   "Roles, cliques and sanctions: Dimensions of patient society." International Journal of Social Psychiatry 9:184–91.

SMITH, RICHARD
1975   "Societal reaction and physical disability: Contrasting perspectives." Pp. 147–56 in Walter Gove (ed.), Labelling Deviant Behavior: The Evaluation of a Perspective. New York: Sage/Halstead.

SNYDER, DAVID, AND CHARLES TILLY
1972   "Hardship and collective violence in France, 1830–1960." American Sociological Review 37:520–32.

SPECIAL TASK FORCE
1973   Work in America. Washington: Department of Health, Education, Welfare.

SPINRAD, WILLIAM
1960   "Correlates of trade union participation: A summary of the literature." American Sociological Review 25 (April):237–44.

STATE OF CALIFORNIA
1940   Special Report to the Governor from the Insurance Commissioner of the State of California.

1970   Annual Report of the Insurance Commissioner for the Year Ending December 31, 1969.

STEADMAN, HENRY J.
1972   "The psychiatrist as a conservative agent of social control." Social Problems 20 (Fall):263–71.

STEER, DAVID
1970   Police Cautions: A Study in the Exercise of Police Discretion. Oxford: Penal Research Unit.

STEFFENSMEIR, DARREL J., AND ROBERT M. TERRY
1973   "Deviance and respectability: An observational study of reactions to shoplifting." Social Forces 51 (June):417–26.

STEPHENSON, JOHN B.
1968   "Is everyone going modern? A critique and a suggestion for measuring modernism." American Journal of Sociology 74:265–75.

STEWART, O. C.
1952   "Indian tribe adjustment to modern living." In S. Tax (ed.), Acculturation in the Americas. Vol. 2. Proceedings, Twenty-Ninth International Congress of Americanists. Chicago: University of Chicago Press.

STONE, CHUCK
1968   Black Political Power in America. New York: Dell.

SUDNOW, DAVID
1972   "Temporal parameters of interpersonal observation." Pp. 229–58 in D. Sudnow (ed.), Studies in Social Interaction. New York: Free Press.

SUTHERLAND, EDWIN H.
1940   "White collar criminality." American Sociological Review 5:1–12.
1968   "White-collar criminality." In G. Geis (ed.), White Collar Criminal. New York: Atherton.

SUZMAN, RICHARD
1973a   "The modernization of personality." Unpublished Ph.D. thesis, Department of Psychology and Social Relations, Harvard University.
1973b   "Psychological modernity." International Journal of Comparative Sociology 14:273–87.
1976   "The individual in the modernizing process." Annual Review of Sociology. Vol. 2. Palo Alto, Calif.: Annual Reviews.

SZASZ, THOMAS S.
1961   "The Myth of Mental Illness." American Psychologist 16:113–18.
1970   The Manufacture of Madness. New York: Harper & Row.

TAIRA, KOJI
1970   Economic Development and the Labor Market in Japan. New York: Columbia University.

TANNENBAUM, ARNOLD S., AND ROBERT L. KAHN
1958   Participation in Union Locals. Evanston, Ill.: Row, Peterson.

TANNENBAUM, FRANK
1938   Crime and the Community. Boston: Ginn.

TAYLOR, GEORGE V.
1972   "Revolutionary and nonrevolutionary content in the Cahiers of 1789: An interim report." French Historical Studies 7:479–502.

TERLECKYJ, NESTOR E.
1975   Improvements in the Quality of Life: Estimates of Possibilities in the United States. Washington, D.C.: National Planning Association.

THERMSTROM, STEPHAN
1973   The Other Bostonians: Poverty and Progress in the American Metropolis, 1880–1970. Cambridge: Harvard University Press.

THIO, ALEX
1973   "Class bias in the sociology of deviance." American Sociologist 8 (February):1–12.

THOMPSON, E. P.
1963   The Making of the English Working Class. New York: Vintage.

THORNE, BARRIE
1972   "Girls who say 'yes' to guys who say 'no.' " Doctoral dissertation, Brandeis University.

THORSELL, BERNARD A., AND LLOYD W. KLEMKE
1972   "The labeling process: Reinforcement and deterrent." Law and Society Review 6:393–403.

TILLERY, WINSTON
1974   "Internal affairs hold the spotlight at the UAW convention." Monthly Labor Review 97 (August):52–54.

TILLY, CHARLES
1969   "Collective violence in European perspective." Pp. 1–42 in Hugh Davis Graham and Ted Robert Gurr (eds.), Violence in America. New York: Signet Books.

1973   "Does modernization breed revolution?" Comparative Politics 5:425–47.

1974   "Town and country in revolution." Pp. 271–302 in John Wilson Lewis (ed.), Peasant Rebellion and Communist Revolution in Asia. Stanford, Calif.: Stanford University Press.

1975   "Revolutions and collective violence." Pp. 483–555 in Fred I. Greenstein and Nelson W. Polsby (eds.), Handbook of Political Science, vol. 3. Reading, Mass.: Addison-Wesley.

TILLY, CHARLES, LOUISE TILLY, AND RICHARD TILLY
1975   The Rebellious Century, 1830–1930. Cambridge: Harvard University Press.

TILLY, LOUISE
1971   "The food riot as a form of political conflict in France." Journal of Interdisciplinary History 2:23–57.

TIRYAKIAN, EDWARD
1967   "A model of societal change and its lead indicators." Pp. 69–97 in Samuel Z. Klausner (ed.), The Study of Total Societies. Garden City, N.Y.: Doubleday Anchor.

TITTLE, CHARLES
1975a   "Labelling and crime: An empirical evaluation." Pp. 157–79 in Walter Gove (ed.), Labelling Deviant Behavior: The Evaluation of a Perspective. New York: Sage/Halstead.

1975b   "Deterrents or labeling?" Social Forces 53 (March):399–410.

TITTLE, CHARLES, AND C. H. LOGAN
1973   "Sanctions and deviance: Evidence and remaining questions." Law and Society Review 7 (Spring):372–92.

TRILLING, LIONEL
1973   Mind in the Modern World. New York: Viking Press.

TROTSKY, LEON
1932   The Russian Revolution. Selected and edited by F. W. Dupee.
              Garden City, N.Y.: Doubleday Anchor, 1959.

TROW, MARTIN
1958   "Small businessmen, political tolerance, and support for
              McCarthy." American Journal of Sociology 64 (November):
              270–80.

TURNER, RALPH H.
1972   "Deviance avowal as neutralization of commitment." Social Prob-
              lems 19 (Winter):308–21.

1975   "Feeling unfree on a university campus." Youth and Society 7.

U.S. BUREAU OF THE CENSUS
1973   Census of Population: 1970. Subject Reports, Earnings by Oc-
              cupation and Education. Washington, D.C.: U.S. Government
              Printing Office.

1974   "Characteristics of American Youth: 1974." Current Population
              Reports, Special Studies, no. 51:23. Washington, D.C.: U.S.
              Government Printing Office.

U.S. BUREAU OF LABOR STATISTICS
1966   Labor Developments Abroad. Washington, D.C.: U.S. Depart-
              ment of Labor (May).

U.S. COMMISSION ON ORGANIZATION OF THE EXECUTIVE BRANCH OF GOVERN-
MENT
1949a   The Independent Regulatory Commissions. Washington, D.C.:
              U.S. Government Printing Office.

1949b   A Report with Recommendations. Committee on Independent
              Regulatory Commissions. Washington, D.C.: U.S. Government
              Printing Office. (Together referred to as the First Hoover
              Commission Report.)

U.S. DEPARTMENT OF LABOR
1956   Study of Consumer Expenditures Incomes and Savings 4: Sum-
              mary of Family Expenditures for Housing and Household
              Operations. Philadelphia: University of Pennsylvania.

VAN DEN BERGHE, PIERRE L.
1967   Race and Racism: A Comparative Perspective. New York: Wiley.

1970   Race and Ethnicity: Essays in Comparative Sociology. New
              York: Basic Books.

VANDER ZANDEN, JAMES W.
1972   American Minority Relations. New York: Ronald Press.

VERBA, SIDNEY, BASHIRUDDIN AHMED, AND ANIL BHATT
1971   Caste, Race, and Politics. Beverly Hills, Calif.: Sage Publications.

VERBA, SIDNEY, NORMAN H. NIE, AND JAE-ON KIM
1971   The Modes of Democratic Participation: A Cross-National Comparison. Beverly Hills, Calif.: Sage Publications.

WALLERSTEIN, JAMES S., AND CLEMENT J. WYLE
1947   "Our law abiding law breakers." Probation 25 (March–April): 107–12, 118.

WARNER, LYLE, AND MELVIN DeFLEUR
1969   "Attitude as an interactional concept: Social constraint and social distance as intervening variables between attitudes and actions." American Sociological Review 34:153–69.

WARNER, W. L., AND J. O. LOW
1947   The Social System of the Modern Factory. New Haven: Yale University Press.

WEBER, ARNOLD
1963   "The craft-industrial issue revisited: A study of union government." Industrial and Labor Relations Review 16 (April):381–404.

WEBER, MAX
1947   The Theory of Social and Economic Organization. New York: Oxford University Press.

1963   The Sociology of Religion. Tr. by Ephraim Fischoff. Boston: Beacon Press.

WEED, PEERY L.
1973   The White Ethnic Movements and Ethnic Politics. New York: Praeger.

WEINER, MYRON (ED.)
1966   Modernization. New York: Basic Books.

WEINER, NORMAN L., AND CHARLES V. WILLIE
1971   "Decisions by juvenile officer." American Journal of Sociology 77 (September):199–210.

WEIR, STANLEY
1973   "Rebellion in American labor rank and file." Pp. 45–61 in Gerry Hunnius, G. David Garson, and John Case (eds.), Workers' Control. New York: Vintage.

WEISS, ROBERT, EDWIN HARWOOD, AND DAVID RIESMAN
1976   "Work: Problems and possibilities." In Robert K. Merton and Robert E. Nisbet (eds.), Contemporary Social Problems. 4th ed. New York: Harcourt Brace Jovanovich.

WELDON, T. D.
1953   The Vocabulary of Politics. Harmondsworth, Middlesex: Penguin.

WELLFORD, CHARLES
1975   "Labeling theory and criminology: An assessment." Social Problems 22 (February):332–45.

WESOLOWSKI, WLODZIMIERZ
1969   "Strata and strata interest in socialist society." Pp. 465–77 in
            Celia S. Heller (ed.), Structured Social Inequality. New York:
            Macmillan.

WESTLEY, WILLIAM A., AND MARGARET W. WESTLEY
1971   The Emerging Worker. Montreal: McGill-Queen University
            Press.

WIDICK, B. J.
1972   "Black city, black union?" Dissent 19 (Winter):138–45.

WILENSKY, H. L.
1961   "Orderly careers and social participation: The impact of work
            history on social integration in the middle mass." American So-
            ciological Review 26 (August):521–39.

WILLIAMS, JAY R., AND MARTIN GOLD
1972   "From delinquent behavior to official delinquency." Social Prob-
            lems 20 (Fall):209–29.

WILLIAMSON, JOHN B.
1970   "Subjective efficacy and ideal family size as predictors of favora-
            bility toward birth control." Demography 7 (3):329–39.

WILSON, JAMES Q.
1968   "The police and the delinquent in two cities." Chap. 7 in Stanton
            Wheeler and Helen M. Hughes (eds.), Controlling Delinquents.
            New York: Wiley.

WILSON, WILLIAM J.
1973a   Power, Racism, and Privilege. New York: Macmillan.
1973b   "The significance of social and racial prisms." In Peter I. Rose et
            al. (eds.), Through Different Eyes. New York: Oxford Univer-
            sity Press.

WINCH, PETER
1958   The Idea of a Social Science and Its Relation to Philosophy. At-
            lantic Highlands, N.J.: Humanities Press.

WINDMULLER, JOHN P. (ED.)
1974   "European labor and politics: A symposium (1)." Industrial and
            Labor Relations Review 28 (October): entire issue.
1975   "European labor and politics: A symposium (2)." Industrial and
            Labor Relations Review 28 (January):entire issue.

WINTER, GIBSON
1966   Elements for a Social Ethic. New York: Macmillan.

WITTY, C.
1975   "The struggle for progress: The socio-political realities of legal
            pluralism." Unpublished doctoral dissertation. University of Cal-
            ifornia, Berkeley.

WOHLSTETTER, ALBERT
1975   "Optimal ways to confuse ourselves." Foreign Policy no.
            29:170–198.

WOLF, ELEANOR
1976   "Social science testimony in the Detroit schools segregation case." Public Interest 13 (Winter).

WOLF, ERIC R.
1969   Peasant Wars of the Twentieth Century. New York: Harper & Row.

WOLFENSTEIN, E. VICTOR
1967   The Revolutionary Personality: Lenin, Trotsky, Gandhi. Princeton: Princeton University Press.

WOLIN, SHELDON S.
1973   "The politics of the study of revolution." Comparative Politics 5 (April):343–58.

WOMACK, JOHN JR.
1968   Zapata and the Mexican Revolution. New York: Vintage Books.

WOOD, GORDON
1973   "The American Revolution." Pp. 113–48 in Lawrence Kaplan (ed.). Revolutions: A Comparative Study. New York: Vintage Books.

WOOD, NEAL
1959   Communism and British Intellectuals. New York: Columbia University Press.

WOODWARD, C. VANN
1968   The Burden of Southern History. Baton Rouge: Louisiana State University Press.

YANKELOVICH, DANIEL
1974a   "Changing youth values in the seventies: A study of American youth—summary report." Mimeographed.

1974b   The New Morality: A Profile of American Youth in the Seventies. New York: McGraw-Hill.

YINGER, J. MILTON
1961–63 "Integration and pluralism viewed from Hawaii." Antioch Review 22 (Winter):397–410.

1965a   A Minority Group in American Society. New York: McGraw-Hill.

1965b   Toward a Field Theory of Behavior. New York: McGraw-Hill.

1968a   "A research note on interfaith marriage statistics." Journal for the Scientific Study of Religion 7 (Spring):97–103.

1968b   "On the definition of interfaith marriage." Journal for the Scientific Study of Religion 7 (Spring):104–7.

ZEITLIN, MAURICE
1967   Revolutionary Politics and the Cuban Working Class. Princeton: Princeton University Press.

ZEITLIN, MAURICE, LINDA A. EWEN, AND RICHARD E. RATCLIFF
1974   "New princes for old? The large corporation and the capitalist class in Chile." American Journal of Sociology 80 (1):87–123.

ZIMMERMAN, DONALD, AND MELVIN POLLNER
   1970   "The everyday world as a phenomenon." Pp. 80–103 in J.
               Douglas (ed.), Understanding Everyday Life. Chicago: Aldine.

ZIMRING, FRANKLIN, AND GORDON HAWKINS
   1973   Deterrence: The Legal Threat in Crime Control. Chicago: Uni-
               versity of Chicago Press.

ZUBIN, JOSEPH, et al.
   1975   "Biometric approaches to psychopathology." In Mark R. Ro-
               senzweig and Lyman W. Porter (eds.), Annual Review of Psy-
               chology 26:621–71.

Name Index

Abel, Theodore, 320
Abell, Peter, 150
Adam, H., 163
Addams, Jane, 22
Adelman, Irma, 104, 105
Ageton, Suzanne S., 237–240
Akers, Ronald L., 228, 234, 236
Alexander, Karl, 334
Alger, Horatio, 89
Almond, Gabriel A., 114, 124
Alston, Jon P., 69–71, 95
Althusser, Louis, 302
Altman, I., 333
Anderson, John, 221
Angrist, Shirley, 238, 241
Apel, Karl-Otto, 327
Arber, Sara, 24
Archer, Margaret S., 63
Arendt, Hannah, 171, 262, 270
Aristotle, 262, 265, 266
Armbruster, Frank E., 77
Armer, Michael, 108, 114–116, 125
Arnold, William R., 240
Aronowitz, Stanley, 52, 54, 64, 89, 90
Attewell, Paul, 339
Attrey, Roshan, 74
Augustine, Saint, 331
Avineri, Shlomo, 272
Avrich, Paul H., 165

Babbitt, Irving, 199
Back, Kurt, 222
Baker, Elizabeth F., 66
Bambrough, Renford, 266
Banfield, Edward, 213
Barnes, J. A., 277
Barton, John, 280
Barton, R. F., 275
Bauer, Raymond A., 128
Bauman, Zygmunt, 53
Becker, Gary S., 42, 311
Becker, Howard S., 220, 222, 229, 231, 234, 240
Beier, Helen, 128

Bell, Daniel, 3, 9, 11, 14, 18, 19, 54, 207, 267, 269
Bell, David, 143
Bellow, Saul, 271
Bemis, S. E., 67
Bendix, Reinhard, 32
Bendix, William, 89
Bengston, Vern L., 77, 127
Berg, Ivar, 42
Berk, Richard A., 147
Berkson, Issac, 187
Bernstein, Basil, 338
Bernstein, Marver, 281, 282
Berquist, Virginia A., 66
Berreman, Gerald, 200, 208
Berry, John W., 105
Biaggi, Mario, 188
Bibb, Robert C., 51, 66
Bierstedt, Robert, 180, 182, 330
Birch, John, 80
Bittner, Egon, 340
Black, C. E., 105
Black, Donald L., 246
Blackmore, Donald J., 60
Blackwell, James E., 179, 180, 187, 191–194, 206
Blackwell, K., 284
Blalock, Hubert M., Jr., 180, 182
Blau, Peter, 32, 33, 41, 106, 333
Blauner, Robert, 64, 180, 303
Bluestone, Barry, 52
Blum, Alan F., 324, 339
Bok, Derek C., 55, 64
Bordua, David J., 228, 234, 236
Borinski, Ernst, 3
Bourne, Randolph, 198
Brandeis, Louis D., 25
Bricker, Victoria Reifler, 197, 205
Brill, Harry, 17
Brinton, Crane, 172
Brislin, Richard W., 105
Brode, John, 105
Brooks, Harvey, 3
Brown, Stanley H., 65

Subject Index